THE ANALOGY (

The Analogy of Grace
Karl Barth's Moral Theology

GERALD MCKENNY

University of Notre Dame

OXFORD
UNIVERSITY PRESS

OXFORD

UNIVERSITY PRESS

Great Clarendon Street, Oxford, OX2 6DP,
United Kingdom

Oxford University Press is a department of the University of Oxford.
It furthers the University's objective of excellence in research, scholarship,
and education by publishing worldwide.

Oxford is a registered trade mark of Oxford University Press
in the UK and in certain other countries

© Gerald McKenny 2010

The moral rights of the author have been asserted

First published in 2010
First published in paperback 2013

British Library Cataloguing in Publication Data

Data available

Library of Congress Cataloging in Publication Data

Data available

ISBN 978–0–19–958267–9 (hbk)
ISBN 978–0–19–967184–7 (pbk)

To Toy,
with love, joy, and gratitude

Preface

Today, some forty years after his death, Karl Barth continues to provoke theological debate, his thought putting into play the same contrary forces of attraction and aversion that swirled around him during his long career. That this theologian, who by his own admission belonged to the nineteenth century, should continue to fascinate readers in the twenty-first may surprise us; it would not have been predicted in the period following his death, when theological trends were moving in other directions. Still, the fascination with Barth among contemporary readers is not equally directed at all aspects of his thought and is not evenly distributed. This point becomes clear when we consider his ethical thought. In the field of Barth studies, the work of a handful of scholars during the past two decades has significantly raised the level of understanding of Barth's ethics and of the place of ethics in his theology and has resulted in a widespread appreciation of Barth as a moral theologian. But in the field variously designated as Christian ethics, theological ethics, or moral theology, Barth's approach to ethics is neither well understood nor widely appreciated.[1] There is irony in this state of affairs, for it has been the explicit task of the most important recent scholars of Barth's moral theology to demonstrate that Barth belongs in the mainstream of Christian reflection on ethics.

Taking aim at the once widely held view that his theology is inherently inimical to ethics, these scholars have succeeded in securing recognition for Barth as a serious moral theologian. But by establishing his place in the mainstream of ethical thought, have they succeeded only too well? Barth himself was well aware that those who enter the realm of his moral theology carrying prevailing conceptions about what ethics is find themselves in 'a strange world,' warning that his approach 'violates at its nerve center what usually passes for ethical reflection and explanation.'[2] The strangeness can be exaggerated, as it was by the early readers who doubted that any genuine ethics is possible at all under Barth's terms, or it can be suppressed, as it has been by the more recent

---

[1] This academic title of the author of this book designates his field as 'Christian ethics.' Barth's preferred term was 'theological ethics' (*theologische Ethik*). Why, then, does this book insist on the term 'moral theology' to characterize Barth's ethical thought? In the past, 'moral theology' was a Catholic undertaking while 'theological ethics' was what Protestants do. The distinction, however, was never perfect—in particular, Anglicans of all kinds often did 'moral theology'—and is much less so now. Given that the term 'moral theology' can now designate the work of a Protestant, there is a strong reason for preferring it in Barth's case, namely, that a nomenclature in which 'moral' is the adjective and 'theology' is the noun is much more faithful to Barth's enterprise than one in which 'theological' is the adjective and 'ethics' is the noun.

[2] CD II/2, 519/575 f.

readers who argue that Barth keeps to the major currents of theological and philosophical thought about ethics. Both types of reader, however, risk obscuring the significance of Barth's moral theology for ethical discourse: the first by denying that he is seriously engaged in such discourse at all, and the second by leaving us to wonder why, if our aim is after all to arrive at the mainstream, we should follow what must be admitted to be an indirect and rather uncertain route to it. If we take an interest in Barth's moral theology beyond any purely historical significance it might have, it can only be because we find some significance in its particular kind of strangeness.

The aims of this book are to bring the reader to an understanding of Barth's moral theology in all its strangeness and to an appreciation of its significance for Christian ethical thought and practice today. The first aim is straightforward. Without making any effort to conceal its strangeness, this book explores Barth's moral theology from both conceptual and developmental perspectives, critically examining its central claims, themes, and arguments while also tracing the lines of their development at different stages of his thought. The accent is on the conceptual, but partisans of both approaches to Barth will find at least something that interests them here. The second aim requires elaboration. To bring the reader to an appreciation of Barth's significance is admittedly a modest aim. This book falls short of an endorsement of Barth's position. One reason it falls short is that to present Barth's position in a form the author is willing to endorse would have demanded a different book, one that would have vitiated the first aim by presenting a position that is strongly influenced by Barth rather than Barth's own position. Another reason has to do with the character of much scholarly writing on Barth. Few people who undertake the immense labors involved in becoming a competent reader of Barth's massive corpus would have kept at the task unless they were strongly disposed to agree with him. The result is that scholarship on Barth is often governed by a presumption of the truth of his position. At times it even mimics Barth's homiletic tone, though usually without the acknowledgments, often made with wit, humor, and mild self-deprecation, with which Barth noted the limits of his own discourse and marked it off from the Word of God itself. By contrast, this book is written by an author whose thought has been deeply influenced by Barth for a reader who is vaguely familiar with his position and at least somewhat skeptical of it. Negatively, it aims to convince this ideal reader that many of the common criticisms of that position are based on misunderstandings or partial understandings. Positively, it aims to convince her that Barth's moral theology, in its very strangeness, articulates a powerful theological vision of ethical thought and practice whose central insights are of vital importance for the church (and therefore also for the world) today yet are difficult or impossible to articulate from other positions.

What is so strange yet significant about this moral theology? Barth distinguishes his ethics from others with his fundamental claim that it is God who, in Jesus Christ, both determines from eternity what is good and brings it about in time. Most other theologies begin with a human moral subject who is capable of at least a partial grasp by reason of a created moral order which is more perfectly known with the aid of historical revelation and who is naturally yet imperfectly oriented to a good which is more fully attained with the assistance of grace. By contrast, Barth begins with the bold and rather startling claims that God alone knows and judges good and evil and that God accomplishes the good in our place. These claims would seem to bring ethics to an end, but Barth insists that it is only with these claims that ethics in its proper form can truly begin. There are negative and positive aspects of both claims. Negatively, the presumption that we are like God, sitting in judgment of good and evil and supposing that the cause of the good rests on us, leads to great moral evils and destroys the moral solidarity of human beings. By contrast, when we know that we stand under a divine judgment which we ourselves are in no position to pronounce, we exist in right relationships to God and to our fellow human beings. Positively, the command of God as God's judgment summons us to participate in the divine knowledge of good and evil as those who hear this judgment (which is always spoken through a fellow human being) and confirm it with our free decision. Negatively, the claim that, in Jesus Christ, God accomplishes the good in our place means that grace radically interrupts our moral striving. Positively, this claim means that the good confronts us from the site of its fulfillment, and that in turn means that it confronts us not as something that it is up to us to do, to bring about, or to become, but as a reality in which we already stand and which therefore addresses us as that which we are now at last free to do and to be, saying 'You may' rather than 'You must.'

In both of these respects, what God does in our place establishes us as subjects who are summoned and empowered to do not what God has already done but what we were created to do. What we are called and enabled to do is a fully human action, one that is entirely consonant with our creaturely nature but which reflects in a creaturely form God's being and doing for us. Barth's moral theology, like his theology generally, is a celebration of the God whose glorification is realized in the glorification of humanity. Its strangeness lies in its insistence on a radical form of divine grace as the only legitimate and sustainable ground of human worth. Its significance lies in its gift to the church (and therefore to the world as well) of a language of human worth in an era when the latter is constantly under assault from forces that either push us to be more than human or treat us as less than human.

Barth's central concern as a moral theologian is to forge a discourse of ethics that is capable of attesting rather than betraying the divine grace that determines and accomplishes the good, and the aim of this book is to critically examine his attempt to do this. Within the scope of this aim, this book can claim to be comprehensive, covering the major stages of the development of Barth's moral theology, treating its major concepts and themes, exploring the relevant primary and secondary texts, and elaborating the traditions of Christian ethics and the schools of modern moral thought that form the background of his moral theology. It is not, however, exhaustive. The account of the development of Barth's ethics ignores his earliest work and assumes, controversially, that the development of his position in the fourth volume of the *Church Dogmatics* is an extension of the position worked out in the second and third volumes rather than a distinct stage in his thinking. As in many other studies of Barth's ethics, there is no extended treatment of the actual content of the moral life of the creature and the reconciled sinner. Unlike many other studies, little attention is paid here to Barth's political theology. Many primary and secondary texts that have relevance for Barth's ethics are ignored. Discussions of other figures and concepts in Christian ethics and moral philosophy are regrettably brief. The most glaring omission, and the one that has caused the author the most unease, is the lack of a sustained discussion of the primary locus of ethical thought and practice in the church and how this relates to its secondary locus in the social and political realms.

Of course, all of these sins of omission could have been avoided—if the publisher and the reader would have been willing to endure a volume of twice the length. What is offered here is a comprehensive treatment of what the author believes to be Barth's central concern as a moral theologian. While the chapters are arranged to present this concern in a logical progression of ideas, each chapter stands on its own and can be read independently of the others.

The German editions and the English translations of the major works of Barth relevant to the topic at hand were both consulted in the research and writing of this book. In most cases, citations are to the English translation with the reference to the German text following a backslash. Where the English translation has been revised, this is explicitly noted. For several of Barth's earlier writings, however, the citations are to the German text and the reference to the English translation follows the backslash. These cases are recognizable by the citation of the German rather than the English edition of the text, either in the footnote itself or in the Abbreviations.

With these prefatory remarks now concluded, the reader is prepared to enter the strange world of Barth's moral theology.

Acknowledgments

Writing a book is never a solitary enterprise. To acknowledge those who have in ways great and small made such an enterprise possible is especially appropriate when the subject matter of the book is the ethics of Karl Barth, for whom acknowledgment was an important moral and theological act.

This book began with an unexpected invitation to deliver a job talk before the Department of Theology of the University of Notre Dame. It is a testimony to the hospitality of my colleagues and students in that department, and to its chair, John Cavadini, that a Catholic theology department has served as the ideal setting in which to write a book on Karl Barth. That this has been the case is due in a special way to my colleagues and students in moral theology and systematic theology. A revised and expanded version of that job talk was presented to the Society of Christian Ethics in January 2000 and published in the *Annual of the Society of Christian Ethics* of that year under the title 'Heterogeneity and Ethical Deliberation: Casuistry, Narrative, and Event in the Ethics of Karl Barth.' The expansion and revision of that essay were substantial enough that Chapter 6 of this volume is now a distant descendant of that essay, but the genetic continuity makes an acknowledgment appropriate.

My study of Karl Barth began in a small seminar at Wheaton College under the late Donald Horne. I am grateful to him and to my Winsor House mates Chuck Bergstrom, Don Carlson, Rich Hannibal, Guy McCaslin, Kevin Meyer, Tom Nicholas, and John Ortberg for providing a lively intellectual setting. In my seminary and graduate studies, I had the privilege of studying Barth in lecture courses and seminars taught by Rebecca Chopp, Mary Potter Engel, Langdon Gilkey, James Gustafson, Robin Lovin, and Daniel Migliore. In addition to these distinguished teachers, my fellow students Per Anderson, Eric Crump, Travis Kroeker, Stephen Pope, and Mark Wallace contributed enormously to my knowledge of Barth and of theology more generally, and still do. At Notre Dame, I have had the daunting challenge of teaching Barth to extraordinarily talented students in moral theology and systematic theology. It is unfair to mention any of them without mentioning them all, but Matthew Loverin and Deonna Neal have taught me much about Barth in the course of writing doctoral dissertations on his ethics.

In writing this book, I have benefited from many people. John Cavadini and Mark Roche, then the Dean of College of Arts & Letters at Notre Dame, extended me the privilege of a year-long sabbatical in 2002–3, during which most of the basic research for this book was completed, and a one-semester sabbatical in the spring semester of 2007, during which the first full draft was completed. During that latter semester, Vaughn McKim graciously assumed my duties as director of Notre Dame's John J. Reilly Center for Science, Technology, and Values, and on both occasions my moral theology colleagues graciously added my various duties in the program to their own. The content of this book owes much to conversations with Nigel Biggar, Eric Gregory, David Haddorff, Kevin Hart, Stanley Hauerwas, Jennifer Herdt, Jean Porter, Cyril O'Regan, Allen Verhey, and Randall Zachman. Special mention must be made of my many conversations on Barth and Judaism with Rabbi Michael Signer which were interrupted by his untimely death. Adam Clark read the first full draft and not only made numerous helpful suggestions and corrections but also entered into a remarkable *Auseinandersetzung* with it. The final version of this book inadequately reflects the thought provocation his comments induced in its author. David Haddorff read a near-final draft and also made valuable comments which resulted in some significant late revisions. Deonna Neal prepared the index. Finally, I am deeply indebted to several people connected with Oxford University Press: first, to the two anonymous referees who took their obligations to the scholarly community seriously and made a number of very helpful suggestions; second, to Lucy Qureshi and Tom Perridge, the two exemplary editors who oversaw the process from initial solicitation to publication; and finally to Elizabeth Robottom and Tessa Eaton for their competence and professionalism throughout the process leading to publication.

These acknowledgments would not be complete without mentioning two people who have exemplified the moral vision described in the book. Before his tragic death, my nephew Peter Andre (1984–2008) was a sign of God's grace to everyone he encountered, and especially to the widows, orphans, and strangers who came across his path and whom he sought out. 'Blessed are the merciful, for they shall receive mercy.' Finally, my wife Phimpmas (Toy) Bunnag has taught me more about grace through her life than I will ever fully comprehend through my mind. To her this book is lovingly dedicated.

Contents

Abbreviations

The following abbreviations will be used in citing works of Karl Barth. Complete references are found in the Bibliography.

CD   *Church Dogmatics*, vols. i–iv (Edinburgh: T. & T. Clark, 1956–75)

CL   *The Christian Life* (Edinburgh: T. & T. Clark, 1981)

Ethics   *Ethics* [1928–9] (Edinburgh: T. & T. Clark, 1981)

Romans₁ *Der Römerbrief* (*Erste Fassung*) (Zurich: Theologischer Verlag Zürich, 1919)

Romans₂ *Der Römerbrief* (*Zweite Fassung*) (Zurich: Theologischer Verlag Zürich, 1922)

Introduction
An Overview of Barth's Ethics

One who assumes the task of giving a general account of Karl Barth's theology faces a monumental difficulty. The difficulty has to do with how to articulate the core of that theology: the basic vision or the central claims on which it turns. The problem is not that Barth's theology lacks such a core or that it is too complex or too esoteric to formulate. Rather, it is that this core seems to be both everywhere and nowhere in his theology. Critics and admirers alike of Barth's dogmatic project have noted his commitment to the rational character of theology and have compared his enterprise with scholasticism.[1] They are right insofar as they have in mind his commitment to consistency, order, and dialectical clarification of concepts. Yet, as in the best instances of scholasticism, what is also striking in Barth's dogmatic achievement is the power of imagination displayed in it. The *Church Dogmatics* is a long series of nonidentical repetitions, of seemingly endless elaborations of a tight circle of ideas that exhibit a remarkable unity across the space structured by its topoi and the temporal span over which its volumes appeared, yet without having recourse to a single origin or a canonical expression to which everything can be traced back. Reaching for the inevitable musical analogy, we could describe the *Church Dogmatics* as a lengthy set of variations on a theme that, while unmistakably in control of each movement, is never presented on its own but appears only in its variations.

What holds true for Barth's theology generally also holds true for those aspects or that dimension of it which may be placed under the heading of ethics. Not only did Barth depart from customary practice by devoting a concluding section of each of his substantive dogmatic topics to ethics rather than confining the latter to one topic or treating it apart from dogmatics. He also wove ethical material through his discussions of issues that were ostensibly purely dogmatic. The result is that dogmatics and ethics are not only inseparable for Barth, they are often indistinguishable. It appears, then, that the core of Barth's ethics, like the core of his theology more generally, can only be culled from its successive iterations in the various topoi of the *Church Dogmatics*—revelation, God,

---

[1] See especially Hans Urs von Balthasar, *The Theology of Karl Barth*, trans. Edward T. Oakes, SJ (San Francisco: Ignatius Press, 1992), xix; and George Hunsinger, *How to Read Karl Barth: The Shape of his Theology* (New York: Oxford University Press, 1991), 49–64.

creation, reconciliation—and their many subordinate themes. This is what this overview will try to do, namely, to reconstruct the theme of Barth's ethics from its variations, and then to discuss the movement and structure of his ethics and the moral vision that animates it. This way of proceeding breaks with a history of scholarship which has looked to a certain feature of Barth's ethics—the relation of dogmatics and ethics, the relation of gospel and law, the correspondence of divine and human action, or the nature and practice of moral reflection—as the key to the whole.[2]

This overview offers the reader a point of entry into the following study. It is not a blueprint or an outline for what follows. Most of the points made here will be taken up in greater detail, but some will be only alluded to or briefly noted. By the same token, many issues treated in the following pages are not mentioned here at all. Nevertheless, this overview articulates the general interpretation of Barth's moral theology that governs the investigation which follows.

1. THEME

For Barth, dogmatics, as the church's critical reflection on its own speech about God, has its criterion in God's self-disclosure in Jesus Christ, the Word and work of God attested prophetically and apostolically in scripture and proclaimed in the

---

[2] While his treatment is difficult to confine to a single theme, Paul Matheny locates the distinctiveness of Barth's moral theology in the relation of dogmatics and ethics which for Matheny is primarily a matter of content and secondarily a methodological principle. See Matheny, *Dogmatics and Ethics: The Theological Realism and Ethics of Karl Barth's 'Church Dogmatics'* (Frankfurt: Peter Lang, 1990). In shorter but still highly significant works, Eberhard Jüngel and Eberhard Busch both view the whole of Barth's ethics from the standpoint of the relation of gospel and law. See Jüngel, 'Gospel and Law: The Relationship of Dogmatics to Ethics,' in *Karl Barth: A Theological Legacy*, trans. Garrett E. Paul (Philadelphia: The Westminster Press, 1986), 105–26; and Busch, *The Great Passion: An Introduction to Karl Barth's Theology* (Grand Rapids, Mich.: Eerdmans, 2004), 152–75. John Webster and, more recently, Paul Nimmo have taken the relation of divine and human action as the key to Barth's ethics. See especially Webster, *Barth's Ethics of Reconciliation* (Cambridge: Cambridge University Press, 1995); idem, *Barth's Moral Theology: Human Action in Barth's Thought* (Grand Rapids, Mich.: Eerdmans, 1998); and Nimmo, *Being in Action: The Theological Shape of Barth's Ethical Vision* (New York: T. & T. Clark, 2007). Finally, Nigel Biggar approaches Barth through the lens of moral reasoning. See especially Biggar, *The Hastening that Waits: Karl Barth's Ethics* (Oxford: Clarendon Press, 1993). To be sure, not all studies of Barth's moral theology focus on one of these features. The most obvious exception is Robert E. Willis, *The Ethics of Karl Barth* (Leiden: E. J. Brill, 1971). Willis takes his readers on a comprehensive tour of the then-published writings of Barth having to do with ethics. Another possible exception is Joseph Mangina's *Karl Barth on the Christian Life: The Practical Knowledge of God.* (New York: Peter Lang, 2001). Mangina focuses on various topics to show how Barth's moral theology exhibits a deep, and multifaceted concern with the human subject. Yet another possible exception is David Clough, *Ethics in Crisis: Interpreting Barth's Ethics* (Aldershot: Ashgate, 2005). Clough focuses on the persistence in later stages of Barth's approach to ethics of the dialectical method of *Romans₂*. However, he does not claim to present a comprehensive account of Barth's ethics from this standpoint but only to trace a way of posing the problem of ethics which, according to Clough, Barth shares with a certain strand of postmodern ethics.

church. In accordance with this criterion, it tells about a God who from eternity resolves, freely yet unalterably, not to be God alone but instead to be God with and for a human counterpart, to identify with this other while remaining God, to include this other in the intra-Trinitarian communion eternally enjoyed by God, and who, to this end, enters into a covenant with this human partner: a covenant that originates in the election from eternity of Jesus Christ and of other human beings in him and is fulfilled in time in the reconciliation of sinful human beings with God accomplished by the incarnation, life, death, and resurrection of Jesus Christ. Creation is the external ground of this covenant, its presupposition, the concrete condition in which God has willed to carry it out, while redemption is its consummation, the final manifestation of God's glorification in the glorification of God's human partner in eternal life with God.

Barth's *Church Dogmatics* is a persistent, indeed relentless narration of this story in the face of tendencies to abstract both God and humanity from it—to start with human beings with their moral experience and capacities, for example, deriving from these a general conception of God as their ground or source, perhaps illuminated and corrected by scripture. As we will see, Barth's rejection of this kind of procedure does not entail the denial of any role for human nature and its moral capacities. It does entail, however, that human nature and its capacities must be understood in light of what accounts for their existing at all, namely the determination of humanity in Christ for fellowship with God. To do otherwise would be to treat humanity (and God) abstractly, as if the being of humanity could be accounted for apart from its true origin and destiny which is given from beyond itself, and from beyond any ground in a metaphysical deity, in God's electing grace.

If the theme of Barth's theology is this covenant of God with humanity inaugurated in election and fulfilled in reconciliation, with creation and redemption constituting its presupposition and its consummation, respectively, then we may find the theme of his ethics in the substance of this covenant which gives it its continuity across all of the events that constitute it, namely, in the relation of election and sanctification. Nowhere in his theology does Barth stand far outside the Reformed tradition of Protestantism which derives from John Calvin, but nowhere is he more an insider than in the fundamental role election and sanctification together play in what transpires between God and human beings, however novel his actual formulations were in the history of that tradition. For Barth, election involves a twofold determination (*Bestimmung*) of divine grace; it includes both God's gracious and free self-determination to be with and for humanity and God's determination of humanity to exist as the one whom God is with and for, that is, to be the recipient of God's grace and the witness to it. In this latter determination, humanity is chosen to glorify God, and in the freedom given by God for this service and commission humanity, too, is glorified. However, this determination is not, as it were, hardwired into humanity as God's elect. It is, rather, a determination of the elect as person and thus as free subject. It therefore confronts human beings with the question of their own self-determination in light of their determination by God. Determined to the service and commission of witness to God's grace, human beings are questioned by God with respect to the expression of this determination in their existence and conduct, and are thereby made answerable to God with regard to it.[3] It follows that '[t]he concept of the covenant between God and man concluded in Jesus Christ is not exhausted in the doctrine of the divine election of grace. The election itself and as such demands that it be understood as God's command directed to man; as the sanctification or claiming which comes to elected man from the electing God in the fact that when God turns to him and gives himself to him he becomes his commander.'[4] Sanctification, as the summons that establishes God's covenant partner as a moral subject who is answerable to her determination or vocation to correspond in her being and conduct to God's gracious election of humanity, is thus the fundamental concept of Barth's ethics. In the terms of God's covenant with Israel, which for Barth is both confirmed and completed in Christ, the covenant includes both the promise of election ('I will be your God') and the command of sanctification ('You will be my people').[5] Dogmatics must therefore consider both God's twofold determination (God's self-determination for humanity and God's determination of humanity to participation in God's being for humanity) and the human self-determination which corresponds to it. Dogmatics, in other words, will include ethics, and ethics, as the account of the kind of activity or form of life which corresponds to the divine determination of human beings for fellowship with God, will lie at the heart of the story narrated by dogmatics—neither a marginal subplot nor an independent story that competes with the dogmatic story or determines it from without.

What is this human self-determination which, in the covenant between God and humanity, corresponds to the divine determination? At its most basic level, God determines humanity simply to be the one whom God is with and for, to be drawn into the fellowship of love that is the divine life itself. Yet, while human beings are thus recipients of divine grace, they are not merely passive objects caught up in the movement of divine love, but are also active subjects of their divine determination, enlisted in God's service and commissioned as God's witnesses. More precisely, then, their determination as God's elect involves 'participation in the life of God in a human being and doing [*Sein und Tun*] in which there is a representation and picture [*Repräsentierung und Abbildung*] of the glory of God itself and its work.'[6] The determination of the elect is to

---

[3] CD II/2, 510 f./565 f.
[4] CD II/2, 512/567.
[5] CD IV/1, 47/49, 53/56, 67/71.
[6] CD II/2, 413/457 (revised).

participate in God's grace as active subjects by signifying it in their being and conduct, thus witnessing to God's glory. The command of God is simply the summons directing human beings to a self-determination corresponding along these lines to their determination by God. 'The summons of the divine predecision, the sanctification which comes on man from all eternity and therefore once and for all in the election of Jesus Christ, is that in all its human questionableness and frailty the life of the elect should become its image and repetition and attestation and acknowledgement.'[7] This summons of election, the command of God, is itself sanctification, and sanctification in turn expresses the very meaning of election, which is the separation of those who belong to Christ: less a separation *from* other human beings (although this too is meant) than a separation *for* human correspondence to God's electing grace. It is this summons that constitutes human beings as responsible and thus as moral subjects, while the modes of mimesis ('image and repetition') and testimony ('attestation and acknowledgement') indicate in a general way the content of the moral life: that our existence as acting subjects should signify in a distinctively human way God's gracious self-determination to be with us and for us in all God's deity, that human life should be lived as an analogy of grace.

Human self-determination is thus a creaturely analogue of the divine determination. In Barth's words, the aim of God's Word and work in Christ 'is that our being and action should be conformed to his. "Be ye (literally, ye shall be) therefore perfect (literally, directed to your objective) even as (i.e., corresponding to it in creaturely-human fashion as) your Father which is in heaven is perfect (directed to his objective)" (Mt. 5: 48).'[8] The church is where the summons to a human life in correspondence to divine grace is explicitly heard and accepted; it is the community, assembled by Christ through the Holy Spirit, in which the human response to this summons occurs on behalf of all humanity and in witness to the rest of humanity. Due both to the grace of God and to the failings of Christians, however, this correspondence to grace is not infrequently exhibited as well as or better outside the church—a fact that must always form part of the church's self-understanding of its nature and mission. And while the church enjoys a special status due to its explicit acknowledgment of the summons, it is also God's will that the social and political orders should correspond to divine grace, bearing an implicit witness in the form of secular analogues to the latter.[9]

---

[7] CD II/2, 512/568.

[8] CD II/2, 512/567.

[9] See 'The Christian Community and the Civil Community,' in Karl Barth, *Community, State, and Church: Three Essays with a New Introduction by David Haddorff* (Eugene, Ore.: Wipf and Stock, 2004), especially 168–80; and CD IV/3.1, 114–22/128–36.

2. MOVEMENT

If election has to do with the determination of humanity for a particular form of participation in God's own life, sanctification has to do with the actualization of this determination in the realm of human existence. In Barth's moral theology, God is the ultimate good. But God's goodness is expressed in God's being with and for the human other whom God elects as God's covenant partner. Human beings actively participate in this good, in God's being with and for them, by their service and commission as witnesses to God's grace in being and conduct that corresponds to God's grace. It is by the command of God that human beings are summoned to this service and commission and God's will for human beings to enjoy this good is done. It is by the command of God, in other words, that 'he sanctifies [them], and the good (which is God himself) enters into the realm of human existence.'[10] This section traces the movement by which the good is actualized in human existence through the command of God which sanctifies humanity.

Both election, with its twofold divine determination, and the sanctification it entails are grounded in the eternal resolve of God and are already established in the election of Jesus Christ from eternity. However, to end the matter here, or even to attempt to construct a moral theology directly from its ground in eternity, would be a mistake. For Barth, the nature, meaning, and purpose of the covenant is revealed and finds its concrete reality not in the election and sanctification expressed in the will of God in Jesus Christ from eternity but in the fulfillment of the latter in the incarnation, life, death, and resurrection of Jesus Christ in historical time. The good is not merely an eternal, transcendent good. It is a good that has also been actualized in human existence in Jesus Christ and thus fulfilled by him. It is in Jesus Christ who obeys the command of God by being the elect one in all that he is and does that the good is actualized. As such, the reconciliation accomplished in Christ is not only the restoration of the covenant in the face of its sinful rejection by God's human partner; it is also the actualization of the covenant in its fullness.[11] In Christ, the divine promise of election ('I will be your God') and the divine command of sanctification ('You will be my people') are both issued ('truly God') and fulfilled ('truly man') concretely, that is, in human history. The command that meets us as the summons to live as God's elect is therefore a command that meets us in Christ as already fulfilled. 'The sanctification of man, the fact that he is claimed by God, the fulfillment of his predetermination in his self-determination to obedience, the judgment of God on man and his command to him in its actual concrete

---

[10] CD II/2, 548/609.
[11] CD IV/1, 13 f./12 f., 36 f./36 f., 47 f./49 f.

fulfillment—they all take place here in Jesus Christ.'[12] It is difficult to exaggerate the significance of this point. The command of God is not a demand that we fill something that is lacking but rather that we confirm what has already been done. The specific subject matter of moral theology, then, 'is the Word and work of God in Jesus Christ, in which the right action of man has already been performed and therefore waits only to be confirmed by our action.'[13]

Barth's insistence on this Christological site of ethics is perhaps the most distinguishing and controversial aspect of his moral theology. Moral theology for him has to do not with a good which human beings find in themselves but with the relation of human beings to a good that has already been accomplished in Jesus Christ. But if the command of God is inaugurated in eternity with the summons to correspond to election and is fulfilled in the midst of time in Christ's obedience, what does this entail for other human beings? Barth's answer is that the command of God is the demand, addressed to us in the present, and thus in every time, for confirmation and proof (*Bestätigung und Bewährung*) of election in our conduct.[14] The summons of election does not simply end with its fulfillment in Christ; it calls for our affirmation of its fulfillment in Christ. We are not merely inert objects of what is accomplished on our behalf in Christ's obedience but are called to participate in it as active subjects. 'The command of God does not hang ineffectively in the air above man. Its particular aim and concern are with him and his real activity.'[15]

Barth goes on to say that 'real activity' involves something 'concrete.' He describes the command of God in existentialist terms as an 'ethical event [*ethische Ereignis*],' namely 'the encounter [*Begegnung*] of the concrete God with the concrete man,' or more specifically, between a 'highly particular, concrete, and special command' and 'a concrete and specific human choice and decision.'[16] The movement of sanctification from its ground in the election of Jesus Christ (and of other human beings in him) from eternity to its fulfillment in history in the obedience of the incarnate Christ as the elect of God, is now concentrated on the present moment, in which a particular command of God demands a particular human decision as the confirmation or proof of election. However, this portrayal of the command of God as an event of encounter is subject to three misunderstandings: that it implies a kind of atomistic individualism, that it is essentially arbitrary, and that it makes the command of God transparent to the human subject, ironically reinstating the latter in a position of moral certitude and mastery. Because these misunderstandings strike at the core of Barth's

---

[12] CD II/2, 517/573.
[13] CD II/2, 543/603.
[14] CD II/2, 512/567.
[15] CD III/4, 5/3 f.
[16] CD III/4, 26/28, 9/8, 8/7.

conception of the command of God, it is appropriate to pause here to dispel them before saying more about the movement itself.

First, Barth is very clear that the kind of decision he has in mind is not atomistic but falls within an ongoing series of actions in which human beings realize themselves as subjects, their past actions conditioning their present choices which in turn condition their future choices. The present, as the moment of self-realization in a decision, is inextricable from the temporality in which one is always also what one has become and will become.[17] Moreover, the ethical event is no exception to Barth's theology generally, which in each of its dogmatic topoi (revelation, election, creation, and reconciliation) locates the individual in a community which precedes her. In the ethical event human beings encounter God not as individuals but in an intersubjective context in which the command of God is always heard through another human person. 'The individual with his actions is not an atom in empty space but a man among his fellows.' In accordance with this fundamental solidarity of human beings, 'not merely ethical advice and direction but the very command of God' is 'given in a very concrete form immediately from one man to another or to many others.'[18] The force of Barth's insistence on the concreteness of the present moment of decision is not to promote atomistic individualism but to secure ethical singularity. Singularity refers to the concrete acting subject as 'this or that man who in his place and skin cannot be compared, let alone exchanged, with any one else.'[19] The point is that while I exist in relation to others, I cannot evade accountability to the command of God as a demand issued to me here and now. Similarly, while my present action occurs in complex relations to my past and future, I cannot evade accountability to the command of God by appealing to what I have already become or might become in the future. Singularity in these senses seems essential to responsibility; it is what keeps the individual from being absorbed into the collective in a totalitarian manner. Solidarity and singularity, respectively, resist liberal individualist and communitarian perversions of the moral subject.

Turning to the second misunderstanding, the ethical event is thought to be arbitrary because of Barth's denial that the command of God is to be specified by formulating principles or rules of conduct which would then be further specified in accordance with circumstances, resulting in a more or less detailed moral code. In the absence of such principles or rules the divine–human encounter seems radically indeterminate, 'a darkness in which anything might be possible and might become actual.'[20] However, the encounter of God with human beings as Barth depicts it is not exhausted in the present event; rather, this event forms and is formed by a history of encounter, or by this encounter as a history—the history

---

[17] CD III/4, 5 f./4.
[18] CD III/4, 9/8.
[19] CD III/4, 5/4.
[20] CL, 34/52.

of the complex, interlocking events of creation, reconciliation, and redemption. 'This history of God and man is obviously the constant factor and therefore the connection or context of all ethical events. Where the divine command and human action meet, there always meet the divine creator and his creature, the divine reconciler and the sinner upheld by his faithfulness, the divine redeemer and perfecter and the child of God with his eternal expectancy.'[21] At this level, moral theology is 'a commentary on this history to be written with particular regard to this encounter.'[22] Substituting a spatial metaphor for the textual one, we might say that it offers a high-resolution map of the places (*Bereiche*: 'domains' or 'regions') within which the encounter occurs, a normative geography of the areas of our lives as creatures, reconciled sinners, and heirs of redemption where God meets us with God's command. The point in either case is that the encounter is not the scene of an arbitrary command of an arbitrary deity. It occurs in a history and in a place that is already morally determinate, not to say fixed. What God commands in the present moment will always be continuous with this history and will conform to the normative contours of these places. From all of this it also follows that the correspondence of our conduct to God's conduct will not simply be an analogue to the divine election but also, and more concretely, to the work of creation, reconciliation, and redemption by which God carries out God's gracious election. In Barth's terms, the three concepts of the command of God the creator, the reconciler, and the redeemer 'characterize in the shortest possible form the act of God who in grace has elected man for the covenant with himself, and in so doing they also characterize the command by which he has sanctified them for himself.'[23]

At the same time, however, what God commands in the present encounter cannot be deduced from a description of the history or place in which it falls. Neither the divine nor the human party is fully disclosed in their encounter, and this brings us to the third misunderstanding. The present is not pure presence; it is not the transparency of the command of God to the gaze of reason or conscience, or even to knowledge of revelation, nor is it the visible proof of election in the life of the elect. God is not fully disclosed, and so moral theology can only instruct, based on its commentary; at the point where the actual command of God itself must be heard, ethical inquiry leaves off.[24] At this point the subject summoned by the command of God stands before God, asking the concrete ethical question, 'what should we do?'[25] This event of encounter is not the presence of the command of God to the moral subject. It is an act of prayer, and the answer to the ethical question comes not as knowledge possessed

---

[21] CD III/4, 26/27.
[22] CD III/4, 26/28 (revised).
[23] CD II/2, 549/610.
[24] CD III/4, 30 f./32–4.
[25] CD II/2, 644–61/717–37.

by a human subject but as the answer to her prayer. Yet to pray for this answer is already to correspond in a human way to God's giving of the command, and to that extent it is already obedience to the demand for confirmation and proof of election. However, the human in correspondence to God is not fully disclosed either. The righteousness and holiness of human beings are not visible in their actions but are 'hidden with Christ in God.' The confirmation or proof of election is a Christological and an eschatological reality; our conduct may and should manifest it, but it does so only partially and imperfectly.

This last point indicates Barth's conviction that ethics remains at its Christological site even when it concerns the confirmation in our own conduct of what Christ has done in our place. The movement of the command of God is Christological at every point. In the election of Christ from eternity the command of God is established; in the obedience of the incarnate Christ it is fulfilled in history; and in the ascended Christ is hidden the proof of election we are unable to supply of ourselves. Moral theologies can be identified in part by the aspect of Christology they take to be fundamental for ethics, and debates in moral theology often turn on claims made for the centrality to ethics of the incarnation, the cross, or the resurrection. What distinguishes Barth's moral theology is the attention he also pays to the election of Christ from eternity, the obedient life of the incarnate Christ, and the ascended Christ with whom, according to Colossians 3: 3, our lives are hidden in God.

We have now seen how sanctification as the actualization of the good in human existence is accomplished in the threefold movement of the command of God from its ground in eternity to its fulfillment in the midst of time and, from there, to its confirmation in every time. In this movement we find the ontological ground and analogical structure of the command of God. Its ultimate ground is in the intra-Trinitarian relation of Father and Son in which Jesus Christ is already from eternity the elected one. The election of Jesus Christ, and of other human beings in him, is an intra-Trinitarian act. 'In the beginning it was the choice of the Father himself to establish this covenant with man by giving up his Son for him, that he himself might become man in the fulfillment of his grace. In the beginning it was the choice of the Son to be obedient to grace, and therefore to offer up himself and to become man in order that this covenant might be made a reality.'[26] The establishment and fulfillment of the covenant are already resolved on in the intra-Trinitarian relation of the Father and the Son, and this can only mean that the divine determination of human beings for fellowship with God and the command of God as the summons to human beings to correspond to this determination are themselves intra-Trinitarian acts. For Barth, moreover, what occurs in God's own eternal being and life is repeated *ad extra* in the being and life of the incarnate Christ, and this repetition

----

[26] CD II/2, 101/109.

is itself repeated, in all its dissimilarity, in the being and life of other humans. Thus the divine determination of human beings for fellowship with God and the command of God as the summons to correspond to it are both issued and fulfilled in Jesus Christ, who is both the electing God and the elected human, and who obeys the command in our place by living as God's elect one in the entirety of his being and activity. And what occurs in Jesus Christ is in turn repeated, however differently and (in our performance) inadequately, as the command of God summons other human beings to action corresponding to Christ's being and work for us.[27]

The command of God is thus grounded in a complex analogy of relations involving the relation of the Father and the Son (and humanity in the Son), the relation of the incarnate Christ to the Father and to other human beings, and the relation of these other human beings to God and to one another. This analogical structure is ontological.[28] While ultimately grounded in the intra-Trinitarian relations, the ontology is centered in Jesus Christ. Because Jesus Christ is truly God, what he is and does in his incarnate life is the being and work of God *ad extra*; it is the execution of what God has resolved on from eternity. Because he is truly human, and in such a way that our humanity is ontologically constituted in its relation to his, what he is and does, he is and does on our behalf and in our place; by virtue of this, our corresponding action is not just a similitude of the intra-Trinitarian communion but a mode of participation in it.

In this threefold movement the intra-Trinitarian fellowship goes forth from itself to become actual in human existence yet without ceasing to be what it is in itself. But Barth's emphasis on the Christ event as the actualization in human existence of an intra-Trinitarian reality prompts two objections. The first objection is that he collapses creation into reconciliation in a Gnostic or quasi-Gnostic manner. The second objection is that in effect he propounds a Hegelian narrative according to which God's being is realized in a historical process. We can begin to answer these objections by pointing out a second threefold movement which crosses the first one, though it is really the same movement viewed from a different perspective. This movement consists of the divine actions of creation, reconciliation, and redemption through which God accomplishes the divine determination of grace.

---

[27] The theme of the obedience of Christ and its fundamental significance of Barth's ethics is treated thoroughly and insightfully by Matthew H. Loverin in his doctoral dissertation 'Obedient unto Death: The Person and Work of Jesus Christ in Karl Barth's Theological Ethics' (unpublished dissertation, University of Notre Dame, 2009).

[28] Caution must be taken to ensure that the term 'ontology' is not taken to imply the metaphysical continuity of divine and creaturely being which Barth rejected under the heading of *analogia entis* or to imply any other form of ontotheology. To establish this point is beyond the scope of this inquiry, but it is clear that for Barth the enhypostatic relation of the human to the divine in Jesus Christ is genuinely ontological yet entails no metaphysical continuity of divine and human being. Barth also attempts to establish a nonmetaphysical ontology in his description of the relation of other human beings to the human being Jesus Christ.

In creation, God brings God's covenant partner into existence in a cosmos with which this human partner of God is inextricably interrelated. For Barth, the being of the human creature is twofold: it includes both its determination as God's covenant partner and its creaturely nature. We begin with the first of these. Fellowship with God as God's covenant partner is the ultimate end (*Ziel*) of human life, but this end exceeds our capability. It is not a state at which we arrive through the exercise of our capacities, even with the power of divine grace; it is ours only in the encounter of our humanity with the humanity of Jesus Christ. In this respect, our very being is ecstatic, constituted by the encounter with an Other which sustains us in being. Of Jesus Christ alone can it properly be said that his being is being with God. The rest of us have our being with God in the relation of our humanity to his humanity.[29] We *are*, then, as we are constituted as the elect of God and as hearers of God's Word (which, as the summons to grace, also takes the form of the command). However, this is not all there is to say about the being of the human creature. Our creaturely nature, too, has ontological status. God's covenant is with a being of a determinate kind. As creation, for Barth, is the external ground of the covenant, our creaturely nature is the presupposition of our being as God's covenant partner. It is *this* being whom God has created to be in covenant with God, and this means that our 'creaturely essence cannot be alien [*fremd*] or opposed [*widerstrebend*] to this grace of God, but must confront it with a certain familiarity [*Vertraulichkeit*].'[30] If this were not the case, the covenant would have required a second creation in order to be carried out, and the nature of *that* creature would have had to have been ordered to its covenant determination.

We can illustrate this point with reference to freedom. For Barth, freedom in its most proper sense is the confirmation in our decision of God's decision for us. It is the freedom of the human covenant partner of God. By contrast, natural freedom is the neutral capacity to choose one action or another. Barth explicitly denies that this capacity to choose is freedom in the proper sense. Yet he also argues that the freedom to confirm God's decision in our own decision presupposes this natural freedom. Without the latter, the former could not occur. God, determining from eternity to be God in relation to a genuine partner, has brought into being a creature whose nature makes it possible for it to be a covenant partner. This does not mean that this creature becomes God's covenant partner through a series of states or modulations of its nature, assisted by divine grace. We do not achieve freedom in the proper sense by progressively making the right use, with God's help, of our natural capacity to choose. It does mean, however, that the being who is God's covenant partner by grace is a being with *this* nature. Our confirmation of what God has done in our place involves the

---

[29] The foregoing sentences are a highly simplified summary of Barth's description of 'real man' (*wirkliche Mensch*) in CD III/2, 132–202/158–241.

[30] CD III/2, 224/267.

exercise of our natural freedom as, with God's help, we decide for God's decision for us. Our nature is suited to our being as God's covenant partner. Grace does not destroy nature but summons, empowers, and directs nature to confirm grace.

Barth's respect for the integrity of human nature is evident in several other respects. First, even when human nature is not actualized in its proper form as the response of the whole human being to the divine determination of grace, it remains intact. Sin distorts human nature but cannot destroy it. Barth's most powerful and eloquent statement of this point is his remarkable discussion of ancient Greek eros. He argues that despite its perversion of the fundamental human characteristic of fellow humanity, Greek eros, in its profound affirmation of life, not only retains a vestige of the natural goodness of creation but also offers Christian love something essential to the latter's own flourishing.[31] Second, this theme of life affirmation is reflected in Barth's disdain for ethical principles or practices that denigrate the instinctual life, fail to respect ordinary human desires, or reject finite human limitations. Third, Barth holds that in sanctifying us through the command of God, the Holy Spirit does not replace natural human capacities or supplement them with infused capacities but quickens them as they are, in their natural form.[32] In all three of these respects, Barth shows profound respect for the integrity of human nature as created by God, and those who hold that grace ignores, overrides, or annihilates human nature in his theology have fundamentally misunderstood his conceptions of both grace and nature.

We may quickly describe reconciliation as the fulfillment of the divine determination of grace in the face of our sinful contradiction of it. Since this divine determination is ontologically constitutive of us as God's covenant partner, our sinful rejection of it contradicts our very humanity, though it does not and cannot destroy the latter. Finally, redemption is the ultimate completion of God's determination of humanity in the adoption of human beings as God's own sons and daughters. Without reconciliation, not only would human beings be left in their sin, but the divine determination of humanity from eternity would never have attained its actualization in time. Without redemption, the movement of God's love outward, towards humanity in Jesus Christ, would never have made its complete return, and had this been the case, we might indeed be left to conclude that Barth holds, with Hegel, the view that the divine realizes itself in its becoming in human history. Instead, Barth, with traditional Christian faith, holds that humanity is fully realized in its sharing in God's eternal life. This is one respect in which Barth's threefold movement departs from Hegel; there are two others. The first has to do with Barth's fundamental claim that in going forth from itself the Trinity nevertheless remains itself. The threefold movement is not required for the actualization of the divine being; rather, the divine being is

---

[31] CD III/2, 274–85/329–44.
[32] CD I/2, 375/412; II/2, 579/643; IV/2, 318 f./356, 557/630.

complete in its intra-Trinitarian communion before it goes forth to include the human other in the latter. The second is that while for Barth ethics does involve the actualization of the good in the world, it is God and not humanity who accomplishes the good, and so the latter is not turned over to human historical action for its actualization.

3. STRUCTURE

For Barth, the determination of election is a determination to fellowship with God, a distinctively and properly human participation in God's intra-Trinitarian communion. 'The glory of God, to participate in which is the intention and purpose of his love for the creature, is the overflowing of the inner perfection and joy of God. God chooses the elect from eternity and for eternity, that he may catch up a beam or a drop of his own blessedness (*Seligkeit*) and live as its bearer, that he may rejoice in him and with him.'[33] That the ultimate human good is defined in these terms is hardly unique to Barth; every moral theology that claims to be Christian says this in some way and at some point. But that God brings this good into the human realm and fulfills it, and in this way accomplishes the divine self-glorification in giving human beings a share in the divine blessedness—the movement we have traced from 'there' to 'here'—is a distinctive emphasis of Barth's. What is most significant here is the role grace plays in this movement—Barth's insistence on the good as something God resolves on, brings into human existence, and fulfills there—and the profound implications this role of grace has for human moral action. For Barth, it is not left to human beings to attain the good or bring it about. The good is not an object of human moral striving assisted by divine grace; rather, it is as already accomplished in the humanity of Jesus Christ that the good confronts us with its demand that we affirm it in our active existence. The moral life is not a human journey from here to there; rather, it is the concrete signification in our conduct of God's movement from there to here. Early in his academic career, Barth presented these contrasting views of the good in terms of a distinction between the theological vision of the Protestant Reformation, especially its Reformed branch, and that of the Christianity which, as he saw it, both preceded and followed the Reformation. In the latter vision, 'Christianity appears as a great pedagogy, a pathway along which the human partly walks, is partly led, and is partly carried along by supernatural power.' By contrast, the Reformed vision 'is thoroughly unpedagogical. It does not begin with human interests, among which emerges finally, ultimately, and as the highest point, the interest in God; rather, it begins with God's interest in the

---

[33] CD II/2, 412/455 (revised).

human person. It does not show the way that the human should seek and follow, but rather, the way that God has already found to him.'[34]

Like much in Barth's earlier work, the contrast between these two visions is drawn too sharply; the *Church Dogmatics* will present a more complex picture of the Christian life in which the pedagogical emphasis on growth in grace will be given a place. But this theme will always be a subordinate one which will never be allowed to challenge the priority or draw the sustained attention accorded to the sufficiency of divine grace. For Barth, ethics is grounded in what God does, and this grounding determines how he understands what human beings do. Neither in the historic Reformed tradition nor in Barth does this priority of grace nullify or even diminish what human beings do, but its implications for the latter are quite radical. In contrast to the pedagogical conception, in which grace partly assists and partly elevates human desires and capacities toward a fulfillment attained through moral striving, for Barth, as we have seen, human ethical activity affirms or confirms what God has already done; it is a human analogue of the divine work of electing and sanctifying grace and is carried out in response to the summons of grace that calls human beings to just such a repetition or attestation of grace in human conduct. It is in this way that human beings participate in the good God has ordained and accomplished on their behalf. '*Mihi Deo adhaerere bonum est.* "For me the good is to cleave to God."'[35] The pedagogical conception also says this. But for Barth, to cleave to God is to affirm what God has already done by corresponding to it in one's concrete existence as an acting subject.

Barth's rejection of the pedagogical conception puts him at odds with important trends in contemporary moral theology. Partisans of this conception might well pose the following objection to Barth: If the command of God is the command of God's grace, and if grace is what God does prior to and unconditioned by what we are and do, then is not the command of God alien to our own being and activity? In contrast to the pedagogical vision, Barth says of the Reformed vision that 'it is very difficult if not impossible for it to integrate itself into what humans otherwise want.'[36] For this reason, and in contrast to the broadly Aristotelian assumptions behind the pedagogical approach, Barth found an affinity between his doctrine of the command of God and the Kantian conception of the moral law insofar as both hold that moral obligation is established independently of what human beings desire.[37] Yet Barth, like Kant, does not finally oppose obligation to desire; he simply denies that we can arrive at

---

[34] Karl Barth, *The Theology of the Reformed Confessions, 1923*, trans. and annotated by Darrell L. Guder and Judith J. Guder (Louisville, Ky.: Westminster/John Knox Press, 2002), 207 f.

[35] CD II/2, 552/612.

[36] *The Theology of the Reformed Confessions*, 208. See also *Romans₂*, 277/294; and CD II/2, 555 f./616 f.

[37] CD II/2, 650/724.

what is morally required through consideration (and cultivation or expression) of what we desire, or would desire if adequately informed. Moreover, ethics for Barth involves conforming ontically, in our existence as acting subjects, to what we already are ontologically, affirming in our life conduct (ontic) who and what we are as creatures who share the humanity of Jesus Christ (ontological). Far from imposing a requirement that is alien to our humanity, the command of God requires the concrete realization of our humanity.

Once we grasp these distinctions between Barth's conception of ethics and the pedagogical conception we can understand how his moral theology is put together and why it has the structure it does. The key is the centrality to his moral theology of his distinctive notions of responsibility and gratitude. For Barth, the command of God is the summons of election, and the content of this summons is grace: the grace in which God resolves from eternity to be with and for an other and to grant this other a particular form of participation in God's own glory. It is this same summons, and the same divine grace, which confronts humanity in the works by which election is carried out: the work of creation, in which God in God's wisdom brings this other into existence in a cosmos, choosing some possibilities as good and rejecting others as evil; the work of reconciliation, in which God takes into God's own life the creature's contradiction to its divine determination and thereby overcomes it; and, finally, the work of redemption, in which the adoption of this human other as God's own child is accomplished, thus completing the determination given in her election. Formally speaking, the divine summons constitutes human beings as those who are responsible or answerable to it, and thus as moral subjects. This summons, however, never stands alone; it is never heard in abstraction from its content, which is grace, so that, substantively speaking, responsibility is exercised as gratitude. In other words, divine grace and human gratitude comprise the material correspondence in which the formal correspondence of divine summons and human responsibility is concretely real. Roughly speaking, the summons of grace occupies the place of the fulfillment to which desires and capacities are (imperfectly) oriented in the pedagogical conception, just as responsibility and gratitude occupy the place of the virtues which, by the empowerment of grace, direct desires and capacities to their fulfillment in that conception.

Responsibility and gratitude are therefore inseparable, but we can consider each of them separately. We begin with responsibility. If grace is what God has done, then to ground ethics in grace can only mean that what God has done takes the form of a summons to human beings to affirm it. Summons in turn implies responsibility: issued to someone, it makes him or her answerable to it. But because this summons is the summons of *grace*, there is an initial displacement of human responsibility: the grounding of ethics in divine grace means that ethics must begin with the responsibility God has taken for us. In placing us under God's command God 'makes himself responsible not only for its authority but also for its fulfillment.'[38] For Barth, this is a matter of God's faithfulness as the divine partner in the covenant. In issuing the divine command, God refuses to abandon us to our own quests for the good by which we subject ourselves and others to the limitations and distortions of human insight and authority, while in fulfilling this command, God refuses to abandon us to our own capability and to a worthiness that depends on our own attainment of the good. In both respects we are relieved of responsibility we were never meant to assume, discharged from the offices of lawgiver and judge and released from the necessity of achieving the good. Yet in taking responsibility for us in these ways, God also makes us responsible; grace is also summons. As answerability to this summons, human responsibility corresponds to divine responsibility as a human analogue to the latter and not a substitute for or usurpation of it. On the one hand, then, the grounding of ethics in grace implies a strong denial of human responsibility: human beings are not responsible for determining the good or bringing it about. On the other hand, human responsibility is fundamental: the moral subject is constituted by her answerability to the command, which summons her to confirm, in the exercise of all of her moral capacities, the good God has determined and brought about.

Barth directs this conception of responsibility against an influential modern conception. In this latter conception, responsibility implies that it is 'up to us' to determine and bring about the good, and (in its theological versions) that ethics marks the turn from what God does for us to what it is now left to us to do. On this view, human responsibility is self-posited, originating in the freedom of a neutral subject. Against this view, Barth holds that human responsibility is posited by God—or, more precisely, that its self-positing occurs as it is posited by God. Freedom consists in affirming the good conveyed in the command, not in a neutral stance between good and evil—or, more precisely, it consists in self-determination in accordance with one's determination by God's command. Ethical reflection is awareness of one's accountability to a law that confronts one from outside oneself; it is not self-reflection on a law within, originating in reason or conscience—or, more precisely, it consists in the exercise of reason and conscience in the awareness that one must hear the law as it is spoken in God's command. In all of this, Barth does not deny or occlude the moral subject but attempts to position this subject in relation to divine grace.

This brings us to gratitude.[39] In all of its works (election, creation, reconciliation, redemption), divine grace confers a benefit which we cannot obtain on our own, and gratitude is the obligation to recognize ourselves as beneficiaries in this sense.[40] The explicit designation of gratitude as an obligation seems to land Barth rather naively in the well-known aporia of the gift in its most elementary form, in

---

[38] CD II/2, 543/603.
[39] CD II/2, 413/456 f.; III/2, 166–74/198–207; IV/1, 41–4/43–5; CL, 30/44 f.
[40] CD III/2, 167/199.

which the requirement or even the expectation of gratitude links the gift to something that returns to the giver, thus implicating it in a circle of exchange which cancels the gift as gift. In fact, Barth is aware that an obligation of gratitude that could be discharged would leave the parties in an economic relation governed by mutual self-interest in which the benefit is repaid and the gift is thus dissolved. However, he explicitly denies that this is what he has in mind. For him, grace is never meant to be repaid—indeed, it would not be gratuitous at all but rather conditional if it were thought of in terms that imply repayment—and the obligation is never meant to be discharged. To understand the sense in which grace is a benefit is precisely not to consider it in terms of an economic exchange. Grace is not an expenditure on God's part for which gratitude compensates; it is an overflow of the divine love. For its part, gratitude is not an expenditure on the part of the recipient, a subtraction from the benefit received, which returns to God in full or partial payment of the divine gift; it is the form in which the recipient participates in the benefit. The movement of divine grace is complete in itself and requires nothing on the part of the recipient to complete it; indeed, any such requirement would nullify grace. Assumptions that imply an economic conception of the covenant relation are thus excluded from the outset. Gratitude returns to God not to complete the gift (it is already complete) but to enjoy it; it is the concrete form in which the gift, precisely as gift, becomes actual in human life. Without gratitude, the benefit would have no reality in the actual life of the recipient.[41] In gratitude, the recipient of grace acknowledges that she lives in and by grace, and with this acknowledgment she really does live in and by grace in her existence as an active subject. It is in this light that we must understand the obligation of gratitude. Grace does not just confer a benefit but summons us to full, active participation in that benefit. The obligation, then, is the gift itself: one lives in and by grace only insofar as one accepts the claim of grace on one's life, making grace the law of one's life.[42] 'Where a genuine benefit calls for thanks, and where genuine thanks respond to a benefit, there exists a relationship which, created by one party, can only be accepted by the other, and not cancelled but continually renewed.'[43] Grace and gratitude exemplify (and in fact constitute) a divine–human relationship in which the fact that everything is done by God does not exclude but establishes human action (a point we will elaborate in Chapter 5).

As the active acceptance of one's status as a recipient of grace, gratitude is also the most general material expression of the correspondence of human conduct to God in the inter-human context. It is as recipients of grace that we are to conduct our affairs with others, treating them in analogy to how God has treated us. This is nowhere more apparent than in Barth's treatment of the Sermon on the

---

[41] CD II/2, 413/457.
[42] CD II/2, 695/776.
[43] CD III/2, 167/199 (revised).

Mount, where he systematically subverts possible economic interpretations of passages in Matthew 5 and 6 where rewards are promised, insisting instead that the behavior of the meek, the merciful, and the peacemakers, of the ones who secretly give alms, pray, and fast, and of those who love their enemies, forgive others, and refrain from judging—that all of this behavior is not motivated by the promised blessing as a reward but is rather expressive of this blessing as a gift already received from God, albeit in the form of a promise. We act graciously toward others because we know ourselves already to be the beneficiaries of grace; we do not do so in order thereby to become the beneficiaries of grace. As he pithily asserts in connection with the Golden Rule, which seems to establish an economic equivalence between one's own actions and the actions of others, 'It is what they have received and would always receive that they are to bring to others.... Not "give and take" [economic exchange] but "take [that is, receive grace] and give [to others]" is the golden rule...'[44] In its correspondence to divine grace, human ethical action is fundamentally non-economic.

Three additional points will allow us to bring this section to a close. First, while for Barth every truly moral action is in some sense an act of gratitude, it does not follow that every action must be a direct expression of gratitude. Concrete human action will always be a specification of gratitude in some deed in the life of a human being as a creature, reconciled sinner, and heir of redemption. It would therefore be a mistake to try to derive the specific command of God directly from gratitude. Still, the criterion of every action will always be 'whether it is an action which exactly and fully corresponds and is adequate to God's Word of grace.'[45] In other words, every action must at least implicitly express the recognition that one is the recipient of grace. Second, responsibility and gratitude imply each other. It is because human responsibility is both limited and established by grace that it can only take the concrete form of gratitude. I owe my responsibility to God's responsibility for me; my responsibility is rightly exercised in the awareness of this fact, and is thus itself an expression of gratitude. Meanwhile, in its limited obligation in response to the gift, gratitude exhibits the limits of responsibility itself. To be grateful is to know oneself as the recipient of the gift rather than to assert one's parity with the giver by paying it back, just as responsibility is properly exercised in response to God's responsibility for us rather than as the assertion of our likeness to God. Finally, responsibility and gratitude exhibit the key features of what Barth means by the correspondence or analogy of divine and human action: In both cases there is, on the one hand, a sharp distinction between what God does and what humans do, ensuring that human action remains a witness to what God does instead of substituting itself for the latter, yet there is also, on the other hand, a mimetic connection between divine and human action, ensuring that what human beings

---

[44] CD II/2, 694/775.
[45] CD III/2, 170/203; see also IV/1, 42 f./44 f.

do retains a similarity to what God does. 'What is involved is that man and man's action should become the image of God: the reflection [*Spiegel*] *which represents* [*darstellt*], *although in itself it is completely different from,* God and his action; the reflection in which God recognizes himself and his action.'[46] For Barth, all human ethical action occurs in the analogical tension between the difference from God's action presupposed by testimony and the similarity to God's action presupposed by mimesis, and the required correspondence to God's action can fail due to the exaggeration of either aspect. Because the good God brings to human beings is participation in the very good God enjoys in intra-Trinitarian communion, human action must be a mimesis of God's action (though because humans participate in this good in a distinctively human way, the mimesis will be nonidentical). At the same time, this good is secured for human beings by God, and this fact finds expression in human action when the latter takes the form of testimony to what God has brought about.

4. VISION

Every moral theology affirms, at least implicitly, a theological meaning or spiritual purpose that provides the ultimate context for human moral life. Barth offers a thorough and radical exposition of the broadly Calvinist conviction that the purpose of human life, both individually and collectively, is to glorify God in the world. His most distinctive contribution to this central tenet of the Reformed tradition is his conviction that God's glorification in the world is accomplished in the glorification of human beings, whose participation in God's glory is expressed in their lives in the world as creatures, reconciled sinners, and heirs of redemption. God's glorification occurs with God's determination from eternity to be in fellowship with this other who is not God and with the fulfillment of this determination in the creation, reconciliation, and redemption of this human other. Human beings glorify God by saying Yes to their exalted status, that is, by confirming it in their life conduct. Human life in the world glorifies God by reflecting God's glorification of humanity.

With this formulation, Barth comes to terms with the irony of the Calvinist vision, noted by observers from Max Weber to Charles Taylor, namely, that an ethic which aimed at the glorification of God became secularized and transformed into a thoroughly humanistic ethic.[47] His moral theology is a sustained critique of the ethos of bourgeois Christianity that is partly the unintended legacy of Calvinist activism and its effort to make the world reflect God's glory. What

---

[46] CD II/2, 575/639 (emphasis added).

[47] See Max Weber, *The Protestant Ethic and the Spirit of Capitalism*, trans. Talcott Parsons (New York: Scribners, 1958); and Charles Taylor, *A Secular Age* (Cambridge, Mass.: Harvard University Press, 2007), especially 61–84.

exactly is this bourgeois Christian ethos? We can succinctly describe it by high-lighting six characteristics: (1) a commitment to human flourishing or well being as the fulfillment of strictly natural human capacities, desires, needs, and aspirations; (2) a deep conviction, accompanied by a sense of urgency, that it is 'up to us' to make the good or the just prevail in the world; (3) an unshakeable confidence in the ability of human beings to remake themselves and their societies in accordance with moral requirements and ideals; (4) the identification of human moral achievements, whether in history and society or in personal lives, with the righteousness or goodness of God; (5) a belief in the moral, economic, and religious self-sufficiency of the individual and a concomitant tendency—deeply embedded in societal norms, practices, and institutions, and in spite of a commitment to the formal equality of human beings—to judge the worth of human beings in terms of what they may or actually do achieve for themselves or for society; and (6) a demand for the reconstruction of Christian belief and the reorientation of Christian practice around the priority of moral ideals and requirements, so understood. This ethos was at the peak of its influence in the time and place of Barth's youth and early adulthood, but it has quite obviously survived the end of the bourgeois era itself.

Barth's rejection of this ethos was by no means total; at the very least, he had high regard for its moral earnestness, its focus on ordinary life, and its respect for the integrity of natural human capacities. Nevertheless, he did reject the bourgeois ethos at its most fundamental level. He came to see that at the root of this ethos is the determination of human beings to be by and for themselves, whereas (for him) the crux of moral theology, and of Christian theology generally, is God's fulfillment in Jesus Christ of God's eternal will to be with and for humanity. We may now state the question that drives Barth's moral theology: How can human ethical inquiry and practice express the reality of God's being as being with and for us, rather than expressing (as in the bourgeois ethos) our determination (in sinful defiance of God's glorification of humanity) to be by and for ourselves? More specifically, how can human ethical inquiry and practice express the fact that in Jesus Christ, God has established the good and accomplished it in our place, rather than expressing the conviction that we are left to ourselves to determine what is good and bring it about? The thesis of this book is that Barth's moral theology is an effort to answer this question. Barth arrives at his answer by reworking his Protestant Reformation tradition in a way that brings ethics unambiguously into the domain of the theology of divine grace as it was articulated in that tradition. By establishing and fulfilling the good in our place, grace interrupts all of our striving for the good and calls it into question. Yet precisely as such, grace summons us and, by the Holy Spirit, empowers and directs us to exist in a human analogy to grace, and thereby to glorify the God who glorifies us.

1

The Problem of Ethics

Imagine a reader encountering Karl Barth's *Church Dogmatics* for the first time. She is startled to find passages where the author equates ethics with sinful human pretensions. What is meant, she wonders, by the assertion that the conception of ethics as the human effort to answer the question of the good 'coincides exactly with the conception of sin,' or that '[w]hat the serpent has in mind [in Gen. 3: 5] is the establishment of ethics'?[1] She then finds, to her surprise, that many experienced readers are undisturbed by such passages. One such reader reassures the scandalized novice by pointing out that Barth can 'safely say' that the problem of ethics 'is *the* theological problem,' '*the* problem of dogmatics,' or the 'most characteristic problem' of theology or dogmatics, and that dogmatics 'has the problem of ethics in view from the very first.'[2] She goes on to mention Barth's high esteem for the Epistle of James as the paradigmatic expression of the proper relation of faith and works, 'gospel' and 'law'—a deliberate reversal of Luther's judgment of the epistle itself and of his antithesis of gospel and law more generally[3]—and notes that the first explicit treatment of ethics in the *Church Dogmatics* is an extended exposition of the Jacobean point that to be a hearer of the Word of God is inseparable from being a doer of it.[4]

These two readers—one new, the other seasoned—are not purely hypothetical, nor is the drama of scandal and reassurance their readings enact. They represent two stages of scholarship on Barth's ethics: an earlier stage in which Barth's polemics against ethics were taken to have simply made explicit what had (it appeared) already been ruled out in principle by his theological emphasis on divine action, and a more recent stage in which Barth's positive remarks are taken as evidence for the view that he opposes only certain kinds of ethics or certain approaches, so that a place can be found for him in the ongoing conversation

---

[1] CD II/2, 518/574; CD IV/1, 448/497.

[2] CD I/2, 790/884, 794/888 (both revised), 793/887; CD III/4, 3/1.

[3] 'There is no New Testament writing that presents the Gospel to men so emphatically and unwaveringly, so consistently from the standpoint of the divine claim, as the Epistle of James' (CD II/2, 588/653 f.).

[4] CD I/2, 362–7/397–403.

about ethics that was only temporarily disturbed by his abrupt entry.[5] But perhaps these negations and affirmations of ethics reflect not only the varying judgments of successive stages of scholarship but also a fundamental ambiguity about ethics in Barth's own thought. This book argues that this ambiguity of ethics, and the problem it involves, is central to Barth's moral theology, and the task of this chapter is to trace the ambiguity through the various stages of his thought, showing how it shapes his understanding of ethics at each stage.

That Barth's work exhibits an ambiguity about ethics is not in itself exceptional. In thinkers such as Nietzsche, Heidegger, and Derrida, ambiguity of one kind or another in relation to ethics becomes a defining feature distinguishing late modern or postmodern ethics from modern ethics.[6] For all three of these thinkers, the ethics to which we look for justice or the good is the scene of a kind of betrayal: It does not accomplish the good or the just, in the name of which it speaks, but betrays them, whether by suppressing a more robust form (Nietzsche), substituting itself for a more originary form (Heidegger), or concealing the violence that it does in its own name (Derrida). For Barth, too, the ambiguity of ethics indicates a betrayal, and for him, as for Nietzsche and Heidegger, the betrayal becomes especially evident in modern ethics while it has in fact occurred much earlier. Yet the ambiguity that concerns Barth is not another instance of the late-modern knowingness that has seen through every deception and is well aware of what lies behind every claim to the good or the just, yet refuses to succumb to the nihilism it has itself exposed in these

---

[5] The first stage as denoted here includes John Cullberg, *Das Problem der Ethik in der Dialektischen Theologie* (Uppsala: Appelbergs, 1938); and Willis, *The Ethics of Karl Barth*. The second stage includes Biggar, *The Hastening that Waits*; Webster, *Barth's Ethics of Reconciliation*; and idem, *Barth's Moral Theology*. Biggar and Webster decisively refute the charge that Barth's theology is inimical to ethics but they tend to understate the tension between Barth's ethics and other forms of ethics.

[6] Nietzsche's attack on morality in the form of the contrast pair 'good–evil' may be said to have inaugurated late modern thought about ethics, yet Nietzsche made it clear that his attack was not directed against the contrast pair 'good–bad.' See Friedrich Nietzsche, *Beyond Good and Evil: Prelude to a Philosophy of the Future* (London: Penguin, 1990), 108–28, and idem, *On the Genealogy of Morality* (New York: Cambridge University Press, 1994), 36. Heidegger's critique of the technological reduction of action characteristic of the age of metaphysics—a reduction he found operative already in Aristotle's ethics—coincided with an effort to retrieve a more originary ethic, which for him was conveyed by the word *ēthos* in the famous fragment of the pre-Socratic, Heraclitus. See Martin Heidegger, 'Letter on "Humanism,"' in *Pathmarks*, ed. William McNeill (Cambridge: Cambridge University Press, 1998), 268–71. Finally, Derrida's exposure of the aporia of justice resulting from its dual demand of adherence to the universalizing rule and response to the other in her irreducible singularity is meant not to provoke skepticism about ethics but to prevent ethics from concealing the violence that is inevitable given the undecidability of the universal and the singular. See Jacques Derrida, *The Gift of Death*, 2nd edn., trans. David Willis (Chicago: University of Chicago Press, 2008), especially 25–7. For Derrida the ambiguity is within the ethical itself, in undecidability as a constitutive feature of the ethical; it is not an ambiguity between different kinds of ethics as it is for Nietzsche and Heidegger. But in each case the question raised by the ambiguity is some variation on the question which opens Emmanuel Levinas's *Totality and Infinity*, namely, whether we have been duped by morality. See Levinas, *Totality and Infinity: An Essay on Exteriority*, trans. Alphonso Lingis (Pittsburgh: Duquesne University Press, 1969), 21.

suppressions, substitutions, and concealments in which the betrayal is accomplished. Rather, the ambiguity that concerns him follows directly from his most basic theological convictions about divine grace.

1. THE PROBLEM DEFINED

To grasp the ambiguity of ethics as Barth sees it and the problem it involves we begin with two central claims on which his mature moral theology rests. The first claim is an assertion of the primacy of God's grace. For Barth, the good with which moral theology is concerned (namely, the fellowship of human beings with God) is both established and fulfilled by God in the revelation and work of God's grace in Jesus Christ. It is not and never was God's will to leave to human beings and their moral capacities the task of determining what the good is or attaining it. 'Even as ethics, theology is wholly and utterly the knowledge and representation of the Word and work of God.'[7] At the same time, while the good is actualized in Christ, it does not remain with him alone, remote from the lives of other human beings. It summons these others to exist as those for whom it has been actualized and thus to participate in it in a distinctively and properly human way. This is the second claim: an assertion that the Word and work of God's grace as presented in the first claim is intimately bound up with human conduct in the form of the summons, or command, to confirm grace. From these two claims it follows that the subject matter (*Sache*) of moral theology is 'the Word and work of God in Jesus Christ, in which the right action of man has already been performed and therefore waits only to be confirmed by our action.'[8]

The task of moral theology, then, is to attest God's grace, which, as pure gift, is unconditioned by human action and thus radically disrupts human moral striving, yet which also demands confirmation in human conduct. We have just presented Barth's mature formulation of this task, but the problem it involves goes back much earlier in his career. As Barth came to see it during the 1920s, while he was working out his understanding of ethics as a Reformed theologian on predominantly Lutheran and Catholic faculties, the failure to carry out this task may take two forms, corresponding to these two claims. First, moral theology may fail to portray the good as that which God determines and brings about. Instead, the good is represented as attainable through human moral activity, though not without the work of divine grace. While it affirms the necessity of grace, what is decisive about this position in Barth's view is that the working of grace presupposes continuity, ultimately rooted in the analogy of

---

[7] CD II/2, 537 f./597.
[8] CD II/2, 543/603.

being, between our moral activity and its final, transcendent end.[9] On the basis of this continuity the moral life is portrayed in gradualist terms, as a transformation from sinfulness to perfection accomplished by the cooperation of human action with divine grace. Moral theology of this kind may make strong claims about the priority of grace, but in Barth's view it cannot sustain these claims. 'Grace which has from the start to share its power [*Kraft*] with a force [*Vermögen*] of nature is no longer grace.'[10] Even when its necessity is acknowledged and its priority to human action asserted, grace in this scheme is compromised, assimilated to a process that occurs in the human subject. For Barth, this portrayal of the moral life expresses the attitude of a subject that 'wishes to remain by itself, and does not wish to hear of something radically different from its own working and its possible changes.'[11] In the end, this subject will acknowledge nothing beyond its own possibilities and limitations, and the good at which it aims will be one that is proportionate to its capability, its activity, its achievements. Barth attributed this failure to Catholic moral theology, which he took to be a sophisticated version of an approach also taken by pietist and liberal forms of Protestantism.

But failure may take another form. This time it is the Reformation-era proponents of a more radical theology of grace who are at fault for failing to demonstrate or maintain the significance of their conception of grace for ethics. According to this theology, grace interrupts human striving by revealing the discontinuity between all human moral activity and the righteousness of God. But while both the Lutheran and (more insistently) the Reformed traditions claimed that their radical conceptions of divine grace gave human moral activity its proper due, neither finally succeeded, in Barth's view, in making good on this claim. Either divine action on behalf of human beings seemed to leave human moral action without a clear status, leading in practice to the marginalization of ethics (the Lutheran failure), or human moral action became independent of divine action on behalf of human beings, leading to a de facto secularization of ethics (the Reformed failure). How can moral theology maintain the centrality and sufficiency of divine grace while also maintaining both the necessity of human moral action and its inner connection to the divine action of grace? This is the question Barth faced in coming to terms with this Reformation heritage whose general theology of grace he fully embraced.

It is important for everything that follows to emphasize that in posing this question Barth takes up what in the early 1920s he identified as the Reformed problematic over against the Lutheran: He will not avoid the question of ethics or diminish its importance in relation to that of grace but will persist in asking

---

[9] Karl Barth, *The Holy Spirit and the Christian Life*, trans. R. Birch Hoyle (Louisville, Ky.: Westminster/John Knox Press, 1993), 3 f.
[10] CD II/2, 531/589; *Ethics*, 31/50.
[11] *The Holy Spirit and the Christian Life*, 25.

what is the significance of grace for human conduct. What does the righteousness that comes to us through God's grace have to do with our conduct in the world? Grace interrupts our striving, yet it also demands to be expressed in our conduct. But how can grace, which only comes to us in radical discontinuity with our moral striving, be expressed in our conduct in the world without the betrayal of grace, without repeating the first failure, namely, the assimilation of the good to the human moral subject? This, for Barth, is the problem of ethics. It is the burden of this chapter to show how this problem, in one form or another, is the force that drives his moral theology, shaping both its development and its content.

We will take up this burden below by showing how Barth's moral theology during its four major formative periods becomes clear when we view it as a series of attempts to pose and solve this problem. But we must first acknowledge the extent to which his way of posing the problem of ethics is determined by the confessional polemics in which he articulated it in the 1920s. Our discomfort with this fact is due not only to an ecumenist sensibility that recoils at Barth's polemical stance against the internal other; it is, more profoundly, due to the fact that his stereotypical portrayals of this other—the Catholic failure to take grace seriously, the Lutheran disregard of ethics—do not accord with our best understandings of these traditions and the similarities and differences between them. This problem is most acute in Barth's tendency to view Catholicism through a Protestant lens, finding in it a sophisticated, ingenious version of a theological position exhibited in a crude, makeshift fashion in pietist, rationalist, and especially liberal forms of Protestantism. Consider in this context the version of a well-known Thomistic dictum quoted by Barth in a discussion of Catholic moral theology: *gratia sanans et elevans naturam* ('grace heals and elevates nature'). For Barth, this dictum, or at least its customary interpretation, binds grace to the possibilities inherent in nature, that is, to human capability. As we have seen, to understand grace in this way is, for Barth, to fail to take it seriously: 'Grace which has from the start to share its power with a force of nature is no longer grace.' However, the dictum is better understood to mean that while our natural capacities are incapable of bringing us to our final end of union with God, which must rather be the work of grace, yet it is our natural capacities, and not some others, which are elevated and perfected in being brought to this end by grace. The continuity between our moral activity and its final end resides in the active exercise of our capacities but not in our capability; in the latter respect, grace does not share its power with a force of nature. For Barth, as we have seen, grace accomplishes our good apart from our activity, actualizing it for us in Jesus Christ. Yet grace also summons and empowers us to participate in its accomplishment with all of our capacities, which were created precisely for this purpose. It is clear that the difference between the Thomist and the Barthian positions cannot be captured by a simple contrast between continuity and discontinuity of our moral activity with the ultimate good. Rather, it is the difference between a notion of grace as working in us to bring about a perfection of our natural capacities which they are incapable of accomplishing, on the one hand, and a notion of grace as bringing about our good apart from our activity and summoning us, from the site of its actualization, to active participation in it, on the other hand.

This difference is nevertheless significant, and Barth will appeal to the Protestant Reformers to insist that grace accomplishes the ultimate good of communion with God for us, apart from our activity, that is, in Jesus Christ, in whom alone it is also ours. But it is just here that Barth corrects what he perceives as the failure of Luther and Calvin and their heirs to establish the proper relation of ethics to grace. For Barth, it is not only our righteousness before God but also our sanctity or holiness that is alien—and yet in both cases what is ours only in Christ also summons and empowers us to active participation in it. What Barth is concerned to do with this schema is to overcome every tendency to represent our acceptance by God and the accompanying renewal of life as involving different forms or operations of grace or different ways in which grace is related to human activity. For him, sanctification is no less the work of grace and the holiness it effects is no less in Christ than are justification and the righteousness it effects— or, indeed, is election itself. The point is best illustrated in the relation of justification and sanctification. Justification involves God's establishment of a relationship with the sinner in which God maintains divine right while also setting the sinner in a right relation to God. In sanctification, the one whom God justifies is also one whom God 'introduces as a new man,' namely, 'a faithful covenant partner who is well-pleasing to him and blessed by him.'[12] It is clear that justification and sanctification, while distinct, are equally the work of God. Barth thus refuses to present them in terms of a 'dualism between an objective achievement of salvation there and then [i.e., justification] and a subjective appropriation of it here and now [i.e., sanctification] . . .'[13] He rejects what he sees as a tendency to attribute justification to Christ and sanctification to ourselves, 'as though his humiliation to death for our justification . . . were his own act, but our exaltation to fellowship with God . . . and therefore our sanctification, were left to us, to be accomplished by us.'[14] Such is by no means the case. 'As we are not asked to justify ourselves, we are not asked to sanctify ourselves.'[15] It is Christ who does both and who, in the case of sanctification, gives to our own action 'the power and significance . . . of a witness to the sanctification of man accomplished in him.'[16]

---

[12] CD IV/2, 499/565.
[13] CD IV/2, 502 f./569.
[14] CD IV/2, 516/584.
[15] CD IV/2, 517/585.
[16] CD IV/2, 528/597 f. There is, of course, much more to say about the relationship between justification and sanctification in Barth's theology. A highly illuminating account of it in relation to Luther and Calvin is found in George Hunsinger, 'A Tale of Two Simultaneities: Justification and

Barth therefore rejects 'the opinion that the goodness, that is, the holiness of the Christian character, in contrast to all the other objective content of Christian proclamation, is not hidden with Christ in God (in spite of Col. 3: 3), but is directly visible...'[17] For him, to hold to this opinion—most notably in the tendency to treat sanctification or the renewal of life, in contrast to justification or election, as a gradual process resulting in visible holiness—can only reflect an interest in qualifying the role of grace in our moral lives, diminishing its force in this domain in comparison with others. And for Barth, that interest is far from harmless. In a post-Reformation context it can only indicate the bourgeois-humanist determination to reserve something for human moral capability over against grace, to reduce the good to what human beings are capable of knowing and bringing about, and to transform Christian faith into a moral religion in which ethics, so understood, has become the criterion of the church's speech and practice. Barth's alternative is to present the entirety of God's Word and work in the same terms: as the Word and work of God's grace which is fulfilled for us in Jesus Christ and which, as already ours in him, summons and empowers us to active participation in it. It is for this reason, and under these terms, that ethics forms a necessary part of every dogmatic topic.

We are now in a position to understand Barth's identification of ethics with sanctification. In its narrow sense, sanctification forms that part of the doctrine of the reconciliation of sinners to God which has to do with human beings as those who now share in Christ's exaltation. In its broad sense, however, sanctification is coterminous with the whole of ethics. It involves the entirety of the human response to God's dealings with human beings, including the hearing and obeying of the Word of God revealed to human beings, the human self-determination that is demanded in response to the divine determination of human beings in election, and the specifications of all of this in the lives of human beings as creatures, reconciled sinners, and heirs of redemption. Our focus here is on the broad sense, but it is significant that in both senses the notion of sanctification is inseparable from that of the command of God. This inseparability has two aspects: it includes *both* the fact that God places human beings under God's command *and* the fact that this command is efficacious in human conduct.

We may summarize these two aspects as follows. For Barth, the first task of moral theology is to understand the Word of God as the command of God, and it begins with the conviction 'that man's action is good insofar as it is sanctified by the Word of God which as such is also the command of God.'[18] In this sense, human beings are sanctified simply by virtue of being placed under the command

Sanctification in Calvin and Barth,' in *Conversing with Barth*, ed. John C. McDowell and Mike Higton (Aldershot: Ashgate, 2004), 68–89.

[17] CD I/2, 782/875 (revised).
[18] CD III/4, 4/2. See also *Ethics*, 16/24 f., 49/81 f., 88/146.

of God, which in itself accomplishes the separation (*Aussonderung*) by which one is claimed for the purpose of attesting God's grace.[19] Moral theology thus proceeds by examining 'the fact and extent that human sanctification and therefore good human action come about through the action of God in his command.'[20] Barth refers to this examination as 'general ethics.' However, moral theology does not stop here. 'For how can we look at the activity of God in his command without being forced to follow its movement and thus being led automatically to man, to what it performs (*ausrichtet*) in him, to what becomes of him in consequence?'[21] In this turn to human conduct, Barth stresses, moral theology 'still has to do with the Word of God as the command of God'—it is not a shift away from what God does to what human beings do—but because the command of God is not inert, leaving it to human beings to act on its determination of their lives, but comes to human beings as an active power, moral theology now turns to human conduct itself, in its concrete reality, to examine 'the fact and extent of the existence of good human action under the lordship and efficacy (*Wirksamkeit*) of the divine command.'[22] Sanctification in this second sense involves 'special ethics,' which by following the movement of the command of God into the realm of human action addresses two questions: First, what is God's command as it is given to us in the distinctive domains of creation, reconciliation, and redemption; and second, how is it that this command (sometimes and to some extent) is actually obeyed by human beings? In both of these aspects—as God's activity of placing human beings under God's command (general ethics) and as the reality and efficacy of God's command in concrete human conduct (special ethics)—sanctification definitively occurs in Jesus Christ and then in other human beings by virtue of their participation in Christ through the Holy Spirit.

The problem of ethics, then, comes down to these questions: How can moral theology be presented as the culmination of the theology of grace rather than as an exception to or a qualification of the latter? How can human conduct express the goodness of God rather than our own goodness? How can ethics express the conviction that God is for us rather than the conviction that we must be for ourselves? For Barth, these are questions the Protestant Reformers (by which he means Luther and Calvin) and their heirs never satisfactorily resolved. As a result of their failure, Protestant theology never developed a moral theology consonant with its theology of grace, leaving the Protestant churches vulnerable to the

---

[19] The notion of separation contains the core meaning of holiness for Barth. See *Ethics* 112 f./ 187 f.; CD II/2, 512/567; CL 157/261 f. In 1929 Barth referred to a preference Luther once expressed for the term 'separated' rather than 'sanctified' to characterize the Christian, holding the former to be more reverent and modest as well as closer to the Greek 'hagios.' See *The Holy Spirit and the Christian Life*, 35, 53 n. 71.

[20] CD III/4, 4/2 (revised).

[21] CD III/4, 5/3.

[22] CD III/4, 6/4 f.

bourgeois-humanist transformation of Western culture during the centuries following the Reformation and depriving that culture of the Christian humanist alternative Barth found to be the essence of Christian faith.

We are moving ahead of our story, which is told more fully in the next chapter. Our task here is to demonstrate the centrality of this problem to Barth's understanding of ethics. It is a problem that Barth explicitly articulated in the early 1920s during his intensive engagement with the classic sources of Reformed theology and resolved, at least to his satisfaction, roughly two decades later with the Christological determination of ethics offered as part of his doctrine of God in the *Church Dogmatics*. But these are simply two reference points in a struggle with this problem which began earlier and continued to reverberate later. This chapter traces the high points of this struggle. It is less an exhaustive developmental account of it than a close examination of points at which significant stages of that development achieve their fullest expression. By showing how Barth's treatment of this problem retained a consistency over time this chapter contributes to the impressive body of literature that finds continuity between Barth's earlier and later ethics.[23] At the same time, this chapter differs from other studies by its focus on the sanctification of human conduct and the problem this involves and by the evidence it provides that Barth's moral theology is implicated in greater tensions than are acknowledged by recent scholars who (rightly) refute the charge that his position leaves no room for genuine ethics.

2. THE RIGHTEOUSNESS OF GOD

Whatever we may conclude regarding Barth's break with liberal theology—when exactly it occurred and how deep the fissure ran—it is indisputable that over the course of his years as a pastor in Safenwil (1911–21) he grew increasingly dissatisfied with liberal Protestant theologies in which God is 'given' in religious experience, moral consciousness, or a historical process. More positively, he became increasingly convinced that theology must recover a sense of what we refer to technically as the aseity of God. An increasingly restless Barth was

---

[23] See especially Christof Gestrich, *Neuzeitliches Denken und die Spaltung der Dialektischen Theologie* (Tübingen: J. C. B. Mohr, 1977), 59–72; Werner Ruschke, *Entstehung und Ausführung der Diastasentheologie in Karl Barths zweitem Römerbrief* (Neukirchen Vluyn: Neukirchener Verlag, 1987), 72–89; Bruce L. McCormack, *Karl Barth's Critically Realistic Dialectical Theology: Its Genesis and Development, 1909–1936* (Oxford: Oxford University Press, 1995), 274–80; Webster, *Barth's Moral Theology*, 11–64. Gestrich focuses on Barth's 1919 Tambach lecture and his 1922 lecture on 'The Problem of Ethics Today,' while Ruschke, as his title indicates, concentrates on the second edition of Barth's commentary on Romans. McCormack discusses the first Romans commentary and the Tambach lecture, but he finds continuity with Barth's later ethics primarily in the second Romans commentary. None of these scholars is centrally concerned with ethics in Barth's thought. This cannot be said of Webster, who insightfully discusses most of the relevant texts in his argument for continuity.

grappling with these still inchoate convictions in early 1916 when he delivered a lecture in Aarau with the title 'The Righteousness of God.' With much of Europe engulfed in death and destruction, that righteousness would surely have been in question among those who heard the lecture. Meanwhile, Barth's spirited protest against what he saw as the failure of the church to take God's aseity seriously in relation to society was already under way, a protest which would culminate in the famous Romans commentaries of 1919 and 1922. 'Above all,' he intoned in an early version of what would become a kind of defining slogan, 'it will be a matter of acknowledging God once again as God.'[24] But if God is not being acknowledged as God it must be because God has been confused with something else— for Barth, in this lecture and at this stage generally, with the bourgeois moral, social, political, and religious order that prevailed before the war, but also with the revolutionary protest against that order in the religious socialist program with which he had strong yet critical sympathies. And so, Barth used the lecture, and the war that occasioned it, neither to defend the righteousness of God nor to despair over its absence but to expose the arrogance and futility of the 'towers of Babel' human beings construct in their vain and ultimately destructive attempts to establish the righteousness only God can establish. Ethics must begin with the recognition of the wide gulf between the true righteousness God brings about and the false semblance of divine righteousness produced by human beings in their mistaken confidence in their own power to accomplish God's will in human history and society. The will of God, Barth proclaims, 'is not a corrected continuation of our own will. It encounters us as a wholly other.'[25]

This theme, put forth so persistently and forcefully during the later years of his Safenwil pastorate (most notably in his famous 1919 lecture at Tambach on 'The Christian's Place in Society,' but also in the first edition of *The Epistle to the Romans* (hereafter, *Romans₁*) of the same year), was one Barth would never abandon; from this time forward ethics for him will always have to begin with the recognition that the good it seeks is found in what God does and not in what human beings do, and that there is no path from the latter to the former. This theme, of course, strikes at the heart of claims to human moral achievement both in history and in individual lives, and it is these claims that Barth, in his struggle during this period to find a way beyond bourgeois moral self-assurance and revolutionary socialism, is most concerned to challenge.[26] Yet his challenge is far

---

[24] 'Die Gerechtigkeit Gottes,' in Karl Barth, *Das Wort Gottes und die Theologie* (Munich: Chr. Kaiser Verlag: 1925), 15 (translation 'The Righteousness of God,' in *The Word of God and the Word of Man*, trans. Douglas Horton (Gloucester, Mass.: Peter Smith, 1978)), 24.

[25] 'Die Gerechtigkeit Gottes,' 15/24.

[26] This is why the point that in this lecture Barth repeatedly refers to the righteousness of God as present to the conscience is not in itself decisive evidence that Barth was still a 'liberal' in early 1916. Claims like this often presuppose that (1) there was a particular moment when Barth ceased to be a liberal and (2) there is a single feature or a precise set of features that distinguish liberalism from whatever Barth became when he ceased to be a liberal. Both are overly simplistic assumptions.

from a pessimistic renunciation of the hope for social transformation. The denial that there is any way from the 'here' of our moral and social endeavors to the 'there' of God's righteousness is matched by a conviction that there is a way from there to here—that there is a movement of the wholly other God in history. 'Then the radically new thing begins to grow in us like a seed that will sprout, overcoming unrighteousness. Where faith is, there is born in the midst of the old world of war and money and death the new spirit out of which grows a new world, the world of the righteousness of God.'[27] This organic metaphor indicates Barth's essentially positive thesis: God is the *living* God, so to acknowledge God as God is not only to reject the identification of God's will with any human program for the social order, whether bourgeois or socialist; it is also to live in hope of the eschatological manifestation of God's will in history.

This is the context in which we must understand the meaning Barth ascribes to human ethical action during this period. Barth held firmly to two convictions. First, the world war and the ensuing crises of industrial society had exposed the bourgeois order as a form of human unrighteousness in opposition to the righteousness of God. There was no going back to the confident assurance of the bourgeois era in the conformity of the existing social order to the will of God. Second, while Christian socialism offers a closer approximation to the divine righteousness, it ignores the most important lesson taught by the collapse of the bourgeois order: that society cannot be brought into conformity with the divine righteousness through human programs, whether bourgeois or socialist, but only by God. No less than bourgeois affirmation of the existing order does revolutionary criticism of the latter belong to this world and its conditions. It is therefore confidence in *God's* action that Barth aimed to impress on his audience of religious socialists at Tambach: 'God in history is *a priori* victory in history . . . The real seriousness of our situation is not to be minimized; the tragic incompleteness in which we find ourselves is not to be glossed over. . . . [But] the last word is the *kingdom of God*—creation, redemption, the perfection of the world through God and in God.'[28] Yet Barth's conviction that God's action is ultimately decisive in history does not make human action superfluous, as his critics often charged. Rather, it is what enables human beings to act with expectant hope. The ground of this hope is the resurrection of Jesus. Just as the resurrection involves 'the appearance in our corporeality of a *totaliter aliter* . . . constituted corporeality,' so the goal of history is 'the summation of the history of *God* in history, its glory veiled to us but manifest to him and to those whose eyes he has opened.'[29] The radical discontinuity between human history and God's righteousness is not final. Barth does insist that to the extent

---

[27] 'Die Gerechtigkeit Gottes,' 16/25 f.
[28] 'Der Christ in der Gesellschaft,' in Barth, *Das Wort Gottes und die Theologie*, 49 (translation 'The Christian's Place in Society,' in *The Word of God*, trans. Horton, 297).
[29] 'Der Christ in der Gesellschaft,' 66/323, 66/322.

that it is overcome (and here we must not forget that the *totaliter aliter* remains *totaliter aliter* even as it is present in our corporeality and in our history), it is not by human action but by God, who establishes the divine righteousness in history. Yet rather than a counsel of inaction, the Tambach address is an exhortation to reorient human action to this eschatological context and away from the false confidence in the power of our moral and social endeavors. 'We need not therefore be apprehensive of any discrediting of our life here and of activity in our life here *if* we conclude with Calvin to fix the place of the Christian in society within the *spes futurae vitae.*'[30]

Barth's basic claim regarding human moral action is thus already in place at this stage. That claim both denies the capacity of human action to do what God alone can do and affirms human action as some properly human form of participation in what God alone does. The problem with Barth's position at this stage is not that he replaces human action by divine action but that he grossly oversimplifies the problem of human action in this eschatological scheme. The first aim of moral exhortation is the reorientation of the will towards divine action, and Barth makes everything rest on this initial move, the one in which we turn from our own righteousness to the righteousness of God. Insisting on our own righteousness, we ignore the righteousness of God, but once we make the shift from human righteousness to the righteousness of God, thus taking up the eschatological standpoint, moral perplexity simply disappears. The major point of the Tambach lecture is not that human action should cease in expectation of the divine action, but rather that once it is undertaken from this eschatological standpoint, human action will exhibit the right balance of acceptance of the social order and radical criticism of it. 'To look from creation and redemption to their consummation, to the "wholly other" of the *regnum gloriae*, means in practice that both our naïve and our critical attitude to society, our Yes and our No, *fall into right relation to each other in God.*'[31] This confidence that good human conduct will follow immediately from orientation to the divine righteousness leads Barth to dismiss questions regarding concrete moral conduct. In the Tambach lecture, for example, he defers to the very end and dispatches in a few meager sentences the deliberative question 'What should we then do?' When we adopt the eschatological viewpoint, 'eternity is set in our hearts,' and if that is so, there is no additional work for ethics to do. '*Sub specie aeternitatis*, why should we not know what is to be done?'[32] In the same spirit, Barth, at a key point in *Romans₁*, dismisses the question of deliberation altogether: '"What should I do?" Above all, stop asking this question! . . . We have to abide in the "body of Christ" (7: 4), in the power of the resurrection inaugurated in him, in which being under obligation proceeds organically from the new "being in the Spirit" (8: 5–9), in

---

[30] 'Der Christ in der Gesellschaft,' 67/324.
[31] Ibid. 68/324 f.
[32] Ibid. 69/326 f.

which the good is not a problematic matter but simply occurs.'[33] Ethics takes care of itself, or rather God takes care of it by bringing to fruition the seed that is already in us as the beginning of our new being in Christ.[34] Good conduct follows immediately, organically, as it were, from the new being in Christ already present in seminal form.[35]

There are two further problems with Barth's proposal at this stage. One problem is that he can understand the expression of the righteousness of God in human action only in terms of some economy of forces already present in the social order. It will consist in some balance of acceptance and criticism of present arrangements, but the content of social ethics will always consist in the possibilities found in these arrangements. Not until Barth develops a stronger doctrine of revelation will his notion of the divine righteousness be capable of generating substantive ethical content. The final problem is rooted in Barth's chief concern regarding ethics at this stage, which, as *Romans₁* repeatedly confirms, was to distinguish, along the lines of the Pauline problematic of law and Spirit, an ethic in which God is the source of an external moral law that confronts us from outside and is impossible for us to fulfill (law) from an ethic in which the good is done immediately, emerging organically out of the eschatological new being in Christ (Spirit).[36] In this immediacy, righteousness, while not a human accomplishment, is nevertheless realized in human beings (albeit eschatologically).

---

[33] *Romans₁*, 263 f.

[34] There is some resemblance here to certain orthodox Marxist theories for which ethics is rendered unnecessary by history so that the only ethical task is to unite with the historical forces from which eventually the good will not be a problematic matter but will simply occur. Of course, in the latter case the good is realized through immanent historical processes while for Barth it is realized through the divine action that brings about the new being in Christ, an eschatological reality that is not fully comprehended in observable history ('Der Christ in der Gesellschaft,' 65 f./321 f.). In both cases, though, the ultimate horizon, be it the classless society or the eschatological kingdom of God, is considered sufficient to guide conduct in present historical conditions, where neither the classless society or the kingdom of God is yet manifest.

[35] In the context of his discussion of the status of the state in Romans 13: 1–7 Barth did accord limited and qualified recognition to a political ethic for the present, but he sharply distinguished this from the Christian ethic of the new being in Christ. See *Romans₁*, 500–22. By the time of the Tambach lecture, however, Barth seems to have dropped this non- or pre-Christian ethic, replacing it, as we saw above, with the assurance that when we set our sights on the eschatological future of God's action we will find the right place between acceptance and criticism of existing social and political conditions ('Der Christ in der Gesellschaft,' 67 f./324.). Both McCormack (*Karl Barth's Critically Realistic Dialectical Theology*, 201 f.) and Webster (*Barth's Moral Theology*, 26) find in this lecture a positive role for analogies between the divine eschatological reality and certain historical events and movements. However, the status of analogy in this lecture is highly complex. On the one hand, from the standpoint of redemption one 'can recognize in the worldly the analogy of the divine, and can take delight in it' (55/305). On the other hand, 'We live by that which is beyond the realm of analogies...' (65/321). Barth's point seems to be this: The synthesis in which *both* the naive acceptance of worldly life as an analogy to the divine *and* the critical rejection of reality (which presumably includes the rejection of reality as an analogy of the divine) is in God, and is thus *itself* beyond analogy. To find the synthesis would presumably mean to find a proper practical relation between affirmation of analogy and denial of it.

[36] See, for example, *Romans₁*, 233.

In Barth's interpretation of the Pauline problematic, then, an ethic that began by asserting the distance and discontinuity between divine and human righteousness ironically culminates in the elimination of this distance and discontinuity in the immediacy with which the new person in Christ relates to the righteousness of God.

This organicist eschatology and with it the notion of a good that no longer confronts human beings as law but emerges out of the immediacy of the new being in Christ will disappear from Barth's theology by the early 1920s, as we will see shortly. Nevertheless, while his formulations will undergo these and other changes, Barth's basic approach to ethics is already in place during this period. The central notion of the righteousness of God which calls human righteousness into question and which is not related to human conduct by any path of human moral activity leading from here to there but only by divine activity from there to here, along with the notion that the task of ethical inquiry is not to determine what specific action or course of action God wills but to describe the situation of human beings in relation to the divine righteousness and to direct them towards the latter, will remain with him. Most important, the central problem addressed by Barth's ethics at this stage—how can the divine righteousness be expressed in human conduct without human conduct becoming the ground of an independent human self-affirmation?—is a first, if rudimentary and ultimately unsatisfactory, formulation of the problem of ethics that will continue to shadow his moral theology.

3. THE FLAME AND THE CURTAIN

The next stage of Barth's moral theology coincides with the end of his parish ministry in Safenwil and his transition to a special professorship of Reformed theology in a predominantly Lutheran faculty at Göttingen. Not incidentally, it also coincides with the political and economic turmoil of Germany in the aftermath of the war. This stage continues the theme of the righteousness of God. 'God is God: this is the presupposition of ethics, and ethical claims are ethical only as elucidations of this...presupposition.'[37] But now this theme means not only that God alone can bring about true righteousness, in contrast to the spurious righteousness resulting from human attempts, but also that the disturbance of all human righteousness by the righteousness of God is a persistent feature of temporal life—a condition moral exhortation must never cease to express. Barth no longer thinks of the righteousness of God as growing organically, as from a seed, in human experience and history; rather, it stands radically over against finite, temporal reality.

---

[37] *Romans2*, 463/439.

This stage can be divided into two parts. The first part is dominated by the second edition of the *Epistle to the Romans* (hereafter, *Romans₂*), which Barth completed just before assuming the duties of his university appointment. Here, his thought is marked by ongoing eschatological tensions between the 'perceptible,' this-worldly character of sinful human existence and the 'imperceptible,' wholly other reality of divine grace and forgiveness, between the old person on this side of the 'line of death' and the new person, an eschatological being in Christ, on the other side of this line. On the basis of such tensions, *Romans₂* is not infrequently read as setting the 'other-sided' against the 'this-sided,' the eternal against the temporal, the (absolutely) infinite against the finite (or the relatively infinite), God against the world of the creature. There is some truth to this reading. However, our treatment of the ethics of *Romans₂* will make undeniably clear that Barth's ultimate concern in this text is with how the other-sided can enter into or be expressed in the this-sided without losing its other-sidedness. Gradually, Barth's engagements with classical Reformed theology in his university lectures will lead him to shift his emphasis from the eschatological distance between divine righteousness and human life to a less dramatized and more positively valorized distance between divine sovereignty and human obedience. This shift makes it possible to speak of a second part of this stage, yet, as we will see in this section, there is a single understanding of the problem of ethics that unifies this extraordinary period in Barth's career and marks it as a distinct stage in the development of his moral theology.

The Quandary of Ethics

We can characterize the problem of ethics as it appears at this stage as follows: If ethics is concerned with temporal human existence, with life on the 'horizontal line,' the line of death, then it seems that ethics is placed under permanent crisis in light of the question mark divine grace sets against every human endeavor, that is, the fact that 'at the center [of the horizontal line], where each of us stands, we willing and knowing humans with our works, there is a break that throws everything into question.'[38] Barth's thought about ethics during this period revolves around this question mark: first in an effort to show that what disrupts temporal existence is the ethical itself, then increasingly in an effort to find a positive ground in this very disruption for some kind of concrete 'ethos,' or moral life on the horizontal line of temporal existence. These efforts involve a quandary. On the one hand, it is not enough simply to repeat endlessly the disruption of temporal existence by the question mark set over against it by the eternal: 'The problem of human life and striving . . . cannot be simply cut off by

---

[38] Karl Barth, *The Theology of John Calvin*, trans. Geoffrey W. Bromiley (Grand Rapids, Mich.: Eerdmans, 1995), 45.

being put under the shadow of its finitude, that is, in the light of its origin.'[39] Temporal existence must, after all, be lived according to *some* standard of conduct, and the question of how it should be lived persists even in the face of the question posed to it by the eternal. On the other hand, in the idiom of *Romans₂*, to treat the horizontal line as a path along which the goal of human striving is found or can be attained is to dissolve the eschatological tension between the perceptible and the imperceptible, the temporal and the eternal, the this-worldly and the wholly other; it is to carry out, in the name of ethics, the insubordination and irreverence which, according to Barth's reading of Romans, are the fundamental sins: those, respectively, in which human beings first assert themselves as divine and then assimilate the divine to the human, making God accessible to them as an object of human knowing and striving.[40] Or, in the less dramatic idiom of classical Reformed theology, to focus on the question of human life is to court the danger, which did in fact materialize in the Reformed tradition, that 'the glorification of God' will end up in 'the worst form of human self-glorification.'[41] Because God cannot be encompassed by the this-worldly or the temporal in these ways, it appears that to attend to what is to be done by human willing and striving is ultimately to ignore God altogether. 'To say ethos is to stride off from God into the world; it is to turn one's back on God.'[42]

Grace, or the ethical (we will see that these are ultimately the same), disrupts every ethos, yet human life cannot be lived without some ethos. This is the quandary imposed on Barth's ethics by his stress on the distance and discontinuity between God and the world of humanity, time, and things during these years. The quandary, however, was far from simply an academic or theoretical matter. We can see in Barth's emphasis in *Romans₂* on the radical disruption of temporal existence a continuation of his struggle to overcome the identification of God's will with bourgeois social and cultural forms, while his denial that human beings can live in a perpetual calling into question of their moral and social ethos can be seen as a rejection of the revolutionary stance that was gathering steam in Germany as Barth was writing. Everything Barth writes about ethics in *Romans₂* and in his 1922 lecture on 'The Problem of Ethics Today' serves his attempt to establish some moral space between the bourgeois and the revolutionary. Yet as he takes up his university appointment we can also see him beginning to locate his struggle in the larger context of the heritage of the Reformation.

---

[39] *Theology of John Calvin*, 49.

[40] *Romans₂*, 19 f./44. See also 184/190, 196/200. In the premodern era, Barth argues, the goal of human striving was located in the hereafter while the modern era locates it in the here-and-now, in nature and history, but in both cases it is a goal to be attained by human willing and striving, and is therefore on the horizontal line.

[41] Barth, 'Reformierte Lehre, ihr Wesen und ihre Aufgabe,' in *Vorträge und kleinere Arbeiten 1922–1925*, ed. Holger Finze (Zurich: Theologischer Verlag Zürich, 1990), 246 (translation 'The Doctrinal Task of the Reformed Churches,' in Barth, *The Word of God and the Word of Man*, trans. Horton, 270.

[42] *Theology of John Calvin*, 90.

The quandary itself and Barth's intention in posing it are most easily grasped by considering, respectively, 'The Problem of Ethics Today' and Barth's lecture course on Calvin, also in 1922.

In 'The Problem of Ethics Today,' Barth sets out the quandary in specifically ethical terms. 'With the question concerning the good, all actual and possible forms of human action, all temporal events in the history of the individual and of society alike, are put into question.'[43] This question of the good, which comes to expression in the fundamental ethical question 'What should we do?', places our temporal existence under the question mark of the eternal: 'In every contingent and temporal "What should we do?" there lies *the* "What?" to which no contingent and temporal "That" can give a reassuring answer, because it is the inevitable and eternal "What?"'[44] In Barth's neo-Kantian terms, what *is*—an existing form of conduct or state of affairs—is always subject to the question whether it *ought* to be. This question is unavoidably posed to every existing condition, including those forms of conduct or states of affairs that are proposed as answers to the question 'What should we do?' Related to temporal human existence in this way, as the question of the eternal to which temporal human life can offer no answer, Barth concludes that the ethical question is a 'deadly assault [*tödliche Angriff*]' against human beings, '[f]or it is the question to which, for human beings, either there are only answers which themselves become questions or an answer for which human beings cannot ask. But human beings cannot live where, for them, there are nothing but questions always being posed anew. Nor can they live by the ultimate answer which is so final that it cannot be an answer for them.'[45]

Barth contrasts the ethical in this, its proper sense with the meaning it held in the years prior to the war, which meaning he associates with the names of Schleiermacher, Rothe, and Troeltsch, among others.[46] During that era the ethical had come to be thought of entirely in terms of the horizontal, as the progressive realization, in the forms and institutions of bourgeois society,

---

[43] Barth, 'Das Problem der Ethik in der Gegenwart,' in Barth, *Vorträge und kleinere Arbeiten 1922–1925*, 104 (translation 'The Problem of Ethics Today,' in Barth, *The Word of God and the Word of Man*, 138).

[44] 'Das Problem der Ethik in der Gegenwart,' 106/141.

[45] Ibid. 116/152. In *Romans₂*, Barth had also described the demand which the new life, the eschatological life of grace, issues as an assault (*Angriff*) on the perceptible person and the dissolution (*Aufhebung*) of all that characterizes her in her concrete existence—a description for which he found the stark neo-Kantian contrast between the subject of moral freedom and the empirical subject of inclination well suited. See Barth, *Romans₂*, 193/197, 196/200, 205/208, and also 'Das Problem der Ethik in der Gegenwart,' 105/139 f., 113/149, and especially 116/152 f., 119/155 f. With this depiction of the moral law as violence against the natural, historical self, Barth seems to combine Luther's problematic of the law with Nietzsche's polemic against Christian-cum-Kantian morality. Of course, Nietzsche would not have accepted as consolation Barth's assurance, later in the lecture, that the death visited on us by the moral law is a door to the deathless God whose grace is revealed in this judgment.

[46] 'Das Problem der Ethik in der Gegenwart,' 110/145, 112 f./148 f.

of the goal of human striving. The ethical question was then posed without any sense of the crisis it involves, as a shared confidence in moral and social progress made it possible for an entire culture to treat the question 'What should we do?' as a merely rhetorical question whose only plausible answers would be those that simply confirm the present course.[47] But to ask the question in this way is not really to ask it at all, at least not seriously. Only now, amid the political and economic chaos of 1922,[48] is it clear what the ethical really is, namely, the perpetual crisis of the 'is' (*Sein*), of temporal human existence in its individual and societal forms, in the face of the 'ought' (*Sollen*), the good as such, posed to it as the ethical question.[49] A question once posed by bourgeois society in the illusory certainty that the answer to it was to be found in its own forms and institutions, along the horizontal line of moral progress, is now posed in all its starkness, as that which renders uncertain every attempt to answer it by pointing to something on the horizontal line.

We can now understand both the ambiguity Barth found in ethics at this stage and the problem this ambiguity posed. First, the ambiguity itself: The ethical question is the question of human existence, a question which theology cannot avoid if it is to discharge its own task. The tendency—one which, most obviously, characterized bourgeois society, but not it alone—is to treat ethics within the horizon of temporal human existence as such: as a matter of a good or right that is to be pursued along the horizontal line of human moral achievement. However, the tumultuous aftermath of the war provides the occasion for understanding ethics properly, namely, as the crisis which the good provokes against all temporal conduct and states of affairs. While ethics indisputably concerns right or good human conduct and is thus the question of human existence as such, the proper theme of ethics is not human willing and striving in itself, with the self-assurance about human capacities and achievements this involves (the horizontal line); rather, it is the assault on human striving and willing carried out by the good itself in the form of the question 'What should we do?' (the vertical line), a question which, when posed seriously (requiring what is (*Sein*) to face the question whether it ought to be (*Sollen*)) disrupts the uncritical identification of the good with present forms of life. Simply put, *ethics* is the calling into question of every *ethos*.[50] Now, the problem posed by this ambiguity: As Barth realizes, ethics in precisely this proper sense means death; human beings cannot

[47] 'Das Problem der Ethik in der Gegenwart,' 109–11/144–6.

[48] Holger Finze, the editor of Barth's lectures and other writings from this period, points out that on the September day on which Barth first delivered this lecture the dollar stood at 1,460 marks ('Das Problem der Ethik in der Gegenwart,' 109 n. 34).

[49] The crisis of post-war Europe thus becomes for Barth the occasion for recognizing again that the ethical is a source of anxiety and terror rather than of bourgeois self-confidence. Significantly, it is Kant who represents the former for Barth and J. G. Fichte the latter. This will not be the last time Kant and Fichte will stand, respectively, for a moral law that calls human beings into question and a moral law that grounds a false and dangerous human claim to mastery.

[50] *Romans₂*, 451/428.

live in this perpetual calling into question of ethos. Temporal life must be lived according to some standard, and it is difficult to see how it can be lived according to a standard which consists simply in putting it in question. But how can one suspend the deadly assault of the question without dissolving it, without returning to bourgeois self-affirmation, without striding off from God into the world?

This quandary of ethics is the product of Barth's strong eschatological perspective expressed in the idiom of neo-Kantian moral philosophy and impressed on his hearers via the crisis of bourgeois society.[51] But it is in his lecture course on Calvin in the summer of 1922 that Barth's intentions in posing the quandary are most clear. These lectures press a distinction between Luther, who for Barth stressed the interruption of human striving on the horizontal line by the vertical line of divine grace, and Calvin, who for Barth returned, in light of this interruption, to an emphasis on the horizontal line.[52] We can best grasp the theological significance of Barth's concern, as well as the difficulty it posed for him, in the role played by a homely simile, inspired by Luther, in which the relation of the vertical to the horizontal is expressed in terms of a flame and a curtain. In Luther's thought, Barth argues, the flame bursts forth and approaches the curtain but never actually touches it. The flame continues burning, but the curtain remains untouched. The point is that the expectation evoked by Luther's theology that the word of divine grace (the flame) would radically reorder human existence (the curtain) is unfulfilled; there occurs only a permanent tension between the grace of forgiveness and life in the world. The case of Zwingli and Calvin is different. Here the flame bursts forth and burns a hole in the curtain, but the fire does not spread; it quickly dies out, leaving only smoke and a few sparks. The curtain is left intact except for the charred hole which registers the fact that the kingdom of heaven really did touch human existence, though in the end it was largely extinguished by the latter.[53]

What the simile lacks in literary merit is offset by its aptness: What Barth desires is a flaming curtain, the ongoing transformation of temporal existence by the gospel—in short, the sanctification of human life. His use of this simile makes clear how in this period he does not simply set the vertical against the horizontal as the term 'theology of crisis' implies, but also aims to demonstrate the significance of the vertical for the horizontal in a way that neither leaves

---

[51] Stepping outside the context of Barth's explicit remarks, we could show how the tension between ethics and ethos repeats, somewhat melodramatically, the modern tension between *Moralität* and *Sittlichkeit*. Modern ethics is to a large extent constituted by this tension between the competing claims of ethics and ethos—paradigmatically, between Kantian *Moralität* and Hegelian (or perhaps Nietzschean, or even Heideggerian) *Sittlichkeit*—and its history is one of continual movement back and forth between these modes and more or less successful efforts at combining them.

[52] *Theology of John Calvin*, 45 f., 49, 67.

[53] Ibid. 72–4.

the horizontal untouched nor absorbs the vertical into it.[54] In both *Romans₂* and in his various lectures on Reformed theology, Barth takes pains to articulate a way of understanding ethics that falls within these parameters.[55] The story of his efforts begins with an exposition of the ethics of *Romans₂*. This exposition cannot avoid being somewhat lengthy, partly because the meaning of ethics in this text is not well understood and partly because Barth's remarks on ethics in the following years indicate efforts to resolve problems left unresolved by *Romans₂*. The exposition of *Romans₂* is followed by a briefer treatment of those subsequent efforts in Barth's various lectures on Reformed theology.

Romans₂ and the Quandary of Ethics

Barth attempts to resolve the quandary of ethics on two levels in *Romans₂*. The two levels correspond, respectively, to justification and sanctification. The key to both levels is the relationship between ethics and divine grace; for Barth, the ethical crisis is itself an expression of a more fundamental crisis of grace. 'There is no genuine or genuinely *ethical* disturbance [*Beunruhigung*] except by grace, and only if the standpoint of grace is held fast at every moment can the *absolute* assault [*Angriff*] on human beings which is the meaning of all ethics be guaranteed.'[56] The relation of the ethical to grace has to do, first, with the role of forgiveness in creating the new person and the opposition of this new person to the old person of sin. As the 'fact of forgiveness,' Barth states, grace 'ignores us as we are and addresses us as what we are not, as new persons.' This is the first level, on which Barth attempts to show how the deadly assault of the ethical question is in fact the paradoxical opening to a new life. However, grace does not simply leave us in this status as forgiven sinners: as this indicative 'it has as its meaning an absolute, categorical imperative.'[57] Precisely insofar as it creates the new person, grace opposes the old person; this opposition is expressed in the

---

[54] See ibid. 73, 77, 80, and Romans₂, 449/426, 454/431. It is in this context that Barth's occasional references to the relation of dogmatics and ethics must be understood. At this stage, which ends almost two years before his first venture into dogmatics, he uses 'dogmatics and ethics' primarily as a formula to suggest that in its proper sense ethics is misconceived if it is taken to be the theme of the horizontal as such, just as dogmatics is misconceived if it is confined to the vertical and does not, as ethics, become the theme of the vertical in relation to the horizontal.

[55] In this respect, what follows is consistent with David Clough's claim that *Romans₂* represents ethics in a genuinely dialectical manner in which apparent negations of the possibility of ethics are kept in tension with apparent affirmations. This is entirely correct as far as it goes, but Clough treats the notion of crisis almost as an end in itself, as if crisis were itself the solution rather than that which confronts every solution. See Clough, *Ethics in Crisis*, 3–31.

[56] *Romans₂*, 454/430. See also 225/225: 'Grace is the crisis from death to life. Therefore, grace is at once the absolute demand [*Forderung*] and the absolute power of obedience against sin.... Therefore, the gospel of Christ is quite simply the disturbance, the tremor, the assault that puts everything in question.' It is also worth noting in this connection that it is God's forgiveness, not the ethical question itself, which was first described by Barth as the 'deadly assault [*tödliche Angriff*]' against sinful human existence (185/190).

[57] Ibid. 185/191, 205/207.

form of a demand, which addresses us as the new person and thus carries out its assault on the old person. This is the second level, on which Barth follows this ethical demand into the horizontal itself and attempts to show how human conduct may attest the crisis under which it stands. Already, then, in these passages from *Romans₂*, Barth has arrived at an early version of his characteristic notion of ethics as an expression of divine grace, of the law as the form of the gospel.

On the first level, Barth can assure us that the death dealt to us by the ethical question is also the beginning of a new life: 'It is because God and God's conduct toward us is the answer [to the ethical question] that, with regard to the question of our own conduct, we can give ourselves only answers which immediately turn into questions or answers which are beyond our grasp.'[58] By exposing our temporal existence as perpetually called into question by a good that always transcends it, as never identifiable with this good, the ethical question and the death it brings is the opening through which the primary determination of human beings by divine grace is disclosed. For Barth, the 'tribulation' of which Paul speaks in Romans 5: 1–3 (of which the assault of the ethical question is surely a primary instance) is an analogue (*Analogon*) to the death of Christ, in which we are 'perceptibly and temporally' one with him and, by virtue of this, also 'imperceptibly' one with the risen Christ.[59] 'The beginning of the new person can become perceptible to us only in the end of the old; the meaning and reality of the resurrection of Christ can become perceptible to us only in his cross.'[60] Thus Barth finds in ethics the same relation to God that is a broader theme of *Romans₂* and is also the theme of 'The Problem of Ethics Today': the deadly assault of the ethical is followed by resurrection, while the new life of the resurrection is accessible to us only through the cross. Barth refers to Colossians 3: 3 to express our paradoxical status as perceptibly united to Christ in his death and imperceptibly united to him in his resurrection: our lives are hidden with Christ in God.

On this first level, this relation of grace and ethics operates within the familiar Lutheran formula *simil justus et peccator*: Perceptibly, we are sinners exposed as such by the law, that is, by the assault of the ethical question which perpetually stands over against us as the embodiment of a goodness or rightness with which our temporal existence will never be equal, and thus we are united with Christ in his death. Imperceptibly, and therefore only in faith, we are the new person in Christ, united with him in his resurrection. The primary relation to God's grace which is opened up in the death-dealing crisis of the ethical therefore consists in the justification of those who remain sinners.[61] Of course, here Barth departs

---

[58] 'Das Problem der Ethik in der Gegenwart,' 131/169.
[59] *Romans₂*, 191/196, 203/206.
[60] Ibid. 137/150.
[61] 'Das Problem der Ethik in der Gegenwart,' 132 f./170–2.

from Luther in identifying grace and law. The genuine ethics of the vertical spells the death of the false ethics of the horizontal and in so doing reveals itself as grace. Barth thus corrects the position of *Romans₁*, which in its commitment to the immediacy of the new being in Christ was unable to assert a justification of those who remain sinners.[62]

But Barth did not let the matter rest here, where it would simply restate the quandary. The unavoidable question posed by human existence—what is the meaning of the vertical for the horizontal?—remains unanswered on the first level.[63] How can the vertical be expressed in the horizontal, the other-sided in the this-sided, ethics in an ethos? This is the question of sanctification. With this question we arrive at the second level on which Barth wrestled with the quandary, where he follows the ethical question onto the horizontal line of human conduct, seeking action that genuinely signifies the vertical without betraying it. On the one hand, grace not only gives death and new life in the form of forgiveness; it is also a refusal to treat sin as the final word, and thus, in the form of the ethical imperative, it demands an ethos in conformity to it. On the other hand, the strong eschatological orientation of Barth's thought at this stage makes any such ethos highly problematic, as we will soon see. An ethos is demanded, yet it is no sooner proposed than it is called into question. If the immediacy with Christ in *Romans₁* made the justification of those who remain sinners unintelligible, the permanent crisis of *Romans₂* seems to make sanctification unintelligible. That, at least, is the conclusion we will draw from the following survey of the second level.

To get some indication of what Barth is aiming at on the second level we begin with his comment on Romans 12: 1a: 'I appeal to you therefore, brothers, by the mercies of God. . . .' Noting that in this verse Paul exhorts his readers 'by the mercies of God,' Barth points out that ethical discourse 'is never only a demand, it is the assertion of grace as demand.'[64] Gospel is asserted as law; dogmatics is ethics. And it is in exhortation that the mercies of God engage temporal human existence without being absorbed into the latter: 'But precisely in their complete other-sidedness [the mercies of God] become this-sided as exhortation.'[65] This last remark makes clear that ethics is far from an ancillary theme in *Romans₂*; indeed, it is in ethics that the eschatological tension which drives the entire text reaches its highest pitch. Grace must take the form of exhortation, must become this-sided (while remaining other-sided), because it is our concrete human existence in this world of 'humanity and time and things,' as Barth refers to it, that is called into question by grace. Yet it is precisely this capacity of grace to become this-sided in the form of exhortation that tempts us to present ethics

---

[62] For this problem see Eberhard Busch, *Karl Barth and the Pietists: The Young Karl Barth's Critique of Pietism and its Response*, trans. Daniel W. Bloesch (Downers Grove, Ill.: InterVarsity Press, 2004), 69 f.

[63] *Theology of John Calvin*, 67.

[64] *Romans₂*, 451/428.

[65] Ibid. 450/427.

as the solution to the eschatological tension. Its success here would be its failure: by resolving the crisis of the ethical with a stable answer to the question 'What should we do?' it would immediately set up a 'high place,' a this-worldly site from which exhortation could now proceed, free from the disturbance of the temporal by the eternal. Grace and the ethical crisis it inaugurates would merely have been a bump on the horizontal line, a temporary suspension of our confidence in our moral and social achievements.

Everything Barth says in *Romans₂* about concrete ethical action aims to express this tension or paradox of absolute other-sidedness and this-sidedness. This tension or paradox is most clearly presented in terms of grace and its opposition to sin. Our actual moral experience, Barth asserts, is always a this-sided, relative contrast of good and evil, a twilight world of ethical indeterminacy where we are unable to make any final, absolute distinctions between good and evil, valuable and worthless, right and wrong; it is a world in which wheat and tares grow up together and in which any action that appears holy could prove to be lawless and vice versa. Neither in our theoretical nor in our practical moral striving on the horizontal line are we capable of giving expression to the absolute opposition of grace to sin.[66] However, this ethical indeterminacy is not final; 'the righteousness of God in Jesus Christ breaks into this twilight,' bringing illumination. Grace is the 'unambiguous criterion,' the only absolute contrary of sin, in the light of which it becomes clear which actions are good and which are evil. Yet grace remains imperceptible precisely in its disclosure, and this limits what ethics can claim to do: 'The presence [of the criterion] will keep making the attempt at an *ethic*, that is, a table of sinful and righteous, of prohibited and commanded ends . . . an inexorably necessary task while it will likewise keep making impossible an ethic which would be more than an attempt.'[67] Human ethical action must in some way reflect the absolute opposition of grace against sin, yet it must do this in full recognition that it remains in this twilight world where the opposition of grace and sin will always remain a relative one.

The problem, in short, is how grace can take form in the this-sided, twilight world of human moral action without losing its other-sided character. How can we avoid both the bourgeois identification of an existing ethos with the ethical itself, on the one hand, and the revolutionary overthrow of the existing ethos by appeal to the ethical, on the other hand? Barth's solution is found in his comments on Romans 12–15. We can depict this solution as occurring in three successive waves. Each wave comes closer than its predecessor to delivering a concrete moral ethos, but each one breaks on the rocks of Barth's eschatology before it is able to deliver its cargo to the shore. The first wave picks up with Barth's comment on Romans 12: 1b, where the apostle urges his readers to 'present [their] bodies as a living sacrifice.' Barth comments as follows:

---

[66] Ibid. 225–9/224–8.
[67] Ibid. 229/228.

'A sacrifice is not a human action in which the will of God is carried out in the sense that the one who sacrifices becomes through his action an agent of God. A sacrifice is rather a *demonstration* for the glory of God, demanded by God (who wills to be glorified) but in itself a human action as good or as bad as any other.'[68] Actions are good or right not by virtue of their material content but by virtue of their form, that is, insofar as they point to the divine action which alone is good and right in the strict sense. In practice this means that perceptible ethical action, as action that is claimed to be materially good or right, effaces itself before its imperceptible origin or ground, in which it is formally good or right. Sacrifice is demonstration, and as such it does attest the crisis under which it (along with all horizontal action) stands. But it attests this crisis only in its own self-effacement, i.e., only under the sign of death. In its sacrificial character ethical action is no exception to the rest of Barth's theology at this point: the imperceptible becomes perceptible only in death. In effect, this form of ethical action simply reasserts the quandary of ethics rather than resolving it.

But in addition to ethical action in this primary form of sacrifice, Barth, following Romans 12: 2, which enjoins readers not to be conformed to the world but rather to be transformed by the renewal of their minds, speaks also of a secondary form in which concrete actions hold the possibilities of expressing either the negation of the form of this world or congruity with its transformation.[69] Riding this second wave, Barth is on the verge of being able to justify actions on the horizontal line itself and thus resolve the quandary of ethics. But of course, he cannot do this without setting up a high place in the world of human existence, and so at the critical moment he pulls back. Secondary actions, he says, are those which 'almost' carry the divine protest against the form of this world and 'almost' make visible the light of the transformation of the world, but in the end the goodness and rightness of all human actions depend on the extent to which they express the primary action of sacrifice.[70] With relentless consistency Barth refers the material rightness or goodness of ethical action to sacrifice, its formal right- or good-making character, in which ethical action effaces itself before its imperceptible origin.[71] 'Whatever possibilities can be designated as positive or negative possibilities are all *human* possibilities. They are ambiguous possibilities, subject to the divine proviso, governed by the authority of the first table, and placed under the crisis of life and death. Precisely in these relations to their origin are they *ethical* possibilities while their ethical character [*Ethos*] is

---

[68] *Romans₂*, 454 f./431.

[69] Ibid. 475/451.

[70] Ibid. 454 f./431 f., 458/434 f., 475/451, 485 f./461.

[71] Barth derives this distinction between the formal and material aspects of the act from Kant's distinction between formal and material grounds of determination of the will, and draws similar conclusions about the moral worth of the material in relation to the formal. See 'Das Problem der Ethik in der Gegenwart,' 116 f./152 f.

betrayed precisely when it is sought in these possibilities themselves, in their material content.'[72]

The second wave thus delivers no more than the first did. Barth's lengthy foray into concrete moral exhortation leaves him right where he began, namely, with the recognition that the non-present presence of grace in the world of temporal human existence makes it impossible to draw up a definitive code of secondary ethical actions.[73] 'What is really alarming here is that all human ethical expression [*Ethos*] can *only* demonstrate, signify, and sacrifice, and that there is no comfort whatsoever in this "only" because precisely in this "only" is the recollection of God through which the question "What should we do?" is posed with inescapable seriousness.'[74] This is to say that in the end, ethos can only keep referring us back to ethics, that is, to the assault of the ethical question itself. And, as Barth himself knows, we cannot live by questions alone or by answers that exceed us. The quandary of ethics is unresolved. The flame touches the curtain but the curtain doesn't ignite; it simply deflects the flame back to itself.

Yet Barth's struggle with the quandary of ethics does not end on this note. He is astute enough to realize that the question of the horizontal still persists. For what shall we say about *our recognition* of the reference of every ethos back to ethics: is not this very recognition an attitude, at least, perhaps even a practice, and in either case *itself* an ethos? Barth tells us that the Epistle to the Romans demands a certain life project (*Lebensversuch*), one characterized by the freedom that follows from the 'disturbing disclosure of the freedom of God' as the answer to the assault of the ethical question.[75] This is a negative freedom: freedom from the relative duties, values, authorities, illusions, etc. whose relativity is exposed by the absolute demand of grace. The epistle thus appears to demand something tantamount to an 'ethos of ethics,' a way of life whose content is precisely the crisis of all content. With this insight, Barth rides on the third and final wave. But how is an ethos of ethics possible? How can such an ethos be prevented from becoming itself yet another high place, in this case a place where one evades the crisis precisely by claiming to have fully embraced it? These are the questions with which Barth grapples in his lengthy discussion of the 'strong' and the 'weak' in Romans 14 and 15.

Like the Apostle Paul, Barth does not question the validity of the ethos of freedom to which the strong appeal (see Rom. 14: 14) but instead questions the grounds on which the strong distinguish themselves from the weak as superior to them (see Rom. 14: 7–12). Is freedom the property of the Pauline Christian or of God alone? Is their strength the possession of the strong themselves or do they

---

[72] *Romans₂*, 486/461.
[73] Ibid. 485 f./461. Indeed, so long is the shadow cast by the inability to determine what actions may be required or prohibited that it is not clear how Barth can even account for why Romans 12: 9–20 enjoins the particular actions it does as secondary actions, and not some other list.
[74] Ibid. 489/465.
[75] Ibid. 530/503.

possess it only in God? Barth will once again press the inescapability of the crisis, this time against the allegedly privileged status of *knowledge* of the crisis, in order to show how this crisis deconstructs the opposition between the strong and the weak (see Rom. 14: 1, 19).[76] 'That which makes us strong proceeds from the crisis, the power of which continually breaks forth, undiminished, on our strength. . . . What, then, are we left with? Nothing perceptible! We can only make clear to ourselves that precisely as those who know, who are pre-eminent, who are free, we are also weak. We can only place ourselves alongside them.'[77] However, this solidarity of the strong with the weak is not total; the former remain differentiated from the latter inasmuch as they are obligated, in the words of Romans 15: 1, to bear the weaknesses of the weak, meaning (for Barth), 'the entire burden of the disturbance which God brings on human beings.' The freedom from all relative duties, etc., is freedom for the other: freedom to live for the other rather than for oneself. This is the ethos or life project (*Lebensversuch*) of the strong, an ethos in which they resemble Christ, who also lived for the other.[78]

Barth finally seems to have found a genuine resolution to the quandary of ethics by gesturing towards this form of human ethical existence that is lived out on the horizontal line yet is constituted by its relation to the vertical. It falls, however, entirely within the logic of *Romans₂*, which never ceases to place the reader before the crisis it depicts, that Barth follows with a final denial that this ethos occupies a high place within the world of humanity, time, and things. 'Our strength consists in bearing [the weaknesses of the weak] in such a way that we ourselves do not appear.'[79] The strong person 'does not come forth, he withdraws. . . . He is nowhere, because he is everywhere.'[80] The action of bearing the weaknesses of the weak is no exception; it, too, must efface itself as a perceptible action. It is precisely here, however, that the failure of Barth's ethics at this stage becomes clear. For it is in their very lack of a *place* that the strong ironically resemble God—an astonishing irony when one considers the intense labors Barth has undertaken in *Romans₂* to prevent just such an outcome. This

---

[76] Much of Barth's exposition of Romans 14 and 15 is a deconstruction of the strong/weak binary opposition. If it is a matter of ethos, is it not the weak with their rich ethical substance who are superior to the strong? If one correctly understands forensic justification then can the strong claim any advantage by virtue of their knowledge? Are the strong in any position to question the claim of the weak that they, too, direct their perceptible actions to the imperceptible God? If the strong presume to judge the weak, do they not themselves become the weak? Is not the very knowledge of the strong—that in which their very strength consists—itself still human knowledge and thus subject to the crisis of all things human? If we 'live to the Lord' and 'die to the Lord' is there any justification for either rigorism or freedom in themselves rather than in Christ? In all these cases Barth shows how, as with all this-sided phenomena, the distinction between the strong and the weak is rendered relative by the relation of both to their imperceptible ground and origin.

[77] Ibid. 552 f./524.

[78] Ibid. 550/522, 552/524, 553 f./524 f.

[79] Ibid. 553/525.

[80] Ibid. 554/525.

irony becomes most obvious at the point where the identification of the strong and the weak with Protestant and Catholic, respectively—an identification Barth has not tried to disguise up to this point—is made explicit in the context of the desire of Protestantism to appear, to occupy a place in the ethical landscape. 'The crisis of Protestantism originates solely in its failure to be the humble (though in reality the decisive!) question mark and exclamation point on the outermost edge of culture, society, worldviews, and religions, in its desire by all means to *be* something, to compete with the Roman vegetable eaters.'[81] The false humility of this (for us) embarrassing identification of the strong with Protestantism is transparent. What is less obvious is that Barth's appeal to it defeats his entire project in *Romans₂*. In the end, it seems, it is the strong/Protestant who puts the world in question—from his standpoint not in eternity but on the outer boundary of this world of humanity and time and things, the no-place that is not a high place, to be sure, but is still a place from where exhortation can proceed in evasion of the crisis. This ethos of the strong has no place to dwell in this world, but precisely as such it threatens the distinction between humanity and God—and thus risks committing what in *Romans₂* is the primordial sin, namely, the self-assertion by which human beings exalt themselves to the absolute. Earlier in *Romans₂*, Barth had written that '[t]he purity of ethos requires... that there be no mixing up of heaven and earth. For the purity of ethos depends on its origin, but its origin must be secured by our persistence, in spite of all romantic urgings, in calling God, God, and humanity, humanity.'[82] Yet it is precisely a romantic urging, and a failure to call humanity, humanity, to pretend to situate oneself on the boundary of the world, not within it, and to suppose that one can from there call everything into question.[83]

The Quandary of Ethics after *Romans₂*

By the end of *Romans₂*, then, the resolution of the quandary of ethics runs as follows: On the first level, the deadly assault of the ethical question is paradoxically the opening to new life, the disclosure of our primary determination by God's grace as forgiven sinners, while on the second level, our actions on the horizontal line can at best only signify the crisis under which they stand. While the first level does establish our status as justified sinners, the second level

---

[81] Ibid. 553 f./525.

[82] Ibid. 455/432.

[83] The liminal position of the strong/Protestant sheds light on a major problem with *Romans₂*, namely, whether Barth's own discourse can sustain itself as a corrective to all other theologies. How is his own discourse in a position to utter this corrective without either substituting itself for the divine correction or becoming one among the theological discourses in need of correction? The analysis undertaken here suggests that for Barth this position is the one occupied by the strong. But if this is correct, *Romans₂* must, for the reasons mentioned, be considered a failure at the very point where it must account for the conditions of the possibility of its own discourse.

leaves our sanctification unintelligible. Barth seems to have recognized the problems with this second-level solution, for his later remarks at this stage involve explicit attempts to show how genuine goodness can be ascribed to conduct on the horizontal line without reducing the distance between this goodness and the divine goodness.

These later remarks occur in the context of Barth's intense engagement, in his role as a professor of Reformed theology, with classical Reformed theologians and confessions. One of Barth's major concerns, especially in his lecture courses on Calvin, Zwingli, and the Reformed confessions, was to highlight the ethical relationship of human beings to God as a distinctive Reformed characteristic.[84] However, two of his occasional lectures from this period attempt direct resolutions to the quandary of ethics. In 'The Problem of Ethics Today,' Barth argues that the forgiveness of sins—the first-level solution from *Romans₂*—both authorizes striving for moral progress on the horizontal line and prevents us from identifying any condition on that line with God's righteousness. On the one hand, forgiveness brings about the justification of those who remain sinners: the 'new creation of man is a *justificatio forensis*, a *justificatio impii*, the renewal of the unrenewable old man, an incomparable paradox.'[85] This means that the ethical crisis, the distance of our conduct from the good, is still in place; our justification as sinners is not the justification of any this-sided moral order, and in Barth's view the Lutheran doctrine of 'orders of creation' (e.g., family, state, vocation) is suspect precisely because it implies that certain this-sided offices and functions are direct reflections of God's will, thus offering a false escape from the crisis. Yet, on the other hand, this first-level solution holds that forgiveness is found precisely in the midst of moral struggle, at the very point of the crisis brought on our conduct by the ethical question.[86] Because it occurs in rather than apart from our moral striving under the ethical demand, forgiveness does not abrogate this demand but rather implies our continuing work for moral progress. And because this ethical striving takes place under God's forgiveness 'there is such a thing as justified human conduct.' Yet because it always remains the forgiveness of *sin*, the righteousness of our conduct will not be identifiable with God's righteousness but will reflect the profane and fallen character of human life in the world. 'Its proper dignity—not as the order of creation made

---

[84] Barth's lectures on these topics sound a consistent theme: that a central and distinctive feature of the early Reformed tradition is the attention it paid to the great Renaissance question of human life—the life of human beings as historical and social agents—in contrast to the Lutheran tradition with its focus on the more narrowly religious question to which grace supplied the answer, and that it was precisely the emphasis on the glory and sovereignty of God in Reformed thought that accounted for this attention to human life, both by creating a space for genuine human action in its insistence on the divine transcendence and by marking this space as one of obedience to God. An illuminating treatment of these matters is found in John Webster, *Barth's Earlier Theology: Four Studies* (New York: T. & T. Clark, 2005).

[85] 'Das Problem der Ethik in der Gegenwart,' 132/170.

[86] Ibid. 134 f./171 f.

manifest but as *testimony* [*Zeugnis*] to, a thoroughly this-sided *reflection* [*Abglanz*] of, an order of creation that is lost to us and hidden from us—is therefore seen neither to require nor to be capable of any distinctive Christianization [*Verchristlichung*].'[87]

In the Lutheran overtones of this lecture, forgiveness—the first-level resolution—is the fundamental answer to the ethical question.[88] However, in the following year Barth presented roughly the same position in the idiom of classical Reformed theology. The Reformed emphasis on knowledge of the sovereign, transcendent God, he proposes, supports the demand for obedience alongside faith as parallel human responses to the gift of divine grace, while the Reformed view of the nature of the humanity of Christ and the eucharistic presence—the strong insistence, against Lutheranism, that Christ's human nature, while united with his divine nature, remains sharply distinct from the latter—keeps one from identifying one's obedience and its results with the will of God. Knowledge of the sovereign, gracious God must be expressed in the glorification of God in the world, but what one does in the world will no more dissolve the distinction between God and the world than the incarnation or the eucharistic presence dissolves the distinction between the divine and human natures of Christ. And so the Reformed believer 'will not too loudly and emphatically commend as *God's* earth this valley of the shadow in which we walk, for he knows that the world as *God's* creation, like the true humanity of Christ, is hidden from us . . .'[89] Here it is Christology rather than eschatology that marks the distance between God and human beings, maintaining this distance even in the hypostatic union and thereby expressing Barth's characteristic emphasis on God's concealment even in God's revelation. The implications for ethics are identical to those drawn in 'The Problem of Ethics Today': on the one hand, there *is* genuinely righteous human action; on the other hand, its righteousness consists in its thoroughly this-worldly reference to what is entirely beyond this world. 'There *is* a sanctification (*Heiligung*) of the individual and the corporate body here *below* which is not to be confused with the holiness (*Heiligkeit*) of God *above*. It is not a matter of good works, is not a bridge to heaven, is not union with the Godhead, is not an anticipation of the end state.' Rather, it is an 'indispensable pointer (*Hinweis*) to the millennial reign' and a 'demonstration we make to the glory of God.'[90]

This solution to the quandary of ethics is an ingenious one: It offers a kind of justification of conduct on the horizontal line and authorizes moral struggle in real social space and historical time while ensuring that such conduct and striving

---

[87] Ibid. 135 f./173.

[88] Ibid. 115/151 f., 130/168 f., 135–9/172–4, 141/178, 143/181. In *The Theology of John Calvin* (80–2) Barth had also argued that the problem of ethics could be addressed only by dialectically moving back and forth between the vertical and the horizontal.

[89] 'Reformierte Lehre,' 238/261.

[90] Ibid. 243/266.

will continue to reflect and will not betray the crisis under which they stand. We have grounds for participating in the existing forms and institutions of society and culture and in the struggle for relative improvements in them, yet in full awareness of the this-sided character of our actions and their results—enabling us to avoid both the smug self-assurance of the pre-war citizen and the incendiary iconoclasm of the post-war revolutionary. At the same time, this solution is fraught with difficulties. There is, first, the instability of any theological position that depends on maintaining such a sharp distinction between the divine and the human. The radical distance between God and humanity does indeed open a space for human moral action, but it also leaves the ethics that follows with a purely secular character. The tension this involves is apparent in the following view, attributed by Barth to Zwingli: 'The majesty and transcendence of God permits, indeed requires human beings to live in a worldly way on the earth, as long as it is done obediently.'[91] This ethic requires us to hold 'obedient' and 'worldly' together. The danger, of course, is that in the proximity of the worldly and the distance of the divine, we will lose sight of the majesty and transcendence of God altogether and become absorbed in exclusively human possibilities, striding off from God into the world. Barth is acutely aware of this danger. 'Everything,' he urges, 'depends on relentlessly holding fast to the awareness that the question of human life is the question posed to human beings by God.'[92] But to keep one's grip on this awareness is difficult; Calvin and Zwingli themselves, Barth admits, nearly let go, and their successors lost hold of it altogether.

Even more troublesome is that Barth's acknowledgment of a genuine sanctity along the horizontal line, far from resolving the quandary of ethics, largely reasserts it. We now hear that there is indeed a sanctification of the individual and community, even as we are reminded that their sanctity differs radically from the holiness of God. But while the distance between the two is evident enough, it is not clear what relates them. Exactly how does this holiness along the horizontal line, in its entirely this-worldly reality, point to the millennial reign or demonstrate the glory of God? How can we be sure it reflects the lost and hidden moral order and not only itself? In short, how exactly is the righteousness of God represented by human righteousness? Barth has no satisfactory answer to these questions, and so the solution to the problem of ethics that he has been striving for during this period—a positive relation of the righteousness of God to human conduct that does not absorb the former into the latter—eludes his grasp. In the end the flame does not touch the curtain at all; it only casts the light in which the merely provisional character of temporal forms and institutions becomes apparent.

---

[91] *Die Theologie Zwinglis, 1922/1923*, ed. Matthias Freudenberg (Zurich: Theologischer Verlag Zürich, 2004), 91.
[92] 'Reformierte Lehre,' 246/270.

Conclusion

Barth fails to solve the problem of ethics at this stage because the unremitting eschatological tension he maintains between the vertical and the horizontal renders it impossible to make intelligible the sanctification of human conduct on the horizontal line. Like that of *Romans₁*, the period of *Romans₂* and its aftermath is marked by the assertion of a radical distance and discontinuity between divine and human righteousness so that sanctification is eschatological: not the product of human moral activity but radically dependent on God. However, in the former period the sanctification of human conduct emerges organically and immediately from the growth of the divine righteousness in human being and conduct, making it difficult to affirm a justification of those who remain sinners, while in the latter period a sharp eschatological tension between divine and human righteousness persists this side of death, so that while it is clear that the justified remain sinners it is difficult to speak of any real sanctification of human conduct. Barth does formulate at this stage an initial version of his eventual solution, which is to treat the goodness of human conduct as a witness, in the form of analogy, to the goodness of God while holding that sanctification itself is accomplished in Jesus Christ. However, at this stage what human conduct chiefly attests is the crisis under which it stands in its distance from the goodness of God, whether in the self-effacement of sacrifice or in obscure witness to a hidden order.[93] As we will see in later chapters, other central themes of Barth's ethics also emerged during this period, most notably the notions of the ethical question as one posed by divine grace in the form of law, and of the permanent gap between the fulfillment of the good in Christ and the questionable goodness of our visible conduct. His task will be to build on these themes in a way that makes the sanctification of human conduct intelligible without making it a human achievement or possession.

---

[93] Ruschke (*Entstehung und Ausführung der Diastasentheologie*, 81) and McCormack (*Karl Barth's Critically Realistic Dialectical Theology*, 278 f.) rightly point out, respectively, the extent to which Barth sees human action in terms of its witness to and its analogy to divine action in *Romans₂*. However, as in the Tambach lecture these positive features of human moral action are more strongly qualified in light of the eternal than Ruschke and McCormack suggest. Given how prevalent is the interpretation of *Romans₂* as one-sidedly negative in its stance towards human action in light of divine action, it is understandable that scholars now emphasize the affirmations of human action in this text. However, Barth always subjects these affirmations to their dialectical counterparts. Clough, too, tends to emphasize the affirmations. But he explicitly does so to correct the opposite tendency, and his overall point is clear (and correct): that Barth offers no escape from the dialectic of affirmation and negation.

4. THE COMMAND OF GOD

A partial breakthrough occurs with Barth's first foray into dogmatics, his 1924–5 Göttingen lectures. The fundamental issue of theology now involves human speech about God: paradigmatically, the speech that is uttered in the church in the form of proclamation. How can human beings speak about God, who, as Barth will continue to hold just as he did in *Romans₂*, is not one among the objects of human consciousness or linguistic representation? Barth's answer is that 'speaking about God can refer only to an original speaking by God . . . ,' to God's self-disclosure. Ethics then becomes 'an attempt at the understanding of human life from the standpoint of this Word originally spoken by God,' while dogmatics is 'the materially prior attempt to grasp this standpoint of the Word of God.'[94] We will see how setting ethics in the context of revelation in this way gives Barth certain means of moving beyond the impasse of the *Romans₂* period. At the same time, we will see that these means are not sufficient, and that despite some advances, the problem of ethics—that grace requires expression in human conduct while it is not clear how human conduct can manifest grace without betraying it—will remain unresolved during this period.

This new understanding of ethics is most thoroughly worked out in a course of lectures first presented in 1928 and 1929 at Münster and posthumously published under the title *Ethics*, and in lectures on 'Das Halten der Gebote' and *The Holy Spirit and the Christian Life*, delivered, respectively, in 1927 and 1929. To some extent this perspective still governs the treatments of ethics in *Church Dogmatics* I/2, published in 1939.

The Word of God as the Command of God

What does it mean to understand human life from the standpoint of the Word of God? Most fundamentally it means that the theme of moral theology will be the Word of God itself, in the form of a command that claims human beings and determines the good of their conduct, thereby sanctifying them. There are several points to set out here. The most basic one is that for Barth we do not look to human capacities, inclinations, or characteristic forms of activity to discover what makes human conduct good. Rather, 'in theological ethics we have to seek and find the goodness of human conduct in the event of an act of God himself toward man, namely, the act of his speech and self-revelation to him.'[95] But this turn to

---

[94] Barth, *The Göttingen Dogmatics: Instruction in the Christian Religion*, vol. i, trans. Geoffrey W. Bromiley (Grand Rapids, Mich.: Eerdmans, 1991), 12 (translation of *Unterricht in der christlichen Religion*, i: *Prolegomena*, ed. Hannelotte Reifen (Zurich: Theologischer Verlag Zürich, 1990), 16).
[95] *Ethics*, 49/81 f.

the Word of God does not imply the erasure of the human moral subject since the Word of God itself includes this subject. 'Theology knows the reality of the Word of God only as that of the Word of God addressed to man.'[96] Ethics, then, will have to do with the way human beings are constituted as addressees of the Word of God in their ethical reflection, decision, and action, in contrast to those modern moral theories which ground ethics in the moral consciousness of the reflective subject. Of course, all of this presupposes that God's address to human beings has to do with their conduct, and thus with ethics. For Barth, the Word of God is the *command* of God insofar as it not only directs a pronouncement to its human addressee but in doing so also claims the latter in the entirety of her life conduct. The theme of moral theology, then, is human life and conduct as placed under the command of God. And the doctrine of the Word of God as the command of God is *moral* theology in the technical sense because it treats the command of God and its claim in ethical terms, as that which makes human conduct good, that is, valid, worthy, or right. 'The good in human conduct is its determination by the divine commanding.'[97] In this claim and determination of the good of human conduct the command of God is the sanctification of human beings, so that 'good' means, precisely, conduct sanctified by God's Word.[98]

With this treatment of ethics in terms of the command of God, Barth has arrived at a position that is familiar to readers of the *Church Dogmatics*. To many of these readers, of course, this assimilation of ethics to the doctrine of the Word of God appears odd, even perverse—the result of a stubborn insistence on refitting ethical categories to the specifications of dogmatics. But what Barth wants to emphasize is that to grasp human life from the standpoint of the Word of God is to grasp it in terms of its determination by God's *grace*. This divine determination by grace, which is declared to us in the self-revelation of God's Word and which claims us as God's command, is the good itself. Echoing the title of Book III of Calvin's *Institutes*, Barth thus describes 'the true substance . . . of theological ethics' as 'the appropriation of God's grace to man on the special assumption that this appropriation consists of the placing of man under God's command.'[99] This brings us immediately to Barth's distinctive thesis of gospel and law, which is first articulated in its mature form during this period. As *Ethics* succinctly puts it, '. . . God by his command primarily claims us as his own, counts us his, sees us as those who belong to him and are loved by him . . .' The command of God tells us both that we fail to meet this claim (we are sinners who reject our belonging to God) and that we stand in God's good pleasure nonetheless (we are justified). Yet because this twofold pronouncement

---

[96] Ibid. 13/19.
[97] Ibid. 50/82.
[98] Ibid. 16/24 f.
[99] Ibid. 88/145.

comes to us as a *command* it is not simply uttered as an abstract truth about us and our situation before God. What God's Word says, 'it says *to* us'; it 'grasps at us and determines us.' It is in this sense that the Word of God is the command of God which sanctifies us: 'This *determination* of our existence by the Word of God is . . . the essence of our sanctification.'[100]

Sanctification, then, is the determination of human conduct by grace. Determination (*Bestimmung*) does not, of course, imply a causal force or fate. We are determined by God's *Word*, not by some cosmic or metaphysical force; what is involved is a divine decision and judgment on our free acts designating us to respond with faith and obedience. 'That we obey in faith and say Yes to God's Word is the determination of our existence by the command of God which meets us in the decision of our acts and decides concerning us and judges us. As God's Word determines us in this way, determines us for obedience, it is our sanctification.'[101] As Barth puts it elsewhere, in terms that recall his 1922 lectures on Calvin, '[t]he *truth* of grace [*what* grace is], which falls plumb down from above, is our judgment and justification [we are sinners and we are justified]. But its *reality*—the reality of our sanctification—consists in this vertical line falling upon and cutting the horizontal line of our existence.'[102] Addressed to us as command, what God's Word has already (prior to and unconditioned by any deed on our part, and thus gratuitously) done for us in our election, knowledge of ourselves as sinners, and the forgiveness of our sin, confronts us as a call for our affirmation in faith and obedience—the appropriation in our concrete existence of God's grace towards us. With this articulation of the complex relationship between grace, command, and faith and obedience Barth's moral theology is close to its mature form, and we can conclude this discussion by saying quite succinctly that for Barth, to understand human life from the standpoint of the Word of God is to understand it as active existence under the determination of God's grace.

The Command of God as the Word of God

But exactly what does it mean to exist under the determination of God's grace? Because this determination has to do with human beings in their concrete, active existence the task of moral theology is to articulate this theological claim in the language of ethics—in terms of the good, the acting, reflecting, choosing subject, and so forth—yet without this language betraying it. Here we have the problem of ethics in a nutshell: Grace must be expressed in ethical terms, as a determination of human conduct, yet it is unclear how ethical terms can express the determination of grace without betraying it. Therefore, much of Barth's energy

---

[100] *Ethics*, 107/177 f.
[101] Ibid. 107 f./177–9.
[102] *The Holy Spirit and the Christian Life*, 33 f.

in *Ethics* goes toward reworking ethical concepts and categories so that they will express the relationship between God's grace and God's command rather than subverting it. That effort consists largely in addressing two questions. First, what does it mean to say that God places our lives under God's command? Later, Barth will treat this as the question of 'general ethics' (or simply 'ethics') in contrast to 'special ethics' (or 'ethos'), which answers the second question: What can we say about the content of the life that is so placed? The notion of the command of God as an *event* is central to the answers Barth gives to both questions.

Barth's answer to the first question, regarding our lives as placed under God's command, begins with a sharp distinction between the command of God as an event and a norm that can be derived from an objective moral order where it would be accessible to theoretical reflection. 'In ethics no less than in dogmatics is the Word of God not a general truth that can be perceived from the safe harbor of theoretical reflection. Nor is it a being from which, among other things, an imperative may be readily deduced.'[103] This denial follows from Barth's doctrine of the Word of God as the event of divine self-revelation which is not conditioned by its human recipient, but it also recalls the neo-Kantian line of thought from 'The Problem of Ethics Today': the ethical question is the critical question posed to what 'is' by an 'ought' that is unconditioned by what is, so that this question is not one we can pose and answer by a theoretical account of what is, but is rather a question posed to us from beyond being.[104] In making this point Barth puts into play a set of contrasts—between event and being, decision and contemplation, the practical and the theoretical—that inevitably lend an existentialist flavor to his account. Not long afterward he will attempt to break with this mode of expression, but even here Barth's concern differs from that of existentialist philosophy. What he wants to stress by describing the command of God as an event is that God is an active subject in it who constitutes the human subject as an addressee, as answerable (*verantwortlich*) to God as the one who decides on her and judges her in her conduct. Thus the command of God is not given as an object but rather '*gives* [*es* gibt] itself to be known, and in so doing it is heard, man is made responsible [*verantwortlich*], and his action takes place in that confrontation.'[105] In rejecting the command of God as given in an objective order in favor of the command of God as event, Barth thus rejects all forms of ethics grounded in a subject who holds the good in her theoretical gaze, self-assured in her mastery over it—the subject for whom the good is an object of self-reflection and who is in a position of neutral choice for or against the good—in favor of a form of ethics in which the subject is confronted by the good from outside, her freedom consisting not in her neutrality in the face of the good but in

---

[103] *Ethics*, 50/83 (revised).
[104] Ibid. 63–7/103–10).
[105] Ibid. 50/83 (revised).

her accountability to it. Addressed to us as accountable subjects in this sense, the question of the good can only be answered by our response to its claim, and this means by our conduct itself. 'Ethics is understanding of the good, not as it is known to us as a general and theoretical truth, but insofar as it reveals itself to us in our doing of the good or not, insofar as the concrete reality of our life-situation is a decision for or against the good.'[106] It follows that ethical reflection is not knowledge of an objective order present to a knowing subject in her self-reflection but rather the awareness that 'at every moment of life, including the very next moment to which our reflection relates, we have to respond by our action.'[107]

This is how Barth describes the ethical as such, but he is not interested in the latter for its own sake; as is typical in his theology, this philosophical concept of the ethical is a formal expression of substantive theological truths about human conduct. In this case, these truths regard the relation of the moral subject to the command of God and the answerability of moral action to a divine decision and judgment, so that in each moment of decision 'our action, as it occurs, is measured and judged and set under an eternal determination.'[108] Human conduct is at each moment the scene of the disclosure of the eternal decision of election. 'Knowledge of the good is knowledge of the judge who, as we decide, pronounces his judgment, declaring salvation or damnation to be our eternal determination.'[109] This reference to the divine judgment is Barth's answer to the first question above: what it means to be placed under God's command is to be subject to God's judgment. Of course, in all of this the command of God is the command of God's *grace*. Barth can therefore insist that the most fundamental point about the judgment of God which takes place in each moment of ethical decision is 'that God *accepts us* in it.'[110] It is in this way that the language of ethics is able to express the relationship between God's grace and God's command rather than betraying grace. But it is striking that in this portrayal of concrete human conduct as the scene of God's gracious judgment the author of *Romans₂* now goes so far as to speak of our concrete life as 'the revelation, the becoming evident of the good' and of our moral decisions as 'the theater of revelation.'[111] At least in principle (and we will soon see why and how Barth qualifies this) the horizontal line—human life in its active existence—is now the site of the revelation of the good.[112] It is where the divine determination of

---

[106] *Ethics*, 66/108 (revised).
[107] Ibid. 89/147.
[108] Ibid. 89/147.
[109] Ibid. 74/121 (revised).
[110] Ibid. 89/148.
[111] Ibid. 67/109, 87/143.
[112] It is notable that in *Ethics*, Barth introduces his account of the command of God via an extended discussion of its truth and of our knowledge of it. Barth's representation of the command of God as an event and his denial that it is an object of our theoretical knowledge do not entail noncognitivism, the view that claims about what is good or right are not susceptible of truth or

human life in the decision and judgment of grace is disclosed, and to exist as a moral subject is to reflect and choose in the awareness of each moment of choice as the site of this disclosure. Barth seems to have gone a long way toward resolving the impasse of the *Romans₂* period.

The second question concerns the moral content of the life placed under the command of God. Here, too, Barth advances beyond *Romans₂* and 'The Problem of Ethics Today.' Unlike the ought that places a question mark against all temporal moral acts, judgments, and endeavors, the command of God as an event of revelation is also a concrete command requiring specific actions and prohibiting others. Moral theology therefore needs only to attend to this command to find moral content. However, because the command of God is an event rather than an object of theoretical reflection, moral theology, as a discipline of inquiry, is in no position to determine the specific actions God commands. Like the Word of God more generally, the command of God 'is not something that "has been given"'—for example, identifiable with the necessities of our natural and social being considered in themselves or even with biblical commandments—'but it consists in God's continual giving.'[113]

At this point, Barth's emphasis on event frequently draws the charge of 'occasionalism,' and it is worth pausing here to show how the charge is misplaced. Barth stands accused of portraying the command of God as a succession of arbitrary, atomistic orders, but the accusation ignores his emphasis on the continuity of God's command. God is not arbitrary, so just as dogmatics more generally is able to serve the task of church proclamation by speaking in general terms about what God will say based on what God has already said, as attested in scripture, so moral theology will be able to speak in a general way about the content of the command of God. Contra the occasionalist charge, for Barth the Word of God itself indicates a certain movement and structure by which moral theology can understand at a general level what God requires. 'What, then, does God's Word say? It is the Word of the divine *creation*, the divine *reconciliation*, and the divine *redemption*.' Thus the Word of God determines its addressee as creature, as forgiven sinner, and as destined to become God's child. Moral theology proceeds by investigating how human life and conduct are claimed and determined in the relations of creator to creature, etc., setting out in general terms the lines along which the actual command itself will fall.[114] So, while Barth does indeed reject the claim that the orders of creaturely life constitute an

---

falsity but are expressions of feelings or attitudes, or that terms such as 'ought' confront us with prescriptivity or alterity as such. Instead Barth presents the command of God as truth that is not conditioned by us as knowers but rather conditions us.

[113] *The Holy Spirit and the Christian Life*, 8.

[114] *Ethics*, 52 f./86–8. It is thus an appreciation of the threefold form of the Word of God and not only a more fully elaborated Christology, as Bruce McCormack supposes, that enables Barth to give content to his theological ethics. See McCormack, *Karl Barth's Critically Realistic Dialectical Theology*, 280.

objective moral order in which the will of God is accessible to human moral reason, he nevertheless affirms natural law and orders of creation, rightly understood, arguing that 'the law of God is in fact no other than the law of the nature created by him.'[115] For Barth at this stage, what God commands will always have as its content the material of our creaturely life found in these orders (as well as our lives as reconciled sinners and heirs of redemption), yet God remains the sole lawgiver who determines in the event of God's commanding *which* specific expression of our life as creatures is required of us.[116]

This completes our discussion of Barth's conception of ethics as the understanding of human life from the perspective of the Word of God. By linking ethics to the doctrine of revelation, this conception seems poised to resolve the quandary of ethics. Barth can now treat human conduct as a site of revelation, making it possible to articulate the positive meaning of the vertical for the horizontal that eluded him during the period of *Romans₂*. The command of God at least appears to go beyond the ought set against all that is and the moral indeterminacy of the twilight world by requiring specific actions on the horizontal line, yet because this command is not given in a moral order accessible to the self-reflection of the moral subject—it must always be heard in the event in which God gives it—the vertical is not reabsorbed into the horizontal. However, these differences belie a remarkable continuity in the way Barth understands the problem of ethics. This is first of all apparent in the inability of moral theology to identify the specific action God commands in a situation of choice. As with revelation generally, 'knowledge occurs here only insofar as its object gives itself to be known,' and this means that the actual command of God 'is an event over whose occurrence we have no control.'[117] This limitation is significant. In Barth's analysis, the determination of human conduct by the Word of God culminates in the notion of a concrete decision as the obedient affirmation of grace, yet moral theology is unable to represent the realization of the good in our decision, to identify our decision in a situation of choice as approved (or not) before the decision and judgment of God on it. In other words, moral theology cannot describe the concrete judgment of grace on human conduct; it can only indicate the latter, pointing to it as something that must speak for itself. It is at the very point where the divine decision and judgment itself is at issue—the specific action that would fulfill the faith and obedience required as the affirmation of grace—that the limits of human ethical inquiry are reached.

Barth's overall doctrine of the Word of God at this stage rests on the notion of revelation as an event in which God's self-disclosure in a human form is also God's self-concealment. The God who is revealed does not cease being God in God's self-disclosure, is not absorbed into that in which God is revealed. The

---

[115] *Ethics*, 209/356.
[116] *The Holy Spirit and the Christian Life*, 8 f.
[117] *Ethics*, 88/145.

same holds for the command of God. Since the command of God simply is the Word of God as the latter claims its human addressee, it will occur as an event in which a divine decision or judgment on human conduct—ultimately, the judgment of grace—is both revealed and concealed. Thus the doctrine of the command of God follows the doctrine of the Word of God more generally: here, too, revelation is also concealment. The revelation of the divine decision and judgment in the human ethical decision and act is also the concealment of this decision and judgment, and in this respect Barth remains within the ambit of *Romans*₂.

The Visible and the Hidden

Once again it is sanctification that exhibits the problem of ethics in its purest form. Sanctification, as we have seen, is human life under the determination of God's grace, and to exist under the determination of grace means, in the first place, that good conduct can be genuinely commanded. Continuing a line of thought from *Romans₂*, Barth argues that the reality of God's forgiveness, expressing itself in the form of the demand (gospel in the form of law), denies the final necessity of my sinfulness. To see myself in light of forgiveness is to see my conduct as freed from sin and thus as the legitimate object of the command (ought implies can). In Barth's words, '. . . as I am forgiven by the gospel the law comes into force with its demand and puts me in this new position in which I must deny the final necessity of my own corruption and affirm a final freedom for my righteousness before God . . .'[118] Here Barth articulates one of the most persistent features of his conception of sanctification, namely, the confidence that the Word of divine grace itself frees human beings from bondage to sin. Forgiveness is not only forensic; it is also creative of the new person. Sanctification, as the divine claim on human conduct, is thus neither illusory nor futile, and it is in this sense that the vertical determination by divine grace has a legitimate meaning for the horizontal line of actual human conduct. However, Barth immediately qualifies this with another persistent feature, also prominent in *Romans₂*, pointing out that we are free to obey only insofar as we are in Christ. 'This order does not point me to myself, of course, but to Christ.' Good works are 'done on hearing the appeal to the new man that I am, not in myself, but in Christ.'[119] In other words, it is only as I am in Christ, and not as I am in myself, that I am the new creature for whom genuine freedom for obedience is possible—and this makes it clear that my sanctification is not identifiable with the visible course of my conduct. In faith, 'we are unable to understand ourselves otherwise than as hearers of the Word and also as doers, as really sanctified and therefore as living in obedience,' yet our obedience is hidden. 'It is hidden

---

[118] Ibid. 111/185.
[119] Ibid. 111/185 f.

because this obedience of ours never, not even partially, becomes perceptible to us unequivocally in itself, and because also, *that* and *how* grace is *actual* on our behalf is hidden in the darkness of faith, in which only the Word itself is the light.'[120] The implications are clear: 'Our sanctification, our new life, is, all along the line, hidden with Christ in God [cf. Col. 3: 3]. Its manifestations are as such unequivocally manifest only to God, as they are really *its* manifestations only by God's act.'[121]

Barth is clearly still struggling with the problem of ethics, torn between his conviction that the significance of grace for the horizontal line is real and his worry that the horizontal line inevitably betrays grace. Sanctification implies both our real freedom for righteousness, which makes a genuine command possible, and the hiddenness in Christ of our righteousness, which means that we cannot presume our righteousness, vouch for it, perceive it, or judge concerning it. We respond to God's command in our conduct, but that we are righteous in it or not is God's decision, hidden in the mystery of election. The remarks quoted above concerning the event of decision as revelation of the good thus receive their decisive qualification: 'In its own way the present moment is itself decision, action, and therefore the revelation of the good. But we may add at once that it is so as a prophecy of the one who comes, who is even at the doors...'[122] Barth will eventually reformulate this point in more explicitly Christological terms, shifting the reality of election from the present event of decision and judgment to the election of Christ from eternity and distinguishing between sanctification that is accomplished by Christ and obedient conduct as our participation in what is already complete in Christ. At this stage, though, the eschatological framework of *Romans₂* is still primary. Yet at both stages Barth's point in insisting on the hiddenness of our goodness is to direct us to God's grace. 'If we have seen the concept of sanctification come to fulfillment in our own Yes to grace, we must emphasize again that it is grace when we say Yes to grace...'[123] Our ethical decision is the point where the divine determination of our conduct is manifest as the realization of election, but we are not in a position to exhibit our own lives or the lives of others as sanctified. That our conduct is genuinely obedient is entirely a matter of God's judgment and decision. 'For this reason our sanctification is reality, but our obedience is a problem that we cannot solve, into the darkness of which we can but enter again and again and be thrown utterly and only upon God.'[124] Insofar as sanctification is real, the Christian life is a life of repentance and conversion; but because the righteousness of the Christian is hidden it must also be a life of vigilance and prayer, lived in constant

---

[120]   *The Holy Spirit and the Christian Life*, 35.
[121]   *Ethics*, 112/186.
[122]   Ibid. 75 f./124.
[123]   Ibid. 113/188.
[124]   *The Holy Spirit and the Christian Life*, 37.

awareness of our dependence on God's grace, yet in the knowledge that because the command of God is the expression of divine grace, the judgment that occurs in our decision will in some way reflect God's grace.

Is the good with which moral theology is occupied found in the Word of God, in its determination of human conduct (sanctification), or is it found in visible human conduct itself, in the pious or virtuous human being (actual obedience, or holiness)? This question now marks a fundamental divide, setting Barth's ethics off from a tendency he finds throughout its history for Christian ethics to seek its ground in a goodness that is visible in the life of the Christian. Against this tendency Barth insists that sanctification is found in God's act, not ours. 'It is *divine* separation when our action is sanctified, not a quality immanent in the action itself.'[125] Barth therefore denies that moral theology can base its account of the good on an ideal or empirical description of the Christian life itself. 'There are Christians only in Christ and not in themselves.'[126] It follows that while the determination of grace culminates in the decision and judgment of God on concrete human conduct on the horizontal line, an account of the good must look for the reality of sanctification and thus for the norm of ethics in the Word of God and its determination of human life rather than in the visible character of human life itself.

Barth's Genealogy of Visible Goodness

While Barth opens *Ethics* by sketching a broad history of neglect of the distinction between sanctification by the Word of God and visible human obedience in Christian ethics, it eventually becomes clear that his accusation has a more specific target. *Ethics* is in no small measure a sustained critique of pietism, and this point offers us a clue to what Barth thinks is at stake in this distinction. 'Our counterquestion to the theology of pietism, then, is whether it is not a theology of impatience, and we believe that Protestant theology has to recognize that seeing the coincidence of the divine Yes with the human Yes is an *eschatological* reality, [namely] Jesus Christ himself. . .'[127] He has the pietism of his day in mind here, but elsewhere Barth treats the identification of the ethical with the visible in eighteenth-century pietism and rationalism as a decisive event in the rise of modern theology, and it is in his critique of these two movements that we can most clearly see what he thinks is at stake for moral theology, and more broadly for the church and its life and thought, in maintaining the eschatological concealment of the good in Christ.

---

[125] *Ethics*, 112/188 (emphasis added).
[126] Ibid. 14/20.
[127] Ibid. 115/191 f. This remark makes clear the extent to which eschatology and Christology are identical at this stage of Barth's thought, as they were in the early 1920s.

Barth argues that in spite of their differences, pietism and rationalism shared the core bourgeois conviction that the meaning of Christian faith lies in 'altering and shaping life in a visible and tangible way, that could be experienced and established concretely and directly, inwardly and outwardly, accomplished by man in particular thoughts, actions, and modes of action.'[128] In this bourgeois imperative to transform or improve ordinary life in a tangible way—whether the pietist effort to give visible expression to the converted heart or the rationalist effort to bring outward life into conformity with moral duties and ideals—and in the tendency to understand this imperative as the central meaning of Christianity, Barth finds the key to eighteenth-century Christianity which continues, he thinks, to shadow his own day. Unbridled confidence in human power to reshape external reality, rejection of a law that confronts human beings from outside, reduction of everything outside the will to material to be shaped by intentional human activity—Barth identifies these as defining characteristics of eighteenth-century culture. Combined with the determination among Christians, in the wake of the devastating wars of the previous century, to emphasize life over doctrine and practice over theory in the hope of avoiding the doctrinal disputes and intellectualist distortions that were seen as the causes of these wars, these characteristics set the agenda for the theology of that century. That agenda was to make the realities about which theology speaks commensurate with human capability and to establish the visible transformation of individual or civic life as the principle of all Christian life and thought, the ultimate criterion of scriptural interpretation and doctrinal reformulation. Ethics, understood as visible human moral achievement, now becomes the arbiter of all that Christians believe, teach, and practice. Modern theology, in this narrative, is inaugurated with this turn to the ethical in pietism and rationalism. Christian life and thought now come to revolve around what is within human power to accomplish, to make visible in or before the world.

For Barth, the commitment of pietists and rationalists to a good that can be made visible in individual and civic life reflects the interest of the eighteenth century in representing the good, like everything else, as attainable by human power and subject to human evaluation. In this light it is neither accidental nor incidental that, as he sees it, both the pietist and rationalist versions of this moral project based their conceptions of the good on Stoic natural law rather than on scripture: Once the good is held to be visible in the life of the pious or virtuous Christian and is represented as capable of realization by human moral activity, it is an immanent good and thus one that can be treated as a form or specification of a general human good grounded in human nature or reason. This turn to nature and reason, which of course is more prominent in rationalism than in

[128] *Protestant Theology in the Nineteenth Century: Its Background and History* (Judson Press Edition, 1973), 91 f. (translation of Karl Barth, *Die protestantische Theologie im 19. Jahrhundert: Ihre Vorgeschichte und ihre Geschichte* (Zurich: Theologischer Verlag Zürich, 1952), 71).

pietism, is the very point, for it is precisely as a natural or rational phenomenon that Christianity can be assimilated to human capability, to the transformation and improvement of human life. For in the eighteenth-century imagination, Barth explains, nature is what is at human disposal, that is, it is material susceptible to shaping by human power, and reason is the capacity to comprehend and assimilate this material, so understood, to human will. It is, therefore, the influence of this moral motive—the effort to render Christianity capable of being realized by human moral effort—and not a speculative or skeptical bent that, according to Barth, fueled the transformation of Christianity into a natural and rational religion during this period.[129]

If rationalism assimilated Christian faith to human capacity by naturalizing and rationalizing it, pietism did so by internalizing it—by making inward what confronts human beings from outside. Pietism is the reduction of the other to the same, 'the interiorization and resultant abolition [*Aufhebung*] of the confrontation [*Gegenüber*] between man and Christianity.' Barth represents it almost as an act of ingestion, 'the taking in [*Hereinnahme*] of all those elements of Christianity which seem to represent an outwardness, a contrast.'[130] This interpretation of pietism as internalization signals what will increasingly come to the fore in Barth's thought: a critique of the self-enclosed subject. The distortion of the Christian ethos will be found less in the identification of a current state of affairs with the will and goodness of God—though that will remain a prominent theme—than in the autonomous solitary subject trapped in its interiority.

His venture into the eighteenth century enables Barth to construct a historical narrative for his critique of the bourgeois religio-moral order, giving the latter the depth that was lacking in his earlier work. But like many of Barth's historical narratives, this treatment of eighteenth-century pietism and rationalism is most plausible if we think of it in genealogical terms, as the exposure of certain formative assumptions of Christian life and thought in his own time.[131] For Barth, there seem to be three such assumptions traceable to 'pietism' and 'rationalism': (1) the identification of the good with the visible improvement of individual and social life; (2) the grounding of moral theology in a general human morality of which the Christian ethos is simply one specification among

---

[129] Ibid. 100–7/80–7.

[130] Ibid. 114/94.

[131] Ibid. 91–100/71–9. Barth's treatment of pietism at this stage and his thesis on the affinity between pietism and rationalism is a highly complex matter. See Busch, *Karl Barth and the Pietists*, 264–85. Busch insightfully points out (270) that in these 1932–3 lectures pietism functions as something of an ideal type deployed for dogmatic purposes; the same can be said of rationalism in these lectures and of both pietism and rationalism in Barth's treatment of dogmatics and ethics in CD I/2. Both this chapter and Chapter 3 will therefore treat Barth's references to pietism and rationalism as ideal types representing a kind of visibility and immanence of goodness in the Christian which Barth associated with the eighteenth century rather than as historically precise characterizations of the particular theologians or texts which might properly be designated as pietist or rationalist.

others; and (3) the priority of the ethical, so understood, over dogmatics, so that the confession and practice of the church are ultimately subordinated to an essentially bourgeois moral vision grounded in a general moral anthropology. Barth's verdict on this transformation of Christianity into bourgeois moralism attacks what he sees as its fundamental presumption: 'Perhaps Christianity, in view of what its creed understands by sanctification and obedience, sets out to be a free, really spiritual power, set over against all human morality.'[132] It is important, though, to be clear about what Barth is and is not arguing here. The problem is not that Christianity is given an ethical meaning in the eighteenth century in contrast, say, to a priority previously given to its doctrinal meaning. This interpretation would pit dogmatics against ethics in a way that would undermine Barth's entire approach. And in fact, the claim by pietists and rationalists to have discovered the ethical meaning of Christian faith and given it its due is one Barth vigorously contests. Nor is Barth advocating that we reverse these modern moves by finding the good in God alone in abstraction from human beings and their conduct. Rather, the good is to be found in the determination of human conduct by the command of God's grace; the proper subject matter of moral theology is thus human being and conduct under this determination. Moral theology must therefore derive its norm or standard from this determination and not from any theoretical or empirical account that treats human capacities and achievements in abstraction from this determination. Thus the question Barth's moral theology poses to pietism and rationalism (and through them, he thinks, to much of the history of Christian ethics) is, how are we to understand human life and conduct if the good is found in this determination and not in anything human beings are able to know and bring about by themselves? It is with this question and its answer that Christianity is 'set over against all human morality.'

Conclusion

Does human moral life in its concrete existence reflect the status of human beings who exist under God's grace or does it reflect a bourgeois commitment to visible moral transformation as the meaning of Christian faith, accompanied by a robust confidence in human powers to achieve it? Does moral theology point to the claim of a good that confronts the moral subject from outside, so that this subject, in her ethical reflection and action, is constituted by her answerability to this claim, or does it reformulate this claim as a ground or a symbolic expression of a good the subject determines and accomplishes out of her own capacities? In raising the question of the good of human conduct do we look for this good in the divine determination and judgment under which human

---

[132] *Protestant Theology in the Nineteenth Century*, 100/79.

conduct stands, in which case it comes to full visibility only in our eschatological being in Christ, or do we assume that we can find this good in human conduct itself, where its visibility would make it possible for moral theology to offer an empirical or ideal description of the good? In putting these questions at the center of his moral theology and in affirming the first alternative presented by each question over against the second, Barth restates the problem of ethics and proposes a bold solution. The ambiguity of ethics will now concern the tension between adherence to the determination and claim of human conduct by the Word of God, on the one hand, and its betrayal in the moral self-confidence that looks for the knowledge and realization of the good in human powers and achievements, on the other hand. At stake is whether the ethos moral theology describes consists in living under the claim of God's grace or in an effort to give visible form to the good by human action.

The implications of this new perspective for Barth's understanding of the problem of ethics are enormous. As we have seen, by grounding the goodness of human conduct in the command of God's grace and thus representing moral conduct as the appropriation of divine grace, Barth is able to make possible the positive treatment of the horizontal line in light of the vertical that had eluded him in the period surrounding *Romans₂*, yet without abandoning the distance between the righteousness of God and human righteousness which it was his concern to uphold during that period. Perhaps most significantly, by linking ethics with the revelation of God in creation, reconciliation, and redemption, he is able to derive moral content, an ethos, from the vertical itself while still acknowledging the eschatological question mark set against every ethos. In principle, at least, Barth can now understand the life of the Christian in its own terms and not just as a negotiation between affirming and negating the forms and institutions of bourgeois society in light of an ultimate origin or as a vague reference to an inaccessible moral order.

Yet, in spite of these advances there is significant continuity with Barth's position in the early 1920s. First, while the betrayal of ethics now occurs in the transformation of Christian goodness along the lines of a natural and rational morality rather than in the opposing stances of uncritical acceptance of the social order and its revolutionary overthrow, both concerns target the bourgeois assurance that the good is knowable and achievable along the line of human moral activity. Second, the problematic of the visible and the hidden in *Ethics* is a continuation of the problematic of the perceptible and the imperceptible in *Romans₂*. While the theology of the command of God makes it possible to understand the sanctification of concrete human conduct, sanctification is still determined by the distinction between a perceptible self as sinner and an imperceptible self as righteous. And while it is now intelligible to speak of sanctification as the revelation of the good in concrete human conduct, sanctification remains an eschatological (while at the same time a Christological) reality.

In these respects the reality of sanctification remains obscure, and to the extent that this is so, the problem of ethics is unresolved.

5. BARTH'S CHRISTOLOGICAL SOLUTION TO THE PROBLEM OF ETHICS

The stage at which Barth's moral theology reaches its mature form is less a new stage than a set of alterations and shifts of emphasis within the general doctrine of the command of God worked out in *Ethics*. What follows largely presupposes the continuing relevance of the position described in the previous section and concentrates on what is distinctive about this mature stage. Most significant in this stage is the prominence of the notion of covenant, with election and sanctification as its two components. Moral theology now rests on Barth's treatment of the command of God as the sanctification which complements election and thus completes the concept of God's covenant of grace with God's human partner. The key point is that election involves both a divine self-determination and a divine determination of human beings. From eternity, God makes a free self-determination to enter into a particular form of fellowship with a human counterpart and also determines this human counterpart for a particular form of fellowship with God. 'God elects himself to be gracious toward man, to be his Lord and Helper, and in so doing He elects man to be the witness of his glory.'[133] Because election involves this 'service, this commission, this office of witness' it necessarily poses to the human partner the question of his response to the divine purpose under which he is placed. 'As election is ultimately the determination of man, the question arises as to the human self-determination which corresponds to this determination.'[134] It is as one who is placed under this question, as answerable (*verantwortlich*) to it, that God's human partner participates in the covenant as an active subject. To be placed under this question, and thus to be answerable to it, is the ethical itself, and the ethical, so understood, is an unavoidable implication of election. 'Unless he accepts this question—however it is to be answered—he obviously cannot be elect.... God cannot draw him to himself without involving him in responsibility [*Verantwortung*: "answerability"].'[135] In other words, there is no gospel without law. Yet by the same token the one who is placed under this question is the one who is elect. 'It is in and with man's determination by God as this takes place in predestination that the question arises of man's self-determination, his responsibility and decision, his obedience and action. To answer this question

---

[133] CD II/2, 510/565.
[134] CD II/2, 510/566.
[135] CD II/2, 511/566.

cannot, then, impose any limitation upon the knowledge of the absolute authority of God's grace.'[136] There is no law that is not also gospel.

The key to Barth's position at this stage is the role of Christ as the one in whom the twofold determination of election is fulfilled. In Christ the God-man both God and God's human partner fulfill the covenant, God's faithfulness overcoming the sinful rejection of the covenant by its human partner. 'What right conduct is for man is determined absolutely in the right conduct of God. It is determined in Jesus Christ. He is the electing God and elected man in one. But he is also the sanctifying God and sanctified man in one. In his person God has acted rightly towards us. And in the same person man has also acted rightly for us.'[137] In Christ, God proves faithful to God's own self-determination to be gracious to humanity, and in Christ, humanity answers the question concerning the human self-determination of the elect by the obedient exercise, in Christ's conduct, of the service, commission, or witness for which God has determined God's human partner—in other words, by existing as God's elect. Barth will continue to stress that our obedience as the fulfillment of our sanctification is in our eschatological being in Christ, but he will also stress that sanctification has already been accomplished in the obedience of Christ. Thus it is now the Word of God in a more explicitly Christological sense that sanctifies human beings. The tension between the uncertain and imperfect reality of the good in our actions and its full reality in our eschatological being in Christ is now overshadowed (though by no means replaced) by a tension between the fulfillment of election in the obedience of Jesus Christ and its (still uncertain and imperfect) confirmation and attestation in our actions. Finally, and for this reason, it is now Jesus Christ, not the Word of God in a less determinately Christological sense, who is identified as the standard of ethics. The theme of Colossians 3: 3, fundamental to Barth's ethics since the period of *Romans₂*, has shifted from a Christologically expressed eschatology to an eschatologically completed Christology—a shift which tracks a similar movement in Barth's theology more generally.[138]

The importance of this Christological focus for the solution to the problem of ethics is difficult to exaggerate.[139] The good is done by Christ, visibly accomplished in his obedient life and death. Now Barth can affirm without reservation that there is a genuine fulfillment of the good on the horizontal line of human conduct. In Christ's obedience the righteousness of God and human

---

[136] CD II/2, 511/566.

[137] CD II/2, 538 f./598.

[138] In accordance with this shift Barth now contrasts the hiddenness of holiness in the lives of Christians and its visibility in Christ, making explicit a Christological realization of the good that was only implicit before. Compare CD I/2, 782/875 with *Ethics*, 6/6.

[139] Failure to give it its due is the primary criticism that can be made of Clough's account of Barth's ethical thought in the *Church Dogmatics*, despite his perceptive analysis of the persistence of the symptoms of crisis in this later period. See Clough, *Ethics in Crisis*, 61–74.

righteousness at last coincide. Now the issue for the moral theologian to clarify is how other human beings share in what has been accomplished in and by Jesus Christ. For Barth, Christ's obedience, his existence as God's elect, involves a special work, inseparable from his person, in which he does the good on behalf of and in place of all other human beings. It is this accomplishment of sanctification in Christ as the obedient one—the one who exists as God's elect in his life conduct—that other human beings are summoned to glorify in their own life conduct: 'In him the obedience demanded of us men has already been rendered. In him the realization of the good corresponding to divine election has already taken place—and so completely that we, for our part, have actually nothing to add, but have only to endorse this event by our action.'[140] The task of these other human beings is not to do again what Christ has already done. So Barth is now free to portray ethics as the expression of the participation of other human beings in Christ in conduct that neither reenacts nor continues Christ's unique work (as if that work were somehow insufficient or incomplete) nor stands independent of it (as if it were done for us in a way that did not involve us) but confirms it, attests it, and thereby glorifies it. In this way, conduct on the horizontal line by other human beings positively signifies the vertical good of grace accomplished by Christ on the horizontal line yet without substituting itself for the latter. The problem of concrete moral action in Barth's thought during the period of *Romans₂* and its aftermath is thus resolved. Human beings are summoned to a form of conduct that is entirely human yet which also, and for the same reason, positively reflects the goodness of God. While Barth's moral theology would continue to develop, it would do so by following the lines set out here.

At every point, Christ is both the exemplar whose obedience is the paradigm of human goodness and the representative or substitute who does the good on behalf of and in place of other human beings; for both reasons, Christ is also the one in whom other human beings have their goodness, so that fundamentally the command of God which sanctifies human beings is the demand that human beings be 'in' or 'with' Christ, which is also a demand that they be a member of God's people.[141] But this is the demand that they express in their conduct what they already *are* by the grace of God in their election and in their creation, reconciliation, and redemption as the acts through which God realizes the purpose of election. Because we are who and what we are as acting subjects, where action is understood in the broadest sense as our 'life act' or our 'act of existence,' as Barth often calls it, the ethical question—the question of the validity or worth of our conduct—is the most urgent and consequential question of our lives.[142] In our conduct will we be those who live in and by the grace of God, expressing in our concrete existence our ontological determination, or

---

[140] CD II/2, 540/599 f.
[141] CD II/2, 569 f./632 f.
[142] CD II/2, 516/572.

will we be those who live in and by ourselves, and who attempt to secure the validity or worth of our lives by submitting to the claim of a good we have discovered or invented?

This question makes it clear that the ambiguity of ethics in Barth's theology has shifted in accordance with this Christological focus. Barth now promotes a more explicitly Christological version of a key point from *Ethics*: Moral theology properly focuses on the righteousness accomplished by Christ in which other human beings participate, not on any righteousness found in those other human beings themselves. Yet what is striking is how the distinction between an ethic grounded in the visibility of the good in human conduct and an ethic grounded in the hiddenness of the good in the Word of God has now yielded emphasis to a distinction between an ethic grounded in the sovereign, self-enclosed subject and an ethic grounded in participation in Christ. 'The man to whom the Word of God is directed and for whom the work of God was done . . . this man, in virtue of this Word and work, does not exist by himself. He is not an independent subject, to be considered independently. In virtue of the death and resurrection of Jesus Christ . . . it is simply not true that he belongs to himself and is left to himself, that he is thrown back on himself.' Rather, this human being exists as a 'predicate' of Christ, who is the proper 'subject,' meaning that 'that which has been decided and is real for man in this subject [i.e., Jesus Christ] is true for him.'[143]

When Barth now criticizes ethics it is almost always insofar as the latter is the activity or expression of the independent, solitary, self-asserting subject. The ethical as an expression of the assurance that God is for us is opposed to the ethical as an expression of the assumption that we must be for ourselves because we are left to ourselves, thrown back on ourselves: that it is left to us to give ourselves the law and judge ourselves, that in the face of moral demands we must reserve our prerogative to secure the worth of our lives, that the ethical question and answer constitute a moral subject whose asking and answering form a self-enclosed circle. Does ethics direct us to live in the grace of God who is for us and who has taken up our cause, or does it throw us back on ourselves, leaving us to secure the meaning and worth of our lives on our own? For Barth, God has taken up our cause and is for us in the most thorough and radical way, opening us up from outside ourselves and granting us, in our human reality as it is, participation in a good that transcends us. To be for ourselves, by contrast, is to be enclosed in ourselves, to be self-sufficient, sovereign, and ultimately alone, and one of the most distinguishing features of Barth's mature thought is this deep conviction of the sovereign, self-enclosed subject as the source of anxiety, loneliness, insomnia, and eventually disillusionment and desperation—less as

---

[143] CD II/2, 539/599.

psychological moods (although this is not excluded) than as modes of existence of a self-positing subject.

Yet, just as the theme of visibility and hiddenness was not really a new theme but a continuation of the earlier problem of the perceptible and the imperceptible, so the theme of the sovereign, solitary subject is not really new but an elaboration of what was implied in the determination to make the good visible. In his 1932 lectures on *Protestant Theology in the Nineteenth Century*, Barth had explicitly grounded this determination in the subject who asserts itself over against all that is other and assimilates all that is other to itself, finding in pietism and rationalism instances of this subject as the most characteristic feature of the eighteenth century as a whole.[144] Similarly, in *The Holy Spirit and the Christian Life*, Barth had frequently contrasted the self-enclosed subject who in its hostility to grace refuses to allow itself to be 'made fit by God for God' with the subject who is open to this determination by grace as a form of activity other than its own.[145] Finally, while it was not named, this self-enclosed subject was implied in Barth's criticisms of the neutral, self-reflecting moral subject in *Ethics*. In the next chapter, we will see that this subject plays a prominent role in Barth's conception of modernity; for now, it is enough to note that this subject seems to Barth to be the ground of the bourgeois ethos from whose captivity he had been striving to free Protestant ethics since the mid-point of his Safenwil years.

6. CONCLUSION

For Karl Barth, ethics begins not with a good to which we are oriented by nature and which we approximate by moral striving with the assistance of divine grace but with our confrontation by a good that consists both in the divine determination of our lives for fellowship with God and in the fulfillment of this determination in Jesus Christ. On the one hand, the divine accomplishment of the good calls all human moral endeavor and attainment into question. On the other hand, it summons human beings to participate in it in a fully human manner by corresponding to it in their existence as active subjects. In the earlier stages examined in this chapter, Barth stressed the interruption of human moral achievement by the divine righteousness and sought to articulate the significance of transcendent grace for this-worldly human moral activity. In the later stages, he stressed the fulfillment of the good in the obedience of Christ and sought to articulate the significance of that fulfillment for the moral activity of other human beings. But in both cases, his task was to show how human moral life can and ought to express what God does for us rather than what we must do or

---

[144] *Protestant Theology in the Nineteenth Century*, 33–135/16–114.
[145] *The Holy Spirit and the Christian Life*, 7, 19 f., 24 f.

become by our striving. This is the problem of ethics in Barth's theology, and we have examined his various attempts to solve it.

The problem of ethics as Barth grapples with it is inseparable from his understanding of the history of Protestant theology and church life. The failure of Luther and Calvin to relate grace to ethics in a satisfactory way eventually made it possible for pietism and rationalism to reorient all of Christian thought and life to a moral project aimed at visible improvement of individual lives and societies, and this in turn set the stage for the complete identification of Christianity with the pre-First World War bourgeois culture which was the object of Barth's early attacks. Barth will eventually go straight to the source of the problem, correcting Luther and Calvin by bringing ethics wholly within the doctrine of grace taught by these Reformers. But are the problem Barth poses and the solution he offers of perennial concern to Christian moral theology or do they reflect a peculiarly modern set of circumstances? This is the question we will pose in the next chapter.

2

Barth's Moral Theology and Modern Ethics

In Barth's moral theology, ethics reflects God's determination of human beings by and for divine grace. Ethical inquiry and conduct are to be carried out under the presupposition that God has established and accomplished the good in Jesus Christ and summons human beings to free and active participation in it. But of course, ethics also can, and often does in fact, reflect the determination of human beings to be by and for themselves. In such cases, ethical inquiry and practice are carried out under the presupposition that it is left to human capability to determine what the good is and bring it about. It is the task of Barth's moral theology to articulate the first and proper understanding of ethics. But what shall we say of a moral theology that opposes these two alternative understandings of ethics to one another and treats this opposition as a fundamental one? Either ethical inquiry and conduct reflect God's grace or they reflect human self-assertion—does not this polarization of the ethical field betray the decisive influence of a distinctively modern set of problems and assumptions? Our suspicions are heightened when we look more closely at the technical ethical terms in which Barth expresses this ambiguity of ethics. We have already seen that he is able to draw on the Kantian conception of morality to describe the command of God as the summons of God's grace, and we will soon see that he is also able to describe the contrasting ethics of human self-assertion in terms of a Fichtean conception of morality in which the moral law is posited by a self-determining subject. The Kant–Fichte axis is, of course, a thoroughly modern one, and this is enough to raise questions about the relation of the ambiguity of ethics, as Barth describes it, to modernity. Does this ambiguity characterize ethics in every era, so that Barth is describing a distinctively modern manifestation of a perpetual problem which moral theology has always faced, whether it has recognized it or not? If this is so, then perhaps we can credit his modern idiom for putting the problem before us with a degree of clarity and urgency it has hitherto lacked. Or is this ambiguity only the product of certain distinctively modern conditions and assumptions, so that Barth's moral theology, whether consciously or not, is an exercise in modern ethics? If this is so, then his modern idiom may bind his moral theology to a particular era, one which (at least as he understood it) may have already passed, or in any case, one whose conditions and assumptions we no longer consider binding on moral theology.

With these questions we have already taken a plunge into the turbulent waters of Barth's relation to modernity. And by identifying Barth with modernity from the outset, we may be going too deep too fast. Let us surface, then, to consider various ways of relating Barth to modern ethics. A superficial reading of Barth might leave the impression that his opposition between the command of God and a law we give ourselves serves an anti-modern cause by reasserting divine sovereignty against human freedom. But Barth's entire doctrine of God is a repudiation of theologies that honor God at the expense of humanity. Far more plausible is John Webster's identification of an anti-modern stance in Barth's effort to ground ethics in the ontology given in God's self-bestowing Word in contrast to modern efforts to ground ethics in the moral consciousness.[1] In concert with Webster, we will encounter an anti-modern streak in Barth's critiques of modern ethical autonomy and interiority, in his refusal of certain conditions and false alternatives (including those of divine sovereignty and human freedom) modern ethics often imposes on moral theology, and in his insistence on retaining themes of premodern ethics, such as ontological participation in the good, which are typically ignored, marginalized, or rejected by modern ethics.

From another angle, Barth's moral theology has been identified with so-called postmodern ethics.[2] William Stacy Johnson argues that Barth validates theology through ethics in a way that reflects the primacy of the ethical over ontology (premodern) and epistemology (modern). He stresses the open-ended and pro-visional character of ethical inquiry for Barth, arguing that these features reflect Barth's understanding of how the mystery of God and the priority of the neighbor disrupt the effort of theological ethics to account for its object.[3] For Barth, however, these characteristics are in the service of particular theological claims about the divine decision and judgment on human action in Christ—claims toward which postmodern thought would direct its suspicion. Neverthe-less, we will see how Barth anticipates certain themes associated with postmodern ethics by pointing out the nihilism inherent in the modern subject, challenging the assumption of the transparency of the good to the reason and conscience of

---

[1] See Webster, *Barth's Ethics of Reconciliation*, 229–30; and Webster, *Barth's Moral Theology*, 42, 54. Webster concisely and insightfully summarizes the broader discussion of Barth's relation to modernity and postmodernity in 'Barth, Modernity, and Postmodernity,' in *Karl Barth: A Future for Postmodern Theology?*, ed. Geoff Thompson and Chrisitaan Mostert (Hindmarsh: Australia Theological Forum, 2000), 1–28.

[2] In his *Ethics in Crisis*, David Clough argues that the crisis of ethics portrayed first in Barth's earlier theology and then throughout his later work can be brought into fruitful conversation with the current of postmodern ethics best represented by Zygmunt Bauman. However, it is not clear whether Clough considers Barth's moral theology itself to be postmodern or only that the conversation between it and genuinely postmodern ethics is a worthwhile one. The latter thesis is the more probable one, and Clough's account largely vindicates it. But for this reason, Clough's interpretation will not be taken here as an instance of a postmodern reading of Barth.

[3] William Stacy Johnson, *The Mystery of God: Karl Barth and the Postmodern Foundations of Theology* (Louisville, Ky.: Westminster John Knox Press, 1997), 153–75.

this subject, and blurring the line modernity draws between itself and the premodern with his mutual intertwining of modern and premodern themes.

It is clear that Barth will not fit easily into the epochal categories by which we often conduct interrogations of thinkers. Nevertheless, we will find good reasons for identifying him as a modern thinker while keeping in mind that to identify a thinker as modern is not to settle the question of the position that thinker occupies within the modern context she or he inhabits. In Barth's case, is this position with respect to modernity that of a critic, a defender, an unwitting victim, a clever appropriator, or an ironic subversive? We, of course, pose this question from our own stance toward modernity. Many Christians today no longer assume that the dominant modern forms of ethics and politics can simply be avoided by defensive moves, as traditionalists have tried for two centuries to do, nor do they assume that Christian witness is best served by embracing these forms as faithful expressions of Christian thought and practice, as liberal forms of Christianity have done. These Christians believe that we are now beyond the old polarization between defensive avoidance and cheerful embrace of modernity, holding instead that our consciousness of the limitations, defects, and unresolved problems of modernity have now placed us beyond its reach, so that we can recover premodern forms of ethics and politics not in a posture of defense but in one of triumph. Yet before they dance over the grave of modernity, these Christians ought to look more closely to see whether there is in fact a corpse inside the coffin. The ability to see through modernity does not amount to seeing beyond it, and it is yet unclear whether contemporary ventures in premodern retrieval do not merely court the nostalgia, *ressentiment*, and ironic repetitions of modernity that have so often accompanied similar ventures during the past two centuries. Barth never pretended to have seen beyond modernity, and we will see in this chapter that he employs a very different strategy for dealing with it—a strategy which neither accepts modernity on its own terms nor refuses its deepest yearnings but instead shows how those yearnings express the determination of human beings to secure for themselves, by their own capabilities and efforts, the good that, in its proper form, God has already given them. It is in this context that we must interpret the opposition Barth sets up between correspondence to grace and self-assertion. However, we cannot avoid asking whether this strategy articulates central Christian moral convictions in modern terms or whether it instead excludes or distorts at least some of these convictions by conceding too much to aspects of modernity that we need not and should not accept.

This chapter will pursue this question by examining Barth's complex relationship to modernity in three sections, covering his overall narrative of modernity, his critique and (critical) appropriation of modernity, and his engagement with autonomy and interiority as two central features of modern ethics. The conclusion will attempt to answer the question of Barth's stance towards modernity.

1. BARTH'S NARRATIVE OF MODERNITY

Narratives of modernity are often less histories in the strict sense than genealogies: efforts to disentangle the author and her reader from certain entrenched ideas or practices by portraying those ideas and practices as rooted in contingent historical circumstances which the author and reader no longer consider binding, thereby enabling them to loosen the grip of those ideas or practices on their thinking and acting. So it is with Barth. Concerned to free the church from the nineteenth-century legacy of bourgeois Christianity, Barth's narratives of modernity consistently focus on the assimilation of Christianity to the bourgeois humanism that progressively gained ground in Europe from the sixteenth century to its triumph in the eighteenth, and which Barth describes as a resurgence of ancient Stoic humanism.[4] Barth's characterization of this form of humanism and its descent into nihilism is a topic for the following section; here we simply note his special concern with how post-Reformation Protestant traditions (especially the Reformed tradition) came to contribute to the assimilation of Christianity to modern humanism. With remarkable consistency over the course of many years, Barth attributes this assimilation to the failure of the Protestant Reformation—whether in the persons of Luther, Zwingli, and Calvin themselves or, more commonly, in the persons of their successors—to maintain consistently its theme of divine grace. This failure was especially notable—and fateful—in matters involving the nature and status of ethics. So important is this theme that we may describe Barth's moral theology as an attempt to overcome this failure and its effects, to bring ethics into line with the theology of grace in a way that would enable moral theology to resist the assimilation of Christianity to bourgeois humanism rather than serving as an indispensable means to that assimilation, as Barth thought had happened.

Barth on the Reformation and Modernity

Barth's portrayal of the Reformation theology of grace, however, involves a highly controversial claim. He holds that with respect to its theology of grace the Protestant Reformation stands apart from both its medieval predecessor and its modern successor and, moreover, exposes an otherwise concealed continuity between the medieval and the modern, which turn out to be united in their portrayal of the good as accessible in principle to human moral capacity and

---

[4] In addition to the 1932–3 lectures discussed in the previous chapter (*Protestant Theology in the Nineteenth Century*, 33–135/16–114), narratives of the assimilation of Christianity to modern bourgeois humanism can be found, in greater and lesser detail and specificity, in *The Theology of Calvin*, 13–68 (much of which is echoed at many points in the lecture courses on Zwingli and the Reformed confessions from the same period); *Ethics*, 5–8/4–10; CD I/2, 783–6/876–80 (this material largely repeats the material from *Ethics*); and CD IV/1, 54–66/57–70, 369–72/407–11.

activity. This claim was formulated early in Barth's academic career, in his lecture courses on Reformed theology at Göttingen, where he portrayed the Protestant Reformation (represented, for him, by its major theologians and its confessions) as neither medieval, as Troeltsch had argued, nor modern, as Harnack had held, but 'as something new and alien, a third entity' set over against what he saw as the common tendency of medieval and modern Christianity to measure the divine by the human in their affirmations of continuity between human moral endeavor and God's righteousness.[5] It is clear that Barth meant that it is the *theme* of the Reformation as he saw it, namely, the disruption of human moral endeavor by God's establishment of a relationship with human beings by grace alone in contrast to all efforts of human beings to establish such a relationship by their own powers assisted by grace, and not its historical actuality, that constituted the Reformation as a radical break with both medieval and modern Christianity. The failure of this theme to take hold as a historical reality during the Reformation and its aftermath, partly manifested in the inability of the Reformers or their successors to articulate the nature and status of ethics in relation to its claims regarding divine grace, is a recurrent topic not only in these early lectures but throughout Barth's career. Yet for him it is this theme that exposes the fundamental continuity of the modern with the medieval, which are held together by a common understanding of the relation of the good to human moral capacities.

However, the continuity Barth finds between the premodern and the modern does not entail the identity of the two. This brings us to an important feature of Barth's understanding of modernity. As he sees it, modernity is continuous with preceding eras in the sense that it in some way makes evident or visible certain features which were only covertly present in premodern thought and practice. What Barth seems to have in mind in this thesis of continuity and visibility is that the relation of human moral capacities to the good in premodern Christian moral thought carry within them the residue of an incompletely suppressed antique humanism, supplying material on which the modern resurgence of humanism will draw. Premodern Christianity is the vehicle that delivers ancient humanism, with its ideals of self-sufficiency and rational autonomy, to the scene of its modern reappearance. What from premodern perspectives would appear to be distorted modern notions of capacities such as reason and conscience (or piety and virtue) turn out to be something that was lurking in them all

---

[5] *The Theology of the Reformed Confessions*, 206 f. The same claim is elaborated in *The Theology of John Calvin*, 25–68; and in *Die Theologie Zwinglis*, 39–49. The notion that the Reformation doctrine of grace stands in opposition to an affirmation of the continuity of divine and human action that is common to both medieval (i.e., Catholic) and modern (i.e., Protestant liberal) theology is echoed in Barth's rather implausible identification of Catholicism and Protestant liberalism in the 1929 lectures on *The Holy Spirit and the Christian Life*, 3, 22, 24. It is also echoed in Barth's opposition of his own view on the relation of moral theology and moral philosophy to those of Protestant liberalism and Catholicism in his *Ethics* lectures, 19–33/30–53; this material is largely repeated in CD II/2, 520–35/577–94.

along. His moral theology thus reflects a conviction about modernity that characterizes his thought more generally and is succinctly stated in his assertion that 'the modern epoch is distinguished from those which precede by the fact that certain tendencies which were previously latent, isolated and in the main suppressed have now become increasingly patent, general and dominating.'[6] In the case of ethics, modern autonomy, interiority, and human self-sufficiency bring into the daylight certain tendencies that were always lurking in the assumption that the good is in principle within the grasp of our capacities, albeit not without the assistance of grace.

It is worth pointing out that, at least in this respect, Barth's interpretation of modernity exhibits some interesting and perhaps unexpected parallels with that of Ernst Troeltsch.[7] Both Barth and Troeltsch emphasize the role played in modern ethical life by the reemergence of late-antique Stoic humanism which, as they see it, had all along been borne (or at least insufficiently suppressed) by Christian moral and social life and thought (paradigmatically, for Troeltsch, in the Christian adoption of Stoic natural law). Characteristic features of modern moral life such as autonomy and emancipation from traditional authorities intensify and make visible what had been concealed and partially suppressed in the Christian appropriation of Stoicism; these features now assert themselves against their erstwhile host, declaring their independence from the need for any grounding or articulation in Christian terms (and, at least in Barth's view, going even further to demand the reconstruction of Christian doctrine and practice in conformity with them). For Troeltsch, this interpretation gave voice to the tension he felt between his commitment to the Christian-bourgeois order, reflected in the primacy he accorded to social ethics and in his fundamental concern with the role of Christianity in maintaining the unity of civilization, on the one hand, and his acute awareness of the historical contingency and, by his time, the apparently permanent loss of the conditions under which Christianity can play a socially constitutive role, on the other hand. By contrast, for Barth this interpretation gives voice to an explicitly theological conviction, demonstrating how the rejection of divine grace as the source and guarantee of human worth in favor of grounding that worth in what human beings can accomplish by their own powers and efforts—a rejection which goes back to the primordial fall but is notably visible in the modern bourgeois order—was made possible in no small part by the failure of Christianity to maintain its theology of grace consistently and without compromise, thereby harboring within itself tendencies that would eventually emerge into full-blown human self-assertion.

[6] CD IV/3.1, 19/18.
[7] See Troeltsch, *The Social Teaching of the Christian Churches*, vols. i and ii, trans. Olive Wyon (Chicago: University of Chicago Press, 1931), especially i. 160 f., 293; idem, 'The Social Philosophy of Christianity' and 'Stoic-Christian Natural Law and Modern Secular Natural Law,' both in *Reason in History*, trans. James Luther Adams and Walter F. Bense (Minneapolis: Fortress Press, 1991), 210–34, 321–42.

Yet if Barth is convinced that the theme of the Protestant Reformation stood apart from its medieval-cum-modern alternative, he does not conclude that the solution is simply to return to the Reformers. The Reformers, after all, were not able to prevent the transformation of Protestantism into bourgeois humanism. But there is also a positive reason for remaining within a modern horizon. Insofar as it brings to greater visibility what was more or less concealed in previous eras, modernity functions for Barth as an epistemologically privileged site. It is also, and for this very reason, the site of a sharp tension. It is in the modern era—especially, as we will see, in modern ethical autonomy and interiority—that the determination of human beings to assert themselves as autonomous self-legislators achieves full expression, but it is also in modern terms—especially in the alterity of the Kantian moral law in relation to the inclinations—that the fundamental theme of moral theology, namely, the claim of God's grace, can be expressed in explicitly ethical terms. The ambiguity of ethics is therefore modern in the sense that modern (specifically, Kantian) ethics discloses with utter clarity an opposition between the claim of divine grace and the determination of human beings to assert themselves as lawgivers. However, this opposition itself is not exclusively modern; it is primordial; in more or less concealed forms, it characterizes every age. Modern ethical autonomy and interiority lay bare a primordial rejection of the claim of divine grace in the determination of human beings to be for themselves. At the same time, Barth apparently believes that it is in the modern notions of the categorical ought and of the ethical as personal encounter that the summons of grace to human beings is most clearly expressed. Just as modernity brings to visibility the self-assertion that lurked undetected in premodern Christian moral thought and practice, it also supplies a formal conception of morality (namely, the Kantian one) in which the proper relation of grace to ethics can be expressed, helping to fulfill at last the unfulfilled promise of the Protestant Reformation. In short, it is in modern ethics that the ambiguity of ethics, which is a primordial ambiguity present in every era, is most visible, and this is what makes a solution to the problem both urgent and feasible.

Barth's view that modernity brings to visibility what was previously concealed echoes, perhaps unwittingly, modernity's own conceit, as does his understanding of modernity as crisis. In these respects, Barth not only speaks in a modern idiom but adopts a characteristically modern self-understanding. Yet, by stressing the continuity of the modern era with previous eras, Barth rejects the notion of modernity as a self-positing, radical break with the past, a notion that is deeply implicated in the oscillations between revolution and nostalgia in modern life and thought. His portrayal of the relation between the premodern and the modern implies that modernity is the truth of what precedes it, and this implication raises suspicions that he gives modernity far too much credit. While Barth nowhere explicitly avows this implication, it is not clear how he can avoid it. But if there is continuity between the premodern and the modern such that the latter brings to conscious expression a form of humanism that lay dormant within the former, it would be a serious mistake to seek the solution to the problems of modernity in a return to some form of premodern ethics. Such a return, assuming that it could be accomplished without self-deception, would not avoid or overcome the problems posed by modernity but would merely reinstate a condition in which the modern is concealed, harder to detect, yet waiting to emerge. In other words, it would risk repeating modernity all over again. '"Back to . . . !",' Barth says in a related context, 'is never a good slogan.'[8] Just as it is in the modern era that the problem becomes especially visible so, it appears, it is in modern terms that the correction can and must be made.

To summarize: The Reformation theology of grace stands against medieval-cum-modern human self-assertion. Modernity brings this self-assertion, concealed in medieval Christianity as the unwitting vehicle of antique humanism, to visibility. Yet in the Kantian moral law, modernity also supplies the conception of morality by which the relation of divine grace to human action can at last be articulated. This position involves two controversial claims: first, that the theme of the Protestant Reformation breaks with a continuity that unites the medieval and the modern; second, that modernity supplies the terms in which the theme of the Reformation can be expressed in an ethical form. We defer consideration of the second question to the following section of the chapter where Barth's use of the Kantian moral law is considered. This leaves us with the first of the two claims. Aside from Barth's tendencies to hypostatize the Reformation and to identify it with its most robust doctrine of grace, we can safely say that few people today would credit his attempt to treat the Protestant Reformation, or what he took to be its theme, in isolation from its historical contexts, as discontinuous with both the medieval period and modernity. Beyond this, it seems just as plausible to reverse the terms of Barth's scheme. It is easy to find continuities between his portrayal of the Reformation and modernity in his turn to the Kantian moral law—which is inescapably modern—to express the ethical relation between divine grace and human action that he thinks is the true teaching of the (allegedly non-modern) Protestant Reformation, while drawing sharp distinctions between premodern notions of the participation of human moral capacities in the good, on the one hand, and modern notions of reason and desire, on the other hand. For both of these reasons, Barth's first claim seems highly implausible. However, if we consider his contrast, described early in Chapter 1, between a theology that asserts continuity between human moral striving and the good at which it aims, however necessary grace is to the attainment of that end, and a theology that asserts that the good radically interrupts our moral striving, Barth's point may be more plausible. While the assertion of continuity may begin with the recognition of the transcendence of the good and the necessity of divine grace, in principle it has already related these

---

[8] CD IV/1, 372/411.

to human moral striving in a way that will allow for the appearance (or reappearance) of an ethic for which the good is wholly immanent and human powers are wholly sufficient. We may suspect that Barth's distinction between these theologies reads too much of the modern form of continuity into the medieval form and thereby threatens certain fundamental Christian moral convictions. But the claim that there is some continuity between these continuities and that there is an identifiable Reformation conception of grace that interrupts this continuity is not entirely implausible.

Two Alternative Narratives of Modernity

We must defer our judgment on these matters until the end of this chapter, but our ongoing consideration of them will be aided by summarizing two major alternative narratives of modern ethics which at certain points in this chapter will serve as points of comparison and contrast with Barth's narrative. One narrative focuses on the demise of the Aristotelian-Thomist tradition in modern ethics. Prior to the modern era, goes this story, there was wide agreement that the kind of being we humans are (our nature) determines the ends we should pursue if we are to live praiseworthy and fulfilling lives. Knowing these ends makes it possible for us to distinguish between what we in fact simply happen to desire and what we would desire if we were adequately informed about the kind of being we are and properly trained, and thus to have a conception of *the* good of human life. Knowledge of the ends that are in accordance with our nature is in principle attainable by reason, though Christian thinkers emphasize that in practice this knowledge must be supplemented by the revealed law of scripture, just as the orientation of our desires to their proper ends requires the assistance of divine grace. However, the story continues, the belief that the moral life consists in the pursuit of certain ends set by human nature was discredited in the wake of numerous developments in the early modern era, including the decline of Aristotelian philosophy, which had provided the metaphysical scheme of nature, end, and desire on which this moral vision rested. The end of the dominance of Aristotelianism was nowhere more clearly registered than in Hume's moral philosophy, with its assertion of the contingency of desire and its instrumental conception of reason. When an effective challenge to Hume was issued, it came not from a retrieval of Aristotle but from Kant, for whom moral reason takes the form of universal and necessary laws and human dignity is found in the capacity of human beings to be motivated by the moral law as such, apart from their inclinations. The stage was then set for Hegel to argue that Kantian morality is merely an abstraction until it identifies itself with the ethical substance of a historical social and political order. From the perspective of Aristotelian-Thomist moral theology, what is missing in both of these alternatives is the rich conception of human nature which in the Thomist tradition grounds ethics in the goodness of God's creation.

This first narrative is complemented by another, which focuses on the demise of a Platonist-Augustinian vision. In this vision there is a rational order to the universe which human beings are, in principle, capable of grasping by reason. In their rational capacity, human beings resemble the divine Logos, who created the universe and who is reflected in its rational order. In the Christian version, the Logos is most fully manifested in Christ, in whom rational order is ultimately revealed as love. This vision, as the story has it, was lost in the modern era. In place of the perception of rational order, the Enlightenment reduced the role of reason to its empirical and technical employment in a fundamentally irrational universe. Especially in its technical form, rationality is merely the expression of human capability, so that a perverse resemblance to God in the form of power over external reality stands in place of the proper resemblance to God in the ability to perceive rational order. To the extent that reason is reduced to these empirical and technical uses, the implications for morality are disturbing. Moral values are relegated to the subjective realm, leaving the calculation of the consequences of acts as the sole task of reason in the moral realm, while the possibilities of rational control of external reality underwrite an ideology of progress. Individual liberty, consequentialist moral reasoning, and the idea of progress thus come together in an unstable union that leaves the fundamental modern commitment to human rights constantly vulnerable to utilitarian calculations and utopian schemes.

Many partisans of these two narratives are careful not to dismiss modern ethics altogether, but they are nevertheless convinced that Christian moral theology must recover aspects of premodern ethics that are excluded by certain dominant features of modern ethics if it is to be faithful to its task. From their perspective, Barth's claim of continuity between premodern and modern treats too many of these aspects as anticipations of modern self-assertion and thereby distorts them along with moral theology as a whole. We will return to these points, but to understand them adequately it is first necessary to examine Barth's interpretation of modernity itself.

2. BARTH'S CRITIQUE AND APPROPRIATION OF MODERNITY

In Chapter 1 we referred to the 1932–3 lectures in which Barth set out his interpretation of eighteenth-century theology and culture. In these lectures Barth describes modern humanity in Promethean terms, as characterized by the discovery and assertion of autonomous power and ability. Along these lines, modern ethics as Barth describes it reflects the desire of human beings to be self-justifying, free of any externally imposed limit, and capable of knowing and realizing the good by human capacities alone: the ethics of bourgeois humanism.

This Promethean theme is, of course, a familiar twentieth-century trope, but the specific form it takes in Barth's thought is indicated by his repeated use of three terms in his treatment of eighteenth-century humanity, namely, the external (*Außen*), the other (*Gegenüber*), and the limit (*Grenze*). Modernity means, first, the self-assertion of the human subject against all that is external, all that stands over against humanity, and its subjection to human authority and power. 'For at the very heart [of this age] was precisely the idea of man grasping everything external and subjugating it to himself.'[9] Autonomous, this subject also lacks an other to whom its power and ability are accountable, by whom they may be called into question, before whom they must be justified. Eighteenth-century humanity 'is able of itself to answer every question but seems not to know of any question posed to it.'[10] The loss of a higher law or authority to which human power is accountable is the theme of Barth's analysis of eighteenth-century politics, which describes two forms of absolutism: that of the sovereign prince and that of the sovereign people.[11] Finally, with no other to confront it, human self-assertion knows no limit; there is nothing to restrain it. The subject who draws everything into itself—opening everything to its gaze, putting everything under its power—is capable of indefinite expansion, of assimilating everything to itself. In the end he or she stands alone, godlike, thrown back entirely upon himself or herself.[12]

Modernity as a Theological Problem

We may gloss all of this by saying that for Barth what is fundamental to modern humanity is its lack of an authority beyond itself (autonomy) and its assertion of itself as self-enclosed and self-sufficient (interiority). In the terms Barth favored, the paradigmatic modern human being is a solitary sovereign. His critique of modernity thus takes the familiar form of a critique of the modern subject. What makes his critique distinctive is that for him this subject exists in a theological form, so that the critique of this subject, and thus of modernity more generally, must also be theological. Barth sums up his description of the modern subject by characterizing the eighteenth century as a renewal of the Renaissance, which itself is explained by the notion of humanism, namely, the 'ideal of the autarky of reasonable man in a reasonable world against the backdrop of the existence and rule of a deity who guarantees this connection and thus also man's autarky.'[13] The modern subject desires to be like God, and in eighteenth-century thought God was understood as both the expression of this desire and its guarantor.[14] This is the significance of

---

[9] *Protestant Theology in the Nineteenth Century*, 56 f./38 (revised).
[10] Ibid. 79/59.
[11] Ibid. 41–54/24–36.
[12] Ibid. 36/19, 52/34, 113/92 f.
[13] Ibid. 76/56 (revised).
[14] We see in this pattern another instance of the twofold theme of insubordination and irreverence announced in *Romans₂*, according to which human beings first exalt themselves to God and then deny the distance between God and them, in this case by making God the guarantor of a human project.

Barth's claim, repeated several times in these lectures, that Leibniz is the most representative figure of this age.[15] Barth invites his auditors to consider the Leibnizian monad, the primordial given of all reality: Is it not an absolutely unique individual, utterly self-sufficient, not limited by anything external but only by its own being, self-transforming, and immortal—in short, like God himself? And, is not God the one who guarantees and justifies the harmony among monads, thereby guaranteeing and justifying man by allowing it to be the case that each monad is the best it can and should be? Finally, and most fundamentally for Barth, is not the existence and rule of God in this scheme established by referring to man himself, specifically, to the act in which he accepts his place in the whole and thus experiences the divinely established harmony, and is not this act of acceptance, in which human beings vouch for the existence of God, 'Stoicism as a triumph of humanism'? In this threefold pattern, in which human beings (1) assert themselves as godlike, (2) conceive of God as one who guarantees and justifies this self-assertion, then (3) vouch for the existence of this God, Barth finds the determinative convictions of eighteenth-century thought.[16]

We may question how accurate or fair this is as an account of Leibniz, but the latter's exemplary status in his account indicates Barth's rejection of the assumption that modern humanism entails a sharp break with Christianity as such. It is crucial to keep this point in mind. Modernity for Barth does not mean the death of God, the wiping away of the horizon, in Nietzsche's vivid image; in the first instance, at least, it means that God becomes the expression of a human ambition as well as its guarantor, with human beings themselves as the ground of certitude. The definitive features of modernity are expressed in a transformation of Christianity along the lines of the threefold pattern before they result in rejection of Christianity; even afterwards, when God is finally dispensed with, it is less in a dramatic gesture of rejection than in exposing God as the mere projection of these human ambitions (thereby bringing the threefold pattern to its logical conclusion). It is therefore a mistake to treat Barth's engagement with modernity as principally a polemic against secularism or atheism.[17] Rather, his concern is to

---

[15] *Protestant Theology in the Nineteenth Century*, 35/18, 37/20, 77/57, 85/65.

[16] Ibid. 78–9/58–9.

[17] From Barth's perspective, to overcome the problems posed for Christian life and thought by modernity it is not sufficient to secure a place in modern discourses for Christian speech or for the existence of God—as it would be if secularism or atheism were the fundamental problem. Graham Ward thus misunderstands Barth when he seeks to claim the latter for his own project of recovering the 'repressed other scene' of modernity, that is, all that modernity in its quest for rationality, objectivity, impartiality, etc. sought to forget or ignore. In this vein Ward credits Barth with recognizing the mysterious as a countercurrent to the demystifying secularization of the Enlightenment and for taking the side of Hamann as a voice of orthodoxy and tradition against Kant and neologism (Graham Ward, 'Barth, Modernity, and Postmodernity,' in *The Cambridge Companion to Karl Barth*, ed. John Webster (New York: Cambridge University Press, 2000), 274–95). But Barth says almost the direct opposite of what Ward attributes to him. He draws attention to the mysterious only to claim that it exhibits the very same self-assertion as does rationalism, and far from opposing Kant, Barth names the Königsberg philosopher along with Mozart as the two

show how the assimilation of Christianity to bourgeois humanism discloses some deeply rooted yet mistaken assumptions within Christian theology and ethics themselves.

From this perspective, to think of God only in terms of difference—as the absolute, the infinite, the unconditioned—is to think of God in terms of human limits, making the concept of God logically dependent on that of the human whose limits it negates and paving the way for Feuerbach's reduction of God to a product of the human imagination, a projection of the desire of modern humanity to overcome these limits in itself.[18] It is in Descartes that Barth finds the relation of this metaphysical conception of God to the modern subject, offering a paradigmatic instance in which God is invoked as the expression of the modern desire to surpass human limits. Descartes's proofs for the existence of God in the third and fifth *Meditations*, Barth argues, merely reflect the necessity under which the thinking subject attributes real existence to the content of one of her ideas. This idea is merely a product of the human mind viewing 'its own characteristics transcended in the absolute, contemplating itself in the mirror of its own possible infinitude, and yet remaining all the time within itself...' Instead of carrying out his proof in obedience to God's self-demonstration (as Barth believes Anselm did), Descartes proceeded from an idea that is fully at the disposal of the thinking subject. 'The circle of the *cogitare* is never broken through.' By thus portraying Descartes's conception of God as the projection of a possible human self-transcendence, Barth no doubt means to suggest that Descartes is vulnerable to Feuerbach's analysis. But (unlike Feuerbach) Descartes is unaware that '[b]y transcending myself, I never come upon an absolute being confronting [*gegenüber*] me and transcendent to me, but only again and again upon my own being.'[19]

How, then, do Christian theology and ethics become the vehicle of Promethean desire, and what error is involved? For Barth, the modern subject asserts itself as a solitary sovereign, as one who is 'not responsible to any other

eighteenth-century figures who recognized the limits of human self-assertion (*Protestant Theology in the Nineteenth Century*, 35 ff./18 ff., 73/53, 266–9/237–9). Ward is troubled by secularism; he therefore applauds the postmodern attention to the countercurrents of mystery and tradition. Barth was troubled by human self-assertion, that is, by the assimilation of all that is other to the self-enclosed totality of the subject. Suspecting that *both* secularism *and* its anti-rationalistic countercurrents are manifestations of the latter, he opposes them both. Less problematic is John Macken's summary and continuation of the line of inquiry opened up by Eberhard Jüngel, which sees modern atheism is central (John Macken, *The Autonomy Theme in the* Church Dogmatics: *Karl Barth and his Critics* (Cambridge: Cambridge University Press, 1990), 19–21). Macken is well aware of the nuances in Barth's thought which preclude treating the latter as a simple response to atheism.

[18] CD II/1, 292/328, 303/341; CD IV/2, 284/315 f., 343/383.

[19] See CD III/1, 358–60/409–13. Jean-Luc Marion argues that the Cartesian ego may not be as self-enclosed as Barth's interpretation supposes. See his 'The Original Otherness of the Ego: A Rereading of Descartes' *Meditatio* II,' in *The Ethical*, ed. Edith Wyschogrod and Gerald P. McKenny (New York: Blackwell, 2003), 33–53.

[*Gegenüber*], not disturbed by any address or claim [*Anderen Zuspruch und Einspruch*], subject to no disposition but his own, controlling himself, sufficient to himself, the first and the last in his [individual or collective] being for himself...'[20] In theological terms, this is the desire to be like God in the divine aseity—or rather, in what this subject misunderstands as God's aseity. Barth calls this desire into question by calling into question the conception of God it presupposes. 'The biblical witness to God sees his transcendence [*Vorzug*] of all that is distinct from himself, not only in the distinction as such,' that is, in God's freedom from being conditioned by anything other or external, 'but furthermore and supremely in the fact that without sacrificing his distinction and freedom, but in the exercise of them, he enters into and faithfully maintains communion with this reality other than himself...'[21] This conception of the divine aseity glosses Barth's concept of God as the one who loves in freedom. 'In the free decision of his love, God is God in the very fact, and in such a way, that he does stand in this relation, in a definite relationship with the other.'[22] For Barth, of course, it is in Jesus Christ that human beings are told that their desire to be like God rests on misunderstanding God as a self-enclosed totality, for it is in the incarnation that God's being-in-self is being for the other, that is, for the human being who is distinct from God.[23] On these grounds Barth can speak quite seriously of the divine grace of election in Jesus Christ as 'the humanism of God,' and of this humanism as the only proper ground of human dignity and human rights, in contrast to the modern humanism of the self-enclosed, self-sufficient, autonomous subject.[24] As always with Barth, modern humanism is by no means entirely rejected.

As is the case with theology proper, to understand God rightly means for Barth that Promethean ethics, with its perverse imitation of a falsely conceived God, will give way to a very different kind of ethics. Yet the substance of this ethics will not consist in any straightforward imitation of God as the one who loves in freedom, for it is both impossible and superfluous for human beings to be and do themselves what God is and does in being for the other. This brings us to an important point. For Barth, the problem with the modern desire to be like God

---

[20] CD IV/1, 420/466. This chapter uses the term 'autonomy' to refer to various aspects of the desire to be like God mentioned by Barth in the quoted passage—aspects which, in John Macken's terms, suggest Fichtean autonomy (the capacity of the subject to posit the moral law) more than Kantian autonomy (the capacity of the will to determine itself by the moral law rather than be determined by inclination) but (as could be said more strongly than Macken does) do not necessarily exclude the latter.

[21] CD II/1, 303/340 f.

[22] CD II/2, 6/4.

[23] CD IV/1, 422/468 f.

[24] The term appears in a lecture delivered at an international conference on humanism held in Geneva in 1949 and is reaffirmed in retrospective summary of the proceedings of the conference. See Barth, 'The Christian Proclamation Here and Now,' and idem, 'Humanism,' both in *God Here and Now*, trans. Paul M. van Buren (New York: Harper and Row, 1964), 3–5, 102.

is not simply that it involves a misunderstanding of God, as if it were necessary only to be right about the character of the God who one is determined to be. He also opposes this desire because it involves the refusal to be human, to recognize that one is not God: specifically, the refusal to be one whom God has chosen to be his covenant partner in Jesus Christ. Ethics as human attestation and imitation of God's freedom and love will accordingly take a distinctively human form, one in which human beings will occupy the position of addressees confronted by the command of God in and as Jesus Christ rather than asserting themselves as lawgivers, with all the catastrophic effects the latter has had in twentieth-century politics (in its totalitarian forms, especially, but also in the individualistic autonomy that is prevalent in modern democratic capitalist societies), and in which human action will *correspond* to God's action rather than attempting to *reenact* it, confirming and attesting God's work rather than attempting to continue and complete it.

We will return to this point in Chapter 5. Here we simply emphasize that it is along these lines that Barth distinguishes his moral theology from the Promethean expression of modern ethics. Barth's description of ethics as the doctrine of the command of God and his conviction that God is the measure of the good can too easily suggest an anti-human ethic, one that reverses the modern turn to the human moral subject with a reassertion of divine sovereignty. It is more accurate to say that he seeks a genuinely human ethic, one that reverses what he sees as the modern human attempt to be like God and thus to be inhuman. And, it is in the humanity of Jesus Christ that this genuinely human ethic is found, so that Christ is both the one in whom the divine being is disclosed as being for the other, for humanity, and the one in whom human correspondence to this divine goodness is fulfilled.

Modernity and the Ambiguity of Ethics

The remarks just made hint that in opposing the Promethean ethics of bourgeois humanism, Barth will not reject modern ethics altogether by setting his moral theology against the latter and returning to some form of premodern ethics as the proper expression of Christian moral theology. As we will now see, the engagement between his moral theology and the ethics of autonomy and interiority is conducted in a distinctively modern idiom, giving us grounds for pressing our questions about whether he is implicated in modern assumptions and ideas to the detriment of his moral theology. We have seen that the key to modernity as Barth understands it is the self-assertion of the solitary sovereign subject against what limits it from outside or confronts it as other. It follows that what is above all at stake for him in ethical discourse is whether the ethical as such consists in the confrontation with a genuine other or takes the form of the self-positing of the free and responsible moral subject. With this concern foremost in his mind, he consistently telescopes the history of modern moral philosophy into the passage from Kant to Fichte and its aftermath.[25]

From early on, Barth credited Kant with presenting the relation to the moral law as a confrontation with an other.[26] Not surprisingly, though, he eventually came to question whether this confrontation is 'so unequivocally attained' in Kantian ethics, for it is unequivocally clear and secure only when its Christological foundations are recognized (a controversial claim which we will consider below).[27] Nevertheless, for Barth the moral law that in Kant confronts me, however tenuously, as a genuine other becomes for Fichte that in which and by which I posit myself; here the moral law reflects the assertion of the subject in its power to posit itself rather than that to which the subject as such is accountable. Fichte's moral thought thus becomes for Barth the paradigmatic ethical expression of the rational autarky he ascribes to modernity more generally. Fichte, says Barth, was determined to view humanity 'as a being which is not confronted by any outward reality [*Außen*] which might call it into question, from which it must receive instruction, by which man is controlled, and at the disposal of which it must place itself.' Thus lacking a limit (*Grenze*) or an other (*Gegenüber*), the Fichtean subject 'is capable of indefinite expansion' which, in the only text of Fichte's that Barth treats in detail (*The Vocation of Man*), takes the form of an identity of the subject with the whole, first in an all-embracing causal determinacy, then (after positing itself as free) in an all-embracing indeterminacy. In short, the Fichtean subject is a self-sufficient and self-enclosed totality, exhibiting in a paradigmatic form the characteristics of modernity Barth identifies in his 1932–3 lectures. Ostensible instances of genuine otherness in Fichte's text—the 'midnight spirit' who addresses the self in its doubt about its reality as a free subject and the eternal One whom Fichte addresses as Thou—turn out to be only apparent. Identical in both cases with the whole, the Fichtean subject lacks all that Fichte wants to ascribe to it: a determinate nature, a ground of resolution and action, and a moral encounter with law, command, duty, and obligation. 'From the very first he has total lack of the other [*Gegenüber*] in relation to which he himself can be.'[28] It is ironic, then, that while the Fichtean subject posits itself through morality, its first victim is precisely its own moral capacity, which disappears with the loss of ethical singularity (*Besonderheit*) in the identity of

---

[25] See, for example, 'Problem der Ethik in der Gegenwart,' 111, 118; and *Ethics*, 86/142.

[26] See especially *Ethics*, 86/142: 'Where there is a real command, there is a will *distinct from our own*. Everything depends on whether the command is understood not to be in any way secretly present in us, but always to imply disruption [*Störung*] and questioning for us. . . . The step from Kant to Fichte, the true fall [*Sündenfall*] of German Idealism, is then impossible. We can only see with Kant and better than Kant that moral knowledge is unattainable without transition to worship.' Years later, Barth more or less repeats this, though without the references to Fichte and to a transition to worship in Kant (CD II/2, 651/725).

[27] *Ethics* 86/142; CD II/2, 650 f./725 f. See also 'Das Problem der Ethik in der Gegenwart,' 116–20.

[28] CD III/2, 103/121 f.

the subject with the totality (whether in the form of an all-embracing causal determinacy or in the form of the all-embracing indeterminacy of the free subject).

Devoid of anything external, any other, and any limit, in the moral subjectivity promoted by Fichte the ethical destroys itself, ending up in a disillusioned nihilism. But before it arrives there in the twentieth century, it passes through Nietzsche. In Nietzsche, Barth finds a champion of humanity without the fellow human, the subject in its 'azure isolation [*azurner Einsamkeit*],' in the words of Nietzsche's Zarathustra quoted by Barth, and in particular, the isolation of the noble, the strong, and the admirable from the weak, the suffering, and the pathetic. Nietzsche is significant for Barth because he shows how the human self-sufficiency over against God already implicit in Leibniz and carried further by Fichte is ultimately expressed in self-sufficiency over against the fellow human—the rejection of the human solidarity to which Barth was so deeply committed. Barth sees in this theme of isolation from the fellow human the culmination of the Stoic-humanist ideal of autarky he found operative in Europe since the sixteenth century and whose earlier stages he saw expressed in Leibniz and Fichte.[29] Nietzsche's rejection of solidarity with the fellow human is thus the ultimate expression of the solitary sovereignty that for Barth characterizes modernity as a whole. In Barth's view, it remains only for the twentieth century to disclose what must inevitably follow as the brash confidence of the eighteenth-century subject gives way to the disillusionment and nihilism of the twentieth-century subject, whose paradigmatic act is suicide—manifested, as he sees it, in the increasing suicide rates of individuals, in Nazism (both in itself and in the suicides of many of its leaders), and in the collective acts of suicide known as the two world wars.[30]

Thus did it appear to Barth, writing in the 1930s and 1940s. There is much to remark on in his account. Surely, the interpretations of Fichte and Nietzsche are open to question.[31] Some will also question whether the subject who asserts itself as an autonomous, self-sufficient, self-enclosed totality is indeed the defining feature of modernity, while others who agree with Barth on this point may be unconvinced by the pessimistic denouement of his narrative of this subject. These critics may suggest that the subject who fails to ground itself and refuses a divine grounding seeks and achieves a partial stability in the recognition of

---

[29] CD III/2, 233 f./279 f., 236/281 f., 239/285.

[30] CD III/4, 406 f./462–4, 452/517. The isolation or solitude (*Einsamkeit*) of the Promethean subject recalls Barth's remarks on Zarathustra's 'azure isolation.' The combination of solitude and sovereignty becomes dangerous, Barth believes, when disillusionment makes its inevitable appearance, as it does, he thinks, in the twentieth century.

[31] With respect to Fichte, Barth would have to show how the otherness of the summons (*Aufforderung*) to free action, prominent in texts of the middle years of Fichte's Jena period, is also merely apparent. Finally, with respect to Nietzsche, Zarathustra's own practice of pedagogy forms a kind of relation to the other that is neither 'azure isolation' nor Christian communion with the weak and suffering.

others, as Hegel held. Or they may suggest that we have by now passed beyond this entire problematic, pointing out that if self-assertion is still a defining feature of our own era, more than half a century removed from Barth's analysis, it seems to take a form that is neither heroic nor disillusioned but merely banal, capable of neither audacity nor despair but only of a kind of insouciance that signifies that the act of assertion itself is no longer necessary. From Barth's perspective such a stage might count as genuinely postmodern; it would mark the point at which 'God' no longer signifies or grounds a human ambition—the point at which Feuerbach's gesture ceases either to offend or to inspire. From our perspective, however, what is notable about this narrative of the modern moral subject is not its trajectory from self-assertion to nihilism, which is, after all, a familiar story, but that Barth's correction does not proceed by restoring one or more of the classical approaches discredited by modern ethics but rather by securing a Christologically corrected Kantian form of morality against what he saw as its Fichtean corruption. This indicates that for him, the crisis of nihilism does not originate in a divide between premodern and modern ethics, as it does in so much contemporary writing, including the Aristotelian-Thomist and Platonist-Augustinian narratives summarized above, but becomes evident in a divide within modern ethics itself, to which both Kant and Fichte quite clearly belong, exposing a primordial fault line which runs through every era but which modernity makes especially visible.

In the first place, then, Barth's fundamental contrast between a subject that asserts itself as lawgiver and a subject constituted as the addressee of law is situated entirely within a modern context, where the problem of ethics is represented in an entirely modern way. Likewise, the contrast between, on the one hand, the moral ought which comes to me from outside, and which alone binds me categorically, that is, apart from my desires or inclinations, and, on the other hand, objects of desire which, as 'what is pleasing and useful and valuable' or even what we think of as 'true and good and beautiful,' bind me only to the extent that I apprehend them as such—this contrast also belongs entirely to modern ethics. That ethical claims are binding only in the form of an ought that is unconditioned by any desire and that the claims made on us by objects of desire are ultimately subjective (because they depend on person-relative apprehensions of them as desirable) are notions that find canonical expression in Kant, who for Barth 'has expressed the essential concern of Christian ethics' in the idea of obligation as that which comes to me from outside myself, as the command of another than myself. Although it involves an overly simple reading of Kant,[32] this point is enough to show that Barth's rejection of Promethean ethics is hardly a rejection of modern ethics as such. To the extent that modern ethics is

---

[32] CD II/2, 649–51/722–6. Of course, for Kant the moral law is within me just as surely as the starry heavens are above me. Barth exaggerates the alterity in Kant, for whom the moral law is a fact of reason and thus does not confront me from outside myself in the way that it does for, say, Levinas.

characterized by an assertion of the priority of the right over the good, Barth's moral theology seems to be an exemplary form of modern ethics. Instead of appealing to a premodern approach to ethics to correct a modern error leading to nihilism, Barth finds the ethical properly (if insecurely) expressed in terms of modern ethics and seeks to reverse the move that led from this proper expression to its nihilistic distortion.

Yet, in the second place, Barth's position is more complex. It is not Kantian alterity as such that he commends. We recall his point that apart from Christological grounds the Kantian ethic, as he understands it, was powerless to prevent the move to Fichte, the first step towards nihilism. More to the point, the contrast that for Barth defines modern ethics, namely, whether the moral law is in us as the expression of a Promethean assertion of ourselves as lawgivers, or whether it addresses us from outside ourselves, as the command of another, is not significant in itself, on its own terms, but only insofar as it makes possible the articulation of the central theme of moral theology. For Barth, what obligates us from outside ourselves is not, as with Kant, the moral law as such, but rather that 'Jesus Christ has died and risen again for us,' making us debtors (*schuldig*) to God. And this means that while the force of obligation confronts the entirety of what is conditioned by our desires and conceptions of what is good, 'it also includes our salvation, namely, what God ascribes to us as desirable and pleasant and true and good and beautiful.' If the concept of obligation means 'not that I demand something of myself [as a good that is conditioned by my desire or perception] but that with all that I can demand of myself, I am myself demanded,' then the fact that the other who obligates me is Christ means that 'everything . . . that we may demand of ourselves [as a good conditioned by us] comes into its own [*zu seinem Recht kommt*] by the fact that it is we ourselves who are demanded.'[33] In other words, the right does not exclude or even precede the good; rather, the right is the proper expression of how the good relates to us.[34]

In short, ethics takes the form of the imperative, the command of the other, yet the other who commands me is Jesus Christ, in whom I find my true humanity and therefore my genuine good—this is part of what it means for 'gospel' to take the form of 'law.' The alterity of the command marks the sense in which my very creatureliness, which, as we will see, is ontologically constituted in

---

However, Kant cannot describe the moral law without representing it as imposing itself on me, considered as a concrete, choosing subject (*Willkür*), as an incentive—to say nothing of its relation to me as an empirical subject of desire or inclination. For Kant also, conscience is properly represented as the verdict of an ideal judge who is another person than myself, even though the subjective necessity of this representation supplies no ground for its objective reality.

[33] CD II/2, 651–3/726–7.

[34] Here as elsewhere, Barth does not diminish the theological and ethical significance of the natural, social, and temporal features of human life. Always for Barth, these features must be interpreted as concrete expressions of our being in Christ, which is the hermeneutical key, rather than vice versa, namely, as capable of disclosing a clear though provisional meaning prior to or apart from our being in Christ.

relation to the humanity of Christ, requires that my true being, which I have or am only in relation to Christ, address me as the command of another, namely Christ. At the same time, because Christ addresses me as the one in whom I have my true being, what confronts me in the form of the imperative is not alien but that which I most truly am. Barth describes the ethical in Kantian terms not because he is committed to the modern concept of morality as such but because this concept expresses the alterity and the categorical nature of the command of God. That his understanding of the command of God is the condition of his use of the modern concept of morality, and not vice versa, is clear from the qualifications he places on his endorsement of this concept in both of its principal features. With respect to alterity he argues that the force of obligation is maintained in its rigor only when 'we see our duty as the content of a decision which confronts our own will—even when it is supremely free in form—in its stark and unlimited sovereignty,' that is, when we see our duty in Christological terms, as the decision of God's gracious election that confronts us as the demand for our conformity to it—a condition, Barth points out, that is obviously lacking in the Kantian tradition.[35] With respect to the categorical nature of morality, Barth, as we have seen, argues that what binds us categorically is not the moral law itself, as an abstract imperative, but Christ, in whom and with whom we have our genuine good. Barth appropriates the concept of morality only because it expresses in a formal way (as command) the divine grace that claims human beings from outside as it elects, justifies, and sanctifies them in Christ, in whom the goodness hidden in the ambiguous character of their actual obedience is visible.

To recapitulate: On the one hand, modern ethics in its Fichtean and Nietzschean forms is the expression of Promethean self-assertion, which culminates in nihilism. On the other hand, in its Kantian form modern ethics also articulates the alterity and the categorical nature of the moral law which enable moral theology to articulate, in formal terms, the manner in which God's grace, taking the form of law, claims human beings. Just as modern ethics brings human self-assertion to full visibility, so it supplies the terms in which the proper relationship between grace and ethics can be clearly expressed. Barth is not committed to modern ethics on the latter's own grounds, but in the divide between Kant and Fichte, modern ethics does provide him with an idiom ideally suited to express, in formal ethical terms, the fundamental divide between the law as the summons of God's grace to us and the law as the expression of the assumption that it is up to us to establish our worth through our moral capabilities and efforts.

---

[35] CD II/2, 651/725 (revised).

Conclusion

Behind Barth's Kant–Fichte axis lies the question whether the moral law meets us from outside ourselves, as the law of an other, or whether it reflects the autonomy and interiority of the sovereign, self-enclosed, self-sufficient, self-legislating subject. What is at stake for Barth in this question is whether ethics expresses the form in which divine grace claims human beings or the determination of human beings to be in and for themselves. And, the transition from Kant to Fichte indicates the vulnerability of every ethic that seeks to maintain the authority and alterity of the law in the face of the autonomy and interiority of the modern subject. Only on Christological grounds, Barth insists, can the Kantian moral law be maintained against the pull of the Fichtean subject and the transition from the former to the latter and all its implications be avoided. We will see that what Barth says about Kant and Fichte and the transition from the one to the other he also says about the Protestant Reformers (Luther and Calvin) and their successors. For now, we simply note that to the extent that Barth's narrative is controlled by the Kant–Fichte problematic, it remains within the horizon of modern ethics, and this raises the question of whether he excludes something which is essential to Christian moral theology but which cannot be expressed in a modern idiom. Critics will complain that his dichotomy between Kantian alterity and Fichtean self-assertion is drawn too sharply, that it represents an instance of modern violence against the Aristotelian-Thomist conviction that the gap between human self-fulfillment and an objective good is mediated by the proper ordering of desire with the assistance of divine grace, and that moral theology therefore has no need of a categorical ought. As we have seen, Barth's response would be that modern humanism only makes explicit an implicit self-assertion that has always been operative to a greater or lesser extent, in direct proportion to the strength of the assumption that the good is found along the line of human moral endeavor. Modern self-assertion makes explicit and programmatic something that at worst was already implicit in premodern moral theology and at best was not decisively excluded by the latter, just as the modern ought enables us to make explicit the relation to the good that was, at best, inadequately articulated in premodern moral theology. The crisis of moral theology in the modern era becomes visible not on a line that separates the modern from the premodern but within modernity itself, on the line which separates Kant from Fichte and exposes a primordial fault line that runs through every era. But can Barth do justice to Christian moral theology from this perspective? This remains to be seen.

3. AUTONOMY AND INTERIORITY

We have referred several times to autonomy and interiority as specifically moral expressions of human self-assertion. Kant, of course, distinguishes autonomy as the capacity of the will to determine itself by the moral law from heteronomy, which involves determination by the inclinations. Here we follow John Macken, who distinguishes this Kantian concept of autonomy from Fichtean autonomy as absolute self-determination in which the subject posits the moral law and has mastery over it, and who argues that Barth's target is the latter, not the former.[36] In what follows we will understand autonomy in this Fichtean sense. By interiority we refer to the treatment of reason and conscience as sources of a moral law given in the self-reflection of the subject in contrast to reason and conscience as capacities to grasp a moral law that is above or outside the subject. Barth's 1932–3 lectures make much of the notion that modern ethics and politics are founded on a moral law that is no longer above human beings but is within them (interiority), and, moreover, is their own law (autonomy); in other words, a law that human beings give themselves, and not the law of another as the lawgiver and judge to whom they are accountable. Here, of course, Barth endorses a familiar story about modern ethics as a turn to the subject and a flight from authority, but we may legitimately ask why these two features figure so prominently in his account.[37] The answer to this question takes us to the fundamentally theocentric character of the moral theology that is entailed by the covenant of grace:

Encountering man in his free love, God becomes the companion of man. . . . But in virtue of his absolute ascendancy, in virtue of the fact that in this relationship he must have both the first and the last word concerning his partner, he is of necessity the judge. . . . God is for his covenant partner both the one by whom he will be judged and also the one according to whom he must judge himself. God is for him the criterion, the standard, the question of the good or the evil, the rightness or the wrongness, of his being and activity.[38]

God is both the judge of human beings and the standard or norm of judgment itself. We will soon see that Barth gives these points their most radical formulation: God alone has the capacity and the authority to know and judge good and evil, and the norm or standard itself is not something within us—reason or

---

[36] See Macken, *The Autonomy Theme in the* Church Dogmatics, 10 f., 13 f. As Macken observes, Barth uses several terms to denote the latter form of autonomy, including 'autarchy' (his preferred term) and 'sovereignty.'

[37] Nearly all of John Webster's work on Barth's ethics shows how Barth carries out a sustained attack on interiority and autonomy as the constitutive features of the human moral subject. See especially Webster, *Barth's Ethics of Reconciliation*; and idem, *Barth's Moral Theology.*

[38] CD II/2, 11 f./10 f.

conscience, for example—but is God. In both respects this radical theocentrism takes a Christocentric form.

These theocentric claims do not, as we will see, entail that human beings stand under the alien law of a heteronomous God. On the contrary, they indicate the conditions under which human beings become who they genuinely are by God's gracious election actualized in the divine work of creation and reconciliation. However, because electing grace itself addresses us as fulfilled in and by Jesus Christ, the command of God in which it is expressed addresses us as the law of another and confronts us from outside, so that autonomy and interiority, with which this command is obviously in conflict, are Barth's principal targets.

Divine Authority and Human Autonomy

The Promethean theme in Barth's treatment of modern ethics—the self-assertion of humanity as its own lawgiver and judge—brings us to one of the most controversial aspects of his moral theology, namely, the portrayal of ethics as the human usurpation of a divine office or prerogative. This Promethean theme resounds in Barth's notorious claim that the conception of ethics as the human effort to know what the good is and how to attain it 'coincides exactly with the conception of sin' and in his provocative assertion that '[w]hat the serpent has in mind [in Genesis 3: 5, where he assures Eve that she and Adam "will be like God, knowing good and evil"] is the establishment of ethics.'[39] Such remarks are likely to exasperate casual readers while prompting seasoned readers to dismiss them as hyperbole or to run off in search of the qualifications and dialectical counter-assertions that can always be found in Barth's work to offset remarks like these. However, the Eden narrative, with its prohibition against eating the fruit of the tree of knowledge of good and evil and the subsequent transgression of that prohibition, is hardly incidental to Barth's moral theology. His assertion that Genesis 2: 16–17, where the prohibition is laid down, 'exhausts and encompasses the whole of ethics' is not made in jest.[40] The issue for us is not how seriously to take this Promethean theme and its derivation from the Genesis narrative but rather how to understand it.

The Promethean theme might at first suggest that at the heart of ethics lies a primordial conflict between divine authority and human autonomy, a zero-sum game in which we are forced to choose between servile submission to an alien demand (heteronomy) and godless self-assertion (autonomy). On this interpretation, Barth's moral theology will have exposed the self-assertion expressed in the human usurpation of the roles of lawgiver and judge which properly belong to God while reasserting God's proper title to an office that God will not be

---

[39] CD II/2, 518/574; CD IV/1, 448/497.
[40] CD II/2, 673/751 (revised).

denied. He will thus have effected a simple reversal of modern ethics, countering a brash and irreverent human assertion of moral autonomy with a solemn declaration of divine sovereignty. It would be difficult not to view such a move as a dubious and somewhat clumsy anti-modern gesture. We will now see, however, that it is precisely Barth's point to reject the terms by which this stark choice is imposed, and thus to reject every form of ethics that pits divine sovereignty and human autonomy against one another in this way.[41]

Barth's extended interpretation of the Eden narrative aims to show how humanity can genuinely participate in the order God created to carry out the purpose of divine election without this participation implying an identity or equality with God as knower and judge of good and evil, on the grounds of which humanity would have the capacity and the right to legislate and judge for itself. To phrase the issue in this way is to claim that Barth aims to retain a traditional Christian understanding of the participation of human beings in a created moral order while foreclosing the possibility of enlisting this participation to serve a modern interest in establishing human beings as lawgivers and judges on equal footing with God. Whether he succeeds remains to be seen. But we will understand Barth's interpretation of the Eden narrative rightly only if we recognize his determination to rule out two erroneous assumptions: first, that human beings in principle possess the same knowledge and authority with respect to the created order as God does, and second, that human beings are merely passive recipients of divine commands. The prohibition, of course, establishes a fundamental distinction between creator and creature.

> To know [*wissen*] good and evil, to be able to distinguish and therefore judge between what ought to be and ought not to be, between Yes and No, between salvation and perdition, between life and death, is to be like God, to be oneself the Creator and Lord of the creature. . . . The Creator distinguishes himself from the creature by the fact that he exercises this power of distinction; whereas the creature is directed to accept and approve what God, who is able and entitled to distinguish, has done, does, and will do.[42]

It is God, and not the creature, who possesses the 'judicial wisdom,' 'judicial knowledge,' and 'judicial freedom,' as Barth variously puts it, to distinguish between good and evil as lawgiver and judge, and it is clear from the first part of the quote that what is at stake here is not simply the capacity to make moral judgments in the strict sense but to determine what the created order itself shall be, as the external ground of the covenant between God and humanity, the concrete condition in which that covenant will be carried out. Yet, as the last clause of the quote implies, there is also a human role, denoted here as the

---

[41] Webster rightly draws attention to Barth's refusal to pit autonomy and heteronomy against one another. See Webster, *Barth's Ethics of Reconciliation*, 211.
[42] CD III/1, 257 f./293.

acceptance and approval of what God has distinguished, of what God has determined the created order to be.

This human role is far from incidental. As Barth sees it, 'God does not in any sense will to exclude man even from his judicial office, but...wills quite definitely that man should participate in it and therefore in his own divine essence [*Wesen*].'[43] This is a strong claim, and it is supported by the central roles played in Barth's interpretation of the Eden narrative by a distinction between two kinds of knowledge of good and evil and two kinds of freedom. Barth consistently uses the term *wissen* and its cognates to refer to the knowledge of good and evil God exercises as creator when, in the divine wisdom, God chooses and rejects, that is, determines what to will and not will, what to do and not do—in sum, what the created moral order shall be. In this strict sense, which is proper to the creator, God alone has knowledge of good and evil. But there is also genuine human knowledge of good and evil; to know the good or the command in this sense is to acknowledge or recognize (*erkennen, anerkennen,* and their cognates) it or to be acquainted (*kennen* and its cognates) with the distinction between good and evil made by God. Hence the chief function of the prohibition is to summon human beings to a life of knowledge (*Erkenntnis*) and praise (*Lobpreis*) of God as the one who has distinguished between good and evil.[44] With this summons to confirm what God has done in the divine wisdom and goodness, we arrive at the very structure of the ethics of the command of God.

The distinction between these two epistemological relations to good and evil correlates with a related distinction between two modes of freedom, which also indicate the structure of the command of God as a summons to human beings to confirm what God is and does for them. It is God, Barth says, who makes the choice (*Wahl*) between good and evil, exercising the judicial wisdom and freedom to determine what constitutes right and wrong, salvation and perdition, life and death. The freedom ascribed to humanity by the Genesis prohibition is not the neutral freedom of choice between obedience and disobedience, the freedom of 'Hercules at the crossroads,' in which the prohibition meets human beings as a test or trial of their obedience. It is rather the freedom given to them to confirm God's choice in an obedient decision (*Entscheidung*).[45] Barth's point is that the human freedom that corresponds to God's freedom is not a creaturely imitation of the latter, in which the human choice of obedience or disobedience is a pale reflection of the divine choice between good and evil, making humanity a sort of lesser god. Rather, human freedom is the free confirmation of God's choice. It is in this sense that, for Barth, the prohibition itself establishes human freedom. 'By reason of this address and summons, and the responsibility thus

[43] CD III/1, 266/303.
[44] CD III/1, 260/296.
[45] CD III/1, 263–5/299–302.

ascribed to him, man becomes and is free; free for what is expected and required of him; free to confirm, not himself, but God's decision accomplished in and with his creation.'[46] Moreover, with this correspondence between divine choice and human decision, freedom stands as 'the true *tertium comparationis*, and therefore the sign of the fellowship already established between God and man at his creation.' Thus, while God is distinguished from human beings by the capacity and right to distinguish good and evil, God does not exercise this capacity and right apart from human beings but in covenant partnership with them. 'It is not without man but with him—and with him in his own decision and act—that God is wise and righteous, the sovereign judge who judges rightly.'[47]

In none of his discussions of and allusions to the Eden narrative does Barth indicate that his target is modern ethics. Nevertheless, it is difficult not to read a critique of modernity into his rejection of a human subject who claims to possess moral knowledge in the same sense as God possesses it and into his denial that freedom is fundamentally a neutral capacity to choose. Against these characteristic modern tenets, Barth's description of a form of participation in a good that exceeds human beings to some extent recalls premodern conceptions of rationality and freedom. Yet, Barth's account differs from these premodern conceptions in two respects. First, he does not distinguish between the wisdom or knowledge God exercises in establishing the created order and the wisdom or knowledge involved in making particular judgments about what that order requires. For Barth, God determines both what that order is and what it requires in concrete situations, and he deliberately blurs the distinction between the two. The result, secondly, is that the notions of moral knowledge and freedom worked out in Barth's interpretation of the Eden narrative do not follow from Augustinian or Thomist premises which hold that human reason participates genuinely though imperfectly in a divine rational order. They follow from premises which characterize human beings as addressees of God's command. Human knowledge of good and evil is recognition or acknowledgment of a command addressed by God, and human freedom is confirmation of the divine judgment regarding good and evil expressed in this command. We will have to wait until Chapter 6 to see exactly what, in this scheme, human moral knowledge consists in and how it relates to God's command. It is important to note here, however, that Barth does not avail himself of the traditional notion of human reason as participation in something which transcends it in order to counter the modern notion of the identity or equality (at least in principle) of human and divine reason, but instead turns to the notion of a command that in some way confers divine moral knowledge and freedom on its human addressee. Do these moves imply that Barth thinks that the Augustinian and Thomist positions already anticipate the

---

[46] CD III/1, 265/302.
[47] CD III/1, 266/303.

modern, Promethean identity or equality of divine and human moral reason, holding that human participation by reason in a rational moral order that exceeds human reason but is accessible to it is finally indistinguishable from the modern position? If so, does this entail that every moral theology that assigns a similar role to reason is complicit in modern self-assertion? Also, while Barth intends to overcome the opposition of autonomy and heteronomy with his notion of human participation in the divine knowledge of good and evil, does his portrayal of the moral subject as addressee of a command end up reinstituting heteronomy? And isn't this portrayal of the moral subject a thoroughly modern one?

We will return to these questions. At this point, there is another dimension of Barth's interpretation of the Eden narrative to consider. For we live in the aftermath of the violation of the prohibition and must therefore ask what it can still mean for postlapsarian humanity. Barth is convinced that the Genesis narrative and the rest of scripture agree that postlapsarian human beings must now live in their possession of the knowledge of good and evil. Human beings now know good and evil in some likeness to God's knowledge. Barth readily acknowledges that natural perceptions of good and evil embodied in moral and legal codes attain some approximation of genuine moral knowledge—a point which must be stressed against those who think he is committed to denying that we possess any intimation or approximation of moral knowledge whatsoever apart from the event of revelation. Barth's position is more subtle, and it will once again appear to involve implicit criticisms of modern ethical autonomy. The prohibition, he points out, is issued with a threat connected with its violation: 'You will surely die.' What is the meaning of this threat and how is it fulfilled in the violation? Barth insists that the knowledge of good and evil can be rightly exercised only by God. 'It is impossible for any other being to occupy the position of God. In that position it can only perish [*vergehen*].'[48] As the term *vergehen* suggests, transgression and death are inseparable here. Transgression is death because the violation of the prohibition means the destruction of the one who now possesses knowledge of good and evil but can possess it only in a deficient sense, as human beings are simply incapable of assuming God's office.

This is so, in the first place, with regard to the moral subject. Knowing good and evil, the human being 'will now have to share with God the whole responsibility of his judicial office, knowledge, and sentence,' but this exceeds human capacity; 'it is absolute in scope and difficulty.'[49] Having assumed the prerogative of distinguishing and judging good and evil, human beings are now exposed to an endless array of claims that never cease to make their demands. Barth depicts the torment of the person in this position, assaulted on all sides by demands coming from every quarter, pushed by them in different directions, forced to rule on all of them. 'His eyes are now open but only like those of a

---

[48] CD III/1, 262/298.
[49] CD III/1, 261/297.

victim of insomnia. He now has to choose and decide and judge on all sides. He has to try to hew a track for himself through the unending primeval forest of claims.' Faced with this endless array of demands, one sets up an ordered system of values, a moral code, to prioritize them, but there is no avoiding the fact that one 'will never satisfy all claims, and . . . will not really satisfy even one.'[50] This is, to be sure, a bleak portrait. In its rigorism provoking despair it recalls the classical Protestant problem of the law, echoing the early Luther in its sense of terror in the face of one's inability to obey. But there is a difference. While the object of Luther's terror was the divine judgment of a wrathful God, the terror Barth describes has no clear object except the infinite moral demand itself. It is a peculiarly modern terror: the terror felt by one who has become like God, who stands alone and sovereign, bearing an infinite responsibility. It is the terror without consolation of the autonomous moral subject.[51]

The inability of human beings to assume the divine office of judging good and evil is also evident with regard to the object of morality. Exercising this office, 'the human decision, unlike God's, will be a decision for evil, destruction, and death.'[52] Barth, writing in the aftermath of the Second World War and in the face of the Cold War, is acutely aware of the propensities to violence and destruction of other human lives and societies that lie within the presumption of nations, groups, and individual persons that the cause of morality, justice, and humanity itself is in their hands, combined with the confidence that what morality, justice, and humanity demand is transparently clear. 'As judge of good and evil, man wants to stand at God's side in defense of the cosmos great and small against the invasion of chaos and disorder and wrong,' to maintain 'the *causa Dei* and the cause of man.'[53] But this combination of responsibility and certitude can only bring about a perpetual state of conflict. 'When man thinks that his eyes are opened, and therefore that he knows what is good and evil, when man sets himself on the seat of judgment, or even imagines that he can do so, war cannot be prevented but comes irresistibly,' whether it is conducted under the

---

[50] CD II/2, 586/651.

[51] Modern moral thought arrives at this point in Levinas's notions of the insomnia involved in moral responsibility and of the moral subject as hostage to the other. Levinas frequently quotes the words of Father Zossima in Dostoevsky's *The Brothers Karamazov:* 'everyone is really responsible to all men for all men and for everything.' There is something morally profound about this insight, but in combination with the modern sense that everything is up to us, this insight contributes to modern hyper-responsibility. That in turn either generates the false paradox of infinite responsibility which Derrida exploits in the third chapter of *The Gift of Death* (to fulfill my responsibility to any other is to sacrifice every other) or drives one to self-exoneration. The second of these is what Barth apparently has in mind when, later on, he will insist that those who begin by appropriating the roles of lawgiver and judge will end by pronouncing themselves at least relatively good (CD IV/1, 388 f./429 f.). The continuity between moral insomnia and lenient self-judgment is sealed when the implication of the former is that no moral agent can possibly do justice to all moral claims, so that sin is after all inevitable.

[52] CD III/1, 261/298 (revised).

[53] CD IV/1, 450/500.

sign of the crescent, the sickle and hammer, or the holy cross; whether it is the war of blood or the cold war.[54] The greater moral danger, for Barth, lies not in the loss of moral confidence expressed in the skepticism and relativism that characterize modern life but in the moral earnestness and self-assurance that are just as characteristically modern. This, of course, is a position which has once again become plausible in our own day.[55] But while others who share this insight call for a Niebuhrian sense of irony or a Derridean recognition of aporia to reign in our moral smugness, Barth calls us to acknowledge a law that we do not give ourselves or a judgment that we do not pronounce. 'I can only live in unity with myself, and we can only live in fellowship with one another, when I and we subject ourselves to the right which does not dwell in us and is not manifested by us, but which is over me and us as the right of God above, and manifested to me and us only by God, the right of his Word and command alone, the judgment and verdict of his Holy Spirit.'[56] For Barth, the primal sin from which Christ delivers us is the usurpation of the role of judge, the presumption to sit in judgment on ourselves and others.[57] Here, this presumption of human beings to stand with God in judgment of themselves and over their fellow human beings is replaced by the solidarity of human beings under the judgment of God—a reversal which will be crucial to Barth's engagement with casuistry.

All of this can only mean that the Edenic prohibition retains its meaning and force for postlapsarian ethics. It remains the case that 'it is God who genuinely knows and disposes over good and evil, salvation and damnation, life and death,' and this is a truth which 'man, having become like God, must now experience to his distress.' If human beings are to avoid destruction from their semblance of God's knowledge, this knowledge must be asked of God and prescribed by God.[58] After Eden, legitimate ethical inquiry can only take the form of prayer, as we will see in Chapter 6. Once again, it is clear that Barth's fundamental contrast is between a Promethean presumption to stand with God or in place of God as one able and authorized to pronounce judgment regarding good and evil, on the one hand, and being positioned as the addressee of God's pronouncement who participates in God's judgment by recognizing it and confirming it in a free decision, on the other hand. And again, the latter seems to replace traditional Augustinian and Thomist notions of a genuine yet imperfect human participation by reason in a rational moral order that reflects the wisdom of its creator

---

[54] CD IV/1, 451/501.

[55] The writing of this book largely coincided with the Bush presidency, which met the murderous moral self-certainty of Islamist extremists with the assurance that the 'war on terror' embodied the cause of civilization itself and justified such moral abominations as the assertion of a right to preventive attacks, the use of torture, and the indefinite detention of prisoners without recourse to basic judicial procedures. It is not without a shudder that we read Barth's mention of the crescent and the holy cross.

[56] CD IV/1, 451/501 (revised).

[57] CD IV/1, 220/241 f.

[58] CD III/1, 287 f./328 (revised).

with a notion of the moral subject as the addressee of a command that, notwithstanding its scriptural roots, seems to be no less modern than the Promethean notion Barth seeks to overturn. There are two issues here. One issue concerns the role moral reason plays in participation in the divine knowledge and judgment of good and evil; the other concerns whether the relation of the command of God to its human addressee is heteronomous. The first issue is taken up in a separate subsection below and in more detail in Chapter 6. Here we take up the question of heteronomy. Does Barth end up contrasting Promethean ethics with a reassertion of divine sovereignty over human beings?

The foremost thing to keep in mind in this context is that for Barth the prohibition is an expression of God's grace: not merely insofar as it is meant to protect human beings from the pathologies that result from taking on responsibility that exceeds their capability but, positively and primarily, insofar as it summons human beings to participate in a properly human way, as covenant partners, in God's knowledge and judgment.[59] Above all, the presumption of human beings to know and judge good and evil involves a mistaken view of how God exercises this office; it is the serpent, Barth points out, who twists the prohibition into the directive of a god who is jealous to maintain divine prerogatives against humanity.[60] Here we recall our earlier observation that Barth wishes to avoid both the assumption that human beings in principle participate in the moral order on the same terms as God does and the assumption that the alternative is to think of human beings as mere passive recipients of divine directives. Consider in this context the following passage:

For man is not content simply to *be* the answer to [the ethical] question by the grace of God. He wants to be like God. He wants to know of himself (as God does) what is good and evil. He therefore wants to *give* this answer himself and of himself. So, then, as a result

---

[59] This sense and its implications are best understood in contrast to the interpretation of Dietrich Bonhoeffer, with which Barth was familiar but which he did not cite in this context. See Dietrich Bonhoeffer, *Creation and Fall: A Theological Exposition of Genesis 1–3* (Dietrich Bonhoeffer's Works, vol. iii), ed. Martin Rüter and Ilse Tödt, English edn. ed. John W. de Gruchy and trans. Douglas Stephen Bax (Minneapolis: Fortress Press, 1997), 85, 87, 103. Against the argument that the ability to distinguish good and evil is already presupposed at the moment when the prohibition confronts Adam, Bonhoeffer, in characteristically Lutheran fashion, distinguishes two stages. Before the fall, the prohibition is an expression of divine grace. At this stage, Adam does not know the prohibition as something that can be transgressed, i.e. as law or command; he therefore does not know good and evil. Rather, he knows the prohibition only as a word of grace in which he is told of his creaturely limits. After the fall, the situation changes radically. The prohibition now becomes law rather than grace. Adam now knows good and evil and therefore knows the prohibition as a command that can be transgressed. For Barth, by contrast, the prohibition does confront Adam prior to the fall as a command. But the command is not only, or even primarily, a law that can be transgressed. First and foremost it calls Adam to confirm God's grace by acknowledging and praising what God has graciously distinguished and judged as good and evil, that is as right and wrong, salvation and perdition, life and death. In this sense (denoted by *kennen* or *erkennen*)—and not in the sense forbidden by the prohibition (denoted by *wissen*)—Adam does know good and evil before the fall.

[60] CD III/1, 259/295; see CD IV/1, 452 f./502 f.

and in prolongation of the fall, we have 'ethics,' or, rather, the multifarious ethical systems, the attempted human answers to the ethical question. But this question can be solved only as it was originally put—by the grace of God, by the fact that this allows man actually to *be* the answer.[61]

The key lies in the contrast between *being* and *giving* the answer to the ethical question. Giving the answer is connected with usurpation; to want to give the answer is to want to be like God in the divine knowledge of good and evil, to possess this knowledge for oneself. As the oblique reference to the sin of Adam and Eve in Genesis 3: 1–6 indicates, this is for Barth the primordial sin, endlessly repeated in ethical theories, codes, and inquiries, all of which imply the assumption that human beings are competent and authorized to determine what is good and evil. But what is meant by *being* the answer? The counterpart of giving is not being but receiving, and Barth surely could have exploited this contrast if he had wished to counter human self-assertion with passive acquiescence in divine sovereignty. The answer becomes clear when we understand what it means for the grace of God to allow human beings to be the answer to the ethical question. 'For it is the electing grace of *God* which has placed man under his command from all eternity. The command of God is therefore the truth from which ... man derives, and which he will not evade. ...' It follows that 'the ethical question ... is put from all eternity as the question to which, on the basis of revelation and the work of grace, man himself will in some way be the answer.'[62] For Barth, human beings were created for the purpose of being, in their distinctively human creatureliness, the covenant partners of God, and they are constituted as such by God's grace. The command of God is the demand that human beings confirm in their existence as acting subjects what they are by grace, that is, that they *be* the answer to the ethical question.

These claims are central to the theological anthropology Barth works out in *Church Dogmatics* III/2. For Barth, human beings are not self-constituted, but are ontologically constituted by the presence of Jesus Christ among them as a human being, for in his presence among other human beings 'a decision has been made concerning the being and nature of every man' by virtue of which the latter 'is something other than he would have been if this One had not been man too.'[63] More specifically, in the presence of Jesus Christ among them human beings are confronted by the divine Other, so that 'to be human [*Menschsein*] is fundamentally and comprehensively to be with God [*mit Gott zusammen sein*].'[64] Barth expands this basic point, explaining that to be with God in the relevant sense is grounded in God's election and consists in hearing God's Word, and what God's Word says is that God is gracious to human beings. Barth continues:

---

[61] CD II/2, 517/573.
[62] CD II/2, 516/572.
[63] CD III/2, 133/159.
[64] CD III/2, 135/161 (revised).

'The Word of God is obviously not only a pronouncement but also a call, not only an indicative but as such also an imperative, because it is the Word of his grace.' It follows, then, that '[the human creature's] being takes its course as it accepts the claim of this Word.'[65] It is precisely in this sense that the command of God is the truth from which human beings derive. This in turn means that for Barth the command of God is always a demand that human beings be who they *are*, namely, God's covenant partners with the creaturely nature God chose as suitable to this status.[66] It is plain that Barth rejects a scheme that pits divine sovereignty against human self-assertion.

The same point is made more fundamentally from the perspective of Christology. In the aftermath of the violation of the prohibition given to Adam the errors involved in desiring to know and judge good and evil—the vast overestimation of the human capacity to assume this role and the mistaken ideas of God involved in the human desire to exercise it—are exposed by the incarnate Christ, who lives a human life devoid of grasping after possibilities that exceed human capacity and in whom God is revealed as one who exercises this capacity not as a prerogative to guard and defend but for the sake of the other.[67] The divine protest against human self-assertion is not a reassertion of divine sovereignty but God's self-revelation in Jesus Christ, who in his willingness to be the answer reveals the human image (*Menschenbild*) with which Adam was created to correspond but failed in his determination to be the one to give the answer:

> How could the Son, who is obedient to the Father, want to ask and decide what is good and evil? How could he regard as the good that which he himself has chosen [*erwählt*]? No, it is because he *is* chosen [*erwählt*] by the grace of God that the good is done here, because as this elected one [*Erwählte*] he is concerned only with obedience without any of his own choice [*Wählen*] between good and evil, because he does not desire to be good of himself and for himself, and therefore is subject in his conduct only to the will and command of God, who alone is good—because of all of this the good is done here; here, in Jesus Christ, the ethical question is answered.[68]

We now live under the restoration of the human image in Jesus Christ rather than in its manifestation in Adam. Ethics in the postlapsarian period continues the ethics of the Edenic prohibition, but only Christ occupies the position of Adam; other human beings do so only by virtue of the relation of their own humanity to the humanity of Christ. Postlapsarian ethics must therefore be Christological: Only by virtue of the revelation of the human image in Jesus Christ is the originary ethic of the Edenic prohibition still valid. Without this

---

[65] CD III/2, 165/197 (revised).

[66] This theme is explored more fully in Deonna Neal's dissertation in progress on Barth's ethics of creation.

[67] CD IV/1, 449–53/498–503.

[68] CD II/2, 517/573 f. (revised).

revelation, this originary ethic would be inaccessible, and the command of God would therefore signify an absence marked by the necessity for human moral inquiry to distinguish good and evil. However, Christ substitutes in this way for Adam only because in a more fundamental sense Adam already substituted for Christ. Created in the grace of election, Adam is the image of Christ, of the one who is elected from eternity. The Edenic prohibition, then, is already Christological.

In sum, Barth's portrayal of the ethical relation between God and humanity is a rejection of the binary opposition between autonomy and heteronomy, of the very terms in which God could confront the moral subject as an alien authority, which would threaten responsibility itself and would thus call for an autonomous subject. It is a repudiation of the alternatives posed by the serpent: either a jealous, sovereign deity or an autonomous humanity. Barth approaches modern humanism not by opposing it but by presenting it as a misguided and tragic effort to secure on humanity's own terms what God has already given. God deals with human beings such that 'on the basis of revelation and the work of grace' they *are* something—the answer to the ethical question—which they are convinced they must grasp by and for themselves. Far from simply a counter-assertion of divine sovereignty against modern self-assertion, Barth understands the command of God as the divine provision for human beings to participate in the distinction God has made between good and evil and thus, as the embodiment of the good in their existence in conformity to the good, to be the answer to the ethical question. The implications of this claim will have to be worked out in later chapters. It is enough at this point to note that, for Barth, what modern human beings think they must secure for themselves in their self-legislating autonomy, God has already provided. As he sees it, modern self-assertion is not only futile and self-destructive. It is also superfluous.

Divine Alterity and Human Interiority

The previous subsection concluded with the claim that we occupy the original position of Adam only in Jesus Christ, and that means only as reconciled sinners. But at this point a second feature of modern ethics distorts the claims of moral theology, namely, interiority. At issue here is not who judges good and evil but rather the standard of judgment, that by which we evaluate ourselves or are evaluated by another. For Barth, God is not only the judge but also the standard of good and evil: the criterion or norm by which something or someone is judged to be good or evil. Because this standard is not within us, it stands in sharp contrast to other standards by which we try to answer the ethical question, all of which, Barth holds, ultimately are within us. 'Man answers the question about the good with these sorts of answers when he is locked in a conversation with himself [*Selbstgespräch*].' In one way or another all of these attempts assume that the good is present to us—in reason, conscience, history, or self—as a norm or law grasped in self-reflection.[69] But for Barth, the assumption that the norm of the good is present to us in such a way that we can identify it through self-reflection is mistaken, precisely 'because Jesus Christ himself is present, living and speaking and attesting and convincing; because in this matter we need not and cannot and should not speak to ourselves. . . . We find our competence to work out the standard by which to measure ourselves denied.'[70]

The contrast is between a divine standard addressed to us in (and as) Jesus Christ and a norm derived from self-reflection. It is a contrast between alterity and interiority,[71] and it raises two questions. The first question concerns Barth's assumption that norms arrived at through reason or given in conscience are internal to the subject, derived from or constituted by self-reflection. On what grounds does he think he can assert this? This poses once again the question of the status of moral reason, and we will once again defer it to the following subsection. The second question concerns the claim that only the Christological standard genuinely or consistently confronts us from outside ourselves. Only if God is known in and through Jesus Christ will moral theology be able to resist the pull of interiority. But how can Barth hold that even those theologies that identify the standard of good and evil with God apart from Christ are ultimately susceptible to the pull of interiority? Before we take up this question we must make clear what is at stake for Barth in this matter.

For Barth, the distinction between alterity and interiority is a distinction between a norm or standard of good and evil grounded in the knowledge of God and a norm or standard of good and evil grounded in self-knowledge. Here he follows Calvin, who in the opening pages of the *Institutes* contrasted the verdict human beings pass on themselves from a purely creaturely standard to the verdict they must accept when measured against the divine perfection.[72] At stake for Calvin in this contrast was the leniency or stringency of our evaluations of ourselves, and the contrast itself was between the relative degrees of goodness and perfection found on an earthly scale and the absolute goodness and perfection of God, which exposes the shortfalls of all human goodness and perfection.

---

[69] Barth, 'Christian Ethics,' in *God Here and Now*, trans. van Buren, 86 f. (translation of Karl Barth, 'Christliche Ethik,' in *Zwei Vorträge*, Theologische Existenz heute NS 3 (Munich: Chr. Kaiser Verlag, 1946)).

[70] CD IV/1, 389 f./431.

[71] The usual contrasts are between alterity and sameness and between interiority and exteriority. This is appropriate since alterity is compatible with a certain kind of interiority and exteriority may be compatible with sameness. In Kant's ethics, for example, the moral law is ultimately within (interiority) even as it confronts me as an other (alterity) while the one who engages in devotional practices with the intention of placating God imagines God as a being outside herself (exteriority) even as she seeks to bring God within her influence (sameness). In Barth's case, however, it is a matter of a contrast between a standard that addresses me as the command of another I (alterity) and a norm that, in principle at least, I can formulate in self-reflection, without having to hear it from another (interiority).

[72] CD IV/1, 366 f./405.

For Barth, however, the matter is more complex. The contrast is not simply between two standards, one divine and one human, but also between two ways in which the evaluator is related to these standards. It is a contrast between a divine norm or standard that addresses us from outside us and a human norm or standard that is grasped through self-reflection. The problem, he argues, is that norms grasped through self-reflection disclose not our sinfulness but only the problematic character of finite human existence: the tensions, imperfections, and limitations inherent in created human nature:

Anything that he accepts in this matter which is not from God but from communing with himself and his fellows, from his own understanding and consciousness of himself, may well be the inner tension between a relative Yes and a relative No, between becoming and perishing, between strength and weakness, between the great and the small, between achievement and will: the dialectic in which human existence has a part in the antithesis or dualism of light and darkness which runs through the whole of creation.

This dialectic, Barth continues, is not sin as such; it belongs to human nature as created by God. Even if by this self-knowledge one should arrive at an awareness of one's own role in generating this dialectic, this would still not be a knowledge of sin but only of one's imperfection—of the limitation of human existence and not of its evil and guilt, and therefore not of its need for atonement by Christ's death on the cross.[73] Evil here is not radical. This brings us to a further problem. In such a norm, human beings encounter only themselves; the problematic character of human existence, therefore, is something they are capable of grasping and addressing through an ethic that remains within the horizon of natural knowledge and capacities and in which, therefore, human beings require no higher power and answer to no higher court. Here ethics is entirely an enterprise of the self-enclosed subject, and sin and reconciliation fall entirely within the economy of this subject.

By contrast, in Jesus Christ the evaluator is confronted by the divine standard as an external standard. As we saw in Chapter 1, the command of God is divine grace itself in the form of the demand that human beings confirm it, and it is in Christ that God's grace is revealed and its human confirmation fulfilled. Thus, in contrast to an ethic for which ethical knowledge and judgment occur in the interiority of the self-enclosed subject, Barth can say that in the person of Christ we are confronted by the divine Other (*Gegenüber*) as the one who elects us in grace and fulfills our election.[74] It is precisely here that the actual situation of human beings as sinners is disclosed. Recall that for Barth '[m]an derives from

---

[73] CD IV/1, 360 f./397. In Chapter 1 we pointed out that in *Romans₂*, Barth contrasted the radical opposition to sin in the grace of God with the relative opposition of good and evil in the twilight realm of this-sided human existence. Barth never abandoned the notion that grace alone can disclose the radical evil of human existence and that natural human knowledge is capable only of grasping the ambiguity and imperfection of human existence as created good.

[74] CD III/2, 134/160, 145 f./173 f.

the grace of God.' The very being of humanity as God's covenant partner is constituted in God's grace by election and the address of God's Word. But to sin is to reject grace, so that sin is an impossible state—one that occurs, to be sure, but that always remains a surd; to be a sinner is to be in contradiction to one's being. Barth's doctrine of sin is designed to show how it is only in Christ that human sin is revealed for what it is, namely, this contradiction. According to his analysis of pride the humiliation of Christ reveals human efforts to be like God as contradictions to the God of grace whose being is being for the other. According to his analysis of sloth the exaltation of Christ reveals the refusal of human beings to live in conformity to electing grace. In both cases, Christ exposes sin as human existence in contradiction (*Widerspruch*) to the good, in contrast to the 'natural inner conflict [*natürliche innere Gegensätzlichkeit*]' between us and itself disclosed by a law or norm within us.[75] And, to the extent that one measures oneself by a normative concept that is in any way 'his own work and therefore a reflection of himself,' it is impossible for one to understand one's aberration in this, its radical character as sin. 'Even in his aberration he will then see and think always of himself together with that norm. He will always be able to order and control his encounter with it, i.e., with himself. He will interpret his transgression as an incident, a point of transition, a stage in development. But he himself will not really be affected by even the sharpest judgment which he may find in it.'[76] Such a norm cannot call one radically into question and will never confront human beings with the need for what can only be done by another, that is, by Jesus Christ.

In Barth's hands, then, Calvin's distinction between divine and human standards for measuring ourselves has become a distinction between an ethic of alterity—of confrontation by an other—and an ethic of interiority, and this turns out to be a distinction between a Christological standard of good and evil and all other standards. At stake in this distinction is whether ethics attests the Christian proclamation of sin and reconciliation or becomes a substitute for the latter. Is ethics the disclosure and the overcoming of a state of radical contradiction involving our very being? Or is ethics the expression of the tensions, imperfections, and limitations of finite human beings which play out in the conflict between human existence and a norm of reason or conscience—a conflict which occurs entirely within the economy of the self-enclosed subject with her knowledge and capacities? The crucial question is whether ethics can express the true situation of human beings as sinners or whether it conceals this situation, just as the question in relation to creation is whether ethics can express the true creaturely status of human beings or becomes a way for human beings to deny this status in their desire to be the creator. At this point, where human beings must understand themselves not only as creatures for whom the command of

---

[75] CD IV/1, 361/399.
[76] CD IV/2, 380/426.

God is the truth of their being as those elected by God in Jesus Christ from eternity and created to correspond to this election but also as sinners who have rejected election and thus violated the command, another facet of the ambiguity of ethics becomes apparent. Ethics in its proper sense can and does express the real situation of human beings as sinners, but ethics can also be a way in which human beings deny and conceal their real situation before God.

Barth's analysis, however, rests on the controversial claims noted above: that natural human capacities such as reason or conscience are forms of self-reflection that can disclose only what is in some way within us, and that only the Christological standard genuinely confronts us from outside. Once again, we defer the first of these claims to the next subsection and examine the second. Barth insists that it is only in Christ that interiority is overcome, yet he acknowledges the traditional claim that the norm by which we measure ourselves is found in some general conception of God apart from Christ, whether philosophical or scriptural in origin. In what sense is a theistic yet non-Christological norm subject to the pull of interiority? Apart from Christ, Barth insists, such a God can confront us only in the grandeur of abstract deity and therefore in the 'infinite qualitative distinction' of God and humanity. In the face of this infinite God, we are confronted with the natural imperfection of our finitude. There are three problems here. One problem is that imperfection is not sin. Another problem is that the distance between the infinite God and finite human beings calls into question the applicability of the divine standard. Why should we hold ourselves up to the perfection of such a God? For Barth, it is precisely because in Christ the divine standard is revealed and fulfilled in a human being that this standard can genuinely bind us. The final problem is that according to Barth we can arrive at knowledge of our natural imperfection through self-reflection, without any confrontation with another. We recall his point that the ascription to God of naked metaphysical concepts such as the infinite and the unconditioned may merely express our consciousness of our creaturely limits and our desire to transcend them. This God, then, may be a mere projection, an object of bad faith: 'In this God do we not have to do simply with a reflection of our own existence . . . in relation to which we have merely sublimated and dramatized and mythologized our own self-communion [*Selbstgespräch*]? Have we not merely imagined that we have heard, in relation to him, a word addressed to us from outside, from another? Have we not, in our relation to him, in fact only spoken to ourselves?'[77]

A metaphysical God whose defining properties are those of an infinite and unconditioned divine nature may well turn out to be a different God than the God revealed in Christ, but most moral theologies that ground moral norms in God apart from God's self-revelation in Christ refer not to these properties but to

[77] CD IV/1, 364 f./402 f. (revised).

God's moral character and governance of the world. Barth's criticism simply ignores this kind of conception of God. Nor does he consider the notion of a moral order that is distinct from God yet created and upheld by God. He goes on instead to consider cases in which the norm is constructed out of biblical laws and commandments treated in abstraction from what for him is the ultimate Christological reference of all scripture. Here he will argue that appeals to biblical law apart from this Christological reference, which once again points us to a standard that confronts us in its fulfillment by a human person, are ultimately unable to resist a rationalist appropriation. The argument takes the form of a historical narrative of the Reformed tradition. Barth begins by noting that Calvin's scriptural starting point enabled him to find the standard of good in Old Testament encounters of human beings with the divine holiness. But without a Christological basis and content, these radical encounters establish only a 'general antithesis' between God and humanity. In effect, these encounters give us in a vivid form what the metaphysical God gives us in a conceptual form.[78] Reformed orthodoxy found a more secure ground for ethics by treating the Bible as a compendium of revealed moral truths. But abstracted from their Christological reference, revealed truths are in principle at the disposal of the one who wishes to construct a norm out of them. Theology has, with respect to these truths of revelation, 'the same assurance and control . . . as man as a rational creature has in regard to himself, his experience, his thinking and therefore his world . . .'[79] At this point biblical revelation ceases to attest a confrontation with the divine goodness. Fully accessible to us and ready to hand for our construction of a norm, the revealed moral truths of the Bible stand in the same relation to us as do the truths of reason and conscience. It is therefore difficult to find in these truths anything other than a revealed double of moral truths already available to reason or conscience, and it comes as no surprise that by the end of the seventeenth century, Reformed orthodoxy was prepared to deny that there is any difference in content between a revealed law addressed to us by God and a natural law we find in our own hearts and even to locate the authority of the former in the latter. While Reformed orthodoxy continued to insist on the usefulness and even necessity of biblical commandments as a set of symbolic precepts to make clear the law that is in principle available in reason or

---

[78] CD IV/1, 363/401, 366 f./404 f. Earlier Barth had argued that Luther and Calvin never lost sight of the Christological basis of Christian righteousness. See CD I/2, 783/876. The present remarks occur in a treatment not of ethics per se but of the Christological basis of the human knowledge of sin. However, Barth points out that to determine what is evil (sin) presupposes a standard of good and its application (IV/1, 365/403), and in decrying what he considers to be the generally insufficient Christological orientation of Luther and Calvin he specifically mentions in tandem their doctrine of sin and the standard by which good and evil are distinguished (366/404). Indeed, Barth's entire discussion of the knowledge of sin concerns the source of the norm by which good and evil are distinguished. These are sufficient reasons for taking this discussion as a treatment of ethics.

[79] CD IV/1, 368/406.

conscience, by identifying the content and authority of biblical law with the rational moral law the shift from a biblical ethic of confrontation to a *Selbstgespräch* involving reason and conscience was complete, and from here it is only a short step to understanding the Bible, with its unavoidable orientation to the radical confrontation of God with humanity, as itself a dramatization and mythologization—a poetic exaggeration—of our relation to a law we find within ourselves, in reason and conscience.[80] The shift from alterity to interiority is thus a shift from God as the indispensable ground of morality to God as its ultimately dispensable figure.[81] In short, there will now be a discourse of evil and its overcoming which, precisely because it remains within the economy of the subject, does not require and will ultimately reject the theological vocabulary of sin and reconciliation. Moreover, an inner conflict of this kind, Barth notes, may be the occasion of remorse, regret, or a wistful irony, but not of the genuine terror (*Erschreckens*) evoked by the contradiction sin involves nor of the genuine consolation given in its overcoming.[82] The loss of this terror and consolation, which Barth lamented in the various forms of humanism proposed in the aftermath of the Second World War, renders the God of scripture and the scriptural depiction of our status questionable even as figurative representations.[83] In the end they are bound to be dismissed as misleading, indeed dangerous and even cruel exaggerations of our real situation before the good or even as threats to our moral identity or resolve.

The distinction is clear and stark: Scripture is either the site of an encounter with the standard that exists outside of us in Christ or it is reduced to a symbolic expression of a standard we find in ourselves. The point of Barth's narrative is to show how Protestant biblicism paved the way for modern rationalist ethics. How did a theology that began, with Calvin, by grounding ethics in an encounter with God as standard of the good end up treating this encounter as an excessive symbol of a rational morality? From the first, this encounter was not understood in Christological terms. Barth will therefore go back to Calvin, correcting his fatal flaw by grounding ethics in an encounter with Christ who exposes our condition as existence in contradiction to the good. He will then reverse the Kantian poetics that treats Christ as the figure of a rational morality, arguing instead that the natural inner conflict between us and the norm within us is properly treated as an analogy of the contradiction in which we stand.[84]

---

[80] CD IV/1, 368/406.

[81] CD IV/1, 373/412.

[82] CD IV/1, 361/398 f.

[83] Barth, 'Humanism,' in *God Here and Now*, 104 f. Barth's narrative could be phrased in terms of two phases in the dissolution of the Protestant moral conscience. In the first phase the terror of accusation and consolation of forgiveness are redescribed in moral terms, as with Kant. In the second phase, both the terror and the consolation are dismissed as cruel or infantile, as with Nietzsche and Freud. The terror may simply be self-hatred or fear of the father, and the consolation may be an illusion that deflects us from ethical maturity.

[84] CD IV/1, 361/398.

Once again, Barth ignores viable alternatives. There are many ways to derive moral content from scripture without either reducing the latter to a mere compendium of moral truths or making explicit references to Christology. By failing to consider these alternatives, Barth once again fails to show how all non-Christological standards entail interiority. Moreover, Barth's narrative of the shift from an ethics of confrontation with a standard outside of us to ethics as the self-reflection of a self-enclosed subject fails on its own terms, as it is not so easily identifiable with the narrative of the transition from the Reformers to the rationalists. The relevant passages in Calvin suggest that he found in the knowledge of the biblical moral law the same ethical relation to God as he found in the biblical encounters with the divine majesty.[85] If so, he already made the initial move in the process by which, according to Barth, the confrontation with God is subsumed into biblical law as a compendium of moral truths at the disposal of human knowers. Meanwhile, as we briefly considered earlier in this chapter, Barth's narrative of the fate of Protestantism, in which an ethic of confrontation made precarious by its lack of an adequate Christology gave way to a rationalistic morality, bears an unmistakable resemblance to his narrative of the fate of idealism, in which an ethic of confrontation made precarious by its lack of a Christology gave way to an ethic in which the subject posits the moral law. Remarkably, Barth finds the same relation between Kant and his successors as he found between Luther and Calvin and their successors. In both cases an ethic of confrontation rendered unstable by the lack of a Christological standard became the occasion for transformation into an ethic of interiority. Thus for Barth, the lack of a Christological standard in Kant is to blame for the fact that the latter was unable to preclude the move made by Fichte, for whom the subject posits the moral law which (as Barth sees it) is therefore unequivocally within rather than (with Kant) equivocally without, and in whom Barth therefore locates the 'fall [*Sündenfall*] of German Idealism.'[86] Barth's concern is to rescue a biblical-Reformation ethics from the rationalistic ethics into which it transformed itself. But the terms in which he carries out his rescue mission—the dichotomy between alterity and interiority and the vulnerability of the former to the pull

---

[85] While Calvin begins Book I of the *Institutes* by referring to God as the sole standard against which human beings compare themselves and refers to biblical encounters with God as instances in which human self-judgments are overwhelmed by the majesty of God, in Book II he explicitly argues that the biblical moral law (the Decalogue) is the standard with which human beings should compare themselves and that it is this standard that confronts and overwhelms human self-judgments. Moreover, in Book II the human self-knowledge that in Book I was attributed to comparison with the majesty of God is explicitly attributed to biblical law as the standard of God's righteousness. See *Calvin: Institutes of the Christian Religion*, ed. John T. McNeill, trans. Ford Lewis Battles (Philadelphia: Westminster Press, 1960), I.1.i–iii (pp. 35–9), II.7.vi (pp. 354 f.), II.8.i (p. 367).

[86] *Ethics*, 86/142.

of the latter—are the terms of the problematic that for him defines the transformation that befell the Kantian tradition.[87]

All of this suggests that while Barth's position quite clearly originates in Calvin's fundamental distinction between measuring ourselves in accordance with the knowledge of God and measuring ourselves in accordance with self-knowledge, the problematic of alterity and interiority in which he expresses this distinction derives from the Kantian tradition. It was here that he found both the notion of ethics as confrontation with the other and the instability of this notion when its Christological ground is not secured, as it also was not, he thought, during the Reformation era. What Barth saw through this Kantian lens was that the divine standard by which Calvin wanted us to measure ourselves proved incapable of resisting transformation into a figure for what is in fact within us. Having witnessed this transformation, Barth thinks, we now know that if the divine standard is to disclose the true situation of human beings in their contradiction to the good it must now be expressed in the Christological form which was always proper to it. In sum, Barth's argument for the necessity of a Christological standard for ethical alterity is inseparable from his narratives of the transitions from Reformed orthodoxy to rationalism and from Kant to Fichte. The extent to which this argument is plausible in other contexts will depend on the extent to which what has occurred in these transitions characterizes those contexts as well.

---

[87] There is another sense in which Barth's narrative unfolds in the discursive space of Kantian ethics. Morality, Kant famously argued, needs neither the idea of another being above human beings in order that they may recognize their duty nor an incentive other than that the moral law in order that they observe it (Immanuel Kant, *Kants Gesammelte Schriften*, vii: *Die Religion innerhalb der Grenzen der blossen Vernunft* (Berlin: Walter deGruyter & Co., 1969); translation 'Religion within the Boundaries of Mere Reason,' in Immanuel Kant, *Religion and Rational Theology*, trans. and ed. Allen W. Wood and George di Giovanni, The Cambridge Edition of the Works of Immanuel Kant (Cambridge: Cambridge University Press, 1996), vi. 3). Rather, religion plays a less fundamental, if still necessary role in morality. By representing duties as divine commands, morality uses both the idea of God and figurative representations of the divine to give morality influence on the will (Immanuel Kant, *Kants Gesammelte Schriften*, vii: *Der Streit der Facultäten* (Berlin: Walter deGruyter & Co., 1969); translation 'The Conflict of the Faculties,' in Kant, *Religion and Rational Theology*, trans. and ed. Wood and di Giovanni, vii. 36; *Religion*, vi. 153 f.). The idea of God involved in the representation of moral duties as divine commands is for Kant not a figurative expression but a rational moral idea. For Barth, however, such an idea can only entail the usurpation of the divine office of knowing and judging good and evil since for Kant knowledge that something is one's duty is prior to, and the condition of, knowing that it is commanded by God (*Religion*, vi. 110, 153 f.). Biblical representations of God and of God's will are for Kant not moral ideas proper but, in his terms, sensible (*sinnlichen*) representations, that is, figurative expressions, of a rational morality. But for Barth this can only mean that they are 'dramatizations and mythologizations' of something that, if not within us, at least does not unequivocally confront us from outside. Once again it seems to be through a Kantian lens that Barth views the formation of modern Protestant ethics. In his account of the latter, just as for Kant reason becomes the criterion by which we know something to be a command of God, the confrontation with the other that defines the ethical turns out really to be within us (even if in Kant's own thought an equivocal otherness remains), and biblical representations of God become figurative expressions for what occurs entirely within us.

Autonomy, Interiority, and Moral Reason

We began this section with Barth's theocentric claim that God is both the judge and the standard of judgment. We have seen that this twofold claim is Christological in both of its aspects. At several points we have raised questions about the implications of Barth's position for moral reason. Does his rejection of an equality or identity (at least in principle) of divine and human knowledge of good and evil rule out classical Augustinian and Thomist notions of human participation by finite reason in the order created and governed by divine reason, assimilating these notions to modern rationalism? Is the human participation in God's knowledge of good and evil described by Barth a rational participation, involving the exercise of human reason, or is it nonrational? Does Barth presuppose a post-Kantian notion of reason as self-reflection in contrast to the Augustinian and Thomistic view that reason participates in an objective moral order, even as it requires the supplement and correction of revealed truth? Does he then assume that any law or norm identified through reason and conscience is therefore within us or constructed by us? Barth's interpretation of the Edenic prohibition seems to imply the voluntarist view that we must choose between a purely rational and exclusively human rational moral law, on the one hand, and a nonrational divine law, on the other hand. And his narrative of post-Reformation moral theology seems to imply the German idealist view of reason as the constitution of the object through self-reflection in contrast to reflection on what exists prior to and apart from reason. Given his critiques of the autonomy expressed in the first view and the interiority expressed in the second, Barth seems to leave moral theology with no genuine place for moral reason—surely an unpalatable result.

At the same time, Barth implicitly and explicitly endorses moral reason. We will treat this topic in more detail in Chapter 6, but we may briefly state a few relevant points here. First, we have seen that human participation in the divine knowledge of good and evil is itself a form of knowledge, and insofar as Barth consistently dismisses mystical and intuitionist forms of knowledge, we may assume that the knowledge he has in mind involves some exercise of discursive reason. That this is indeed what is involved becomes clear in his description of what is entailed in hearing the command of God which, as we will see in Chapter 6, gives a prominent though not ultimately decisive role to the evaluation of reasons for and against a proposed course of action in an intersubjective context. Finally, the command of God itself is rational in form, addressing its hearer as a categorical imperative which possesses the formal property of universality even in its singularity. In all of these respects the hearing of the command of God is a rational process.

What all of this suggests is that what governs Barth's position is not a distinction between a rational and a nonrational moral theology but between two economies in which moral reason is exercised: that of the sovereign, self-enclosed subject, and that of the addressee of the command of God. In the former case, the relation of reason to the good takes the form of mastery and assimilation. Here we recall Barth's account, presented in his 1932–3 lectures, of modern humanism as the reappearance of Stoicism in the form of rational autarky and his view, presented in the same lectures and discussed in Chapter 1, that the attempted humanization of Christianity in the eighteenth century—its assimilation to human capability—was carried out by the re-description of Christianity in natural and rational terms. His criticism of rational morality is not a rejection of moral reason but of reason as a tool of self-assertion, of its role in giving the subject a sense of certitude in a moral law that is transparent to her gaze, at her disposal, under her control. This criticism clearly does not apply to the exercise of moral reason in the hearing of the command of God.

That all of this presupposes a modern context is, however, indisputable. Barth's acceptance of rationality as formal universality, his concern with reason as possession of its object, and especially his opposition between the position of the addressee and that of self-assertion seem remote from classical Augustinian and Thomist notions of moral reason as participation, with the necessary assistance of grace and revelation, in a created moral order that reflects the rationality of its creator. We can no longer defer the questions this raises: Does Barth concede too much to an entirely modern problematic, leading him to jettison a traditional Christian view of moral reason that is superior to anything that can result from accepting the modern problematic? Or does he see that by virtue of the role they assigned to moral reason the Augustinian and (especially) the Thomist position, if not actually complicit in modern rationalism, are at least unable to keep the latter at bay? Are the ethics of autonomy and interiority a radical departure from the Augustinian and Thomist visions of human participation by reason in a rational order created and governed by God? Or were the ethics of autonomy and interiority latent in and only partially suppressed by the Augustinian and Thomist visions, especially the latter, with its confidence in human moral capacities?

We can best answer these questions by placing them in the larger context of the relations between divine grace, the good, and human moral capacities. For Barth, grace interrupts the continuity between our moral striving and its object, accomplishing the good in our place and summoning us to a joyful confirmation of its actualization. From this perspective, to insist that divine grace is a necessary condition for knowing and attaining the good is not enough; if one still holds to the continuity of human capacities with the attainment of the good, one keeps the good within an economy of human moral striving in spite of one's acknowledgment of the necessity of grace, and when (with modernity) the good is eventually reduced to what is consonant with our capability, this will have involved a shift (to be sure, a significant one) within the same paradigm. This is the point of Barth's insistence on the continuity of the medieval and the modern, his conviction that the Protestant Reformers' doctrine of grace interrupts this continuity, and his evident agreement with Troeltsch that antique Stoic humanism was given a haven in premodern Christianity, with its commitment to the continuity of human striving and its object, from which it finally reemerged in the form of modern human self-assertion. From Barth's perspective, then, while Augustinian and Thomist notions of the participation of human reason in a divine rational order differ significantly from the notions of modern rationalistic ethics, they nevertheless till the soil in which the latter will sprout. Of course, the Thomist will rightly respond that Barth fails to understand that in the Thomistic tradition, too, grace operates by granting human beings a genuine participation in what grace does, though this participation primarily takes the form of cooperation with grace rather than confirmation of it. From this perspective it is precisely his insistence on the radical disruption of grace that puts Barth (and perhaps his Reformation-era predecessors as well) in continuity with modernity by forcing a crisis that will eventually make human action altogether independent of divine grace. We have now arrived at the most fundamental question: Does modernity result from a gradual slippage from Thomism to rationalism or from the crisis forced by a radical doctrine of grace? This question may never find a definitive answer. But Barth's moral theology, by contrasting an *ethic* of divine grace to an ethic of human self-assertion, at least shows how the result can be avoided from his side; it is two different conceptions of human action (one established by divine grace, the other asserted against divine grace) that are contrasted, not divine grace and human action. Nevertheless, we will have a positive reason for choosing Barth's formulation over its Augustinian and Thomist rivals only if we have reason for thinking that this contrast is not only one that belongs to a certain phase of modernity but one that in one form or another poses a perpetual problem for moral theology. This brings us to the conclusion of this chapter.

4. CONCLUSION

God is with and for us in all of God's deity, yet we insist on being by and for ourselves. In accordance with this most basic conviction, Barth's approach to modern ethics is determined by the dichotomy between the claim of divine grace and the determination of human beings to assert themselves. There is, of course, much that is not visible through this lens, and we are tempted to remind Barth of the obvious: that there is more to modernity than self-assertion; that some modern thinkers know how to cultivate piety, gratitude, and humility even in a godless cosmos; that modern desires and ambitions flow in other streams than the *Feuerbach*. But he knows all of this. His concern is not to identify a defining characteristic of modernity as such but to show how modern self-assertion brings to visibility a human stance that characterizes every age because it is the primordial and always repeated sin. Moral theology focuses on this characteristic because it is what is always at stake, in the modern era, to be sure, but in every other era as well. However, this only brings us to the most critical questions. Is Barth's dichotomy between the claim of God's grace and human self-assertion a primordial opposition in which ethics is perennially ensnared, as he thinks, or is it produced by the volatile encounter of a certain Protestant theological vision with a certain strand of modern life and thought? If modernity for Barth is the site where this dichotomy is most visible, is this because it was always there but relatively concealed, as he thinks, or because his entire portrayal of ethics as the scene of an opposition between divine claim and human self-assertion is itself inescapably modern? Has this critic of the notion of modernity as an epochal break unwittingly succumbed to the opposite modern tendency, in effect treating premodern and even primordial history as proto-modern, and has the theologian who counseled humility in the face of the theological task offered up a self-serving variant of a now discredited Protestant narrative, one in which the Reformation restores the first century—and now itself requires correction in the form of Barth's Christocentric ethics?

We subject Barth to these questions from a stance that is in part removed from modernity as he understood and experienced it. We have suggested that we are less inclined to take modernity as our point of reference and thus less inclined to credit a position whose problematic can be made clear only in modern terms. We have also suggested that we are less inclined to see our reflection in the mirror of Promethean ambition. In a crucial sense, Barth belongs to the last stage of an era of humanism whose catalyst he identifies in his 1932–3 lectures, where he points out the significance of the fact that the eighteenth century was the first in which human beings had fully absorbed the lessons of the recent past and were aware of the insignificance of humanity in the spatial and temporal vastness opened up by modern discovery. No longer did history or the cosmos reflect back to human beings their incomparable worth. They would now have to assert this worth for themselves, with God as both the content and the guarantor of their self-affirmation. The subjugation of the world to human power, the rejection of a higher law to which human beings are accountable, the expansion of human power beyond every limit and assimilation of everything to humanity—these, of course, were the ways in which modern humans asserted their worth. We, however, may think that we are beyond this horizon, that we seek less to assert our own worth and the possibility of morality in an impersonal, amoral cosmos than to form our identities in a world that is global yet fragmented and inundated with information yet afflicted with amnesia; to find worthy objects of desire amid the pointless production and proliferation of desires in a world of consumer capitalism; to fashion new forms of solidarity in a networked yet faceless world; and to connect with the sacred in a world that is at once permeated with spiritualities and disenchanted.

However, we have also questioned the assumption that we are now beyond modernity as Barth knew it, and it is precisely in the context of ethics that the persistence of modernity may be most evident. Nothing is more characteristic of our social world than the assumption that our worth depends on what we achieve. This is quite obviously so in the crass and often cruel ways in which we measure and evaluate human lives according to norms of productivity, but it is likewise so in the role ethics has come to play in the self-vindication of modern human beings. This role is most apparent in the concept of responsibility, which, as various commentators have noted, comes to assume a privileged place in modern ethical thought. In its distinctively modern sense, responsibility is the ethical form taken by the consciousness that (1) the basic moral shape of our lives, of our political and social institutions, and of the course of history itself is not given by God, nature, or the cosmos but must be determined by us so that we now become conscious of being, in a radical sense, the authors and actors of our individual and collective lives (even when we recognize the limits nature and history impose on our scripts); (2) moral endeavors, like all human endeavors, must be carried out without the confidence, rooted in divine providence, that however it may appear, our moral endeavors go with 'the grain of the universe,' so that it is now incumbent on us to give our moral causes visibility and effectiveness in the world; (3) because the good is now 'up to us' to determine and bring about, all forms of consolation and of dependence on divine assistance are suspected of compromising the earnestness of human moral effort; (4) the good at which ethical action aims is an immanent good, so that human aspiration, at least insofar as it is a concern of ethics, is directed towards the fulfillment (and perhaps the extension) of natural human capacities and desires, to the appropriation of a historical identity, to ethical or spiritual self-cultivation, or to the creation—whether through technology, revolution, or the slow, persistent work of reform—of a new human order; and (5) due to global social and economic linkages and to modern technology the range of what is affected or is capable of being affected by human action is much greater than was once thought, so that the limits of action are no longer confined to a geographical or historical site or even set by nature itself.

It is plausible to interpret Barth's entire approach to modernity as an effort to draw a connection between this modern form of responsibility and the Reformation-era problem of 'works righteousness.' In the struggle with a conscience burdened with the knowledge of one's sinfulness and of the righteousness of God, the question of the Reformation era was, how can I gain God's favor and avoid God's wrath? The analogous question of modernity is, how can humanity be assured of its ultimate worth when God, the cosmos, and history can no longer be counted on to do it? It is here that Barth's approach to modernity addresses contemporary readers. For while we no longer lose sleep worrying about whether our works are sufficient to please God, we (at least many of us) do look to ethics for the ground of our dignity or worth, for the vindication of our form of life over against those of our predecessors or contemporaries, and for the ultimate validation not only of our lives but of human existence generally, and we think of the responsibility for this burden of the ethical as one that falls, and must fall, on ourselves, without the support of God or the cosmos. This in turn accounts for the urgency of modern responsibility, which will not let us slumber while justice is delayed or suffering is unalleviated. Our insomnia is moral. It is precisely this insomnia that keeps us in the position of the judge, convinced that the cause of humanity depends on us.

While he does not explicitly articulate it, Barth seems to recognize that the new insomnia bears a certain similarity to and continuity with the old one, and he wagers that the Protestant Reformers' solution to the old insomnia can, in a revised and corrected form, address the new insomnia as well. He can take up this wager because from his perspective works righteousness and modern responsibility involve the same problem: both are forms of human self-affirmation in denial or rejection of the divine affirmation of human beings through grace. Yet, just as Luther and Calvin did not intend their polemics against works righteousness to induce moral complacency, so Barth recognizes that, rightly understood, the modern primacy of the ethical is a great achievement as well as a great temptation. He will attempt to do justice to it by treating the human response to God in ethical terms and including it as an integral part of every dogmatic topic, as we will see in the next chapter.

Early in this chapter we posed the question whether Barth's position within modernity is that of a critic, a defender, an unwitting victim, a clever appropriator, or an ironic subversive. We conclude with an answer to that question. We have pointed out Barth's denial that modernity accomplishes an epochal break with all that precedes it. It follows from this denial that Barth does not look for features unique to modernity on the grounds of which either apologies for modernity or polemics against it can be instigated. He is neither critic nor defender, then, because he is convinced that modernity simply brings to a high level of visibility what has always been the case. Yet at the same time, it is for this very reason that Barth treats modernity as an epistemologically privileged site, and it is difficult to imagine how he could express his dichotomy between the command of God's grace and human moral self-assertion in any other than modern terms. This leads us to wonder whether Barth might be an unwitting victim of modernity, allowing a specifically modern form of rationalistic ethics to stand as the truth of what preceded it and thus exaggerating the extent to which classical Christian moral theologies need correction. Nevertheless, it is also precisely at this point that Barth proves himself to be a clever appropriator who is able to draw on the Kantian moral law to express the claim of God's grace and thereby meet the unfulfilled promise of the Protestant Reformation to bring ethics under the canopy of its theology of grace.

Barth thus seems to be at once an unwitting victim and a clever appropriator, yet neither of these positions represents his fundamental theological intention. That intention can be found in his essentially pastoral and evangelical attitude to the self-asserting subject. In the subject determined to assert its worth, Barth was able to look beyond its will to power in which it sought to exercise mastery over everything external, beyond its rejection of a higher authority to which human power in all its forms and expressions is accountable, and beyond the impiety of its desire to transcend human limits and become godlike, seeing in this subject the desire of human beings to attain on their own, and thus in a distorted and ultimately futile form, what God has already from eternity determined to give them. Barth accepts modernity's deepest desire—the desire for the affirmation of human worth—finding in it an echo of God's own will, yet he rejects its own understanding of that desire, knowing that the echo is a distortion. He therefore directs the self-asserting subject to the interruption of her desire by grace, which both calls her self-affirmation into question and confers on her a more profound affirmation than she could ever achieve for herself. In this sense, Barth appears to be an ironic subversive who inserts himself into the modern self-understanding only to turn it against itself. But it would be more accurate to say that he gestures beyond modernity's own horizon, pointing to the theology and ethics of grace to indicate what is genuine and what is distorted in modern yearning and thus attesting in his own speech the negation within (and for the sake of) affirmation of the Word of God itself.

3

Dogmatics and Ethics

In a compact statement at the end of his dogmatic project Barth reaffirms the fundamental convictions about ethics that had guided that project from its beginning. 'Comprehensively,' he asserts near the beginning of his posthumously published draft of the ethics of reconciliation,

ethics is an attempt to answer theoretically the question of what may be called *good* human action. Theological ethics...finds both this question and its answer in God's Word. It thus finds it where theological dogmatics as the critical science of true church proclamation finds all its questions and answers....The Word of God...is, however, Jesus Christ in the divine-human unity of his being and work. In God's Word, then, we are dealing both with God and with man...And the Word of God is the command of God to the extent that in it the sure and certain goodness of God's goodness confronts the problematical goodness of man's as its standard, requirement, and direction.

Human action, he continues, is therefore good insofar as it is commanded by God and obedient to him. It follows that 'ethics cannot be understood and ventured as an independent discipline working on its own presuppositions and according to its own methods, but only as an integral element in dogmatics.'[1]

This passage is exemplary not only because it offers a pithy summary of the most basic claims of Barth's moral theology but also because it announces, as an implication of these claims, the enclosure of ethics within dogmatics. What does this enclosure of ethics within dogmatics signify for ethics as Barth understands and practices it? At one level it simply means that ethics may not be treated as an exception; that it will be subject to the same rules that govern the rest of Barth's theology. Beyond this, it signifies a bold wager that ethics can indeed be carried out from within dogmatics. Finally, it signifies a provocation, a summons to question the almost universal practice, taken nearly for granted in modern and contemporary moral theology, of treating ethics in at least relative independence of dogmatics.

This enclosure of ethics within dogmatics troubles many readers of Barth's moral theology, presenting a seemingly insuperable obstacle. The very movement

---

[1] CL, 3 f./1 f.

of the passage just quoted exemplifies the problem. Ethics is introduced in its own name—the name of the good as such—but is no sooner mentioned than it is immediately absorbed into dogmatics. The enclosure of ethics within dogmatics appears to be its erasure, where only a trace of the ethical as such would remain in the dogmatic language of righteousness and command. The suspicion which this enclosure of ethics within dogmatics arouses is a marker of our commitment to an ethic that stands at least somewhat apart from dogmatics—an ethic that can be articulated on its own terms even if its ultimate grounds are held to lie in theological claims. The reasons for this suspicion are far from trivial. They involve, first, the worry that to enclose ethics within dogmatics is to remove it from the sources and contexts of concrete moral activity and reflection. The first section below examines Barth's proposal in light of this worry that there is something abstract and artificial about an ethic enclosed within dogmatics. A second reason for suspicion is the thought that Barth's wager cannot be won, that ethics cannot really be carried out as part of dogmatics without slighting ethics or doing violence to it. The second section below presents Barth's proposal in detail, showing how he attempts to make good on his wager. A final reason for suspicion is that to enclose ethics within dogmatics is to engage in a totalizing project, a thorough assimilation of the other, in which there is no place for a nontheological discourse of ethics. In response to this concern, the third section below treats Barth's complex view of the relation of moral theology to moral philosophy. But before we turn to an exposition of Barth's position in light of these concerns, it is necessary to examine the rationale for that position.

Why did Barth insist on this enclosure of ethics within dogmatics? The thesis of this chapter is that Barth's conception of the relationship of dogmatics and ethics is his methodological solution to the problem of ethics discussed in Chapter 1. If ethics is to attest God's grace to humanity (the ethics of human correspondence to divine grace) rather than betraying it (the ethics of human self-assertion), then it must be carried out as the investigation of human life and conduct from the standpoint of God's self-revelation and thus as a part of dogmatics. It would be unwise, however, to focus on this methodological point for its own sake. As always with Barth, method is dictated by subject matter, and we will see how certain substantive convictions about God and God's grace require the enclosure of ethics within dogmatics. These same convictions will show us that it would be just as accurate to describe Barth's position as the expression or even the realization of dogmatics in ethics. Nevertheless, a very brief overview will show how successive formulations of the relationship of dogmatics and ethics in Barth's theology generally track his formulations of the ambiguity of ethics as we traced them in Chapter 1. This overview will provide the basis on which we will later show how his mature formulation can be understood as a solution to the problem posed by that ambiguity.

The theme of dogmatics and ethics seems initially to have simply expressed Barth's conviction of the inseparability of the questions of faith and the questions of conduct. As early as *Romans₁*, he used the formula 'dogmatics and ethics' to refer to the inseparability of these questions.[2] This conviction would later find expression in the inseparability of hearing the Word of God and doing it—the point from the Epistle of James which is the theme of Barth's first treatment of ethics in the *Church Dogmatics*.[3] Gradually, however, the relation of dogmatics and ethics would move from a formula to a program. We have already seen that it was during the crucial phase that began with the publication of *Romans₂* that Barth's characteristic sense of the ambiguity of ethics began to take shape. For grace to be grace it must express itself in this-sided human life and conduct, yet ethics presents a danger precisely because of its this-sidedness. Ethics can either be the alibi by which some of this-sided ideal or program can proclaim itself to be the realization of the will of God in this world, thus abolishing the eschatological tension in which God puts all human achievements in question, or (in the language of Romans 12: 1) it can take the form of exhortation, a discourse in which the mercies of God become this-sided while retaining their essential other-sidedness.[4] It is thus in ethics that the theme of *Romans₂* reaches its height of expression. In the 1922 lectures on Calvin's theology, this ambiguity of necessity and danger gives rise to a more programmatic statement of the unity of dogmatics and ethics. Lamenting the failure of Luther and Calvin to unite the 'vertical' dimension of grace, forgiveness, and faith with the 'horizontal' dimension of obedience and sanctification, Barth refers to the necessity of 'so relating dogmatics and ethics that each dogmatic statement would also be an ethical statement and vice versa'—a necessity, he points out, which no theology can adequately meet.[5] For Barth at this stage, ethics is the site of an intractable problem for theology: It is a this-sided, horizontal, human endeavor, yet the grace of God itself, in all its vertical, other-sidedness, requires expression in this inescapably human realm. The only recourse of theology in the face of this unsolvable problem is to dialectic: theology must maintain a continuous motion back and forth between the vertical and horizontal.[6]

It was in his 1924 lectures on dogmatics at Göttingen that Barth began to resolve the impasse. Here he developed his programmatic statement from two years earlier in light of his nascent theology of the Word of God, as we noted in Chapter 1: Insisting that 'speaking about God can refer only to an original speaking by God,' Barth now defines dogmatics as 'the materially prior attempt to grasp this standpoint of the Word of God' and ethics as 'an attempt at the

---

[2] *Romans₁*, 250, 251, 262, 348.
[3] CD I/2, 362–7/397–403.
[4] *Romans₂*, 450 f.
[5] *The Theology of John Calvin*, 80.
[6] For Barth this meant moving back and forth between Luther, the theologian of the vertical, and Calvin, the theologian of the horizontal. *The Theology of John Calvin*, 81, 88, 90.

understanding of human life from the standpoint of this Word originally spoken by God.'[7] This program was carried out in the opening pages of Barth's 1928–9 lectures on ethics and continued in roughly the same form in the first volume of the *Church Dogmatics*.[8] The crucial move here is the assertion that the Word of God establishes and fulfills a relationship between God and humanity which includes humanity in its entirety, and therefore in all its being and activity.[9] We have seen that in Barth's doctrine of the Word of God as first articulated in this stage of his thought, the command of God simply is the Word of God as the latter claims human life and conduct. It follows that dogmatics, as the theological discipline that measures the speech and activity of the church by the Word of God as its criterion, will necessarily include ethics. This mature formulation of the relation of dogmatics and ethics is inseparable from Barth's new understanding of the ambiguity of ethics, which now involves the distinction between human life and conduct as determined by the Word of God, on the one hand, and human life and conduct as the expression of human capability, depicted in an ideal or empirical description of the life of the Christian and understood as an instance of human moral conduct in general, on the other hand. This distinction corresponds to the distinction between ethics within dogmatics and ethics independent of dogmatics. Ethics is still both a necessity and a danger. But the problem moral theology now faces is posed by an ethic that asserts itself in independence of dogmatics. For Barth, such an assertion can only mean the substitution of a human standard and achievement for the Word of God.

The Word of God establishes and fulfills a particular form of relationship between God and humanity, and this relationship includes human life and conduct. God having freely decided from eternity to enter into this form of relationship with a human other, dogmatics is not free to abstract God from it, and thus from human life and conduct; and God having also from eternity determined humanity for this relationship, ethics is not free to abstract human life and conduct from it. The implication is plain: 'Dogmatics itself is ethics; and ethics is also dogmatics. . . . God in his relationship to human existence is necessarily the theme of dogmatics.'[10] However, this relationship of God and humanity is grounded in God; it is not self-grounded nor grounded in humanity. It follows that, in the language of the Göttingen dogmatics quoted above, the 'standpoint of the Word of God' really is 'materially prior' to 'the understanding of human life from the standpoint of this Word.' 'That dogmatics has always to be ethics cannot alter the fact that it is first and foremost and in itself

---

[7] Karl Barth, *The Göttingen Dogmatics: Instruction in the Christian Religion*, vol. i, trans. Geoffrey W. Bromiley (Grand Rapids, Mich.: Eerdmans, 1991), 12. (Translation of *Unterricht in der christlichen Religion*, vol. i, ed. Hannelotte Reiffen (Zurich: Theologischer Verlag Zürich, 1990).)

[8] *Ethics*, 15 f./23 f.

[9] CD I/2, 788/881 f.

[10] CD I/2, 793 f./888.

dogmatics.'[11] From this perspective, as Barth points out, '[i]t is not self-evident that there is in theology a particular discipline which bears the name of ethics and addresses itself to the ethical task.'[12] Denying that moral theology possesses the status of a theological discipline in its own right, Barth defined it instead as an auxiliary discipline (*Hilfswissenschaft*) to dogmatics.[13] While he held out the possibility that one could assign ethics this role while presenting it apart from dogmatics (in, say, a separate volume), Barth rejected such a procedure for himself, announcing his intention to present his ethics within his dogmatics by asserting that 'so-called ethics I regard as the doctrine of the command of God.'[14] It is these assertions of the priority of dogmatics to ethics that prompt concerns that Barth's enclosure of dogmatics in ethics fails to do justice to ethics.

1. DOGMATICS AND ETHICS AS A PROBLEM IN MORAL THEOLOGY

Christians in Europe and North America today are occupied with the ethical, political, and cultural roles of Christianity in a civilization whose Christian heritage is now being contested. The ethical task, in this broad sense, is accordingly invested with an urgency that is at least equal to that accorded to the apologetic task in the face of modern challenges to Christian belief. The urgency of this task is proclaimed both by those who think that Christianity remains a necessary support for moral principles or values that are at the basis of Western civilization and by those who think that Christianity is a critical alternative to the principles and values of a civilization that no longer is and perhaps never was Christian. There are, of course, 'conservative' and 'liberal' versions of both of these stances. But in both cases there is concern that to enclose ethics within dogmatics is to risk getting in the way of the ethical task of Christianity, whether by fueling suspicions that the ethical claims Christians make are merely particularistic after all or by obscuring the clarity of Christian witness with abstract doctrines which fuel irrelevant controversies. In one case, dogmatics seems remote from the natural and social contexts in which ethical questions arise and are contested; in the other case, dogmatics seems remote from the practices and forms of life that constitute the church. These arguments against Barth's proposal are pressed in exemplary fashion by two recent theologians.

---

[11] CD I/2, 794/888.
[12] *Ethics*, 5/4 f.
[13] *Ethics*, 3/1, 18/28.
[14] CD I/1, xvi/XII (revised).

Dogmatics and Ethics According to Rendtorff and McClendon

Trutz Rendtorff argues that dogmatics and ethics should be treated as distinct yet complementary components of systematic theology, each with its own approach to 'the question which is basic to all theology, that of the structure of our relations to reality.'[15] Independently of dogmatics, but still as a branch of systematic theology, theological ethics articulates the meaning of the reality in which human beings participate as agents. With this approach, Rendtorff notes, dogmatic debates no longer determine the agenda of theological ethics, and the latter is now free for engagements with nontheological inquiries into ethical reality. James McClendon emphasizes the complementarity of dogmatics and ethics over their distinctness, but he, too, denies that ethics belongs within dogmatics. Like Schleiermacher, McClendon treats both dogmatics and ethics as normative descriptions of the life of the church. But unlike Schleiermacher, he grants ethics, which identifies 'the shape of the common life in the body of Christ,' procedural priority over dogmatics, which investigates 'the common teaching that undergirds that common life...'[16] While Rendtorff wants to free theological ethics from the agenda of dogmatics and for engagements with nontheological forms of ethics, McClendon wants to renew theology as a pedagogy, as training in Christianity, in which ethics enjoys procedural priority over dogmatics on the grounds that one learns Christianity as a way of life before one understands it as a form of knowledge.

Not only do Rendtorff and McClendon represent two influential approaches in recent theological ethics—one holds that the task of theological ethics is to articulate the theological grounds of ethical meanings that are found in natural and social reality prior to theological reflection, while the other holds that this task is to articulate the convictions and practices that constitute the way of life of the church as a community distinct from the world in which it finds itself—they also illustrate how these two approaches embody two different kinds of dissatisfaction with dogmatics. Rendtorff's specter of a moral theology constrained by dogmatic issues and debates and thereby cut off from other inquiries into the realities with which ethics is concerned portrays dogmatics as insular and

---

[15] Trutz Rendtorff, *Ethics*, i: *Basic Elements and Methodology in an Ethical Theology* (Philadelphia: Fortress Press, 1986), 9. Translation of *Ethik: Grundelemente, Methodologie und Konkretionen eine ethischen Theologie* Band I (Stuttgart: W. Kohlhammer Verlag, 1980). An earlier discussion is found in Trutz Rendtorff, 'Der Ethische Sinn der Dogmatik,' in *Die Realisierung der Freiheit: Beiträge zur Kritik der Theologie Karl Barths*, ed. Trutz Rendtorff (Gütersloher Verlaghaus Gerd Mohn, 1975), 119–34. However, Rendtorff's major interest in this text is in the relation of divine and human action, which is the concern of Chapter 5. Our presentation of his position here will therefore be drawn from his *Ethics*, vol. i.

[16] James Wm. McClendon, *Ethics: Systematic Theology*, vol. i, 2nd edn. (Nashville: Abingdon, 2002), 43. Procedural priority, of course, is fully compatible with McClendon's claim that, logically, dogmatics and ethics along with 'witness,' which for him is the third branch of theology, all imply each other.

inattentive to voices other than its own; in short, as dogmatic in the pejorative sense. It is from this perspective that Rendtorff attributes to Barth—wrongly, as we will see—a position according to which moral theology is unable to engage in discussion with other forms of ethical inquiry because of its determination by dogmatics.[17] McClendon explicitly grants ethics only a procedural priority to dogmatics for pedagogical purposes, but he betrays a second type of dissatisfaction with dogmatics when he invites us to consider 'how different might have been the history of Christianity if after the accession of the Emperor Constantine the church's leaders had met at Nicaea, not to anathematize others' inadequate Christological metaphysics, but to devise a strategy by which the church might remain the church in light of the fateful political shift—to secure Christian social ethics before refining Christian dogma?'[18] This question reflects a broadly Anabaptist (or as McClendon prefers, 'baptist') sensibility, suggesting that his priority of ethics over dogmatics is rooted in a historic Christian tradition. But it also reflects a broader sensibility—not uniquely Anabaptist—that dogmatics is an abstract, theoretical affair, remote from the concrete life of the church, which is most directly and properly expressed in its ethics.

A Barthian Rejoinder

Dogmatics is either insular or abstract; in either case its remoteness from the proper sources and contexts of ethics renders it an unsuitable location for ethics. These are the charges leveled against Barth's enclosure of ethics within dogmatics. Are they sound? Rendtorff's complaint that doing ethics within dogmatics holds the former hostage to the issues and debates of the latter begs a key question: If ethics really is a part of dogmatics then the issues and debates of dogmatics are by definition those of ethics as well. In fact, this complaint presupposes an alternative conception of ethics, one which holds that contemporary life poses questions about the shape human life itself is to take, that ethical theory articulates the reality of human life implied in those questions, and that the task of ethical theology is to show how these questions and that reality involve humanity in its relation to God. Ethical theology is logically dependent on questions and accounts of reality that come from outside theology. Barth, of course, rejects the logical dependence of theological ethics on extra-dogmatic material. He argues (as we will see) that the Word of God does in fact pose (and answer) questions of ethics and offers its own account of the reality of human life. Yet he also holds that within these parameters, moral theology is (and must be) open to conversation with other disciplines that impinge on the problems of ethics.

---

[17] Rendtorff, *Ethics*, i. 18.
[18] McClendon, *Ethics*, 41.

Rendtorff is less interested in an accurate interpretation of Barth's position than in using it as a foil for his own. Nevertheless, his remarks pose a legitimate question: Can Barth's enclosure of ethics within dogmatics do justice to the natural and social reality of human moral life? Recall Barth's distinction between understanding human life and conduct in its determination by the Word of God and understanding human life and conduct as depicted in an ideal or empirical description. If we are to understand ethics from the standpoint of the Word of God, does this exclude understanding it as a natural and social reality?

To answer this question, we will have to take a short detour into Barth's theological anthropology. In accordance with his doctrine of creation more generally, Barth's theological anthropology is structured around the twofold claim that the human creature has its ultimate ontological determination in its being as God's covenant partner and that this determination presupposes a creaturely essence that is distinct from it yet suited to it. Theological anthropology must therefore consider both the being of humanity as covenant partner, and thus as the one elected by God and summoned by God's Word, and also the being of humanity as the creature whose nature is not neutral, much less hostile to the determination as God's covenant partner, but is its presupposition, the condition God deemed (and made) suitable for the realization of the divine purpose, whose most fundamental feature is humanity's being with the other but which also includes the body–soul character of human existence and its temporality. In accordance with the *analogia relationis*, the humanity of other human beings possesses these characteristics in an analogical form by virtue of their ontological participation in the humanity of Jesus Christ, who is in the most real sense the elect one and the one for others, while the humanity of Jesus Christ itself is the repetition *ad extra* of relations proper to God's Trinitarian being. On these grounds, it is clear both that Barth's moral theology cannot at any point lose sight of or abstract from the natural and social reality of human life and conduct (to do so would be to ignore or deny the creaturely condition in which humanity exists as God's covenant partner), and that the ethical significance of this reality must always be understood with reference to the ultimate determination of human beings as God's covenant partners. This position is best summed up in Barth's own words: 'There is no law and commandment of God inherent in the creatureliness of man as such, or written and revealed in the stars as a law of the cosmos. . . . But in his creatureliness, in his nature—which is the sum of his possibilities and destiny and nothing more—man is called to hold to the grace of his Creator, to be thankful for it, to bow to it and adapt himself to it, to honor it as truth.'[19] Whether on these grounds Barth can (or does) do justice to these natural and social features of human justice remains to be seen; it can be determined only by an examination of specific topics in his ethics of creation.

[19] CD IV/1, 140/154.

But there is no reason to suppose prior to such an examination that the enclosure of ethics within dogmatics precludes doing justice to these realities.

McClendon's charge is not that dogmatics is insular but that it is abstract. He distinguishes between ethics as the description of the order and practices of the church and the moral formation that is effected through them, on the one hand, and the investigation of the doctrine that undergirds this way of life, on the other hand. It follows that *both* the 'shape' of the church's life *and* inquiry into that life are prior to and can be characterized apart from the church's beliefs and inquiry into them. Under this assumption, both the church's life and its ethics as the normative description of that life are distinguished, as first-order discourses, from the church's teaching and its dogmatics as the normative description of this teaching, as second-order discourses. Like McClendon, Barth distinguishes between first- and second-order discourses to depict the activities in which the church talks about God (paradigmatically in proclamation) and critically examines its talk (dogmatics).[20] However, dogmatics for him is not the abstract discourse McClendon has in mind. First, the standard by which dogmatics measures proclamation, namely the Word of God, is itself the source and object of that proclamation. Thus, second-order dogmatics and first-order proclamation are alike subordinate to the revelation of the Word of God, which is the necessary condition for the successful performance of either. Second, dogmatics is itself talk about God—it is not abstract reflection on talk about God; and, moreover, it is the church's own self-examination of the claim it makes in its proclamation—it is not an examination conducted from above or outside. For both of these reasons, Barth rightly points out that dogmatics does not occupy a higher stage of faith or of knowledge of faith even if it is a second order of discourse.[21] Third, dogmatics is not a theoretical inquiry. To fulfill its role in relation to proclamation, dogmatics aims at the formulation of pure doctrine, and according to Barth, doctrine differs from theory in two respects: First, unlike theory it is not formulated in a relation of reciprocity between the inquirer and the object but rather in relation to an object that transcends human thought; second, the one who formulates doctrine is responsible not only to the object and to herself (as in theoretical inquiry) but also to her neighbor, to whom, by its very

---

[20] CD I/1, 3/1, 51/52. At the risk of exaggeration one may say that Barth's entire conception of theology is rooted in the conviction that Christian proclamation can, by God's grace as the necessary and sufficient condition, be itself the Word of God. The task of dogmatics is to investigate what is implied in this claim. Barth's emphasis on proclamation is inseparable from the notion of the Word of God as addressed to human beings in an event. Proclamation is talk that explicitly claims and expects to declare the Word of God to human beings and therefore must be evaluated with respect to that claim and expectation. Dogmatic inquiry, then, is necessarily critical inquiry since the actual proclamation of the church cannot be accepted in its mere facticity; the church can err in its proclamation, and so the latter must be evaluated in relation to the Word of God, which constitutes the church. The following discussion of dogmatics presupposes the centrality of these convictions to Barth's dogmatic enterprise.

[21] CD I/1, 4/2, 83/85, 250/263 f.

nature, doctrine is directed.[22] Hence, like McClendon and others who espouse 'cultural-linguistic' understandings of theology, Barth stresses the responsibility of dogmatics to the ecclesial community. But unlike the latter, Barth stresses the nonreciprocity between the theologian and her transcendent object.[23]

The unique character of the object of dogmatic inquiry brings us to two additional reasons why dogmatics for Barth is not a remote, theoretical discourse. As a divine address to human beings the Word of God is given only in the event of its saying (*Sagen*); it is a matter of an encounter, not a matter of an object that, like natural or historical objects, can be assimilated to human knowing.[24] At the same time, dogmatics is never carried out in the pure presence of the Word of God but always only in the recollection (*Erinnerung*) and expectation (*Erwartung*) of God's saying, and therefore in *faith* in God's promise that the Word of God can and will be present in proclamation.[25] For the same reason, that is,

---

[22] CD I/2, 761 f./851 f.

[23] Lindbeck's intratextuality presents Christian theology as an immanent discourse on religion. For Lindbeck '[t]he task of descriptive (dogmatic or systematic) theology is to give a normative explication of the meaning a religion has for its adherents' (George Lindbeck, *The Nature of Doctrine: Religion and Theology in a Postliberal Age* (Philadelphia: Westminster Press, 1984), 113). Despite his efforts to distance himself from Schleiermacher, this definition, with its emphasis on description, already places Lindbeck in the latter's camp, though for Lindbeck the religious meaning that is set forth in speech is grounded in a community's form of life rather than in religious affections. Lindbeck's 'cultural-linguistic' method of normative description locates religious meaning in the 'intratextual' uses of a particular language which Lindbeck distinguishes from 'extratextual' objective realities or experiences. Thus for cultural linguists, as Lindbeck explicitly points out, religious meaning is immanent (114). Lindbeck suggests that his notion of intratextuality derives, albeit at second hand, from Barth (135). Yet it is difficult to comprehend how Lindbeck can make such a claim when he announces that his intratextual approach is grounded in a general theory of religion that is neither Christian nor theological but derives from philosophy and the social sciences (7) and when he recommends his cultural-linguistic model as better suited than alternative models to the nontheological study of religion (25). Most importantly, Lindbeck differs from Barth in that for Barth the idea of doctrine is inseparable from the idea of what transcends human observation and thought (CD I/2, 761/851). For Barth the entire problematic of doctrine arises out of the relation between proclamation as the divinely appointed task of speaking the Word of God in human words and the dependence of this task on the divine promise to speak in human words. Lindbeck is of course free to construct his own theory of doctrine, and the value of his theory for explaining doctrinal disagreements is unsurpassed. But neither his cultural-linguistic theory nor the 'cognitive' or 'experiential-expressivist' alternatives to it come close to grasping doctrine as Barth understood it, namely in the context of the relation of immanent human speech to the transcendent Word of God. Barth's position is succinctly presented in his 'Fate and Idea in Theology,' in *The Way of Theology in Karl Barth: Essays and Comments*, ed. Martin Rumscheidt (New York: Pickwick Publications, 1986), 26–30.

[24] CD I/1, 132/136.

[25] CD I/1, 249/262 f. For Barth, God is able at any time to speak his word in human talk. The church lives in and by the promise that God does this in the case of church proclamation. It is in faith in this promise that dogmatics undertakes its examination of proclamation with respect to its agreement with the Word of God. But in this examination dogmatics does not have direct access to the Word of God. The Word of God is always what it is in the event of its being spoken; any account of it, in dogmatics or otherwise, is necessarily a matter of recollection and expectation. In this sense dogmatics for Barth is a deconstruction of dogma to the extent that the latter is identified with the truth of revelation itself. As Barth says of dogmatics, 'its office cannot be to tear down the barriers of faith [i.e., the limitations of recollection and expectation] that are set for the Church. Part

because its object of inquiry is the Word of God addressed to human beings, dogmatics is a discourse of *obedience*. 'Its truth can only be apprehended in one way—as the truth that is said to us. Anything we might say to ourselves in this regard must always begin and end with obedience, and obedience cannot be grounded in anything but the truth said to us.'[26] True dogma is not only or primarily propositional truth. It is that, to be sure, but only insofar as more fundamentally it reflects a relation of obedience to the Word of God which, in addressing itself, issues the demand that the church proclaim it, and that its proclamation agree with the Word of God.[27] It follows from this that dogmatics is itself an ethical performance in the strict sense, as Barth implies by repeatedly describing dogmatics as the self-examination (*Selbstprüfung*) the church carries out in its responsibility (*Verantwortung*) to God, and by insisting that it is carried out in a position of obedience to God and responsibility to the neighbor.

In sum, dogmatics for Barth is not the abstract, theoretical discourse removed from the concrete life of the church that McClendon fears. Dogma for Barth cannot be abstracted from its pragmatic context in which it is always spoken from the position of the addressee of the Word of God in the church. Genuine dogma is the linguistic expression of the proper relation of the church, in its speech and

---

of its task is rather to make these barriers known as such, to say what can be said and therewith to warn against violations or illusions regarding things one cannot say' (ibid.). For Barth demonstration (*Aufweisen*) of the agreement of church proclamation with the Word of God, i.e., dogma, is therefore an eschatological concept (CD I/1, 269/284). Unlike most modern theologians Barth's theology is not an attempt to show how human consciousness or language is capable of representing the divine. Since his theology is not logocentric in this sense, it is not susceptible to deconstruction. However, this does not mean that dogmatics for Barth is itself a form of deconstruction. The extent to which that is true depends on the extent to which deconstruction is compatible with Christian eschatology.

[26] 'Fate and Idea in Theology,' 51.

[27] CD I/1, 269–75/285–91. Barth's criticism is directed against what he sees as a Roman Catholic tendency to treat dogma in terms of dogmatic propositions to which one may adhere theoretically, that is, with mere assent. Dogma as Barth understands it is inseparable from the Word of God as a summons to a decision or commitment—something like what Stanley Hauerwas and McClendon intend by speaking of 'convictions' rather than 'beliefs.' For Barth, any account of the Word of God or of the sense in which human beings may know the latter will be mistaken if it abstracts from its character as a summons to obedience in this sense. His point seems to be that dogmatic inquiry into the Word of God does not establish or determine the inquirer's relation to the Word of God; rather, her relation to the Word of God is already established by the Word of God itself, which determines inquiry as an act of obedience. Here, inquiry is responsible to that which it investigates, and it cannot properly represent its object except insofar as it also and thereby attests its condition of obedience to its object. Only in this context can the status of the propositional content of dogma be properly understood. Charged with evaluating the claim and expectation that church proclamation genuinely declares the Word of God, dogmatics cannot presume to be able to represent them from the neutral position often presupposed when dogma is reduced to its propositional content; it must rather carry out its inquiry from a position of obedience. Even in this position, as we have just seen, dogmatics does not stand in the luminosity of the presence of the Word of God; it always recollects and anticipates in faith. All of this is to say that dogmatics itself does not supply and cannot secure the conditions for the truth of its representations, and any formulation of dogma itself must reflect this limitation.

activity, to the Word of God which constitutes it. While dogmatics remains a second-order, critical discourse for Barth, it stands in close proximity to the church's first-order discourses. Barth thus shows how ethics can be carried out within dogmatics while preserving the concrete, ecclesial determination of ethics McClendon seeks to uphold, yet rejecting the reduction of theology and ethics to an immanent horizon that occurs whenever theology loses sight of the transcendence of the standard by which the church measures its own discourse. At the same time, McClendon's charge is not entirely off the mark: Dogmatics for Barth is not only descriptive but critical. As such, it may put more distance between itself and the concrete ethical speech of the church—even as it, too, remains part of the speech of the church—than does McClendon's normative description. The critical posture of Barth's dogmatics follows from the transcendence of the Word of God as its standard, while McClendon's normative description seems to presuppose an immanent horizon.

To conclude, Barth's enclosure of ethics within dogmatics does not in itself mean that ethics will be carried out in isolation or abstraction from its natural and social or its ecclesial contexts. But neither will Barth's ethics be grounded in those contexts in the ways Rendtorff and McClendon desire. Neither human life as grasped by reason and experience nor the church's own speech and practice will be accepted on their own terms by an ethic enclosed within dogmatics. Both will be subjected to critical examination in the light not of an abstract moral principle but of the concrete Word of God.

2. DOGMATICS AS ETHICS IN BARTH'S MORAL THEOLOGY

We have approached Barth's enclosure of ethics within dogmatics from the outside, interrogating it from two opposed perspectives in contemporary theological ethics from which two related suspicions against Barth's proposal may be expressed. It is now time to turn to that proposal itself in order to face a second kind of suspicion, namely that ethics cannot finally be carried out within dogmatics.

Dogmatics as Ethics: What is at Stake

The first task is to determine what is at stake in the very question of the relation of ethics to dogmatics. In both Protestant and Catholic theology the separation of ethics from dogmatics was largely accomplished in the seventeenth and eighteenth centuries.[28] What dissatisfaction would call for revisiting an issue

---

[28] There are many accounts of the independence of ethics from theology. Barth, like

that seems to have remained amicably settled for centuries? Already in the early nineteenth century, Schleiermacher could identify certain pernicious conse- quences that follow from this separation of ethics from dogmatics: Christian ethics becomes separated from the life of the church (where, he emphatically insisted, all theology, doctrinal or moral, belongs); it is assimilated too closely to rationalistic ethics; and the relationship between Christian thought and Christian behavior is obscured or distorted.[29] Concern over these three factors is, of course, widely voiced today, most often by moral theologians who by no means claim an affinity with Schleiermacher. What they share is a worry that ethics has become identified with the notion of a universal rational morality, leaving the church without adequate means to articulate its own moral life, which is inseparable from its convictions and practices. However, in spite of his interest in bringing them closer together, Schleiermacher cited a common rationale for treating Christian ethics separately from dogmatics, namely that in treating ethics as part of dogmatics, Protestant orthodoxy had failed to give ethics its due, doom- ing ethics to a stunted development in comparison with dogmatics.[30] For many, though not unambiguously for Schleiermacher, this condition alone warrants a separate treatment for the sake of ethics. Ethics must be treated in separation from dogmatics because it is only in this way that ethics can be assured of a proper treatment at all.

Where Schleiermacher sees the separation of ethics from dogmatics as prob- lematic yet necessary in order to give ethics its due, Barth sees a very different ambition at work. For him, the separation of ethics from dogmatics cannot properly be invoked as a condition for doing justice to ethics; it is, rather, the alibi for a radical transformation of theology and the church itself along the lines of an ethic grounded in a general conception of human nature or reason:

[A]n independent ethics has always shown at once a tendency to reverse the roles, replacing dogmatics as the basic theological discipline, absorbing dogmatics into itself, transforming it into an ethical system with a Christian foundation, and then penetrating

---

Schleiermacher, identifies the *Epitome theologiae moralis* (1634) of George Calixtus as the culprit (CD I/2, 785/878). This, of course, reflects the interest of both Barth and Schleiermacher in the Protestant origin. A Catholic origin might go back as far as Suarez. Some historians of moral philosophy point to Grotius as the turning point (see J. B. Schneewind, *The Invention of Autonomy: A History of Modern Moral Philosophy* (Cambridge: Cambridge University Press, 1998)). In any case, the prevalence of Jesuit and Anglican moral treatises in the seventeenth century indicates how quickly the trend caught on.

[29] See Friedrich Schleiermacher, *Brief Outline for the Study of Theology*, trans. Terrence N. Tice (Atlanta: John Knox Press, 1966), §§ 23–31; idem, *Introduction to Christian Ethics*, trans. John C. Shelly (Nashville: Abingdon Press, 1989), 33–49.

[30] It is ironic that Schleiermacher, who wanted to give ethics its due, never completed the *Sittenlehre* that was to have complemented his *Glaubenslehre*. This point is not lost on McClendon, who cites this failure to complete a definitive treatment of Christian ethics as evidence of what he thinks goes wrong when dogmatics comes before ethics (see *Ethics*, 39). It could also serve Barth as evidence of what goes wrong when ethics is presented separately from dogmatics.

and controlling biblical exegesis and pastoral theology in the same way. Since independent ethical systems are always in the last resort determined by general anthropology, this inevitably means that dogmatics itself and theology as a whole simply becomes applied anthropology. Its standard ceases to be the Word of God. It is the idea of the good which controls its investigation of the goodness of the Christian character. But this idea is both sought and found apart from revelation. The Word of God is retained only in so far as it can be made intelligible as the historical medium and vehicle of this idea. The Church which sanctions this theology has subjected itself to an utterly alien sovereignty.[31]

Barth makes three claims here regarding the independence of ethics from dogmatics: (1) that it involves an assertion of the primacy of ethics over dogmatics and an absorption and transformation of dogmatics into ethics; (2) that it thereby subjects the whole of theology to a norm ultimately grounded in a general anthropological conception of morality rather than in biblical revelation; and (3) that it reduces the meaning of revelation to its role as a historical medium and vehicle of this morality. When all of this happens the church subjects itself to an independent moral norm, one grounded in anthropology, for example, in a general conception of human nature or reason. While he is not named at this point, Barth almost certainly has Kant in mind here. For it was Kant's *Religion within the Boundaries of Mere Reason* which gave paradigmatic expression to claims from the side of philosophy which, if adopted as a program for theology (which Kant did not do), would likely result in these three claims, while also drawing the conclusion which subordinated the church, as a visible historical entity, to rational morality. This program is, of course, the attempted humanization of Christianity which Barth found in eighteenth-century bourgeois culture and which we discussed in Chapter 1. It could not be clearer what Barth thinks is at stake in the enclosure of ethics within dogmatics.

The influence of Kant's position on modern attempts to formulate the relation of theology and ethics is undeniable. But Barth's account claims something much stronger, namely, that every effort to treat ethics in separation from dogmatics will repeat the Kantian paradigm. This is a far more controversial assertion. On what grounds does Barth press this sharp disjunction between the enclosure of ethics within dogmatics and the Kantian paradigm—a disjunction which leaves no space for a theological ethic between dogmatics and moral philosophy? The answer to this question will bring us to the heart of Barth's methodological solution to the problem of ethics.

Barth's argument is partly conceptual and partly historical. We begin where he does, with the conceptual point. In every case, he insists, the presupposition behind efforts to treat ethics separately from dogmatics is 'the opinion that the goodness, that is, the holiness of the Christian character, unlike the other objective content of Christian proclamation, is not hidden with Christ in God

---

[31] CD I/2, 782 f./875 f.

(in spite of Col. 3: 3), but can be directly perceived and therefore demonstrated, described and set up as a norm.' This assumption in turn 'seems always to have involved' treating that character as a specific form of human conduct generally, so that the norm is ultimately grounded in a general conception of human nature. We are back, of course, to the complementary tendencies of pietism and rationalism. Once again, Barth is determined to link these two phenomena, namely, the visibility of goodness in the Christian and a natural conception of the good. The claim is that when goodness becomes a human property, accessible to an ideal or empirical description of the life of the Christian, it can only be understood as a specification of a general norm of human goodness. For Barth, of course, the proper presupposition is opposite to the one that gives rise to this view, namely, 'that the holiness of the Christian character is not less visible in Jesus Christ, but also not less hidden in the life of Christians, than the remaining content of Christian proclamation.'[32] Under this presupposition, as we saw in Chapter 1, holiness as the reality of sanctification—no less than righteousness as the reality of justification—must be found in Jesus Christ rather than in our own moral and spiritual achievements, and to the extent that this presupposition has prevailed over the alternative, Barth asserts, the project of an ethic that is independent of dogmatics is rendered difficult or impossible. To enclose ethics within dogmatics will therefore entail treating sanctification on the same terms as justification, or as election, for that matter—that is, as accomplished in Christ and calling for our confirmation of its accomplishment in him. Thus will Barth apply himself to bar the door through which an independent ethic can enter the house and subdue its inhabitants.

The presupposition that the holiness of the Christian is hidden with Christ clearly rules out an ethic that is independent of dogmatics. Under this presupposition moral goodness must be articulated in terms of Christological dogma. If moral theology is determined to avoid the Kantian paradigm, this is surely the definitive solution. But is there really a problem here that requires a definitive solution? Is it really the case that the presupposition of the visibility of goodness in the Christian inevitably leads to the Kantian paradigm? Barth does not claim that the connection between the two is a necessary one; he cautiously remarks that the assumption of visibility 'seems always to have involved' treating the visible goodness of the Christian as an instance of a general conception of human goodness. This brings us to the historical part of his argument. The connection is a contingent one which must be demonstrated historically, as Barth attempts to do by tracing the coincidence of visible goodness with a general philosophical norm and linking both to the separation of ethics from dogmatics.[33] The problem for Barth, as his own historical narrative indicates, is that through most of its history, the assumption of the visibility of goodness in the Christian and the presence of norms drawn from a

---

[32] CD I/2, 782/875.
[33] CD I/2, 783–6/876–80.

general anthropology did not in fact coincide with a separation of ethics from dogmatics. As is often the case, Barth is least convincing when he tries to stretch to the middle ages and even to antiquity an analysis that is properly directed to the modern conditions of bourgeois society which were the focus of his concern (though, as we saw in the previous chapter, it is another question whether earlier periods somehow harbored the relevant modern conditions and yet another question whether these conditions can be overcome by retrieving aspects of these earlier conditions).[34] In this case the modern conditions that are his real target are found along the arc in continental European Protestant theological ethics which runs from eighteenth-century pietism and rationalism to Troeltsch. In tracing this arc, Barth begins by rejecting the claim that the separate treatment of ethics arose as a necessary corrective to the neglect of ethics by Protestant orthodoxy. Orthodoxy did not slight ethics, he argues; it simply refused to grant ethics the primacy and independence which pietism and rationalism, in distinct yet related ways, now demanded.[35] It was pietism that affirmed the centrality of the visible effects of grace in the life of the Christian (making goodness visible in the Christian) and rationalism that identified the moral law with the law of nature (grounding the goodness of the Christian in a general anthropological norm). Together, they inaugurated the agenda to transform Christianity into an ethical religion as expressed in the Kantian paradigm. The anti-orthodoxy narrative now stands exposed as a legitimization of this agenda rather than as an effort to give ethics its due, while Kant is credited simply with bringing to philosophical precision a project that was being carried out in theology itself. According to Barth's narrative, this agenda continued through the nineteenth century, notably in the school of Ritschl; that Ritschl's famous students, Herrmann and Troeltsch, who disagreed on so much, were both committed to the fundamental status of ethics for theology—their definitive debate was largely over what kind of ethics is suited to play this role—is for Barth evidence of the influence the initial moves made in pietism and rationalism continued to exercise up to his day.[36]

---

[34] Barth is compelled to admit that in pre-Reformation moral theology both the visibility of Christian goodness and the acceptance of norms drawn from outside biblical revelation were often operative without subverting the proper relation between dogmatics and ethics. None other than Augustine, John of Damascus, Peter Lombard, and Thomas Aquinas are credited with maintaining a proper order here (CD I/2, 783/876). This obviously prompts the question whether on Barth's own analysis it is only in modern Christianity that visible righteousness and independent norms lead to the situation of which Kant is the paradigm. Barth, of course, is convinced that the errors his theology corrects are found not only in modern Christianity but in much of early and medieval Christianity as well, so that one cannot appeal to the pre-Reformation era to correct the errors of the eighteenth and nineteenth centuries. He must therefore treat the instances of visible goodness and extra-Christian norms in premodern moral theology as something like a Stoic sleeper cell waiting for the Enlightenment as a signal to strike.

[35] CD I/2, 785/878.

[36] CD I/2, 786/879. See the analysis of the Herrmann–Troeltsch debate found in Brent Sockness, *Against False Apologetics: Wilhelm Herrmann and Ernst Troeltsch in Conflict* (Tübingen: J. C. B. Mohr, 1998).

In short, where Schleiermacher and his many followers (most of whom dispense with his reservations) claim only to be giving ethics its due by treating it separately, Barth sees instead an ambition, whether covert or overt, to transform Christianity into an ethical religion grounded in a natural or historical conception of human goodness—a transformation which for him was already inaugurated by pietism and rationalism and then fully carried out in nineteenth-century theology. The independence of ethics from dogmatics coincides with the primacy of ethics and with the subordination of Christian life and thought to a general ethical conception. This, at least, is Barth's conviction—a conviction which sets him against modern theological ethics to the extent that the latter defines itself around the quandary with which Schleiermacher struggled. Where one party claims to be doing justice to ethics while keeping it within a theological context, the other party is convinced that this claim conceals a sinister ambition. Here lies a point of fundamental divergence between Barth and nearly all of modern theological ethics, and it is at this point—though it is seldom recognized as such—that Barth's dismissal of the terms set by Schleiermacher's quandary seems obstinate and exaggerated and his worry over the ethical transformation of Christianity idiosyncratic.

How persuasive is Barth's account? The answer seems to depend on the extent to which the line he traces from the unnamed pietists and rationalists to Troeltsch subtends modern and contemporary theological ethics as a whole. Do the developments Barth describes, which have their epicenter in the modern German theological tradition, characterize the past two centuries of theological ethics generally? Against Barth, one could point out that the historical connection between the presupposition of the visibility of Christian goodness and the Kantian paradigm appears to be much less inevitable than he assumes. We can easily find counterexamples to the claim that an ideal or empirical description of the Christian character always treats this character as a specification of human conduct more generally and to the claim that to identify the norm with a general conception of human nature entails the reduction of revelation to a historical medium or vehicle of this idea.[37] In support of Barth, however, one could point to a widespread tendency in both theology and church life to assert the

---

[37] In *The Peaceable Kingdom: A Primer in Christian Ethics* (Notre Dame, Ind.: University of Notre Dame Press, 1983) and in other writings Stanley Hauerwas denies that his description of the Christian life is derived from any norm of human goodness as such, in part because he denies that there is any normative conception of the human as such. He thus provides a counterexample to the second point of the Kantian paradigm. In *Resurrection and Moral Order*, 2nd edn (Grand Rapids, Mich.: Eerdmans, 1994), 85–8, Oliver O'Donovan articulates the norm of conduct in terms of a metaphysical order of natural kinds and teleological relations while arguing that the privileged disclosure of this order is found in biblical revelation. The moral order is cosmic: O'Donovan does not understand it in terms of human nature or reason; rather, he understands human nature and reason in relation to man's ordering in the cosmos. Still, the norm of human conduct lies in this natural order even if its knowability as well as its normativity are ultimately grounded in Christ. Assuming that it is scripture that interprets the metaphysical order and not vice versa, O'Donovan supplies a counterexample to the third point of the Kantian paradigm.

primacy of ethics by articulating the rest of theology in ethical terms, submitting dogmatics, exegesis, and pastoral theology to reconstruction on the basis of ethical criteria, along with a similar tendency, also widespread, to derive moral norms from a general conception of human reason or nature while assigning revelation a purely ancillary role.[38]

Perhaps the best way to characterize the present situation, at least in Protestant ethics, is to think of it as one in which certain heirs of Kant face off against certain heirs of Schleiermacher. We may describe as Kant's theological successors those who hold that the content of the Christian moral life is found in natural morality, however far they may depart from Kant's distinctive theses regarding the unconditional nature of moral worth, the categorical imperative as the principle of morality, and duty as the necessary and sufficient motive of morality. These latter-day Kantians, if we may call them that, seek to establish a theological discourse about ethics that is at least relatively independent of dogmatics but which also chips away at the sharp distinction Kant drew between God as a concept of moral reason and God as the object of a historical faith, and which assigns greater roles to God as the ground of the moral principle and for religion as a motive for morality than Kant allowed. What remains essentially Kantian, however, is the notion that Christian faith and life are to be evaluated in terms of their conformity to natural morality, however the latter is understood.[39] We may describe as Schleiermacher's theological successors those who respond to this priority of natural morality as Schleiermacher responded to Kant, namely, by treating Christian ethics as the description of the ethical life of the church as a historical community, while either conceding universal morality to philosophical reason (as Schleiermacher's nineteenth-century heirs did) or dispensing with universal morality altogether (as his contemporary heirs tend to do).[40] Proponents of this position often appeal to Barth, and they do so legitimately insofar as they return ethics to the discursive space of the church. However, their departures

---

[38] The first tendency is more prevalent in Protestant and the latter in Catholic moral theology. Examples of the first tendency include both Troeltschian liberals such as Rendtorff and Anabaptists such as McClendon. Examples of the second tendency include Catholic theologians, the most influential of which was Josef Fuchs, who in the aftermath of the Second Vatican Council found in Christian revelation the ultimate motivation for a morality whose ground and content are in human nature or reason.

[39] We may include in this category James Gustafson, *Ethics from a Theocentric Perspective*, 2 vols. (Chicago: University of Chicago Press, 1981, 1984); Trutz Rendtorff, *Ethics*, 2 vols. (Philadelphia: Fortress Press, 1986); and William Schweiker, *Responsibility and Christian Ethics* (New York: Cambridge University Press, 1995). Of course, none of these theologians considers himself a Kantian in the strict sense, but our point here is only that Kant gave classical expression to a way of relating theology and ethics that is widespread in modern theology.

[40] We may include in this latter category Stanley Hauerwas, in his many writings, and James McClendon, as already discussed. Again, neither Hauerwas nor McClendon considers himself a follower of Schleiermacher, and mostly for good reason; however, Schleiermacher gave classic expression to the notion of Christian ethics as the description of an ecclesial form of life over which no rational morality can claim normative authority.

from Barth are quite significant: their discourse on ethics is not a strictly dogmatic discourse; their descriptive method implies the assumptions about the visibility of goodness Barth rejects; and they relieve theological ethics of the burdens which a universal ethic must assume.

We might, in a polemical vein, attempt to identify these two positions with positions Barth explicitly rejected, namely, an apologetic effort to find a ground for theological ethics in moral philosophy and a defensive effort to place theological ethics beyond the hegemonic reach of moral philosophy by confining it to a region where the latter has no jurisdiction (namely, the church).[41] But today's heirs of Kant and Schleiermacher are more sophisticated than the positions Barth criticized. From his perspective, however, it is sufficient to point out that both positions rely on the viability of an extra-dogmatic theological discourse, and such discourses, for Barth, inevitably end up speaking about God in a way that abstracts from God's self-revelation in Christ, and therefore from what God does for us in Christ and summons us to confirm, substituting for this an ethic based on what we must make of ourselves. The answer to our question of how persuasive Barth's account is must ultimately be decided here. His argument rests less on the extent to which the whole of modern theological ethics can be assimilated to the legacy of pietism and rationalism than on the inability of ethics outside of dogmatics to sustain the proper relationship of ethics to divine grace.

Where does Barth's rejection of the separation of ethics from dogmatics leave him? It would be a mistake to interpret his historical narrative as a call for a return to Protestant orthodoxy. While he refuses to indict orthodoxy for a neglect of ethics, Barth does charge the latter with three errors. While treating ethics within dogmatics, orthodoxy (1) confined ethics to a few doctrines (usually the topoi of law, sin, and sanctification) rather than engaging in a comprehensive treatment of the ethical aspects of doctrine; (2) treated Christian goodness as visible rather than hidden; and (3) inaugurated the articulation of a naturalistic ground of ethics which culminated in the Enlightenment.[42] In other words, it was orthodoxy which set the terms in which its pietist and rationalist successors would declare the independence of ethics from dogmatics. Rather than returning to orthodoxy, then, Barth will reformulate what he takes to be the position of Luther and Calvin, a position from which orthodoxy, by committing the three errors just noted, made the first significant departure.[43] What is this position of

---

[41] *Ethics*, 21–8/33–44; CD II/2, 520–8/577–86.

[42] CD I/2, 785/877 f.

[43] This narrative offers one instance of a pattern in Barth's moral theology, which consists in part in an effort to reformulate certain themes that earlier Protestant ethics failed to stress sufficiently or state unambiguously—failures that led to certain modern aberrations that became explicit in pietism and rationalism and remained in subsequent Protestant ethics. Barth's self-appointed task is to eliminate these aberrations by restating the earlier themes with the rigor and emphasis that, he thinks, was either lacking or was compromised in Protestant orthodoxy and in some cases in the Reformers as well.

the Reformers to which Barth turns? Against the first error of orthodoxy Barth asserts that the Reformers never treated any matter of faith or its object without regard to the conduct of the believer.[44] He will follow their precedent by including extensive treatments of ethics in each of his dogmatic topoi (revelation, God, creation, reconciliation, and redemption). Against the second error of orthodoxy, Barth asserts that it is because 'they held the insight of Col. 3: 3 so firmly' that '[t]he ethics of Luther and Calvin is to be sought in their dogmatics and not elsewhere.'[45] He will once again follow them by treating the good, as it is formulated in the context of each dogmatic topic, as established and fulfilled in Jesus Christ and as summoning other human beings, from this Christological site, to confirm it in their own being and conduct. Finally, because of this conviction of the hiddenness of goodness with Christ, the Reformers avoided the third error of orthodoxy, rejecting a naturalistic ground of ethics in spite of their general acceptance of the existence of a natural law apart from divine revelation.

Here, then, is Barth's methodological solution to the problem of ethics: Ethics will attest grace rather than betray grace if its place in every dogmatic topic is clarified and if in each topic its proper relation to Christology is maintained. Ethics will be found everywhere in dogmatics, and everywhere it will be found playing under the very same Christological rule. Election, creation, justification, sanctification, vocation—each topic will yield its own ethical content, but in each case that content will involve the establishment and fulfillment of the good in Christ and its summons to others to confirm what is accomplished in Christ. This is what is meant by the enclosure of ethics within dogmatics, though as we will now see, it is just as appropriate, and perhaps more so, to speak of dogmatics expressing itself as ethics, yet without ceasing to be dogmatics.

Dogmatics *as* Ethics

We will have to wait until Chapter 5 to see whether Barth succeeds in treating human moral action under these terms. At this point we are investigating the methodological aspects of his proposal to do ethics as an exercise of dogmatics in light of the suspicion that this proposal is doomed to failure. Having now established what is at stake for Barth in this proposal, we are in a position to state more precisely what that proposal is. What exactly does it mean to do ethics as an exercise in dogmatics? The key to the answer is found in Barth's determination to place human conduct under the same terms that govern the rest of the reality of human beings as beneficiaries of God's grace. In his insistence that Christian goodness or holiness is hidden with Christ, Barth denies that this goodness or holiness constitutes an exception to the objects of the rest of

---

[44] CD I/2, 783/876.
[45] CD I/2, 783/876 f.

Christian proclamation, which are also hidden with Christ. It is this assumption that Christian goodness or holiness is an exception that makes possible the ambition expressed in pietism and rationalism. It follows that the critical examination of church proclamation on human conduct will fall to the same discipline as that which examines the rest of Christian proclamation, namely dogmatics, and it will be subject to the same dependence on the divine revelation of what is hidden. By contrast, under the assumption that the goodness of which Christian ethics speaks is found in the pious Christian (and therefore ultimately in the natural human being) ethics marks a transition from what is revealed in Christ to what can be discovered in the Christian herself, that is, in the visible effects of grace (pietism), and expressed in terms of a general moral norm, that is, a rational moral law (rationalism).

Of course, ethics does mark a shift from what God does for human beings to what human beings are to do (or refrain from doing) in response. But, Barth denies that a theological consideration of human conduct must undergo the 'fatal interchange of the subjects God and man' that with such a transition 'becomes the true constitutive principle of ethics.'[46] He denies that there is any change of subjects because the Word of God itself poses and answers the question of its addressee and therefore of human conduct:

Even in its conception and doctrine of revelation dogmatics itself already gives an account of what becomes of the person to whom God's revelation comes. What should we do, we who claim that we have heard and believed the Word of God? Because in its fundamental considerations it already recognizes and treats the problem of the Christian person as its own problem, dogmatics takes ethics into itself and therefore makes a separate theological ethics superfluous. For dogmatics itself, without ceasing to be reflection on the Word of God, is also ethics.[47]

It follows that ethics is properly constituted not by a turn from the divine to the human subject but by the determination of the human subject made by the Word of God and the summons to the human subject to correspond to this determination. This in turn means that ethics belongs to the same inquiry that investigates the Word of God in all its other respects, namely dogmatics.

Only now are we in a position to understand Barth's controversial proposal regarding dogmatics and ethics. In order to rule out an independent ethic it is not sufficient that dogmatics determine the place of ethics or authorize the latter. One may insist on this determination or authorization while still undergoing the change of subjects Barth rejects. For example, one may argue, on exclusively dogmatic grounds, that justification is what God does and ethical action is what human beings do in grateful response to God. Alternatively, one may argue, still on dogmatic grounds, that the relative independence of the human being as

---

[46] CD I/2, 790/884.
[47] CD I/2, 371/408.

creature is the ground of a natural goodness grounded in human nature. In these and similar cases dogmatics itself may certify an independent ethic precisely because dogmatics itself effects the change of subjects from a goodness hidden with Christ to a goodness visible in the nature or conduct of the Christian. Barth must therefore show instead how dogmatics, whatever else it is, is *itself* also ethics.

We can understand Barth's entire moral theology as an effort to vindicate this claim. We will illustrate it here with reference to the doctrine of election. The initial assertion that the Word of God determines the goodness of human conduct follows the path of dogmatics to its fuller development in Barth's treatment of the God revealed in God's Word, that is, in the doctrine of God. God is known and knowable only in Jesus Christ, and this means that the doctrine of God is not only about God but also about God in God's freely chosen, but once chosen, essential relationship with that which is other than God, namely the human being Jesus and all human beings who are included in him. This relationship is the election of divine grace, in which God establishes God's covenant with human beings. But, as we have seen, this covenant relation is not exhausted by electing grace. God does not elect human beings without electing grace itself also claiming them. 'There is no grace without the lordship and claim of grace. There is no dogmatics that is not at the same time necessarily also ethics.'[48] Dogmatics learns in the course of its own inquiry that God does not elect human beings without also commanding them to confirm their status as God's elect in their being and doing. It follows that a dogmatic treatment of the doctrine of God must include not only a doctrine of election but, along with it, a doctrine of the command of God.

To the extent that Barth can show with reference to every dogmatic topic how the Word of God itself determines the goodness of human conduct, he vindicates his claim that a moral theology separate from dogmatics is superfluous, that at every point dogmatics is 'at the same time necessarily also ethics.' The Word of God, of course, is in the most proper sense Jesus Christ himself, so that the initial claim that the Word of God determines human conduct is from the start a Christological claim. Again, the doctrine of election exhibits this point clearly. 'What right conduct is for man is determined absolutely in the right conduct of God. It is determined in Jesus Christ. He is the electing God and elected man in one. But he is also the sanctifying God and sanctified man in one. In his person God has acted rightly towards us. And in the same person man has also acted rightly for us.'[49] Dogmatics does not change the subject when it turns to ethics because the goodness of the Christian—whether we are speaking of the norm of that goodness or of its actual fulfillment—is hidden with Christ. Dogmatics, without ceasing to be reflection on the Word of God, is itself ethics.

---

[48] CD II/2, 12/11 (revised).
[49] CD II/2, 538 f./598.

It is appropriate to illustrate Barth's proposal with reference to the doctrine of election since the relation of election and sanctification comprises the basic structure of ethics that will be repeated in particular forms under the headings of creation and reconciliation. The ultimate test of the proposal will be whether it can succeed in comprehending creation, justification, and sanctification under these terms without distorting them. We must once again defer this matter to Chapter 5. Our point here is simply to illustrate methodologically how Barth places ethics under the terms which govern the rest of dogmatics and thus claims to rule out the need for an ethic independent of dogmatics.

Dogmatics as Ethics

If dogmatics is itself ethics in the sense we have just described, this means that moral theology will conduct its inquiries as a dogmatic discipline. Here is where the suspicion arises that dogmatics cannot do justice to ethics. Barth himself fuels this suspicion by readily conceding that ethics undertaken as a dogmatic discipline will differ quite radically from ethics as we generally think of it. Just how radical the divergence will be is expressed sharply and succinctly by Barth himself:

The problem of ethics generally—the law or good or value which it seeks as a standard by which human action and modes of action are to be measured, and according to which they are to be performed, the problem of the truth and knowledge of the good—is no problem at all in the ethics immanent in the Christian conception of God, in the doctrine of the command of God. For in virtue of the fact that the command of God is the form of his electing grace, it is the starting-point of every ethical question and answer. It is the starting-point which is already given and to that extent presupposed and certain in itself.... And, conversely, that which is no problem at all to ethical thought generally, or only a problem which can be lightly pushed aside and left open—the actual situation of human beings in face of the question by which they are confronted when they answer the ethical question, their actual commitment to the good, their actual distance from it and the actual overcoming of this distance (not by themselves, but by the actuality of the good itself)—this is the burning problem in Christian ethics, the very aim and content of the whole ethical enquiry and reply.[50]

This formulation raises major questions about the viability of the execution of ethics as a dogmatic discipline. First, how can any ethic presuppose its starting point in this way? In what sense is the norm or standard of ethics already given prior to ethical inquiry? Why is it not the task of ethical inquiry to determine this norm or standard? Can an ethic that presupposes its starting point in this way count as a rational inquiry at all? Even if these formal problems can be surmounted, on what grounds is the command of God as the form of electing

---

[50] CD II/2, 519/576.

grace to be presupposed as the starting point? Second, what exactly does Barth mean by saying that the problem of the doctrine of the command of God is not the determination of the good but the relation of human beings to a good that is already determined?

These questions take us to the heart of Barth's moral theology. We begin with the questions regarding how the doctrine of the command of God can presuppose the standard by which human conduct is measured and in what sense it does so. The doctrine of the command of God is an aspect of dogmatics; as such it exists in the same relation to the Word of God as does the rest of dogmatics. The doctrine of the command of God 'only intervenes with its distinctive method because, long before it arose, its subject matter [*Gegenstand*] proclaimed itself,' demanding a rationally disciplined (*wissenschaftliche*) treatment, that is, one appropriate to its nature.[51] Negatively, this means that the doctrine of the command of God cannot submit its standard to human inquiry. 'We cannot first make a problem of the reality of the good in the command of God, or the reality of the command of God as the sum of the good, and then come back to the affirmation of them in the form of a solution to the problem.'[52] To submit the standard of ethics to inquiry in this way is to place it under the epistemic authority of the human subject, and this is, however subtly, to make it an object of human choice. But like the rest of dogmatic discourse, ethical discourse, if it is to be rational in the sense of appropriateness to its object, must be a discourse of obedience precisely because its subject matter is the Word of God. The Word of God constitutes its hearer as its addressee; any inquiry into it is possible only from the position of this addressee, and thus from the position of obedience. It follows that the ethics of the command of God cannot treat the ethical question as a question for human inquiry to answer. 'We do not know any human action which is free, i.e., exempted from decision in relation to God's command, or neutral in regard to it. And for just the same reason we do not know any free investigation [*Fragen*] of good and evil.'[53] The ethical inquirer is therefore in the same position with respect to the good as is the agent who is bound by it: 'This good is chosen only in obedience . . . because we are chosen ourselves and can only make this one choice.'[54] Positively, then, the doctrine of the command of God 'represents the awareness . . . that "what is good" has been "said" to man (Micah 6: 8) so that man is prohibited from wanting to say it to himself and commanded to repeat [*nachzusagen*] plainly and faithfully what has been said to him. This is what theological thinking calls ethical reflection [*Besinnung*] and understanding.'[55] In these stark terms—perhaps too stark, since the mechanical

[51] CD II/2, 537/596 (revised).
[52] CD II/2, 536/595.
[53] CD II/2, 535/594.
[54] CD II/2, 536/595.
[55] CD II/2, 537/596 (revised).

kind of repetition denoted by *nachsagen* is hard to reconcile with the reference to reflection and understanding and, as we will see, with Barth's actual view and practice of ethical inquiry—the distinction between a standard presupposed by ethical inquiry and a standard we establish through inquiry becomes the distinction between what is said to us by the Word of God—and therefore addresses us from outside—and what we say to ourselves, a distinction we examined in the previous chapter.

We now know why the doctrine of the command of God *must* presuppose its standard. But *can* it do so? How can any moral theology avoid becoming an inquiry that identifies a standard of the good through a certain rational procedure? And if it is not such an inquiry, what exactly is it? Barth's answer to these questions is that to the extent that the doctrine of the command of God holds to the Word of God as its proper subject matter, the Word of God constitutes it as its witness. 'Like theology in general, it is not concerned to penetrate to the foundation of things. It can only bear witness to the foundation which all things actually have . . .'[56] As we have seen, for Barth the Word of God itself claims the discourse that speaks about it, and it requires that this discourse speak about it in a way that is appropriate to its nature—appropriate, that is, to something which no human speech is adequate in and of itself to represent. We are left, then, with a reversal in the relation of ethical inquiry to the good. Whereas ethics in general attempts to establish the good through ethical inquiry, in the doctrine of the command of God the good itself—electing grace established and fulfilled in Christ—establishes ethical inquiry as its witness. Moral theology arrives after the good has already addressed itself to us and has placed us, its addressees, in the position of obedience to it; its task is now to attest and explain this good and the position in which it places us. Once again, ethical inquiry is in the same position as the ethical agent whose obedient action also attests the grace of God.

Can we say that Barth's own discourse of ethics is constituted as witness in this way? Does it attest and explain the command of God without establishing it and thereby betraying it? Does it remain in the position of the addressee? A definitive verdict on these questions can be pronounced only after a thorough examination of Barth's ethics. But the conviction that moral theology must be a discourse of obedient witness is apparent in Barth's avoidance of the genre of philosophical argument—much to the annoyance of readers who think that ethics must assume this genre. For Barth, the fundamental difference between theology and philosophy is that the former begins where the latter ends, thinking from what has already been given to human inquiry rather than thinking towards what must be established by human inquiry.[57] We will see in the following section that philosophy nevertheless has a legitimate and necessary role to play in moral

---

[56] CD II/2, 536/595.
[57] 'Fate and Idea in Theology,' 51–60; 'Philosophy and Theology,' in *The Way of Theology in Karl Barth*, ed. Rumscheidt, 79, 87 f.

theology. Indeed, for Barth the very decision to articulate the *doctrine* of the command of God as the *ethics* of the command of God—a decision dictated by the subject matter itself—inevitably places moral theology in a relationship with moral philosophy. But Barth's moral theology is not a theory of ethics whose plausibility or lack thereof rests on philosophical criteria for what a justifiable moral theory must be. It is not a *theory* at all, but rather a *doctrine* of the command of God, and we have seen that for Barth this means that the inquirer exists in a nonreciprocal relation to the object and in a relation of responsibility to others.

It is in precisely this sense that moral theology presupposes its standard. And because its relation to its subject matter requires it to presuppose its standard in this way, moral theology must rigorously maintain its focus on Jesus Christ. This brings us to our second question, regarding ethics as the relation of human beings to a good that is already determined. We repeat a point made in the previous subsection: 'What right conduct is for man is determined absolutely in the right conduct of God. It is determined in Jesus Christ. He is the electing God and elected man in one. But he is also the sanctifying God and sanctified man in one. In his person God has acted rightly towards us. And in the same person man has also acted rightly for us.'[58] Jesus Christ is therefore both the standard (*Maßstab*) of ethics, that is, the rule by which human conduct is measured, and the fulfillment of this standard. In him 'the command of God is established and fulfilled and revealed as such.'[59] The precise sense in which dogmatics is ethics now becomes clear: 'If dogmatics, if the doctrine of God, is ethics, this means necessarily and decisively that it is the attestation of that *divine* ethics, the attestation of the good of the command issued to Jesus Christ and fulfilled by him.'[60]

Once again, this requirement involves a fundamental alteration in the method of moral theology. Barth articulates it in opposition to the tendency to identify the standard of human conduct not with Jesus Christ but with an ideal or empirical description of the life of the Christian. Moral theology thereby undergoes the fatal transition from the goodness of God to human goodness as its focus. This brings us full circle to where we began: with Barth's objection to 'the opinion that the goodness, that is, the holiness of the Christian character, unlike the other objective content of Christian proclamation, is not hidden with Christ in God (in spite of Col. 3: 3), but can be directly perceived and therefore demonstrated, described and set up as a norm.'[61] It is a mistake to find the norm or standard of ethics in empirical or ideal descriptions of the good or holy person because the latter does not exist in herself but in Christ. What moral

---

[58] CD II/2, 538 f./598.
[59] CD II/2, 539/598.
[60] CD II/2, 518/575.
[61] CD I/2, 782/875.

theology must investigate, then, is '[our] participation in the righteousness of [Jesus Christ] and not [our] own abstract immanent righteousness.' The content of ethics for Barth is the analogical relation between the goodness realized in the humanity of Jesus Christ and our own goodness, a relation that expresses our participation in Christ, which itself is grounded in the intra-Trinitarian relation of Father and Son. Good human action will in every instance confirm the actualization of the good in Christ. In all its inquiry into the goodness of human action, moral theology is therefore concerned with 'the question whether and to what extent human action is a glorification [*Lobpreis*] of the grace of Jesus Christ.'[62] This is precisely what Barth means by his claim that the doctrine of the command of God is not preoccupied with the standard of the good (which is already given) but rather with the position of human beings with respect to the good.

Dogmatics as *Ethics*

Thus far we have established that insofar as the Word of God determines the goodness of human conduct, dogmatics need not, and cannot, go outside or beyond itself to establish ethics. Yet, the suspicion is likely to arise that the determination of good conduct by the Word of God does not really count as ethics. What exactly does it mean to say that the claim of electing grace on human conduct is an *ethical* claim? What precisely is Barth saying when he describes dogmatic inquiry into the command of God as *ethical* inquiry? On what grounds is the *doctrine* of the command of God also the *ethics* of the command of God? These questions cannot be answered by simply repeating the fact of the determination of the goodness of human conduct by the Word of God. To account for that determination, Barth refers to notions of law, command, sanctification, and the like. These are not necessarily ethical notions, and the question is in what sense they allow or require articulation in terms of ethics. The answer to this question requires a consideration of the relation between the doctrine of the command of God and a general conception of ethics. The stakes are high: On the one hand, if the doctrine of the command of God does not genuinely count as ethics, the call for a separate moral theology to supplement dogmatics will sound again in spite of Barth's demonstration that the Word of God determines the goodness of human conduct. On the other hand, if the doctrine of the command of God falls under a general conception of ethics, moral theology may turn out to be simply one instance or specification of something that can be characterized apart from dogmatic claims.

Barth begins with a programmatic point: Dogmatics is free to appropriate whatever concepts it finds useful without being bound to the meanings such

---

[62] CD II/2, 540/599 f.

concepts may have in extra-dogmatic contexts. In the present case, this means that dogmatics will determine in what senses the doctrine of the command of God counts as ethics rather than subjecting the doctrine of the command of God to one or another conception of ethics.[63] In what follows, Barth will engage in a dialectical process of determining in what senses the doctrine of the command of God is and is not ethics in the sense of a general conception of the latter. Like ethics in general, the doctrine of the command of God 'seems in some way to be a matter of the investigation of the goodness of human action.'[64] As such, it raises a distinct type of question with respect to human action. Following Kant, Barth formulates this question in its practical or agent-centered form; it is the question 'What should we do?' To ask this question as an ethical question is to interrogate particular actions from the standpoint of general modes of action, inquiring as to their conformity to the laws or continuities that govern human behavior. But unlike other inquiries into these laws or continuities, ethical inquiry questions the latter with respect to their validity, that is, their 'genuineness and rightness and value.' On what grounds can one claim that a certain action should be performed because it is an expression of a valid continuity, one that deserves recognition as normatively binding? For Barth, this question of validity is what distinguishes ethical inquiry from other inquiries. So defined, the ethical question is an open one: the question of validity is not settled by a description of one or another kind of continuity of behavior (for example, the conformity of human actions to laws of nature, to custom, to positive law, to historical processes). Ethics is therefore a critical discipline; to ask the ethical question is to interrogate, in the name of the good, the various continuities to which normative force may be uncritically ascribed. The ethical as such is thus the crisis of the 'ought' on every 'is.'[65] Finally, the ethical question is not simply one question among others but is *the* question of human existence. 'For it is as he acts that man exists as a person.'[66] The question of the genuineness, rightness, and value of human action is thus also the question of the genuineness, rightness, and value of human existence as such. For Barth as for the strand of modernity examined in the previous chapter, the ethical question is the question of the meaning and significance of human existence.[67] It is important to keep in mind that he, too, accords a certain primacy to the ethical, albeit within the terms set by dogmatics.

---

[63] CD II/2, 513/568 f.

[64] CD II/2, 520/576.

[65] CD II/2, 515/571.

[66] CD II/2, 516/572. While this may appear to be a general anthropological claim surreptitiously smuggled into theology, it follows from Barth's understanding of the divine claiming of human self-determination (through human activity) in correspondence with God's determination of human beings (through divine activity).

[67] These two properties of distinctiveness and primacy appear to matter more for Barth at this point than the question of whether the ethical is primarily a matter of the good or the right, as the ambiguity of the phrase 'genuineness, rightness, and value' indicates.

For Barth, the ethical question so understood is a general human question, one that in its concrete form is inescapable. 'What is the right choice? What ought I to do? What ought we to do? This is the question before which every person is objectively placed.' There is nothing distinctively theological or Christian about this question; it is the question of 'philosophy, politics, and pedagogy' just as it is the question of the church.[68] Here, ethics in general is a semantic notion: it refers to a shared question by virtue of which the doctrine of the command of God may count as ethics. Because the doctrine of the command of God is an investigation of this question—it, too, raises the question of human conduct in its relation to a valid law or continuity—it is appropriate to refer to it as the *ethics* of the command of God, as Barth does and as we will now do. However, ethics in general refers not only to the question itself but also to the act in which it is posed (its pragmatics). Who addresses this question? To whom or to what is it addressed? At this level, the ethics of the command of God and ethics in general diverge. The general conception of ethics treats the ethical question as a question to be posed and answered by a philosophical inquiry that identifies (that is, discovers or invents, depending on whether one is a realist or a constructivist) and justifies a notion of the good or right as a valid norm of conduct. But we have already seen that the ethics of the command of God cannot treat the ethical question in this way. For this ethic, the answer to this question is already given in the electing grace of God. Therefore it is the electing grace of God itself, taking the form of the command, which poses the ethical question. 'We cannot understand the ethical question . . . as if there were an ethical question in itself and for itself, as if it were not first posed by the grace of God—and not only posed but already answered by the grace of God.'[69] It remains an open (that is, a critical) question—not in the sense that human inquiry poses to the various continuities of human action the question of their validity but only 'in the sense and to the extent that our human life and will and action are put in question by the command of God and the revelation of the good which takes place in it . . .'[70] For the ethics of the command of God, then, the ethical question ('What should we do?') is not posed in a search for the good. In that sense, the question is already answered.[71] Rather, the ethical question is posed in response to the demand of electing grace that human beings confirm in their conduct their status as the elect of God. When we ask, 'What should we do?' we are not trying to determine the identity of the good. Rather, we are attesting that we in our action are interrogated by a good that addresses us and in that sense is

---

[68] CD II/2, 535/594.

[69] CD II/2, 518/574.

[70] CD II/2, 518/575.

[71] Once again, it is in 'Fate and Idea in Theology' and in 'Philosophy and Theology' that the claim that theology takes as its starting point what philosophy posits as its ending point is articulated most clearly. See *The Way of Theology in Karl Barth*, 51–60, 79, 87 f.

already known. As we will see in Chapter 6, ethical inquiry for Barth is the test or examination of our conduct with regard to its conformity to grace.

Barth thus finds a double ambiguity in ethics as generally conceived. On the one hand, the doctrine of the command of God is expressed in terms of ethics because God's grace itself is put to us as the inescapable demand that we confirm it in our conduct. Insofar as ethics in general treats the ethical question as a categorical question posed to human conduct, ethics in general 'confirms the truth of the grace of God which as it is addressed to man puts the question of the good with such priority over all others that man cannot evade it and no other question can completely hide or replace it.'[72] On the other hand, ethics in general refers to the human effort to determine for ourselves, in disregard of the claim of divine grace, what is good. In this sense it must be rejected, for divine grace has already answered the ethical question; any human effort to answer it can only be, in the strictest sense, a rejection of grace, and thus sin. (We examined this notorious identification of ethics in general with sin in the previous chapter.) Ethics in general is also ambiguous insofar as its generality may be understood in two ways. On the one hand, there is the generality of the ethical question itself, the question of the goodness of human conduct which, as we have seen, retains its semantic identity across the radically different pragmatic contexts in which it is posed. On the other hand, generality may imply that the ethics of the command of God is a particular mode or specification of a conception of ethics which must be acknowledged as prior to or independent of the doctrine of the command of God. Barth, of course, denies this; with regard to this sense he consistently contrasts the general conception of ethics with the ethics of the command of God. When the doctrine of the command of God expresses itself as the ethics of the command of God it does not place itself under a general conception of which it is one instance among others.

The relation of the ethics of the command of God to ethics in general can now be made clear and succinct. The ethical question is a question about the goodness of human conduct and therefore of human existence. Insofar as it too raises this distinctive question, the ethics of the command of God coincides with the general conception of ethics. It *coincides* with this conception; it does not *derive* from it. The ethics of the command of God is not merely one form of a question about human conduct and human existence that is posed by human thought or human life in general. As the answer to the ethical question, electing grace is not the answer to a general human question. Instead, the ethics of the command of God, in its effort to attest the reality of electing grace, appropriates the general conception of ethics in order to show how electing grace expresses itself as the demand that human beings confirm it in their conduct. The ethics of the command of God never ceases to be a doctrine; it does not depart from its

[72] CD II/2, 518/574.

dogmatic site in order to place itself under a general conception of ethics. At the same time, its coincidence with the general conception of ethics permits and even requires it to hold a continuous conversation with ethics in general, as we will see in the next section.

Before turning to that conversation, we must face a final problem. The question of the good as the question of validity, the sharp distinction between the form of morality and its content, the relation between 'ought' (*Sollen*) and 'is' (*Sein*), and the categorical status of the moral norm—all of these features reflect in rough form the neo-Kantian contexts of Barth's formative years.[73] Can Barth's ethics of the command of God stand independent of this particular and, today at least, controversial moral theory? More to the point: Can the ethics of the command of God coincide with *any* general conception of ethics, or are various general conceptions more and less compatible with it? It would seem that the ethics of the command of God requires a conception of the ethical that (1) can express the command of God as an obligation which commands categorically and addresses us from outside ourselves; (2) can distinguish between the semantics of the ethical question itself and the pragmatic contexts in which it is posed; and (3) can retain a formal character that does not prejudice the claim that the command of God is not derivable from conditions outside of or prior to its own occurrence. These requisites clearly favor and perhaps require a Kantian conception of some kind, though not necessarily a neo-Kantian one. If so, the formulation of the doctrine of the command of God in terms of ethics is not nearly as theory-neutral as Barth implies, and moral theology cannot be as indifferent to the fate of moral theories outside of theology as he assumes.

---

[73] It is difficult to overemphasize the extent to which Barth's ethics of the command of God will assume a basically Kantian structure, a structure Barth took so for granted that he did not seriously consider alternative formulations of the ethical question—eudaemonistic formulations, for example, which do not treat the good as something by which human beings are radically questioned. The notion of the ethical as a critical enterprise, as an 'ought' that calls every 'is' into question, was strongly stated in the opening paragraphs of Barth's 1922 lecture on 'The Problem of Ethics Today.' At this stage ethics for Barth repeats, or participates in, the eternity–time dialectic of the second edition of Barth's *The Epistle to the Romans*: The good is eternal and cannot be identified with any achievement or state of affairs in time; to raise the question of the good, the ethical question, is therefore to bring the crisis of the eternal (= the ought) on everything temporal (= the is), including oneself as a temporal creature. Twenty years later, the eternity–time dialectic is gone and the identity between the ethical crisis and the crisis of divine grace has given way to a more complex coincidence between them, as we have seen. However, the neo-Kantian context remains in the sharp distinction Barth draws between the moral law as normative and all other laws of human conduct as descriptive as well as in his understanding of the ethical question as a critical interrogation of all attributions of normative status to (descriptive) constants of human behavior (CD II/2, 514 f./569–71). There is now a wide body of literature in analytical moral philosophy questioning the distinction of normative and descriptive on the grounds that in ordinary language and practice the evaluation and description of human conduct and character are often inseparable. See especially Iris Murdoch, *The Sovereignty of Good* (London: Routledge and Kegan Paul, 1970) and Bernard Williams, *Ethics and the Limits of Philosophy* (Cambridge, Mass.: Harvard University Press, 1985).

3. MORAL THEOLOGY AND MORAL PHILOSOPHY

We have already seen how the ethics of the command of God makes use of a general concept of ethics, and this use raises questions regarding the status of the latter from the standpoint of the former: Can moral theology, the discipline which attests and explains the command of God, recognize as valid another, nontheological form of ethical inquiry? Again, much is at stake in this question. An affirmative answer would seem to authorize, on theological grounds, a discourse of ethics apart from dogmatics—precisely what Barth has taken such pains to rule out; while a negative answer would seem to court an objection to the enclosure of ethics within dogmatics that is the most serious objection of all precisely because it is a moral objection, namely, that dogmatics is an imperialistic or even a totalizing discourse which either eliminates or absorbs every other ethical discourse. And since for Barth, the matter of the relation of church and state is never far from that of the relation of theology and philosophy, the question before us has a political as well as a strictly ethical dimension.[74]

By posing the question in this way, as a question concerning moral theology and its other, we may be accused of demanding that Barth take up a position outside of his own dogmatic project and subject that project to an alien question. But for Barth himself, the question of the relation of moral theology to a nontheological form of ethical inquiry is not only the methodological question of how to relate two possible approaches to or sources of ethics; it is also the question of the relation of moral theology to its other. Speaking favorably of Kant's acknowledgment of the possibility of a theology based on divine revelation which is 'not only relatively but absolutely different' from the theology (if we may call it that) which Kant undertakes from within the boundaries of reason alone, Barth remarks that '[w]ith such a man a conversation from the other point of view, from the point of view of a completely different theology, is possible . . . ,' while with those who do not recognize this other form of theology as 'a distinct opposite of their own possibility' but who in one way or another confuse it with a theology based on reason—here Barth mentions Rousseau, Lessing, Herder, Schleiermacher, and Hegel—'it is fundamentally impossible to conduct a conversation . . .'[75] It is the recognition of the other as other that makes genuine conversation possible. If Kant has extended this recognition to the other from the side of philosophy, should we not expect Barth to do the same from the side of theology? Yet, as we will see, Barth will struggle to determine precisely what kind of recognition moral theology can legitimately accord moral philosophy and what exactly is to be gained from the conversation. It will also

---

[74] Barth explicitly relates the issue of the relation of theology and philosophy to that of the relation of church and state in 'Fate and Idea in Theology,' 27, 30, 31.
[75] *Protestant Theology in the Nineteenth Century*, 267/237 f.

become clear that the encounter of moral theology and moral philosophy will involve an irreducibly agonistic element which seems to be inseparable from the post-Enlightenment context in which the encounter takes place.

A Complex Interrelation

It is already clear that our question will not allow for an easy answer. Our attempt to give an answer begins where we left off in the previous section. Moral theology and moral philosophy share a common metaethical concept of the good as the critical question posed to human conduct, a concept which for Barth is implied in the normative ethical question of moral deliberation, 'What should we do?' To ask this question in the practical context of moral deliberation is to ask the critical question of human conduct. At the same time, we have seen that the doctrine of the command of God and ethics in general understand this ethical question in opposite ways. In one case, it is the question human beings raise as those who are summoned by a good that is already known and which now questions them as to their conformity to it. In the other case it is the question human beings ask themselves in their attempt to identify the good through the self-reflective activity of reason or conscience. Given this distinction, and its importance to Barth, it is not clear how the question regarding nontheological ethics can be seriously entertained in the first place. The sharp distinction between the question addressed to human beings in and as Jesus Christ and the question human beings address to themselves in their efforts to determine the good seems to imply an obvious answer to the question of the validity of any nontheological ethic: *Nein.* If by a nontheological ethic we mean an ethic grounded in the 'know thyself' which one addresses to oneself, that is, 'a self-reflection, a self-understanding and a self-responsibility in which man has to tell himself what is good,' then the answer is resolutely negative. 'For there is no good which is not obedience to God's command,' and '[w]hat begins with the human self cannot end with the knowledge of God and of his command.'[76]

Yet, as is so often the case with Barth, the issue is more complicated than it first appears. We will consider two ways in which moral theology for Barth engages nontheological forms of ethics. Each way involves both opportunities and temptations for moral theology. The first way is familiar. We have already seen that at a formal or semantic level the ethics of the command of God coincides with what Barth calls ethics in general, that is, moral philosophy. At this level, moral theology has limited yet legitimate recourse to moral philosophy. The limits are clear: Moral theology must not forget that the ethical question is posed and answered by the grace of God, and that the formal treatment of ethics as question and answer in moral philosophy therefore has its origin and meaning

---

[76] CD II/2, 540 f./600 f.

(*Sinn*) in the command of God rather than in philosophical reflection. In no way, then, will moral theology treat moral philosophy as an authority before which it must legitimize its own question and answer—the grace of God in the form of command—by showing how it is grounded in or included in the philosophical question and answer. To do so would be to forfeit its object or theme (*Gegenstand*): For moral theology, as we have seen, the answer to the ethical question is already given, and an already given answer which interrogates the questioner cannot be derived from a question both posed and answered by the questioner. Barth therefore insists that 'there is no general moral reality autonomously confronting the Christian moral reality.'[77]

It follows from this that moral theology cannot allow itself to be positioned by philosophical moral inquiry as the ground of its own inquiry but must rather position moral philosophy with respect to its own claims, approaching the latter 'with the understanding that it has its origin and meaning from the divine command, which objectively applies to man, whatever attitude man may take to it.' The moral theologian will approach moral philosophy knowing that the Word of God is addressed there, too, even though it is concealed in the philosophical articulation of the question and answer and not acknowledged by the philosopher. On this ground, moral philosophy can be for moral theology a witness (*Zeugen*) to the ethical knowledge moral theology obtains from the command of God, and to that extent a legitimate, and indeed a necessary conversation partner (*Gesprächspartner*) from whom moral theology, in faithfulness to its own task, must be prepared to receive instruction and even correction (*Korrektur*), since after all its own witness is only human and thus fallible.[78] It is in precisely these terms that Barth treats Kant in the *Church Dogmatics*, rejecting the latter's claim that the principle and motive of morality are established independently of appeals to a divine revelation in history while also articulating the command of God as a categorical demand in terms that clearly reflect instruction and perhaps also correction from Kant.[79]

Does this recognition of moral philosophy as a conversation partner amount to the recognition of moral philosophy as a distinct other with its own proper claim to validity? We must say that it does not. The terms of engagement are set by the relation of moral theology to the Word of God itself, or more precisely, to its form as the command of God, and this has implications for both the stance of moral theology towards moral philosophy and the ultimate status of the latter. On the one hand, because it occupies the position of the addressee, the position of obedience, moral theology is in no position to assert exclusive rights with

---

[77] CD II/2, 543/ 603 (revised). This is the most fundamental difference between Barth and Rendtorff, for whom the world in which human action occurs poses unavoidable ethical questions which theology interprets in its distinctive way, i.e., in light of the relation of humanity to God (*Ethics*, i. 3–7, 19).

[78] CD II/2, 523 f./580 f.

[79] CD II/2, 665–7/742–4.

respect to its object. Its own faithfulness to its object therefore requires it to remain open to the voice of the other, knowing that the Word of God is free to (and does) speak through that voice as well, whether this is acknowledged or not. On the other hand, moral philosophy is recognized only on the grounds that it, too, is objectively in the position of the addressee of the command of God, though it is subjectively unaware of this. Moral philosophy is accorded recognition, but only as the unwitting double of moral theology itself.

We turn now to the second way in which Barth's moral theology engages nontheological forms of ethics. The moral theologian could be tempted to approach moral philosophy not as an allegedly autonomous reality to which she looks for the ground of her own enterprise (as just considered) but as a distinct and complementary form of ethical inquiry which appeals to reason and experience, leaving moral theology free to concentrate on the spheres of revelation or the church. In the first case, it was assumed that moral theology and moral philosophy share a common space of articulation of the ethical question and answer; at issue was the temptation of moral theology to seek its ground in moral philosophy. In this case, however, what is involved is a temptation to assign moral theology and moral philosophy separate spaces of articulation of the ethical question and answer. What is proposed here is that moral theology yield reason and experience to moral philosophy, along with the claim to universality, restricting itself to a particular, distinctively Christian or ecclesial region of human conduct. This, of course, would be to acquiesce in a classic liberal solution to the problem of religious moralities, and Barth will have none of it. Since 'all ethical truth is enclosed in the command of the grace of God' moral theology cannot concede truths of reason or experience to a nontheological inquiry and must itself speak with the binding force of the universal. In other words, the truth attested and explained by moral theology is not true only for Christians or only of an ecclesial reality, nor can there be any question of acknowledging two different and perhaps conflicting truths. More positively, if all ethical truth is enclosed in the command of God then every claim to ethical truth either properly belongs to moral theology or it is not ethical truth at all.

For Barth this means that the relation of moral theology to every other form of ethics is at once comprehensive and exclusive. It is comprehensive in the sense that '[i]t has to take up the legitimate problems and concerns and motives and assertions of every other ethics as such, and therefore after testing them in the light of its own superior principle. It has to listen to all other ethics insofar as it has to receive from them at every point the material for its own reflections.'[80] More colloquially, 'Christian ethics runs through this whole world of morals, tests everything and preserves the best,' that is, 'those things by which from time to time God's grace is best praised.'[81] However, moral theology is exclusive of

---

[80] CD II/2, 527/585 (revised).
[81] Barth, 'Christian Ethics,' in *God Here and Now*, 90.

moral philosophy to the extent that the latter 'tries to deny or obscure its derivation from God's command' and generates content that is inconsistent with the command of God.[82] 'Insofar as a nontheological ethics has for its content a humanity which is grounded in itself and discovers and proclaims itself, theological ethics will have to deny the character of this humanity as humanity and consequently the character of this ethics as ethics.'[83] Once again, this is how Barth in fact treats moral philosophy. For example, he takes from Albert Schweitzer's religious philosophy the principle of reverence for life, tests it in light of what moral theology knows from its own sources about the command of God in the domain of life, and revises the principle accordingly, adopting certain aspects of it as true and discarding others as false.[84] These are also the terms under which, in the period after the Second World War, Barth approached philosophical humanism. In this case, the exclusion extended to the term 'humanism' itself, which Barth was willing to admit only with the greatest caution, but comprehension is also evident in Barth's own emphasis during this period on 'the humanity of God' and in his deep concern with human dignity and its theological grounds.[85] Finally, it is also in this light that we must view Barth's deep though by no means uncritical respect for the joyful affirmation of life he found in Greek eros and, it seems, in Nietzsche.[86] Indeed, much of Barth's special ethics consists of borrowings from diverse sources under the discipline of carefully elaborated theological criteria which determine on a case-by-case basis what is borrowed and what criticism and correction it must undergo.

It seems clear that in this second case, moral theology does not recognize moral philosophy as a distinct other with a legitimate claim to validity. Such recognition would entail the capacity of philosophy not to articulate what it shares with moral theology (as in the first case) but to propose its own substantive claim to moral truth. It follows that moral theology cannot treat this case like the first one, where it had only to approach moral philosophy as objectively confronted by the command of God, but must directly deny the claim of moral philosophy to preside over the truth of reason and experience. In the first case, some form of alterity remains in the instruction and correction moral theology must be

---

[82] CD II/2, 527/585.

[83] CD II/2, 541/600.

[84] CD III/4, 324/366 f., 349 f./397 f.

[85] See Barth, 'The Christian Proclamation Here and Now,' and 'Humanism,' in *God Here and Now*, 1–10, 94–108; 'The Humanity of God,' in *The Humanity of God*, trans. John Newton Thomas (Atlanta: John Knox Press, 1976), 37–65; and CD III/2, 339 f./385 f.

[86] Barth discusses Greek eros in CD III/2, 274–85/329–44. His discussion of the positive requirement of respect for life in CD III/4, 344–97/391–453 seems to owe not a little to Nietzsche, with its celebrations of *Triebleben*, *Freude*, and even *Wille zur Macht*, albeit expressed in a form and content Nietzsche would have scoffed at. Was Barth answering Nietzsche's charge that Christianity is life-denying, not by defending Christianity directly but by his characteristic method of showing how God gives modernity what it most deeply wants, yet not in the way it thinks it wants it and tries to get it?

prepared to receive from moral philosophy as a conversation partner. In this second case, moral theology denies recognition to moral philosophy as a distinct bearer of substantive moral truth, absorbing into itself whatever material content it can claim as its own truth and discarding as false whatever it cannot.

This is not the whole story about the second case, however, as Barth does allow for the possibility of a nontheological discourse of ethics that presupposes a knowledge of the Word of God which it does not make explicit. Fully aware that as an activity of human self-reflection it cannot speak the final word regarding human conduct, such a discourse would be one which reflects on human life in its limitations, pointing out the questionability and uncertainty of its goodness, and thus indirectly attesting the position of humanity under the command of God's grace.[87] As possible instances of such a discourse, Barth mentions the works of certain novelists and social and political theorists as well as 'the studies of the philosophical moralists.' However, it is not clear how moral philosophy as an academic discipline could be recognized by moral theology on these terms. The criterion of the validity of such a nontheological discourse is whether its principles, if made explicit, would be identical to those of moral theology.[88] But how can moral philosophy, as an academic discipline (*Wissenschaft*), avoid making its own presuppositions explicit? And, if it were to do so, it would either turn out in fact to be moral theology or it would be based on different presuppositions than those of moral theology, and would fail to fulfill the criterion. We are therefore back to where we started: moral philosophy in this case is either comprehended by moral theology or excluded by the latter. For Barth, 'in principle ... correct [*richtige*] ethics can only be Christian ethics, and Christian ethics, if it speaks academically [*wissenschaftlich*], is indistinguishable from theological ethics.' Strictly speaking, 'in an academic form there is only one ethics: theological ethics.'[89]

In summary, we have found that while there is a degree of recognition of moral philosophy as a distinct other, it can be recognized as a valid form of ethical inquiry only to the extent that it can be comprehended under the ethics of the command of God. With regard to its usefulness in the articulation of the ethical question and answer by moral theology, it is sufficient for the latter to treat moral philosophy as objectively positioned as the addressee of the Word of God; there is no expectation that the former will acknowledge the Word of God that speaks through its voice. With regard to the claim of moral philosophy to articulate substantive moral truth in the language of reason or experience (or both), moral theology can recognize the validity of moral philosophy only if, and to the extent that, it implicitly knows the command of God and thus is, once again, itself a kind of moral theology. In both cases, then, the command of God is the sole

---

[87] *Ethics*, 42 f./69 f.; CD II/2, 527/584, 541 f./601 f.
[88] CD II/2, 542/602.
[89] CD II/2, 542/603 (revised).

criterion of the validity of moral philosophy, or of any other nontheological ethic. At the same time, in its own obedience to the command of God, moral theology will continually listen to moral philosophy and to other forms of nontheological ethics, thus acknowledging, at least to this extent, their irreducible alterity. Moral theology neither concedes the independent validity of moral philosophy nor absorbs the latter into itself. It is indeed a complex and possibly unstable position at which Barth has arrived. How did he get there?

Theology, Philosophy, and the Post-Enlightenment Condition

Barth is in the position of recognizing the de facto reality of a moral philosophy standing independent of dogmatics while not according it, in its independent form, de jure recognition. This position is best understood as his attempt to maintain something like a traditional Christian appropriation of philosophy in a historical situation in which moral philosophy not only resists such an appropriation but asserts contrary claims. Up to now we have examined Barth's thought on the relation of moral theology to moral philosophy in its mature form, as it appeared in 1942. A brief review of the development of his thought on this matter will clarify how he got to this point, and this will shed additional light on his position. During the period of *Romans₂*, in the early 1920s, the central distinctions Barth drew between time and eternity and the perceptible and the imperceptible, along with the eschatological gulf between them, relativized the distinction between moral theology and moral philosophy. The critical concern was that ethics, precisely in its orientation to the world of humanity, time, and things, would be treated as a this-sided solution to the crisis of time and eternity and would then cease to be what it is, namely an other-sided exhortation addressed to this-sided existence.[90] The distinction between an ethic that maintains this tension and an ethic that does not cuts across the distinction between theology and philosophy. Thus Barth can credit the Apostle Paul and Kant alike with maintaining the tension, while liberal theologies of progress, conservative theologies of orders of creation, activist religious socialism, and the philosophy of Fichte are all alike denounced for identifying the ethical with the realization of a human capacity, attainment, or state of affairs.[91]

By 1928–9, the distinction between moral theology and moral philosophy is still secondary but has become far more explicit. Barth's discussion in *Ethics*, which is at least in part a response to a philosophical treatment of practical reason by his brother Heinrich Barth, can be summarized in terms of two related claims.[92] First, both theology and philosophy may offer genuine witness to the Word of God, and for that reason both may be called 'Christian.' Both moral

---

[90] See *Romans₂*, 450–64/426–30.
[91] These points are pressed throughout 'The Problem of Ethics Today.'
[92] *Ethics*, 33–45/53–74.

theology and moral philosophy, insofar as they are Christian, acknowledge that they cannot speak the ultimate word on ethics themselves but must rather begin with the knowledge that this word has already been spoken. With this knowledge, moral theology and moral philosophy in their distinct ways both bear obedient witness to the Word of God. Indeed, both can be claimed as activities of the church. A moral philosopher such as Kant who, Barth says, recognizes that morality leads to worship stands with a moral theologian who faithfully proclaims, while both differ sharply from a Fichte who refuses to acknowledge that moral knowledge requires a transition to worship.[93] Thus far, there is no fundamental difference between the two disciplines. Nevertheless, the two are not identical. Christian theology, as a positive science, bears direct witness to the Word of God; its *object* (*Gegenstand*) is God's self-revelation. Philosophy, insofar as it is Christian, bears witness not as a positive science but as human self-reflection, a transcendental inquiry, and therefore indirectly; the Word of God is its *presupposition*, which it knows and hears but with respect to which it keeps silent as it reflects on human existence in light of this presupposition. This difference brings us to the second claim.[94] Both moral theology and moral philosophy understand ethics as the claim of an other, but they do so in different modes. As a direct witness to the Word of God as its object, moral theology speaks of God as the other who claims us in the *actuality* (*Wirklichkeit*) of God's self-revelation, while moral philosophy, as an indirect witness, speaks of the fellow human being as the other who claims us in the *possibility*, grounded in the actuality of God's self-disclosure, that this claim will be a claim God in actuality makes through the other.[95] In the end, however, the distinctions between theology and philosophy still count less than the economies in which each stand. What is decisive for both moral theology and moral philosophy is whether, in their distinct ways, they acknowledge the Word of God as the ultimate word in moral matters or not. When moral philosophy fulfills this condition, moral theology recognizes its validity (*Berechtigung*).[96]

Barth's 1929 lecture on 'Fate and Idea in Theology' sharpened the distinction between theology and philosophy by dropping the theme of a Christian philosophy. In part directed at the Jesuit philosopher Erich Pryzawara, the lecture is a lesson on how theology is to avoid becoming philosophy in spite of its recognition that it, like philosophy, is an entirely human form of thought and speech. Here Barth continues the theme first worked out in his 1924 Göttingen lectures on dogmatics: Theology has as its object the God who is proclaimed in the church, but this God is known only in God's self-revelation. Therefore, theology

---

[93] Ibid. 86/142.

[94] Ibid. 19/30, 28/44, 41–5/67–74.

[95] In Barth's terms, the fellow human '*can* bring God's Word to us *when* God wills to speak his Word through him. On the grounds of this possibility we have to receive him.' Ibid. 44/73.

[96] Ibid. 19/30.

cannot establish the conditions for the success of its own speech, which depend entirely on the freedom of God in God's self-revelation. It can speak about God only in the stance of faith in God's promised self-revelation. Theology is thus in the perpetually awkward position of bearing witness to divine revelation while speaking in an entirely human language, a condition which presents a constant temptation to the theologian to speak of God in terms appropriate to human language as an object of reason or experience—and thus to become a kind of philosopher. Despite a hesitation to pronounce a final judgment on him, Schleiermacher represents for Barth the paradigmatic instance of succumbing to this temptation. For its part, philosophy is an activity of human self-reflection, and it must recognize the limits of such an enterprise. Specifically, the philosopher must recognize that for philosophy the idea of God can only mark a question that arises at the limit of self-reflection; it cannot constitute the final synthesis of thought and reality ('idea' and 'fate') at which philosophical reflection aims. The temptation of philosophy is to forget this limit and to attempt to fulfill its aim by becoming a kind of theology. Here it is Hegel who paradigmatically succumbs to the temptation.

This lecture is important for our purposes insofar as it expresses from the side of theology the counterpart to the position Barth ascribes to Kant from the side of philosophy.[97] Just as Kant rightly recognized the limits of reason and so left room, on his own terms to be sure, for the other of philosophical reason, namely, reason as the addressee of revelation, yet without taking responsibility for the ultimate viability of the task of theology, so Barth recognizes the right of philosophy to aim at a synthesis of thought and reality so long as it remains aware of the limits of human self-reflection and so distinguishes the question of God which arises at those limits from an alleged positive knowledge of God through self-reflection as the attainment of the synthesis.[98] Here, Barth seems to have arrived at an ideal solution to the 'conflict of the faculties.' Each discipline attends to its own task and recognizes the right of the other to its task yet without having to vouch for the ultimate viability of the other's task. Alterity is secured in the awareness of each that it is unable to speak the ultimate word in relation to its subject matter. Theology must therefore heed Kant's reminder that while it thinks and speaks about divine revelation, it does so as a discourse of human reason, while philosophy must be reminded that it lacks the positive knowledge of God that would complete the synthesis at which it aims. Finally, each has the right to appropriate the other so long as each remains cognizant of the rules of appropriation and of the dangers and confusions involved in ignoring these rules. Since she speaks in the voice of reason, the theologian recognizes that she is inevitably a kind of philosopher; only she must never lose sight of the fact that her object is given only in the miracle of revelation and not through the

---

[97] *Protestant Theology in the Nineteenth Century,* 266–312/237–78.
[98] 'Fate and Idea in Theology,' 53.

self-reflection of reason or experience.[99] For his part, the philosopher is free to examine religion as a necessary aspect of a priori reason so long as he respects the boundary between this religion of reason and the positive religion of a revealed faith.[100]

The peaceful coexistence of moral theology and moral philosophy envisioned in this proposal is, however, somewhat illusory; underlying it are disputed claims to sovereignty over the territory of ethics. Barth describes Kant's own self-understanding as a philosopher in his relation to theology as that of a victor who imposes the terms of a dictated peace (*Friedensdiktat*), who with respect to religion claims for philosophy what reason can master and leaves to theology what reason cannot master.[101] In this case, it is the philosopher who sets the conditions under which the theologian must operate while (in Kant's case at least) leaving the theologian free to conduct her affairs under those terms. The implication is that the philosopher has claimed title to the entire territory, granting the theologian a semi-autonomous zone where the philosopher is not able or does not wish to exercise effective rule. For his part, Barth disputes the title of the philosopher to the territory, arguing that even if the theologian is a late arriver, she nevertheless bears the right of an original inhabitant and is therefore entitled to annex it from the occupying power and to reduce its present inhabitants (the philosophers) to service providers (handmaids?) for theology. The moral theologian will hear from her philosophical colleagues the claim to be the original inhabitants of the ethical domain but by no means is she to accept this claim, for 'the Word of God, and in its faithful proclamation the preaching of the church, and with this dogmatics, and at the head of dogmatics the Christian doctrine of God, are in relation to everything else, to general human thought and speech, not the object of aggression but the aggressor [*Angreifer*]. When they enter the field of ethical reflection and understanding they must not be surprised at the contradiction of the supposed (but only supposed!) original inhabitants of this land. . . .'[102] Nor may they yield to this contradiction. Moral theology 'must not and will not disarm [*verharmlosen*] its distinctive Whence? and Whither?' in order to gain legitimacy in the ethical realm; rather 'it must and should disarm . . . the opposition which confronts it in the discussion.'[103]

Barth's concern is plain enough; moral theologians are answerable to the command of God and must not allow themselves to suppose that they must derive their legitimacy from another authority. Nevertheless, the language of aggression and annexation, with its violent imagery, is problematic, to say the least. Its resonances are multiple: they include the ancient Israelite conquest

---

[99] Ibid. 27–31.
[100] *Protestant Theology in the Nineteenth Century*, 281–305/250–72.
[101] Ibid. 278/248.
[102] CD II/2, 520/577 (revised); see also *Ethics*, 19–21/30–2.
[103] CD II/2, 524/581.

of Canaan, which is for Barth the source of the metaphor, the Christian appropriation of antique moral philosophy, to which he seems to allude with his acknowledgment of the late arrival of Christian moral theology, and—this is our suggestion—the task Barth assigns to the modern Christian moral theologian in the face of the Enlightenment. Barth seems intent on reinstating, in some form, the premodern subordination of philosophy to theology which the Enlightenment reversed, or more accurately, to keep moral theology from acquiescing in the Enlightenment reversal. Yet, Barth does not proceed by attempting to restore any premodern schema. Just as Kant, on Barth's reading, shared the Enlightenment confidence in the superiority of reason to ecclesial Christian faith but did not think that he could (and perhaps did not want to) ignore the latter or count on its disappearance, so Barth retains confidence that the doctrine of the command of God has rightful possession of the moral territory but knows that he cannot ignore the claim of moral philosophy to independence of Christian faith or count on philosophy to cease making this claim. By attempting to reintroduce a premodern Christian schema in this context one would succeed only in either assimilating moral theology to a non-Christian moral philosophy or baptizing a non-Christian moral philosophy. Christendom, with its permanent possibility of a genuinely Christian philosophy, is over. There is a close analogy here to Barth's treatment of the relation of church to state. The Christian community can neither ignore the de facto independence of the civil community with respect to the gospel and the church nor accord de jure recognition to this independence but must remind the civil community of its limits while remaining confident that the Word of God is spoken there as well.[104]

Closing Remarks

We now understand both how Barth arrived at his position and why that position exhibits tensions. What remains constant in his attempts as a theologian to come to terms with philosophy is his confidence in the Word of God which addresses itself to both theology and philosophy. What are variable are the degrees to which or the senses in which the resonances of that Word are registered in philosophy. At the end of the day, moral theology must recognize the de facto independence of moral philosophy while refusing to concede its validity on its own terms. This point is well illustrated in Barth's last major statement on theology and philosophy.[105] Just like Karl Barth and Heinrich Barth, the theologian and the philosopher will be inseparable, bound together by a common subject matter, yet will also be passing one another in different

---

[104] See 'The Christian Community and the Civil Community,' in *Community, State, and Church: Three Essays* (Eugene, Ore.: Wipf and Stock, n.d.), 149–89.

[105] We refer to the 1960 essay 'Philosophy and Theology,' which originally appeared in a Festschrift for Heinrich Barth.

directions, their common subject matter bound to its origin in opposite and ultimately irreconcilable starting points (namely, divine revelation and human self-reflection). In the ideal case, each will learn from the other, though not necessarily what the other wanted him to learn. Each will make demands the other will find intolerable, yet, again in the ideal case, each will also acknowledge that he is not in a position to compel the other to accept those demands.

Despite their conflicting claims to sovereignty, a tense peace will nevertheless reign over the land if both the theologian and the philosopher acknowledge the inability of their own discourse to pronounce the final word on ethics.[106]

4. CONCLUSION

Insofar as dogmatics is the activity in which the church critically examines its own speech and practice in light of the Word of God as its criterion, it must therefore concern itself with ethics; and insofar as it is to carry out this activity in obedient responsiveness to the Word of God, it will not be free to formulate an ethic that is independent of the Word of God. This methodological principle follows from a substantive point, namely, that the Word of God, or as he increasingly came to put it, the Word and work of God's grace in Jesus Christ, not only confronts us with what God has done for us but also claims us in our concrete existence as acting subjects. These methodological and substantive points at first may appear to leave Barth with an abstract, narrow, and isolated moral theology, but we have seen that this is not the case. First, while moral theology does not derive its content from the natural or social orders treated independently of God's grace in Jesus Christ, the claim of that grace pertains to all of human life in its creaturely reality. Because the meaning and purpose of our natural and social existence are misunderstood apart from their reference to God's determination of humanity as God's covenant partner, Barth does not acknowledge the legitimacy of any natural morality as such. But the reason for rejecting natural morality as such is also a reason for insisting that the command of God has to do with the entirety of our natural and social existence and cannot abstract from it without denying the claim of God's grace. Second, far from restricting moral theology to a narrow horizon, Barth's methodological and substantive claims expand the theological range of ethics beyond the confines set for it in many theologies. As we saw in Chapter 1, Barth places all of dogmatics under the same terms with respect to God's grace. In whatever divine acts it is expressed, grace does not simply leave us as we are but, without ceasing to be sufficient, summons us to active participation in what it has done for us. For Barth, *all* of God's work has this structure, and it is

---

[106] In Karl Barth's case, the cause of this peace might be furthered by making unambiguously clear that it is not finally the moral theologian but Jesus Christ who in his death and resurrection has disarmed the original inhabitants of the land. See CD II/2, 524/581.

the task of dogmatics to articulate every topic in a way that expresses this point. Finally, to restrict ethics to its dogmatic site is not to isolate it from other discourses of ethics. It is precisely its status as the addressee of the Word of God that compels moral theology to listen to the voices of others, for it cannot occupy this position without renouncing every illusion that it is the exclusive addressee of this Word and has mastery over it. It expects this Word to be spoken elsewhere and listens to the voice of the other with this expectation. Thus, while Barth refuses to authorize a theory of natural law, holding that the knowledge of good and evil human beings possess due to their own powers is capable of only dim approximations of the divine knowledge of good and evil, he is also convinced that the Word of God is spoken everywhere and is not bound to speak only where it is explicitly acknowledged.

We have noted that Barth's position on dogmatics and ethics depends on the notion that it is the Word and work of God's grace that claims human beings in their conduct. But is this notion defensible or even intelligible? We turn next to Barth's controversial thesis on gospel and law.

4

The Divine Claim

Karl Barth's moral theology puts forth an ethic of the good.[1] From eternity, God elected humanity in Jesus Christ to enjoy communion or fellowship with God as God's covenant partner. And in time, God actualized this good in the human being Jesus Christ. 'The good is done here.'[2] It follows that the subject matter (*Sache*) of moral theology is 'the Word and work of God in Jesus Christ, in which the right action of man has already been performed and therefore waits only to be confirmed by our action.'[3] It is clear from all of this that grace—God's realization of the good in our place—is itself the standard or measure of human conduct in Barth's ethics.

It is only in this light that we can understand what Barth means when he describes moral theology as the doctrine of the command of God. For him, the command of God is itself the Word of God; it, too, must therefore be understood as God's self-offer even as it claims our conduct. It, too, addresses us as the revelation and work of God's grace in Jesus Christ. 'If we hear this Word of God, then we hear—grace.'[4] The command of God does nothing more (and nothing less) than summon us to be in our life conduct what we already are thanks to what Christ has done in our place. From *Romans*$_2$ through the *Church Dogmatics*, Barth presses a consistent point, however much the details vary and the emphases fluctuate: The grace of God addresses us as what we are not (yet) in ourselves but are (already) in Christ, such that what we are in Christ becomes determinative for what we are in ourselves, in our existence as acting subjects. We have stressed that for Barth, ethics is no exception to what holds in dogmatics generally. Jesus Christ takes our place here, where our sanctification is at issue, just as he does in the case of our justification (see 1 Cor. 1: 30). He accomplishes the good on our behalf so that the good confronts us not as something still to be accomplished by

---

[1] CD II/2, 552/612. It is no accident that the first substantive treatment of ethics in the *Church Dogmatics* begins with the Augustinian dictum. '*Mihi Deo adhaere bonum est.* "For me the good is to cleave to God."' There are, of course, treatments of ethics in prior volumes of the *Church Dogmatics*, and a methodological paragraph precedes this statement in this volume. Nevertheless it is significant that this statement opens Barth's substantive exposition of the command of God.

[2] CD II/2, 517/573.

[3] CD II/2, 543/603.

[4] Barth, 'Gospel and Law,' 73.

us but as a demand to be what we are, and are now free to be. The command of God is the claim of God's grace.

More, perhaps, than any other single factor this fundamental normative role assigned to grace distinguishes Barth's moral theology from other ventures in this field. We may illustrate this point by referring to two classical examples. For Luther, grace in the strict sense is what God does for us in the face of our inability to meet a requirement which itself expresses something other than grace; it is the consoling word of forgiveness in the face of accusation by a law that is without grace. For Aquinas, grace is God's healing and assisting power that brings us to a perfection of our created nature which we would otherwise be incapable of reaching. For both of these theologians, though in different ways, the law in one form or another is the principle of human conduct, and grace, in the strict sense, is God's provision in the face of our inability to fulfill the law by our own powers. Of course, it would be a mistake to draw the contrasts too sharply here: Barth, Luther, and Aquinas all find places in their theological vision for grace as both divine forgiveness and divine empowerment. But what distinguishes grace in Barth's ethics from these classical accounts is that for him grace in the strict sense, as what God does on our behalf and in our place, is also the source and content of the ethical requirement itself: 'What God wills *of* us is the same as he wills and has done *for* us.'[5]

It is no exaggeration to say that Barth's moral theology depends on the viability of this simple yet enigmatic statement. Yet in spite of their fundamental importance, statements like this have received remarkably little attention in recent scholarship on Barth's ethics, perhaps because they resist efforts to assimilate his ethics to more familiar models. This account, however, pays this theme the central attention it is due. We have seen that the concern of Barth's moral theology is to show how human life and conduct may express the determination of humanity by God's grace rather than the determination of humanity to be for itself. This concern can be met only if Barth can show how grace takes the form of law without losing or distorting either grace or law. But can he show this? This chapter examines his attempt.

1. BARTH'S GOSPEL–LAW THESIS

In Protestant theology the relation of law and grace is typically expressed as the relation of law and gospel, so it is no surprise that Barth's peculiar identification of grace as the norm or standard of ethics takes the form of a controversial thesis regarding law and gospel, one that involves a reversal of the customary law–gospel relation. Barth's gospel–law thesis entails three affirmations: (1) the

---

[5] CD II/2, 568/631 (emphasis retained from German original). The same point is made with minor variations at 560/621 (see 'Gospel and Law,' 78) and 562/624.

inseparability of gospel and law; (2) the priority of gospel to law; and (3) the inclusion of the law in the gospel as, in some sense, its 'form.' These three affirmations are by no means arbitrary; they reflect, respectively, three fundamental tenets of Barth's theology: (1) the unity of God and God's Word against all notions of a duality in God's nature or self-communication; (2) the priority of grace and mercy to holiness and righteousness in the perfections of the divine nature, which corresponds on the human side to the priority of love of God to fear of God; and, finally, (3) the conviction that sanctification is implied in election.

These tenets, along with the gospel–law thesis itself, are ultimately rooted in Barth's insistence on the ontic and noetic determination of the doctrine of God by Christology. God is known in God's self-revelation, and that means in Jesus Christ, in whom the fullness of the Godhead dwells bodily (Col. 2: 9). But in Jesus Christ, God is revealed precisely as one who 'in the free decision of his love' wills to be God, and is God, only in relationship with a human other. Thus grace, as this fundamental divine self-determination for humanity, 'is the basis and goal of all God's works,' which, it follows, are all works of grace, even when they are works of divine judgment.[6] Simply put, from Barth's perspective we learn in Jesus Christ that all God is and does is grace. The term 'gospel' expresses the entirety of this self-determination of God for humanity in Christ and thus has a broader meaning for Barth than the word of forgiveness to the sinner whom the law has convicted of sin and driven to grace. It is in relation to gospel in this broad sense that Barth understands law. As 'gospel' encompasses the entirety of God's being for humanity in Jesus Christ (that is, grace), so 'law' refers to the claim this being for humanity makes on human beings, its normative force: that what God has done for humanity in Jesus Christ should determine human being and conduct. To put it abstractly, in Jesus Christ, God is for humanity in all God's deity (gospel) and summons humanity to exist as the one whom God is for (law).

Grace is the expression of the love of God who from eternity, in Christ, 'willed even in all his divine glory to share his life with another, and to have that other as the witness of his glory.'[7] The divine self-determination (in which God wills to be gracious to humanity) thus includes a determination of humanity (in which God wills that humanity actively participate in God's graciousness), and from eternity, insofar as Jesus Christ is from eternity the electing God and the elected human, the divine determination is expressed in a summons to God's human partner as a free subject. Gospel and law are thus already established in the will and resolve of God's grace from eternity. The ultimate ground of the gospel–law thesis is intra-Trinitarian. But it is in God's self-revelation in Jesus Christ that the divine determination of grace is revealed and addresses human beings, and so it is

---

[6] CD II/2, 9/8; 'Gospel and Law,' 72 f.
[7] CD II/2, 9 f./8.

in the Word and work of Christ that we find the actuality and meaning of gospel and law. In Christ as God incarnate, 'the grace of God has become truly human grace,' and in this 'revelation and actualization of grace' in Christ, humanity is 'jolted and impelled' by a summons or call to live in and by this grace.[8] It is above all here, where God's will is fulfilled in the execution of God's eternal resolve in a temporal human life, that what is accomplished on our behalf by Jesus Christ calls for our active confirmation, that gospel takes the form of law. Thus we arrive at the basic ontological and analogical structure of Barth's moral theology: The good is established in the intra-Trinitarian relation of Father and Son in which the divine self-determination and determination of humanity already occur; it is fulfilled in the incarnate life of the Son who in his humanity realizes for all of humanity the divine determination of humanity for fellowship with God; and in its very fulfillment in Christ's humanity it summons the rest of humanity to confirm it by existing as those for whom it has been fulfilled in Christ.

Gospel and Law: What is at Stake

As with many of Barth's most fundamental convictions—one thinks of his doctrine of revelation with its rejection of natural theology—the gospel–law thesis comes with a kind of exigency driven by a sense that everything depends on getting right something that virtually everyone except Barth has gotten wrong. But why is Barth convinced that moral theology stands or falls with this thesis? What is at stake for him in his conviction that moral theology must rest on the grace of God in Jesus Christ as its norm or standard? This question takes us beyond an important body of scholarship which examines the gospel–law thesis in relation to the legacy of the Protestant Reformers who first posed key questions of soteriology in terms of law and gospel.[9] The work of these scholars has brought to light Barth's deep and often subtle engagements with both the specific formulations of Luther and Calvin and their broader theological contexts, but it does not explain why it was a matter of such urgency to Barth that the Reformation heritage prevail in what he took to be its proper form.

---

[8] CD II/2, 567/629 (revised).

[9] The literature is extensive. It includes Simon Rae, 'Gospel Law and Freedom in the Theological Ethics of Karl Barth,' *Scottish Journal of Theology* 25 (1972): 412–22; Bertold Klappert, *Promissio und Bund: Gesetz und Evangelium bei Luther und Barth* (Göttingen: Vandenhoeck & Ruprecht, 1976); Wilfried Joest, 'Karl Barth und das lutherische Verständnis von Gesetz und Evangelium,' *Keryma und Dogma* 24 (1978): 86–103; Jüngel, 'Gospel and Law,' 105–26; Ulrich H. J. Körtner, 'Noch einmal: Evangelium und Gesetz: Zur Verhältnisbestimmung von Gesetz und Evangelium bei Karl Barth und Calvin,' *Theologische Zeitschrift* 49 (1993): 248–66; Jesse Couenhaven, 'Grace as Pardon and Power: Pictures of the Christian Life in Luther, Calvin, and Barth,' *Journal of Religious Ethics* 28 (2000): 63–88; and idem, 'Law and Gospel, or the Law of the Gospel? Karl Barth's Political Theology Compared with Luther and Calvin,' *Journal of Religious Ethics* 30 (2002): 181–205.

In Chapter 2 we saw how Barth blamed the Reformers for failing to secure the Christological referent of the law and thereby setting in motion a process by which scriptural commandments came to be identified with and were eventually superseded by an independent rational moral law, which ended up becoming the criterion of Christian belief and practice. As this process unfolded the role of Protestant moral theology changed, shifting from the articulation of scriptural law to the justification of a rational law or a cultural norm. This new task indicates the distinctive challenge posed to modern moral theology: How can we know that an independent moral law is really an expression of the will of God and not only the product of autonomous human reason? And how can we know that the justification theology offers is not simply an act of legitimization, the claim of divine authority for norms that merely reflect particular social and political arrangements? In this context the lordship of Christ over other lords is at issue, so that the first question of ethics and politics is one of idolatry: How can I in my moral activity and my political allegiances be sure that I am obeying God rather than merely myself or someone else who asserts the authority to direct me?[10] It is clear, from this angle, what is at stake in the claim that grace is the norm of ethics: With the appearance of a moral law articulated independently of theological claims and the prevalence of ideological uses of notions of divine law to claim divine authority for norms underlying particular social and political arrangements, to obey a law that is independent of the gospel is to risk idolatry by acknowledging and serving in one's moral obedience a lord other than Christ.

This concern with idolatry in moral and political contexts is crucial to Barth; it plays a central role in his critique of the assimilation of Christianity to bourgeois society in modern Europe. The only question is how fundamental this concern is to his gospel–law thesis. A second body of scholarship on this thesis focuses on this concern. This scholarship rightly emphasizes Barth's view that it was the Lutheran separation of law from gospel that led to the theological validation of a moral order entirely independent of the revelation and work of grace while also showing how his gospel–law thesis, in overcoming this separation and reversing its order, is at once a rejection of theological validations of law in the form of autonomous moral orders and an act of resistance to moral and political authorities that claim our obedience and allegiance by appealing to such orders. Barth's 1935 lecture on 'Gospel and Law' appears from this angle as the paradigmatic expression of his stance, and the gospel–law thesis is thereby placed in the context of the rise to power of National Socialism and the ensuing German Church Struggle. This kind of interpretation is especially attractive to Barth's defenders because it suggests that his claims regarding the inseparability of gospel and law and the priority of the former to the latter are vindicated by the role played by

---

[10] Posed in this way this question might be thought of as the ethico-political corollary of a central question of Barth's theology in general, and especially his doctrine of revelation: When I speak of God how can I be sure I am not merely speaking about myself?

two important corollaries arising out of the twofold modern context mentioned above—namely, the rejection of a law that is prior to or independent of the grace given in Christ, and the rejection of authorities who claim human beings apart from Christ—in his resistance to the theological legitimization of National Socialism.

This interpretation is not without its merits. It is true that Barth arrived at his clearest exposition of his gospel–law thesis in the wake of efforts by German Lutheran theologians, including his former *confrère* Friedrich Gogarten, to enlist the notion of a law independent of the gospel to argue for absolute submission to the authority of the *Führer* and his regime. It is also true that the gospel–law thesis strikes at the heart of the claim of these theologians that the church has no standing to criticize the laws of the state, which, qua law, are independent of the gospel, and their claim that the very grace-less character of these laws confirms their legitimate status as laws. In opposition to such claims, Barth insists that no law is binding except insofar as it is an expression of the gospel. Finally, the linkage of the gospel–law formula and opposition to National Socialism is underscored by the vivid image of the pastor of the Barmen church reading Barth's 'Gospel and Law' lecture in October of 1935 to an audience under the watchful eyes of the Gestapo, who then escorted the defiant author, who had not been permitted to deliver the lecture himself, back to the Swiss border.[11]

Despite these points, it is a mistake to associate Barth's thesis too exclusively with his opposition to the neo-Lutheran theology of law and gospel and its disastrous connection with National Socialism. For one thing, the convictions behind the gospel–law thesis and even the formula itself were in place well before the German Church Struggle, as we will soon see.[12] Moreover, the 'Gospel and Law' lecture itself attributes the misuse and misunderstanding of the law to a form of human self-assertion that has to do with human sinfulness in all its manifestations, not only with the evils that unfolded in Germany in the 1930s. To understand the lecture itself and the gospel–law thesis it develops, this wider picture must be kept in view. Finally, if identified too closely with this context, Barth's thesis may appear as a reaction (and possibly an overreaction) to

---

[11] The incident is recounted by Eberhard Busch in *Karl Barth: His Life from Letters and Autobiographical Texts*, trans. John Bowden (Philadelphia: Fortress Press, 1976), 265 f.

[12] As early as *Romans₂* (see especially 188 f./207 f.), Barth had spoken of grace as an indicative that also entails an imperative, as that which both creates the new person and takes up arms against the old person. Early in his Göttingen appointment, which began shortly after he had completed *Romans₂*, Barth asserted the inseparability of gospel and law as a way of referring to what he was now pointing out as the Reformed emphasis on ethics as inseparable from dogmatics, in contrast to the relative neglect of ethics he found in the Lutheran tradition; it was in this context that he clearly stated both the inseparability of gospel and law and the reversal of the customary order, according to which, especially in the Lutheran tradition, the gospel announces the forgiveness of sins to those driven to despair at their inability to obey the law. See especially Karl Barth, *Unterricht in der christlichen Religion* (*Göttingen Dogmatics*) (Zurich: Theologischer Verlag Zürich), i. 207–44/ 168–98, iii. 18–25.

the neo-Lutheran position rather than as a positive thesis which deserves attention on its own terms. In retrospect, while doing full justice to Barth's courageous
stance, we may wonder whether his gospel–law thesis is so important after all if
this is its paradigmatic context. For while his formula certainly rules out the
abhorrent conceptions of law and authority propounded by the neo-Lutherans
while also underlying Barth's courageous opposition to the Nazi regime, it is not,
as is sometimes assumed by his defenders, the only effective weapon against
them, nor is it clear what relevance it would have outside of the (mercifully)
limited time and place in which those conceptions held sway. To this last point,
proponents of this second interpretation would rightly respond that Barth
implicated the neo-Lutheran law–gospel formula in a wider context of autonomous moral orders and their ideological uses, and that there is no shortage of
times and places where this context prevails. But this brings us to the more
general phenomenon of human self-assertion which, as Barth saw it, accounted
for autonomous ethics in the first place, and this in turn brings us to the positive
thrust of the gospel–law thesis which both exposes and overcomes human self-
assertion.[13]

The underlying problem with the foregoing interpretation is its concentration
on the negative task of overcoming problematic conceptions and uses of law
rather than on Barth's positive affirmation of grace. The gospel–law thesis is
primarily a thesis about grace, and it is only in light of grace that the misuse of the
law is properly understood. Barth's claim is that grace is determinative of human
life, that it is God's will from eternity that human beings live in and by what God
does on their behalf and in their place. Because *grace* in this sense is thus the
norm or standard of human conduct, it puts before us, in the form of a
command, the fact that God is for us, thereby exposing and opposing our
determination to be for ourselves. 'It is the fact that God is for him which
binds and commits man himself, and that unconditionally. It is this which
completely excludes, therefore, everything which would in any way mean that
he for his part wanted to be for himself.'[14]

The problematic of the law, and thus of ethics, unfolds in this fundamental
opposition of God's being and doing for us to our being and doing for ourselves.
Law will either express the fact that God is for us, requiring only our active
affirmation of what God does and has done for us, or it will express our
determination to be for ourselves as we misuse the law to assert ourselves, to

---

[13] A historian of ethics and politics might raise the troubling question whether the entire theo-
political discourse of gospel and law is implicated in the events that unfolded in Germany from the
bourgeois era to the Nazi era. Are law and gospel in whichever order an unstable combination which
is bound to oscillate back and forth between law–gospel and gospel–law, generating ever more
extreme forms of legitimization and disruption? Do they inevitably put into motion the distinctively
modern dialectic of revolution and reaction? These questions cannot be avoided, but they are
best delegated to the historian.

[14] CD II/2, 597/663.

make ourselves morally worthy, and to establish ourselves as moral subjects, with all the consequences this will have in the lives of individuals as well as in the social and political orders.[15] We will see that Barth's theological exposition of divine grace and human self-assertion is thoroughly intertwined with his exegesis of the Pauline problematic of the law in Romans 7–8 and other passages as he continually contrasts the law of grace which requires only that we live as those whom God is for with the misused law as we appropriate it, in our desire to be for ourselves, as a means to our moral self-realization and self-vindication.

These two economies once again indicate the ambiguity of ethics and pose the problem of ethics, namely, how to articulate the proper meaning of law as the expression of divine grace in opposition to law as the expression of human self-assertion. Yet it would be misleading to assume that we are dealing with two moralities locked in a Manichaean struggle. For Barth, it is only as the expression of divine grace that morality can be sustained at all. God is for us and not against us—this declaration of divine grace, which grounds the command of God and is expressed in its very form, establishes morality, which is imperiled and distorted by our assumption that we are left to ourselves and must be for ourselves.[16] Barth intends his gospel–law thesis to show how the law does not in any way leave us to ourselves (as a demand confronting us prior to grace) or bring us back to ourselves (as a demand imposed on us in the wake of grace) but positions us with respect to what has already and decisively been done for us by Christ, who is our sanctification in the same sense as he is our justification (1 Cor. 1: 30). Far from bringing us back to ourselves, the law as the form of grace conveys to us a reality in which we already stand. We are both free from the condemnation the law pronounces on us in our misuse of it and free for our life in Christ who has fulfilled the law, in its proper sense, in our place. It is only under these terms, Barth believes, that morality can be sustained.

Lutheran Criticisms and their Continuing Relevance

Central to Barth's view is the claim that God's will is revealed in Christ's accomplishment of it in place of other human beings and that the law therefore addresses us from this Christological site. For Barth, it is a mistake to look for the summons or claim of God anywhere else. 'We must seek it only in what happened in Bethlehem, at Capernaum and Tiberius, in Gethsemane and on

---

[15] This distinction determines the structure of 'Gospel and Law,' in which Barth, drawing on the conceptuality of his 'Fate and Idea in Theology,' distinguishes between the 'truth' of gospel and law, that is, their ultimate nature, and their 'reality,' that is, the form they assume in the factual (and absurd) condition of human sin. The former concerns the proper relation of gospel and law in which the law is the expression of the gospel. The latter concerns the situation in which the gospel announces God's forgiveness to human sinners who have misused the law to establish their own righteousness and thus fallen under its condemnation.

[16] CD II/2, 557/618 f., 592/658, 597/663, 602/669.

Golgotha, and in the garden of Joseph of Arimathea.'[17] During Barth's lifetime this claim encountered vigorous opposition, especially from his Lutheran critics. Too often, these critics presented skewed or superficial versions of Barth's position and countered it by simply reasserting familiar Lutheran convictions while Barth for his part never fully engaged their attacks, with the result that a nuanced debate never occurred.[18] Moreover, the terms of the debate largely reflected mid-century Lutheran–Reformed polemics that did not resonate outside those communions. Nevertheless, the criticisms of these Lutheran opponents take us straight to points of vulnerability in Barth's thesis which are of relevance beyond the Lutheran and Reformed traditions, and it is in light of this more general relevance that we will formulate them. The first criticism, which is not confined to moral theology, is the charge that Barth empties history of any meaning by staging the entire drama of human salvation in an eternal intra-Trinitarian divine decision and act.[19] The Lutheran theology of law and gospel as it was articulated by Barth's opponents emphasizes the decisiveness of the historical Christ event as the division of history into distinct eras of law and gospel represented, respectively, by the Old and New Testaments of the Christian scripture. From this perspective, moreover, the distinction between the law which condemns and the gospel which forgives ensures that the question of damnation and salvation is continually decided in the histories of actual persons as the Word of God is heard first as law and then as gospel. By contrast, these Lutherans charge, Barth subsumes the salvation-historical dialectic of law and gospel into a timeless Word in which the tensions between judgment and grace, damnation and salvation, are eternally overcome by absorbing the former into the latter, thus depriving the historical Christ event and the response of the believer of any determinative significance.[20] So, they conclude, while Barth claims to give decisive significance to the historical Christ event, this event simply enacts what has been the case from eternity.

Today, of course, many Lutherans recoil from stark contrasts between an Old Testament law of condemnation and divine wrath and a New Testament gospel of forgiveness and divine love, contrasts which have been rendered problematic

---

[17] CD II/2, 559/621.

[18] A partial rebuttal is made to his opponents *en masse* at CD IV/3, 370 f./427 f. It offers a handy register of Barth's objections to the law–gospel formula of his opponents but is mostly a set of counter-counter-assertions to their counter-assertions rather than a proper critique and defense of his position against theirs.

[19] For this criticism, see especially Paul Althaus, *The Divine Command*, trans. Franklin Sherman (Philadelphia: Fortress Press, 1966); and Helmut Thielicke, *Theological Ethics*, i: *Foundations* (Philadelphia: Fortress Press, 1966).

[20] These Lutherans rightly attribute their disagreement with Barth to differing views of revelation. Rather than restricting theology to the historical revelation of God's wrath and love and rescinding from speculation on God apart from this historical revelation, for Barth theology has to do with the self-revelation of God who is concealed as well as disclosed in this self-revelation but who is not other than who and what God is therein.

by biblical scholarship and by a rethinking of the relationship between Christianity and Judaism, not to mention by a more nuanced understanding of Lutheran teaching, which need not presuppose that the distinction between law and gospel corresponds exactly to the distinction between the two Testaments. Still, the charge that Barth's gospel–law thesis can succeed only by subordinating the historical Christ event to an eternal divine decision and act remains a serious charge. But is it a legitimate one? To hold that for Barth, the Christ event is simply the temporal enactment of what is eternally the case is to miss what for him is the central point, namely, that it is God's will that the good become a fully and distinctively human good and that this happens decisively in the Christ event. It is not correct to say that on Barth's view, something which was already complete in eternity simply took temporal form in Christ. It is more accurate to say that what was resolved on by God from eternity was accomplished in Christ's human existence, which is the only place where it could be accomplished because from eternity the divine resolve was that the good which God enjoys in the form of intra-Trinitarian fellowship also become a human good. For Barth, the Christ event is not merely a stopgap measure to deal with human sin but is the fulfillment, in the face of humanity's sinful contradiction, of an eternal divine plan whose very meaning consists in its temporal actualization.[21] Both the Old and New Testaments point, in distinct ways, to this actualization of God's plan, and the drama occurs in the entirety of Christ's incarnate life, especially in Gethsemane, where the actualization of God's will for the whole of humanity rests on his obedient decision for God's will (which is itself the actualization in time of the eternal obedience of the Son to the Father), as well as in every moment of every human life, as human beings are confronted with the decision for or against obedience to God's grace in Christ.

However, the Lutheran concern that Barth empties history of meaning by treating both law and gospel in Christological terms can take the form of a second criticism. Consider three claims Barth makes in his lecture on 'Gospel and Law': (1) grace *is* Christ; (2) sin is hostility to grace (and thus to Christ); and (3) Christ saves us from our sin.[22] It follows from these three claims that Christ both precedes our sin (as the grace rejected by sin) and responds to our sin (by saving us from it). Consider also that for Barth, the law summons us only as it is fulfilled by Christ in our place.[23] If this means that Christ obeys in our place a law that is in force prior to his obedience, then it appears that there is a law that precedes the gospel after all. However, the alternative—that the law itself is somehow inaugurated in Christ's obedience to it in our place—is also

---

[21] In this respect, Barth of course resembles Hegel, but the resemblance is superficial insofar as for Barth, God remains God in God's becoming human in Jesus Christ and insofar as Barth speaks of actualization in Jesus Christ as a particular, unrepeatable, nonsubstitutable event that does not have its ultimate meaning in anything beyond or outside itself.

[22] Barth, 'Gospel and Law,' 73–5.

[23] Ibid. 77 f., 81 f.

problematic since it implies that there was no law prior to Christ's obedience, and if this is so then it is not clear in what sense Christ can be said to fulfill the law 'in our place' or what the Old Testament legislation could possibly mean—or, indeed, how human beings could be said to be sinners prior to Christ's obedience. In short, there seems to be a vicious circle here: Jesus Christ is the gospel precisely insofar as he fulfills the law in our place, yet the law itself is nothing other than the demand addressed to us in and with the gospel.

To break out of this circle, Barth relates Christ's obedience to the summons to humanity issued in the determination of human beings from eternity by divine grace and explains Old Testament law as a form of this summons which points forward to Christ's fulfillment. By existing as God's elect, as God's covenant partner, Christ fulfills the divine determination of humanity in our place. Yet from eternity it was not God's will that we come to know and fulfill this determination by our own powers; rightly understood, neither the command given to Adam nor the Mosaic legislation required this of its addressees but rather directed them to God's grace, thus pointing them to Christ's fulfillment of the law.[24] By treating the Old Testament law as a sign pointing to Christ, this solution shows how the law can exist prior to the incarnation as an event in history even as it ultimately issues forth from its fulfillment in Christ, which itself refers us back to its ultimate ground in the eternal divine determination of humanity in the election of Christ and of other human beings in him and the eternal obedience of the Son to the Father. These last moves, however, exact a cost as they seem to require us to read the incarnation back into the eternal divine determination. Some momentous issues are at stake here including, in Trinitarian theology, how we understand the identity of the eternal Son of God with the incarnate Christ and the obedient decision of the Son to become incarnate (though the major concern of the Lutheran critics, namely, the historical integrity and decisiveness of the Christ event, has already been resolved in the response to the first criticism). It is beyond the scope of this chapter to address all of these issues. But Barth's cardinal theological principle—that God is not other than who God is in God's self-revelation in Jesus Christ—rules out the possibilities of an eternal divine law, a law of the created order, or a law given in a historical covenant that differ from the law which is manifested in the obedience rendered by the incarnate Christ in our place and which summons us to confirm its fulfillment by him.

This last point brings us to a third criticism, one which is by no means only a Lutheran one. It has to do with the status of laws that pertain to our nature and the societies in which we live. Barth holds that no law or moral demand issued apart from God's grace in Christ can count as the command of God or enjoy the backing of divine authority. This seems to deny the legitimacy of all laws and

---

[24] CD I/2, 310–12/339–40.

moral demands except those that are directly given in the event of God's self-revelation in Christ, whatever they turn out to be, and that grace is the direct content of every command, whatever that would mean. In practice, this would almost certainly amount to an extreme form of Gnostic antinomianism. But this is not at all what Barth has in mind. He explicitly states that 'the claim of God's command always wears the garment of another claim of this kind,' namely, of a demand arising from our natural, social, and cultural existence.[25] It is true that he grants normative status to these demands only as concrete forms of the grace that summons us out of its fulfillment in Christ, but it is also true that the summons of grace has to do with the entirety of our natural, social, and cultural existence. Grace, for Barth, never meets us apart from a claim on us, as if God had done something for us without calling us to share in it as active subjects, and the claim of grace never addresses us apart from the claims of our natural, social, and cultural existence, as if we could somehow be active subjects in abstraction from all that constitutes our creaturely being.

The final Lutheran criticism is the most challenging one. It can be expressed in the form of several questions raised by Barth's claim that the law is the form or expression of grace. If grace concerns what God has done for us, how can it have the force of law, demanding something of us? How can it actually bind human conduct? Does law not lose its capacity to compel our obedience if we know all along that it is really the expression of grace? And if *grace* takes the form of law, this can only mean that the requirement of the law has already been met, but in what sense can we then speak of the law as *law*? Again, if grace concerns what God has done for us, how can it assume the form of a law of our own activity without either compromising its gratuitousness (by taking the form of a *nova lex*, a new law of grace) or diminishing the significance of human activity (by reducing it to passive acquiescence in what God has done)? If grace is to assume the form of a command, one or the other of these alternatives seems inevitable.

These questions go to the heart of the Lutheran conviction that not only theology but also the entire situation of the Christian before God are thrown into confusion unless law and gospel are rightly and rigorously distinguished. From this perspective, Barth's gospel–law thesis imperils both law and gospel and makes a coherent understanding of both faith and ethics impossible. The previous three criticisms all fail to take into account certain key aspects of Barth's position, as we have just shown. But this criticism goes to the heart of Barth's position and finds there a fundamental confusion. To respond to this criticism will require a lengthy exposition of Barth's position, to which we now turn.

---

[25] CD II/2, 584/649.

2. THE COMMAND OF GOD AS THE CLAIM
OF GOD'S GRACE

Eberhard Jüngel points out the 'startling' fact that there is no specific section of the *Church Dogmatics* devoted to the topic of gospel and law.[26] While it is true that no section or subsection has the gospel–law formula in its title, Barth's first substantive exposition of his doctrine of the command of God, placed under the title of 'The Command of God as the Claim of God,' is in effect a lengthy exposition of the gospel–law thesis.[27] This section, which, strangely enough, is almost entirely ignored by Jüngel, presents the gospel–law thesis in its most mature form and is the primary source for the exposition of Barth's position in this section. But we will understand his position more clearly if we first understand how it developed, especially during the crucial period beginning with *Romans₂* (completed in 1921) and culminating in the 1927 lecture 'Das Halten der Gebote,' where the mature position expressed in his 1928–9 ethics lectures and later crystallized in 'Gospel and Law' received its first extended formulation.

Development of the Gospel–Law Thesis

In Chapter 1 we noted that by the time of *Romans₂*, Barth had already arrived at an early version of his gospel–law thesis, referring to grace as an 'indicative that has an absolute categorical imperative as its meaning' and as 'an absolute demand,' and describing the law, 'rightly understood, [as] nothing other than the demonstration, justification, and revelation of the faithfulness of God.'[28] As we saw, in the forgiveness of sins grace creates the new person, opposing her to the old person as it takes the form of the demand. All three aspects of Barth's thesis—the inseparability of gospel and law, the priority of gospel to law, and the law as the form of the gospel—are at least implicit in these and similar remarks in *Romans₂*, though explicit articulation of the gospel–law thesis is still to come. More important, the most crucial point of Barth's mature position—that grace brings about a new reality, one in which the law is both legitimate and effectual—is already in place here, if in a somewhat rough form.

---

[26] Jüngel, 'Gospel and Law,' 111.
[27] CD II/2, 552–630/612–701.
[28] *Romans₂*, 188/207 f., 207/225, 91 f./116. Michael Beintker shows how these and other remarks link up with the broader thematic of *Romans₂* and indicate the extent to which the mature gospel–law formula is anticipated in that text in the relation between divine grace and divine judgment, in Barth's emphasis on the creative and transformative nature of grace, and in his doctrine of election. See Beintker, 'Das Krisis-Motiv der Römerbriefphase als Vorstufe von Barths Zuordnung von Gesetz und Evangelium,' in *Theologie als Christologie: Zum Werk und Leben Karl Barths: Ein Symposium*, ed. Heidelore Kökert und Wolf Krötke (Berlin: Evangelische Verlagsanstalt Berlin, 1988).

A significant step in the direction of explicit articulation of the gospel–law thesis was taken in the course of Barth's intensive engagement with historic Reformed theology during his years at Göttingen (1921–5), which culminated in his first venture in dogmatics. During these years, Barth, reworking a theme from *Romans₂* in the context of Reformed theology, frequently highlighted what he saw as a Reformed focus on *God* as the *object* of faith, contrasting it favorably with what he saw as a Lutheran focus on the situation of the believing subject. The Reformed focus, he argued, makes it impossible to separate gospel from law. For while the Lutheran emphasis is on the forgiveness of sins as the answer of the gospel to the predicament of the sinner before the law, the Reformed stress 'the one God [who] stands behind both [gospel and law].' In the unity of God in God's revelation 'God's gracious answer [that is, gospel] never stands alone. With it, and not before or behind it, there comes the question which is thrust into our lives by this answer [that is, law].'[29] It is significant that Barth asserts the inseparability of gospel and law (the first aspect of the thesis) on the grounds that both derive from God, thus treating his gospel–law thesis as primarily a statement about God; only as such is it also a statement about faith and obedience (which correspond, respectively, to gospel and law) as the response to God's sovereign will by the human subject.[30] Barth establishes the priority of gospel to law (the second aspect) in much the same way as he establishes their inseparability. This priority is derived from the fact that God's covenant with humanity is a covenant of grace. 'For in fact the *gospel*, the *New* Testament, the *good* news, the divine *Yes* to humanity is primary, the first and last, the meaning of the covenant.'[31] Gospel and law belong together under the primacy of grace, which establishes both gospel and law, and in that order.[32] Here Barth unambiguously locates law in the economy of grace, but what is lacking during this period is an explicit statement of the third aspect of the thesis, namely, law as the form of the gospel. In what sense the law is an expression of grace is therefore unclear— less clear, in fact, than it was in *Romans₂*—and the lack of attention to this point means that Barth's ethics do not undergo any significant substantive development during this period despite his important elaborations of the centrality of ethics in Reformed theology. As he sought during these years to highlight the distinctiveness of the Reformed tradition in its ethical thrust, Barth was largely content to set the law on the same footing as the gospel, though second in order

---

[29] Barth, 'The Doctrinal Task of the Reformed Churches,' 264/241; *Göttingen Dogmatics*, 172/212. See also *The Theology of the Reformed Confessions*, 93 f., 148; and *Die christliche Dogmatik im Entwurf*, i: *Die Lehre vom Worte Gottes*. Edited by Gerhard Sauter (Zurich: Theologischer Verlag, 1982), 425 f.

[30] We can see in these programmatic statements some of the fault lines later traced by Barth's Lutheran opponents, who understood his distinction between God's will and the situation of the believer as a distinction between eternity and history.

[31] Barth, *Unterricht in der christlichen Religion*, iii. 20.

[32] Barth, *The Theology of the Reformed Confessions*, 101.

to the latter, and to ground both in God, whose grace confronts us as both gift and task, demanding both faith and obedience.

A major step forward is taken with the March 1927 lecture 'Das Halten der Gebote.'[33] Here Barth's mature position on gospel and law is stated for the first time. It can be distilled into three claims. First, God's command to human beings must be understood as an expression of God's will to be with and for human beings, to have human beings as God's own. 'As he commands me . . . he obviously wills, as Calvin (*Inst.* III, 6, 1) said, that *symmetria et consensus* occur between his will active in the commandment and my *obsequium*, my obedient decision. But this means that he wants me, and wants me for himself. He wills not to be without me. He wills that I, as the one who I am, be with him . . . The origin of the command is love, grace, election.'[34] Second, only in this relation to the gospel is the law genuinely binding. 'The law receives its power and truth through the gospel. Apart from the gospel I have not heard the law as law, as the Word that binds me.'[35] Finally, the law that binds me in this way is the demand to confirm the grace of election in my life conduct, my 'act of existence'; by it I am 'summoned to be who I am, and therefore no longer to choose but to be chosen and to confirm my election.'[36]

It would be difficult to find a more succinct expression of Barth's entire moral theology than is found in these three claims. The three claims give rise to three questions: First, how is law established by grace? Second, how and in what manner or form does grace bind us? Third, what conduct does law as the expression of grace actually require of us? These three questions correspond to the three subsections of Barth's most sustained treatment of gospel and law in the *Church Dogmatics* under the heading of 'The Command of God as the Claim of God,' where Barth answers the three questions by considering, respectively, the ground, the form, and the content of the divine claim (though not in that order).

Grace Establishes Law

Barth consistently emphasizes that 'the grace of God never stands alone,' that 'it is the summons which draws man's attention to the fact that when God is gracious to him, he himself is meant, and therefore what he is and does.' Speaking more metaphorically, it is never unveiled; it is always clothed in the law, concealed in the summons to grace.[37] Grace cannot become concretely present without also putting in place the law: 'When grace is actualized and

---

[33] Barth, 'Das Halten der Gebote,' in *Vorträge und kleinere Arbeiten, 1925–1930*, ed. Harmann Schmidt (Zurich: Theologische Verlag Zürich, 1994), 99–139, especially 120–3. The perspective of this essay continues in Barth's 1928–9 ethics lectures. See especially *Ethics*, 89–93/147–54.
[34] Barth, 'Das Halten der Gebote,' 120 f.
[35] Ibid. 122.
[36] Ibid. 123.
[37] CD II/2, 563/625.

revealed [*Ereignis und Offenbarung wird*], it always means that the law is established.'[38] The reason for this has to do with the nature and reality of grace itself. Grace is not 'self-circumscribed and self-exhausting.' It is not enclosed within God's own being and willing, as if it concerned only a divine self-determination and determination of humanity resolved upon and carried out by God in isolation from human life. Rather, the determination of humanity for fellowship with God is expressed in the form of a summons of grace issued to humanity. 'Grace is the movement and direction [*Bewegung und Richtung*] of man in accordance with his determination.'[39] And because God's determination of human beings for fellowship with God is not to a mechanical or passive but to a free and active participation, it follows that grace cannot become manifest without summoning human beings to respond freely to grace. 'God cannot draw [man] to himself without involving him in responsibility.'[40] We have already seen that this point is a Christological one, both in regard to the election of humanity in Christ from eternity and in regard to the incarnation. 'Docetic' conceptions of grace, which treat the latter solely in terms of a divine determination resolved on and carried out in isolation from concrete human life, are ruled out on Christological grounds.[41] As it is manifested in the incarnation of God in Christ, it is clear that grace has become a human reality, that 'grace does apply to *us*, it does concern us.'[42] Law is the expression of this concern of grace with and for our human reality; it is the mode in which God's undeserved favor towards human beings, actualized in Christ, becomes normative for them, that is, in which the divine determination of humanity confronts human beings in their actual existence as the summons to live in and by God's grace, 'to be one who stands and walks and lives and dies within the fact that God is gracious to him, that God has made him his own.'[43]

Thus it is that grace establishes law. But is the grace that establishes the law still grace? And is the law it establishes really law? The answer to the first question is twofold. First, as the final sentence of the previous paragraph indicates, and as 'Das Halten der Gebote' explicitly notes, the law is the expression of God's will to be with and for human beings, to have us as God's own. That this is the case is already apparent, Barth claims, in the Old Testament legislation, where the meaning of the Decalogue is given in the first commandment and especially in the pronouncement which Christians have generally taken as the preamble but which Judaism, as Barth notes, recognizes as the first commandment itself: 'I am the Lord your God who brought you out of the land of Egypt, out of the house of slavery' (Exod. 20: 2). The purpose of the law, Barth remarks, 'is to give us the

[38] CD II/2, 562/624.
[39] CD II/2, 567/629.
[40] CD II/2, 511/566.
[41] CD II/2, 567/629 f.
[42] Barth, 'Gospel and Law,' 78.
[43] CD II/2, 558 f./620.

very presence of God himself in the act in which he himself is ours, in which he binds himself to us to save us.'[44] What holds in this paradigmatic case holds for scriptural law in general, and this in turn governs the theological and ethical meaning of law. 'The thing we are to hear as we hear the command of God is that we may belong to him.'[45] In the words of 'Das Halten der Gebote,' the origin of the command is love, grace, election. Grace 'is not exhausted by the fact that God is good to us. As he is good to us, he is well-disposed towards us. And as such, he wills our good. The aim of the grace actualized and revealed in God's covenant with man, is the restoration of man to the divine likeness and therefore to fellowship with God in eternal life.'[46] The command of God is the form in which God's will to be with us and for us claims us.

But how can grace express itself in this claim without ceasing to be grace? This brings us to Barth's second answer to the first question. Grace is still grace because it is Christ's fulfillment of the law in our place that claims us and binds us as law. The law established by the actualization and revelation of grace is not a law which human beings are commanded to fulfill but one which, precisely insofar as it is the law of God's grace, has already been fulfilled in Christ, and, moreover, it is precisely this fulfillment of the law in Christ that gives the law its validity. 'The law is valid because God himself is the doer of the law, because God orders and only orders on the basis of the fact that he himself has given and realized and fulfilled what he orders.'[47] The law is issued from the site of its fulfillment; its demand addresses us as already having been accomplished. 'The law which really binds us is the law which was fulfilled once and for all in Jesus Christ.'[48] It is precisely in this sense that Barth can legitimately claim that 'the gospel is the content of the law.' The gospel declares what Christ has done in our place, and the law summons us to appropriate as our own what is already accomplished for us by Christ.

However, this answer immediately poses the second question: In what sense can a law that is already fulfilled for us by another still be a law that calls for our obedience? Is law understood in this sense really law? There are in fact two questions here. First, how can the law both express what Christ has done for us and demand something of us? Barth's answer, which is considered in more detail in the following two subsections, is that the law frees us to be who and what we are in Christ and that what it requires is our active agreement with or confirmation of what God has done for us. Second, how and in what sense does God's fulfillment of the law in Christ establish the validity of the law as law? This question, which is our present concern, has been pressed most pointedly by

---

44 CD I/2, 274/299.
45 CD II/2, 738/824. See, more generally, CD II/2, 734–41/820–9; and *Ethics*, 89–93/147–54.
46 CD II/2, 566/629.
47 CD II/2, 565/627.
48 CD II/2, 563/625. See also 'Gospel and Law,' 81 f.

Lutheran critics, but it obviously has relevance beyond that context.[49] Barth addresses this question under the assumption that the validity of law entails both its right (*Recht*) and its force (*Kraft*): its legitimacy and its power to bind; in a word, its moral authority.[50] The success or failure of his answer will depend on the senses he gives to these two terms.

In raising this question of validity, Barth does not depart from his fundamental conviction, discussed in the previous chapter, that moral theology is not in a position to ground the command of God but only to attest and confirm it. This same conviction governs his account of the validity of the claim of God's command. Right and power to bind are not lodged in us and are not conferred by us. Any account of the validity of the divine claim must therefore explain how the command of God establishes its own authority. This conviction has an unmistakable voluntarist flavor, and Barth will take some pains to avoid the problematic implications of voluntarism. This is nowhere more apparent than in his response to the notion that the divine claim is grounded in God as one who has the power (*Macht*) to compel our conformity to a divine order (or, in more personalistic terms, our obedience to divine commands). Barth's scathing response to attempts to ground moral right in divine might in part reveals his deep humanist sympathies as well as his awareness of the political implications of strong voluntarism. Human beings, he says, have not only the capacity and the right but also the duty to maintain themselves against power as such and thus to resist religion in this form as 'an outrage to the essence of man' and a source of tyranny.[51] No claim based on power as such has any right to demand our obedience. However, the vigor with which Barth opposes the appeal to divine power also indicates his determination to dissociate himself from a position which, as we will soon see, is dangerously close to his own and must therefore be resisted all the more strongly. Another appeal to God as the ground of the moral law identifies God as the ultimate object of human desire, understanding the moral life as the ordering and direction of desire to this its only proper and genuinely satisfying object. In Barth's view, while it is true that God does satisfy the deepest and most genuine human desires, what these desires are is apparent only in light of the command of God, not in advance of it. To appeal to the satisfaction of desire as the ground of the divine claim makes the good

---

[49] See Helmut Thielicke, *Theological Ethics*, i: *Foundations* (Philadelphia: Fortress Press, 1966), 99 f. The Lutheran position expresses a twofold conviction that law must be presented in its starkness in order to accomplish its two purposes of restraining evil and convicting of sin, and that law so understood is unable to resolve the problem it opens up.

[50] The assumption here is that the notion of authority combines both legitimacy and force (which is not compulsion or coercion, in which case we would speak of power rather than authority). It is unclear what use a concept of authority could have if it simply repeated, perhaps in a loud voice, what is already conveyed by legitimacy, the notion that a moral claim or directive has right on its side. Authority adds something to legitimacy; it involves a surplus of persuasive force over and above right.

[51] CD II/2, 552–4/613–15.

conditional on a contingent human desire, and so it too fails to ground the divine claim.[52] Neither by compulsion nor by attraction, then, is God the ground of the validity of the law. Nor is this ground given by a natural participation of human beings in God as the ultimate good. Here, too, participation in the divine good is what the command of God bestows on us apart from what we already possess in ourselves; it therefore cannot be the condition of the validity of this command.[53]

In contrast to these positions, Barth holds that the God who legitimately and effectually claims us is the God who 'has made himself ours,' 'has taken our place and taken up our cause,' and 'is for us in all his deity.' In the incarnation, life, death, and resurrection of Jesus Christ, God has realized on our behalf the fellowship with God which God willed for us from eternity, assuming our humanity into God's deity, saying Yes to grace in our place, and bearing the judgment of God against our No to grace. In place of attraction, compulsion, and natural participation, Barth finds the ground of the divine claim in the actualization of the good God has resolved on from eternity. In Jesus Christ, God has accomplished the good in our place, realizing it as the human good, and it is only on this ground that God claims us—not as a God to whom we are forced to submit or as one who completes an economy of desire but as the God in whom we *may believe.*[54]

But how is it that God's claim on us has legitimacy and force by virtue of what God has done for us? On what grounds do God's benefit and favor towards humanity confer right and power to bind on God's claim to humanity? Barth's reply to these questions is twofold. The first reply has to do with God's self-vindication as God in being for us. Barth argues that 'the grace of God in Jesus Christ is the proclamation and establishment of his authority over man' insofar as it is here that God shows decisively that 'all that he proposes to do and wills to have will finally achieve its goal and end.' Thus 'what God maintains in this way in relation to man is his own glory, his authority and majesty.'[55] Here legitimacy, the right to command, is closely related to sovereignty, yet sovereignty is not conceived as arbitrary power, as it is in strong versions of voluntarism. For Barth, God's power is not abstract might and God's will is not arbitrary freedom. God's power and will must rather be understood as power and will to fulfill God's eternal self-determination to be with and for a human other. Divine sovereignty must therefore be understood as God's power to uphold the covenant God has made with humanity. God's self-vindication in Christ is God's self-vindication as lord of the covenant. God proves faithful to the covenant from its divine side, and it is, therefore, as already fulfilled on God's side that the claim of

---

[52] CD II/2, 555 f./616 f. This point recalls Kant's argument that moral principles based on desires or inclinations lack the universality and necessity morality requires.

[53] CD II/2, 554/615 f.

[54] CD II/2, 557–59/618–21.

[55] CD II/2, 560/622.

God addresses us. 'It is as he makes himself responsible for man that God makes man, too, responsible.'[56] It is in this way, Barth holds, that what God has done for us establishes the legitimacy of God's command. In contrast to the cases of power, desire, and participation in the good by nature, here God meets us in God's self-disclosure, and thus unambiguously as God rather than as the projection of human ambitions and ideological constructs.[57]

Second, Barth argues that what God has done for us establishes moral authority because it alone claims us in a complete and decisive way. If the first point had to do with the legitimacy (*Recht*) of the divine claim, this point has to do with the power to bind (*Kraft*) that accompanies its legitimacy. 'The God who is the basis of the ethical claim,' Barth argues, '. . . must have authority over man, and therefore the power to deprive him of recourse to his own freedom or weakness, to his own alleged identity with the good.'[58] No other command can claim us wholly because other commands leave us to ourselves: to our neutral freedom to obey or disobey them, to our ability or inability to meet their demands by our own capacities and powers, to the necessity and prerogative of determining exactly what is required of us. In all of these respects the law is conditioned by us and both expresses and perpetuates our being for ourselves. By contrast, the command of the God who is for us in Jesus Christ is unconditioned because it nullifies appeals to our freedom to obey or disobey it, our relative strength or weakness in the face of what it demands, and our prerogative to determine what it requires. These appeals are nullified precisely because Christ has already done the good in our place.[59] There are therefore no grounds on which we are free to consider whether to do the good or not, but only to freely affirm its accomplishment in Christ; no grounds for despair or self-exoneration in the face of our inability to do the good; and no grounds for attempting to determine what that good is, as if it had not already been determined in Christ's accomplishment of it. The law thus requires only what the gospel has already given: that we exist in and with Christ who has accomplished the good in our place.

For Barth, then, it is in these two respects that grace—what God is and does for us in Jesus Christ—establishes the law. If Barth is right, then he has successfully addressed the charge that grace is incapable of establishing a truly binding law. Yet his position is problematic in both of its aspects. First, God establishes the authority to command in the fulfillment of the covenant from its divine side. But exactly how does this establish the legitimacy of the divine claim to human obedience? If the legitimacy of the divine claim rests on the fact that it is in God's grace in Jesus Christ that God meets us unambiguously as God, how is this not simply a more subtle

---

[56] CD II/2, 511/567.
[57] CD II/2, 560 f./622.
[58] CD II/2, 564 f./627.
[59] CD II/2, 565/627.

form of the voluntarist appeal to God's power which Barth has rejected, notwithstanding that the God who meets us here is the one who has fulfilled the covenant
from its divine side? Why is this act by which God claims us not an act of divine self-
assertion, in which case Barth's God (as some, writing from somewhat different
perspectives than this one, have held) ironically resembles the modern subject? And,
if legitimacy in this case has to do with what God has done for us, how is it that
God's command of grace establishes a genuine human partner rather than a mere
object of divine benefit? Second, God's claim over us gains its force by foreclosing
our retreat into ourselves. But why should we not view this as the annihilation of the
human subject claimed by grace? How is it that the moral subject is established in its
proper reality by the command of God rather than eliminated by blocking the paths
of its withdrawal to itself? Does grace bind us only by humiliating or destroying us?

In sum, it is far from clear why we should not see the command of God's grace as
the benevolent tyranny of a divine philanthropist who is for us at the expense of our
existence as free subjects and whose gifts are simply calculated to instill a deeper and
more lasting sense of obligation than fear of divine wrath ever could. And if this is
so, it is difficult to see how grace has established either the right of the law or its
effective force. The response to these problems is found in Barth's claim that the law
as the form of the gospel is a law of freedom, and to that claim we now turn.

Law is not Law apart from Grace

For Barth, there is no grace that does not also establish law—that was the first
point. But there is also no law that is without grace. This is the second point. For
Barth, just as grace never stands alone, so also the 'divine claim never stands
alone'; the law is always the 'concealed repetition' of grace.[60] This brings us to the
second claim from 'Das Halten der Gebote': Apart from the gospel, I have not
heard the law as law. But what does it mean to hear the law in the proper sense, as
the concealed repetition of grace? It is to hear it as the law of freedom. 'The
command of God orders us to be free. How can it be otherwise? The command is
only the form of the gospel of God, in virtue of which—not in and by ourselves
but in and by Jesus Christ—we are free.'[61] The distinctiveness of the command
of God thus 'consists in the fact that it is permission—the granting [*Gewährung*]
of a wholly determinate [*ganz bestimmten*] freedom.'[62]

It is in this sense, as Barth suggests, that the law is the form of the gospel.[63] By
this he appears to mean at least two closely related things. First, as the form of the

---

[60]   CD II/2, 563/625.
[61]   CD II/2, 588/653.
[62]   CD II/2, 585/650 (revised).
[63]   Gerhard Ebeling argues that Barth's oft-repeated formula stating that the law is the form of
the gospel and the gospel the content of the law is logically incoherent insofar as content and form
must always refer to some factor X of which they are the content and the form. He also argues that
the notion of form intended by the formula is not specified and that Barth presents inconsistent

gospel, the law confronts us with a moral reality in which we already stand. Rather than confronting us, as other commands do, with what it is up to us to do or become, the command of God 'wills only that we make use of the given permission by the grace of God to be what we are . . .'[64] Responsibility thus rests on its proper ground: As the form of the *gospel,* the law presents us with what has already been done for us and not with what we must do for ourselves. It is only in this context that we can understand the otherwise puzzling claim that the command of God takes the form of permission, that it addresses us by saying 'You may,' rather than 'You must.' Barth does not deny that the command of God confronts us with an imperative; it too says 'Do this and do not do that.'[65] But these imperatives command us to live in the freedom made possible by God's grace, to appropriate for ourselves a reality that is already opened up for us in and by Christ's fulfillment of the law in our place, a reality in which, by virtue of our participation in Christ, we already stand. What we may be is what in Jesus Christ we are now free to be, so that the form of the law is permission, yet what we may be is also what we ought to be, so that it also confronts us as an obligation.[66]

With this identity of permission and obligation we have already arrived at the second point implied in the claim that the law is the form of the gospel. In the command of God as the form of God's grace, 'the right obligation is the true permission, and the right permission [is] the true obligation.'[67] It follows from this that an act of obedience is also and as such an act of freedom, and vice versa. This fundamental point clarifies the alternative Barth is seeking between compulsion and attraction, or power and desire, as grounds of the divine claim. The 'may' and the 'must' preserve, in radically altered form, the legitimate features of attraction and compulsion, respectively, so that this coincidence of permission and obligation replaces the contrast between attraction and compulsion. What we are by the grace of God in Jesus Christ is, for Barth, the fulfillment of our being, and in this sense Barth preserves the fundamental insight of teleological, 'attractive' conceptions of ethics even as he rejects the notion that we have a natural affinity or capacity for our telos.[68] This lack of natural affinity between desire and the good is precisely why permission must also be obligation, the 'compulsion' of law. Permission alone would leave us free to be or not to be

versions of the formula. See Gerhard Ebeling, *Word and Faith* (Philadelphia: Fortress Press, 1963), 267 n. 1. Ebeling is right to criticize the formula itself on both of these grounds. However, Barth's central idea is clear enough. 'The one Word of God is both gospel *and* law' (CD II/2, 511/567). As gospel, it tells us what Jesus Christ has done for us in our place (content, indicative). As law, it tells us that what Jesus Christ has done in our place claims us (form, imperative) by summoning, empowering, and directing us to make it our own (see 'Gospel and Law,' 73; and CD II/2, 557/619).

[64] CD II/2, 588/653.
[65] CD II/2, 587/652.
[66] CD II/2, 587/652, 593/659, 602/669.
[67] CD II/2, 602/670.
[68] CD II/2, 566 f./628 f., 571/634, 650/724.

who and what we truly are and would thus reaffirm the false freedom of the subject that is for itself.[69] Hence, without ceasing to be permission the command must also take the form of obligation—not, however, obligation without permission, for the demand on its own addresses us as something we are to accomplish by our own will and action, thus canceling grace, while the command of God frees us from living for ourselves.

This coincidence of permission and obligation is paradoxical, and for good reason. Barth points out that it is only in Jesus Christ and therefore eschatologically that the coincidence occurs; for us, this coincidence is a matter of faith rather than a fact of experience. Empirically, our moral life will always exhibit a preponderance of one at the expense of the other as we lean now towards legalism (obligation alone) and now towards antinomianism (permission alone). At no point in our moral experience itself, then, will the law unambiguously express the gospel. Barth is no utopian. The best moral theology can do in this situation is what theology must always do in the case of an eschatological reality, which is to tack dialectically back and forth, in this case between permission and obligation in the confidence that they do indeed coincide in the Word of God itself and thus in the command of God given to us. But because they do coincide there, our moral theology, as well as our moral lives, can and must be carried out in this confidence.[70]

With this identification of the law with freedom in place, we are in a position to address the suspicion that the divine claim of grace is an expression of divine self-assertion that destroys the human moral subject. It is only after we have understood exactly how Barth links the law with freedom—and what this linkage implies for notions of responsibility and the moral subject—that we will be able to see how divine grace is other than mere divine self-assertion and how the human subject is established rather than annihilated as this grace takes the form of law. Barth's linkage of law with freedom, however, is highly complex. It combines the Pauline problematic of the law in Romans 7–8 with the Reformation-era polemics against works righteousness which appealed to that problematic, and it treats all of this in the context of modern tensions between freedom and authority in relation to the moral subject. The remainder of this subsection clarifies this complex linkage of law and freedom in response to the suspicion regarding the divine claim.

The key to Barth's position is his distinction between the true meaning of the law as the expression of God's grace and its distortion in our attempt to establish our moral worth. As the demand to live as those whom God is for, the law 'requires only that we be satisfied with the grace of God.' But when the law encounters us, it awakens our desire to be for ourselves; this desire appropriates the law, taking advantage of its very normativity in an effort to establish our

---

[69] CD II/2, 599/666.
[70] This paragraph states Barth's major points in CD II/2, 602–8/669–76.

moral worth: to justify, sanctify, and glorify ourselves.[71] In Pauline terms, this is the law that arouses sinful passions, the law through which sin finds an opportunity to assert itself, with the result that the law that promised life brought death instead (Rom. 7: 5, 8–11). How so? Precisely as that by which we would secure our own moral worth, this law is without grace; it throws us back on ourselves, making us responsible for determining its requirements and fulfilling them.

Since the law in this distorted form is how the law is experienced in our factual (though absurd) reality as sinners, we will begin with it. Barth's characterization of this condition in which we are left to ourselves under the law seems to revolve around a twofold indeterminacy of the law in this condition. The first indeterminacy has to do with responsibility. Apart from grace the law confronts us as unfulfilled and thus demands of us that we meet its requirement. It confronts us with the gap between itself, as an ideal or an obligation, and reality, and it imposes on us the burden of making reality approximate the ideal or conform to the obligation. Law instills in us the sense that it is 'up to us'; it thus appeals, Barth says, to our anxiety and fear.[72] Second, the law in this condition is indeterminate insofar as it is left to us to determine what the law specifically requires. In our effort to secure our moral worth we are confronted with the plethora of demands which present themselves to us as requisites of our natural, social, or cultural existence, commend themselves as norms through which we may achieve moral goodness, and claim the authority of the law of God. The ideological abuse of law—investing merely human norms with divine authority—is of course prominent among Barth's concerns here. Just as important, and closely related, is the threat of tyranny. These multifarious demands all confront us with their imperative force which we, committed to making ourselves morally worthy, are not free to ignore. Having taken the law to be the means by which we establish our own righteousness, we must evaluate and do justice to all its demands. Above all, insofar as we have, in this project of moral self-realization, taken upon ourselves the task of judging good and evil, we are delivered over to human judgments—whether our own or those of others—of what those demands are. We are therefore slaves, even when the laws we impose on ourselves and others commend themselves to us, as they regularly do, by appealing to our desires or interests. In this condition, as human beings assert themselves as judges of good and evil in God's place and over each other, the law becomes vulnerable to the truly horrific abuses of the German Christians as well as to much more banal abuses in everyday life.[73]

In short, when Barth looks away from the command of God fulfilled in Christ, what he sees is a form of morality in which neutral freedom of choice is constrained by the moral law, leaving the moral subject with a perpetual tension

---

[71] CD II/2, 590/654 f.
[72] CD II/2, 585/650.
[73] CD II/2, 586 f./651 f.; 'Gospel and Law,' 88 f., 91.

between obligation and freedom; in which the moral law confronts us with the gap between itself and reality, demanding that we close this gap yet without giving us the power to do so; and in which we must assume the prerogative to determine what the law requires, subjecting ourselves and others to our power to pronounce the judgment of good and evil. All of this, Barth holds, is inevitable when we misuse the law to establish our own moral worth. But we should be clear what Barth is and is not saying here. The problem for him does not lie in the notion of law itself, that is, the fact that our lives are placed under a binding norm or standard to which we are responsible in all our life conduct. Obviously, the command of God itself is law in this sense. Nor is the problem necessarily with individual laws themselves, the specific requirements issuing out of our natural, social, and cultural existence. We have already seen that for Barth 'the claim of God's command always wears the garment of another claim of this kind,' and he will go on to devote hundreds of pages to detailed moral instruction about the command of God in these aspects of our lives as creatures.[74] Rather, what Barth targets in his depiction of law as the expression of human self-assertion is the burden of responsibility we assume for ourselves by taking on the dual task of determining what the good is and realizing it in our conduct. The problem with the law as the expression of human self-assertion is that it is not the expression of God's grace, and apart from grace it can only address us as something we are left to ourselves to fulfill while its concrete imperatives can only subject us to norms that do not attest God's grace but serve other interests. For Barth, there is a close relationship between our mistaken belief that the law, unfulfilled in itself, confronts us with the necessity of fulfilling it, on the one hand, and our treating the law as something we are left to fulfill by giving it our own content, on the other hand. Both result from failure to understand the law as the summons of grace. If the law is something other than the summons of grace it will hold us responsible to bring about the good, and the good we resolve to bring about will be something other than the good fulfilled in Christ. It is true, of course, that we *are* responsible and that content apparently other than Christ may in fact be genuine attestations of Christ. But responsibility and moral content in these proper senses depend on the law addressing us in its proper form, namely, the form of the gospel.

What should we make of this bleak portrait of life under the misused law? As is frequently the case, Barth's rhetoric reaches its highest pitch precisely where he must convince us of something that first strikes us as implausible. Is it really such an intolerable burden to be confronted with an unfulfilled demand or to place oneself under laws determined by human judgment to be morally binding? Barth speaks of the person in this condition as 'vexed and tormented,' filled with 'anxious fears,' 'a victim of insomnia,' 'delivered up, like a hunted beast to the

---

[74] CD II/2, 584 f./649.

hounds, to what the world and life and men want of him, to what, above all, he himself must continually want of himself.'[75] Yet he is aware that our subjective experience of moral responsibility may be very different from this depiction; we may in fact feel quite comfortable in our self-assertion.[76] What is it, then, that in his mind makes self-assumed moral responsibility the thoroughly dismal affair he describes?

To answer this question let us look more closely at the form the law takes in our being for ourselves. In addition to the twofold indeterminacy we have just discussed, the law in this condition is also the counterpart of neutral freedom of choice. Here we recall Barth's portrayal of the subject who maintains itself in its neutral freedom as well as in its prerogative to judge good and evil. In the economy of this subject, laws impose themselves on us as necessary limits to an essentially neutral freedom which itself is dangerous because it is fundamentally anarchic, while human judgments of good and evil have undue authority and power over those who have determined to assert the human prerogative to judge good and evil.[77] In both cases, our being for ourselves turns out to be domination by an alien law. For Barth, no law of this kind—not a biological necessity or social requirement or even a law of conscience—'has the power to press us so closely that we cannot keep our distance from it, remaining within ourselves, or constantly returning to ourselves, behind and in all that we think and say and do in submission to its claim. It belongs to the nature of all other commands that in the face of them we necessarily have to come back again and again to ourselves . . .'[78] We retain in the face of such a law our freedom to decide for or against it and our prerogative to judge it. But this means that the law in this economy of self-assertion is subject to a twofold failure. Insofar as it stands over against the human subject, leaving this subject intact in its being for itself, it cannot genuinely bind, while for its part this subject can never wholly identify with it, which means that its obedience can never be joyful and whole since in its very being as the subject it is—in its freedom, its inability to obey, and its position as judge—it maintains itself over against the law. In its being for itself it can recognize as law only what it freely chooses in accordance with its judgment of good and evil, yet the law which it chooses stands over against its neutral freedom to obey or disobey and its prerogative to determine what it requires. A subject who, qua moral subject, is free to obey or disobey—indeterminate like Hercules, who (in one of Barth's favorite images) is free to choose between good and evil—possesses a fragile freedom because the determinacy of obedience necessarily threatens it and the subject constituted by it. Its obedience will always be servile submission to an other, even when it is freely chosen. The subject who

---

[75] CD II/2, 585/650, 586 f./651 f.
[76] CD II/2, 593 f./659 f., 594/660.
[77] CD II/2, 585/650, 586 f./651 f.
[78] CD II/2, 595/662.

asserts itself in its being for itself is thus caught in an unrelieved tension between freedom and obligation which appears destined to play out in other tensions— between alienation and self-assertion, authoritarianism and rebellion, legalism and antinomianism—which are all too prevalent in modern (and not only modern) moral and political life.[79]

In this economy of our being for ourselves the law as the tool of human self-assertion takes the form of tyranny. Yet it is still the law of God, and as such it now plays the role of exposing us as sinners. Grace itself, in the form of the law, as a demand to live by grace, exposes our hostility to grace: our sinful self-assertion against grace in our desire to establish our moral worth as the product of our own efforts and abilities. In Pauline terms, the law becomes 'the law of sin and death' (Rom. 8: 2), the law under which (viewed retrospectively from the perspective of the new person) we were in bondage (Gal. 3: 23 f.) and from which we are now free (Gal. 3: 25; Rom. 7: 6, 8: 2). It is from this condition, Barth holds, that Jesus Christ has delivered us, doing what the law could not do (Rom. 8: 3). It is at exactly this point—where the law as the form of grace exposes us as sinners hostile to grace and therefore as disobedient—that the more familiar priority of law to gospel has its proper though limited place. The law now takes on the familiar Lutheran role of conviction of sin that drives us to the gospel, which now meets us as the consoling word of forgiveness and reconciliation. Yet the sin exposed by the gospel in the form of the law is, as we have noted, not a violation of a grace-less law but of the law of grace itself.[80] And the gospel that consoles is not a law-less gospel but a gospel that both frees us from condemnation (negative) and reestablishes the law of grace (positive): 'The law of the Spirit of life in Christ Jesus has set me free from the law of sin and death' (Rom. 8: 2). Before turning to the positive freedom given by the command of God, it is worth quoting Barth's summary of the liberation it offers. 'As the command of the grace of God, it circumvents the person who would save and purify and justify and sanctify himself. It circumvents all the submissions to other commands which he would make to this end. More than that, it circumvents all the permissions he

---

[79] The notion that the determinacy of an object of choice nullifies the indeterminacy of freedom has a Hegelian ring to it (see Hegel, *Elements of the Philosophy of Right*, § 15). However, the terms 'indeterminate' and 'determinate,' used here to characterize the neutral freedom to choose and what is required or obligatory, respectively, do not have a Hegelian meaning here. For Hegel, the will is both indeterminate freedom (the abstract capacity to act otherwise than our inclinations or desires dictate) and determinate content (desires or inclinations) and must overcome this opposition in order to actualize its freedom (*Elements of the Philosophy of Right*, § 7 & R, A). The indeterminacy Barth has in mind here is simply the capacity to choose, and if this interpretation is right, his point is that insofar as the moral subject is constituted by its indeterminacy in this sense, it cannot identify itself with a moral obligation, since the latter entails determinacy.

[80] This explains why Barth can portray even the terror and accusation of the law as an expression of grace (II/2, 595/662). The law opposes me only in my self-destructive being for myself, and in that sense it expresses the grace of God who is for me and will not abandon me to my being for myself. Judgment, for Barth, is always an act of the God who wills to have us as God's own.

would give himself to this end. Above all and decisively, it circumvents his retreat into himself, the further exercise of his office as the judge of good and evil.'[81]

We are now ready to consider the law in its proper nature, as the expression of God's being for us. Precisely as the form of God's grace the command of God confronts us with what has already been done for us in Christ, and thus with a reality in which, in our being in Christ, we already stand. Because the law has already been fulfilled in the obedience of Jesus Christ, it confronts us by placing us before the reality in which we are now free to live, not by imposing on us a norm or ideal that it is up to us to realize. It is difficult to overemphasize the significance of this last point. For Barth, the fact that the law comes to us already fulfilled means that it does not confront us as an obligation, ideal, or end for us to meet, actualize, or approximate through our moral activity but as a reality in which we already exist by virtue of our participation in Christ and in which we are summoned to remain. In this connection, Barth draws attention to the frequency of the commands to 'abide' and 'stand' in the New Testament. 'Christians who are summoned to an "abiding" and a "standing" have a possibility in what is given to them in Jesus Christ and through life with him and in his Church; and the sum of all that is demanded of them is to make use of this possibility, or rather to let it realize itself.'[82] We recall that for Barth the command of God 'wills only that we make use of the given permission by the grace of God to be what we are,' namely, those who in Jesus Christ are free. To hear the law in the proper sense, as the form of grace, its 'concealed repetition,' is to hear it as this summons to freedom which, in Jesus Christ, we already possess. To speak again in terms of Barth's scriptural exegesis, the law in this, its most proper sense is the 'law of liberty' (James 1: 22 f.), the 'law of the Spirit of life' (Rom. 8: 2), and the law that according to Romans 7: 12 and 14 is 'holy and righteous and good' and 'spiritual.' This is the law that is not opposed to the promises (Gal. 3: 21), is attested by the Torah and prophets (Rom. 3: 21), and whose righteous demand is fulfilled by those who walk according to the Spirit rather than the flesh (Rom. 8: 4). The law in this proper sense is the command of God which 'requires only that we be satisfied with the grace of God.'[83]

It is clear that the kind of freedom indicated here goes beyond negative freedom, that is, liberation from the false freedom of our being for ourselves. The law of the Spirit of life is not simply liberation from the law of sin and death, leaving a space altogether empty of law; it is, after all, the *law* of the Spirit of life. This brings us back to the claim that the command of God is permission. Permission grants something. The law is a 'gift of freedom.' But in what sense is this so? We recall that it is a *determinate (bestimmten)* freedom that is commanded; the command of God 'will always set us free along a definite

---

[81] CD II/2, 596/663.
[82] CD II/2, 600/667.
[83] CD II/2, 590/655.

(*bestimmten*) line.'[84] For Barth, 'God freely makes himself available to man by granting him the freedom he is meant to have.'[85] But the freedom that fulfills this divine purpose is a certain kind of freedom and not mere indeterminacy, the capacity to choose one way or another. In the proper sense, freedom can mean only the affirmation, in our own choice, decision, and act, of what God has done for us. 'Man becomes free and is free by choosing, deciding, and determining himself in accordance with the freedom of God.' It follows that to choose, decide, and determine oneself otherwise is not to exercise freedom wrongly; it is to contradict freedom altogether.[86]

Of course, Barth is aware that to refer to choice, decision, and act is to imply a kind of natural freedom that belongs to human creatureliness.[87] Nothing in his position requires the denial of this natural human voluntary capacity. To the contrary: freedom in this sense is the presupposition, the condition of the possibility, of affirming grace; it is a constituent of created nature as that which God has chosen to bring into being as the external ground of the covenant. Without this freedom, obedience would be merely mechanical—not the fully human form of obedience God willed in electing and creating a genuine partner. What Barth does deny, though, is that this natural freedom is the ontological ground of the moral subject. This follows from a central point in Barth's theological anthropology, which propounds an ontology of the subject in place of a substance ontology. 'The human subject is not a substance with certain qualities or functions. It is the self-moving and self-moved subject in responsibility to God, or it is not a subject at all.' Ontologically, therefore, freedom is the act of a subject rather than a capacity. 'Freedom is not to be found in a background which enables him to live freely. It is the freedom lived out and exercised in the act of responsibility before God, or it is not freedom.'[88] For Barth, to be human is ultimately, in terms of its ontological ground, 'to be with God [*mit Gott zusammen sein*].'[89] Theological anthropology is grounded in the doctrine of the incarnation, in the bond of our humanity with the humanity of Jesus, which is ontologically constituted by its enhypostatic relation to the divine, so that to be with God, and thus to be human, is to be with Jesus. But because the existence of Jesus is determined by his election from eternity and is the sum of the Word of God addressed to the human creature, to be with Jesus is to be elected in him and to be addressed by the Word of God in his existence. 'Summoned because chosen' is Barth's pithy way of expressing the human reality.[90] The

---

[84] CD II/2, 586/651.

[85] Barth, 'The Gift of Freedom: Foundation of Evangelical Ethics,' in *The Humanity of God*, trans. Thomas Wieser (Atlanta: John Knox Press, 1976), 75.

[86] Ibid. 76 f.

[87] Ibid. 75.

[88] CD III/2, 196/233.

[89] CD III/2, 135/161.

[90] CD III/2, 150/180.

human subject is ontologically constituted by the summons to appropriate the grace of election, that is, to determine oneself, by one's own choice or decision, in accordance with one's divine determination. To respond freely to this summons is to be ontically (in one's concrete existence) what one is ontologically (elected and summoned by God to participate freely in God's freedom for humanity); it is to confirm one's election.

In the law as the form or the concealed repetition of grace, then, freedom and obedience coincide, corresponding to the coincidence of permission and obligation. Of course, the coincidence is in principle. As we have seen in the case of permission and obligation, it occurs in Christ, and therefore eschatologically rather than in our moral experience itself. But it is from this Christological site that the law is issued, summoning us to appropriate a reality that is already ours in Christ. And it is only now, in view of this coincidence of freedom and obedience, that we are finally in a position to respond to the suspicion that in Barth's moral theology grace annihilates the human subject.

As grace takes the form of law it brings ethics into crisis, forcing the two alternatives we have been exploring in this chapter and in this book as a whole: Either ethics expresses the radical espousal of the human cause by God (radical because it is ultimately God's own self-determination) or ethics expresses the determination of human beings to take up their own cause in rejection of God's grace. What we can now see is that these two fundamental forms of ethics involve two fundamentally different conceptions of the moral subject in relation to freedom and obedience—that is, two different conceptions of responsibility. The discussion of the law as the form of the gospel in the *Church Dogmatics* presses the quasi-Kantian contrast between a law that is in tension with our freedom and a law that is identical with our freedom.[91] In the first case, freedom is 'free will,' 'self-will,' indeterminate choice.[92] Here, as we have seen, the moral law is the correlate of a freedom grounded in ourselves, a freedom which may be equally exercised in obedience or disobedience to that law, so that freedom and obedience remain in constant tension while the moral law always returns us to ourselves.[93] The moral law is, paradoxically, both grounded in us and alien to us. It is therefore subject to the double failure noted above: because in the end it must appeal to our arbitrary freedom, it is both unable genuinely to bind us

[91] CD II/2, 585 f./650 f.
[92] CD II/2, 594/660.
[93] The most concise formulation of this contrast occurs in Barth's treatment of 'the form of the divine claim' in CD II/2, 583–630/648–701. From a superficial perspective Barth seems in this section to engage in a rather crude version of the kind of reversal of valuation Nietzsche ascribed to the slave morality and its *ressentiment*: the freedom of human self-assertion is really servitude and the servitude of obedience is true freedom. However, this interpretation makes clear that for Barth the question is whether freedom and obedience converge or remain in tension. This in turn determines, as we will see presently, which position can solve the problem of freedom and alterity, and all of this, finally, depends on whether ethics is grounded in the radical 'for us' of God's grace or in the 'for ourselves' of modern humanism.

(rendering responsibility itself precarious), since we retain in our freedom the power and right to decide for or against it; and it is unable to demand our full identification with it, since our obedience to it is always qualified by our freedom to reject it.[94] There is here a permanent tension between freedom and obedience, leaving in its wake an unstable moral subject for whom autonomy (false freedom) and tyranny (false obedience) are never far apart.

In the second case, freedom is 'our own decision . . . which corresponds to our determination.'[95] The law is 'the given permission by the grace of God to be what we are';[96] it 'imposes freedom on man' and 'sets man free with the obedience which it requires of him,'[97] and it 'secures obedience by itself setting us free.'[98] Here, the moral law is expressive of the freedom to fulfill the divine determination of human beings to be covenant partners of God, a freedom which grace has already won for us, in which it has established us, and which it summons us, as law, to confirm in our conduct. The moral law as the expression of divine grace confronts us from outside ourselves, in Christ's obedience (thus genuinely binding us), yet it confronts us as the fulfillment of our true being, that is, as the accomplishment of our determination by the divine grace of election over against a false, spurious, and ultimately ruinous self-determination. Freedom and obedience are thus (in principle) perfectly conjoined, and we are constituted as moral subjects by this summons to be in our conduct what we already are in and by God's grace. In this way the command of God addresses us as the command of the God who is for us and not against us; it 'takes our side.'[99]

In sum, to hear the law rightly is to hear it as the renewed offer of grace.[100] In place of our effort at self-justification is Christ who has fulfilled the law in our place. In place of the gap between the demand of the law and our moral capability is the possibility opened up for us by Christ's own obedience, a possibility in which we already stand as those who participate in Christ and in which the law summons us simply to remain. In place of an alien law confronting our neutral freedom is the coincidence of permission and obligation, freedom and obedience, eschatologically fulfilled in Christ and issuing forth to us as law from that Christological site.

---

[94] It would be interesting to compare this line of criticism of modern responsibility with Hegel's criticism of Kantian morality in his *Elements of the Philosophy of Right* (see especially §§ 133–8). Hegel thought that the Kantian moral law was capable of binding the subject but unable to supply the content that would enable the subject genuinely to identify with it. For Barth the moral law so understood (which he recognized as more post-Kantian than Kantian) is unable to do what Hegel thought that it could do.

[95] CD II/2, 595/661.
[96] CD II/2, 588/653.
[97] CD II/2, 596/663.
[98] CD II/2, 593/659.
[99] CD II/2, 595–7/661–3.
[100] CD II/2, 594/660.

Jesus Christ, the Content of the Law

To hear the law as law in the proper sense is to hear it as the form of the gospel, but this implies that the *content* of the law is Jesus Christ himself. It is this content that is expressed in the form of the law. Apart from Christ as the content of the law, sin takes advantage of the normative form of the law, its imperative or 'ought' character, to establish moral worth by human moral striving, filling this form with whatever content recommends itself to our judgment as plausible for this project, investing that content with divine authority, and imposing it on oneself and others.[101] It is this grace-less (because Christ-less) law that condemns us. But what does it mean to say that Jesus Christ is the content of the law? More specifically, what is the law which Christ fulfills in our place, and what does his fulfillment of that law demand of us? These questions bring us to the third and final point of our discussion, namely, that what the law demands is the confirmation of God's grace in human being and conduct. This point prompts what may be the most challenging question posed to Barth's gospel–law thesis, namely, how is it that the demand to confirm grace does not constitute a *nova lex*, a new law which nullifies grace? It is easy to see how this question persists despite all that we have said in the previous two subsections. For if Christ has fulfilled the law in our place it is not clear how his fulfillment of it can demand anything of us without compromising the meaning and reality of 'in our place,' and thus nullifying it.

To respond to this question let us first consider what it is that Christ has done in our place, the law he has fulfilled on our behalf. For Barth, Jesus 'does not crave to be good of and for himself.' Unlike Hercules at the crossroads, he is not good on the basis of an autonomous choice of good over evil but rather as one who is subject 'to the will and command of the God who alone is good.'[102] As such, his obedience is that 'of the one who is received and accepted by God in free goodness'; it is 'the obedience of the free man to the free God.'[103] In other words, it is the obedience of faith. It is in saying 'Yes' in this way to grace that Jesus fulfills the law in our place. He believes and obeys in our place, both substituting for us and representing us before God.[104] It is in this light that we are to see what is demanded of us. What the law requires is that we allow his fulfillment of the law, his obedience of faith, to count as our own and thus 'to be one for whom God has intervened in this way . . . to be one for whose human existence Jesus Christ himself stands before God. . . .'[105] We are to think and act and live as those who have their lives not in themselves but hidden with Christ in God.[106]

---

[101] Barth, 'Gospel and Law,' 87 f., 91.
[102] CD II/2, 517/574.
[103] CD II/2, 561/623 (revised).
[104] CD II/2, 558 f./620.
[105] CD II/2, 559/620.
[106] See Barth, 'Gospel and Law,' 82–4, II/2, 559/620 f., 579–83/643–8.

It is clear from these considerations that the law addressed to us from Christ's fulfillment of it does not demand that we do anything as a condition of grace, as if grace were not entirely gratuitous, or as a supplement to grace, as if grace were insufficient in itself to establish the good and were in need of a law to complete it. In either of these cases it would be necessary to speak of a *nova lex* that is not the law of the gospel. As Barth formulates it, however, the law requires only that we confirm grace, say 'Yes' to it, endorse it—and that not merely in passive acquiescence to it but as the active subjects God determined to have as genuine partners in God's covenant. 'When man is summoned to do the right, primarily and decisively he is summoned only to adhere to the fact that the gracious God does the right.'[107]

If we have now allayed the suspicion that the command of God's grace is a *nova lex* that nullifies grace, we have not yet explained what it means for Jesus Christ to be the content of that command. The explanation takes us back to where we began, namely, to the reason why grace establishes law in the first place. 'The aim [*Ziel*] of the grace actualized and revealed in God's covenant with man, is the restoration of man to the divine likeness [*Bilde*] and therefore to fellowship with God in eternal life.'[108] God wills to have us as God's own: this is God's determination of humanity from eternity, and the law is simply the summons to human beings to be God's own, to enjoy fellowship with God. But Jesus Christ is the one who obeys the summons and thus fulfills this determination on our behalf. Jesus Christ himself is thus the content or substance of the law, and what the law therefore summons us to do is simply to be with Jesus. The fellowship with God which is the aim of the law is fellowship with Jesus Christ who has already fulfilled that aim. It follows that the most fundamental expression of the command of God is the call to discipleship: 'Follow me!' The command of God is God's self-offer. It is inseparable from the grace of God who wills not to be without us. But what is the discipleship to which we are summoned? In the first instance, as the command issued to Jesus' disciples, '"following" means simply to be there, to be with Jesus, in his proximity.'[109] However, because 'Jesus never exists alone and for himself, but always as the first-born among many brethren,' to be with Jesus is to be with his people. The fellowship with God that is the aim of God's grace is fulfilled by membership in Israel and the church. 'The law of this people's life is the Law of God. In the fact that he wills and creates this people, God says what he wants of it and what he wants of all other men.'[110] We will have much more to say in the next two chapters about the human action that is demanded with this claim. In this chapter our task has been to understand the claim itself as the claim of God's grace, a task we are now prepared to conclude.

---

[107] CD II/2, 579/643.
[108] CD II/2, 566/629.
[109] CD II/2, 570/632.
[110] CD II/2, 571/634 f.

3. CONCLUSION

For Karl Barth, Jesus Christ takes our place and represents us before God not only in justification but also in sanctification—not only in making us righteous before God but also in making us holy. Beginning with Calvin, the Reformed tradition struggled to affirm both the strong claim of the sufficiency of God's grace articulated by Luther and the reality of sanctification. Yet neither Calvin nor his successors were able consistently and unambiguously to demonstrate the compatibility of the sufficiency of grace and the reality of sanctification. From Barth's perspective, to fail to treat the goodness or holiness of the believer on the same terms as her righteousness before God is to open the door through which the bourgeois-humanist vision will eventually enter the church and subvert its proclamation and practice. We will have more to say in the next chapter about Barth's attempt to close this door. We close this chapter with a final assessment of Barth's claim that the command of God confronts us with the good which Jesus Christ has accomplished in our place.

At its best, Barth's claim keeps ethics closely tethered to the central Christian story of God's saving grace to humanity in Christ, and it puts sanctification on the ground of a genuine rather than a spurious hope. Barth combines Lutheran realism about the powerlessness of a demand addressed to us apart from grace with confidence in the power of a demand addressed to us from the site of its fulfillment. Consider this passage: 'For how can the man who is against God become a new man merely by being asked to make a decision which is really quite alien to him and to be for God? ... It would simply be an abstract law—a law without any locus in a life fulfilling it and embodying it. ... The revealed truth of the living God in his quickening Spirit has its content and force in the fact that it is he first who is for man, and then and for that reason man is for him. ... The law which he obeys has its locus in his life as it is freed by the gospel.'[111] Barth's gospel–law thesis is meant to establish the grounds on which God's gracious purpose for humanity can be realized in human lives and thus to assure us that the command of God and the sanctification it accomplishes is not an illusion in spite of the ambiguity of our own lives and the lives of those around us.

The epiphany of Jesus Christ—the appearing of what has been done for us through him, the disclosure of our life with him as eternal life, the appearing of what we are (I Jn. 3: 2)—has not yet taken place. ... But even here and now, in the concealment in which we now live it, this life does not lack anything of that reality, and therefore of significance and power, of truth and force. What has happened—happened for us—has really happened. What is demanded of us is really demanded, and what is given us is really given. We cannot be more strictly, more intimately, more completely subject to a demand

---

[111] CD IV/2, 579 f./655 f.

than when we stand in this expectation. Nor, again, can we be more lavishly endowed than we are already in this expectation.[112]

Much as Kant pointed us away from our empirical desires and inclinations to the moral law which discloses a kind of freedom of which we would otherwise be ignorant, Barth points us away from the factual reality of our moral lives to a moral reality which, precisely as an eschatological reality in Christ, makes available to us a freedom and power for the good which would otherwise be inaccessible to us. Much as for Kant, the moral law obligates us only on the ground of transcendent freedom, so for Barth, it is the reality of what Christ has done for us that grounds the demand issued to us from his obedience in our place. Barth's entire moral theology requires us to understand ourselves as moral subjects placed in the position of addressees of the command of God. But the command of God addresses us with a demand that is already fulfilled in Christ and confronts us as an eschatological reality which is ours in faith. Rather than confronting our misplaced confidence with the hyper-Augustinian emphasis on what we cannot do because of our bondage to sin, Barth confronts us with what Christ has done in our place and urges us to confidence in its reality and power. The hyper-Augustinian theme is there too, of course, but it is placed in this latter context. Not 'You must but cannot,' but 'You may' is what the command of God principally says. To stand in the position of the addressee of this command, then, is to live and act as one who is free and empowered to do the good.[113] At its best, Barth's claim that the command of God confronts us with the good Jesus Christ has accomplished in our place instills our moral lives with realistic hope.

At its worst, however, Barth's claim seems to deny that anything finally rests on our own moral striving. The summons to confirm what Christ has accomplished in our place is a real one, and there can be no question that Barth's theology leaves room for genuine human moral activity, contrary to what was once widely charged. However, it is still unclear what significance this activity can have for him. If the human good itself—fellowship with God—is attained by Jesus Christ and is ours only in Christ, then the command of God itself summons us not to strive toward the good with the assistance of divine grace but rather to confirm what has been attained by Christ in our place. In other words, the command of God is issued only after what is finally at stake in it has already been settled. What meaning and status, then, can human moral action possibly have? This question points us to the topic of the following chapter.

---

[112] CD II/2, 608/676.

[113] It is difficult to understand how Jesse Couenhaven, whose discussion of Barth's position in relation to Luther and Calvin is generally insightful, can conclude that Barth thinks of grace in terms of pardon rather than power. See Couenhaven, 'Grace as Pardon and Power,' 81–4.

5

Human Moral Action

The old question that hounded Barth in the wake of *Romans₂* and never entirely went away, namely, whether the emphasis on the divine initiative in his theology leaves room for genuine human action, may now be regarded as settled. A considerable secondary literature supports the thesis that Barth not only allows for human action distinct from God's action but that the relationship between divine and human action lies at the very center of his theology.[1] Also settled are fundamental questions regarding the nature of human action and its relationship to divine action. So thoroughly and competently have matters related to these questions been treated during the past two decades that taxing the reader with yet another discussion of this topic requires some justification. The justification in our case has to do with the significance of the fact that for Barth, it is Jesus Christ who accomplishes the good in our place.[2] If this is so—if the good at which our

---

[1] No one is more responsible for this felicitous state of affairs than is John Webster. See Webster, *Barth's Ethics of Reconciliation* (Cambridge: Cambridge University Press, 1995); idem, *Barth's Moral Theology: Human Action in Barth's Thought* (Grand Rapids, Mich.: Eerdmans, 1998); idem, *Barth*, 2nd edn. (London: Continuum, 2004), 141–63; idem, *Barth's Earlier Theology*, 22–8, 51–3, 57–9. Throughout these works, Webster convincingly shows how human action that is distinct from divine action yet not independent of the latter is far from marginal to Barth's fundamental theological vision, much less incompatible with it, but is integral to its most fundamental claims. Webster's account also explains why so many readers have missed this point, showing how it is when we approach Barth's theology with the modern assumption that human action must be grounded in the self-reflection of an autonomous subject that we fail to see the reality and integrity of human action in his thought and to appreciate his challenge to precisely that assumption. The first step down the path Webster cleared with his early work on Barth's ethics of reconciliation was taken in a seminal essay by Eberhard Jüngel, who exposited Barth's notion of human action as correspondence to God's action in 'Invocation of God as the Ethical Ground of Christian Action: Introductory Remarks on the Posthumous Fragments of Karl Barth's Ethics of the Doctrine of Reconciliation,' in Eberhard Jüngel, *Theological Essays*, vol. i, trans. and introd. J. B. Webster (Edinburgh: T. & T. Clark, 1989), 154–72. Alongside these works of Jüngel and Webster, we must now place that of Nimmo, *Being in Action*. Nimmo develops what he calls the 'actualistic ontology' of divine and human action (and their interaction) in Barth's thought, and from this vantage point he interprets the whole of Barth's theology. Finally, a treatment which appreciates the importance of human action in Barth's theology but is more critical of Barth's conception of it is found in Reinhard Hütter, *Evangelische Ethik als kirchliches Zeugnis* (Neukirchen-Vluyn: Neukirchener Verlag, 1993).

[2] Why, for Barth, must there be human action at all? Webster correctly points out that it is because God's election of humanity is teleological; in electing human beings, God endows them with a purpose for which they are to live. But how can human action have any significance if Christ accomplishes this purpose of election in our place? Webster deflects this issue, which stands at the center of Barth's struggle with ethics. See Webster, *Barth's Ethics of Reconciliation*, 49, 53.

actions aim has already been realized for us—it is unclear what meaning and status our moral action can have for Barth even if we are not in doubt regarding the reality of human action in his theology.

To clarify the question before us it is useful to recall how the question of human action originates in the context of God's eternal determination of humanity for fellowship with God.

As election is ultimately the determination of man, the question arises as to the human self-determination which corresponds to this determination....As the one who is determined in this way, what sort of a man will he be and what will he do? It would not be his determination if he were not asked these questions, if to the divine decision there did not correspond a human one in which the partner in the covenant has to give his answer to what is said to him by the fact that God has concluded it.[3]

It is the command of God that poses these questions, confronting us with the determination of divine grace and summoning us to answer with our life conduct to what we are in and by this determination of grace. It is evident in this light why human moral action is necessary. The divine determination of grace itself calls for an active human subject. The other who is determined for fellowship with God is not an inert object but a genuine covenant partner, and as such this determination calls for a free response on the part of the one it determines. Yet Barth also insists that it is Jesus Christ who has made this response in place of other human beings, fulfilling the divine determination of grace and thus obeying the command of God. 'For it is our place, the place which belongs to us, that is the place which this man has chosen for himself, and for which he is chosen. It is our election and sanctification which are resolved on [*beschlossen*] and fulfilled in him.'[4] This brings us to a point made early in Chapter 1, namely, that our sanctification is no less the work of Christ than is our justification, and indeed our eternal election. 'Sanctification does not mean our self-sanctifying as the filling out of the justification that comes to man from God. It is sanctification by and in Jesus Christ, who, according to I Cor. 1: 30, is made unto us both justification and sanctification.'[5] Thus Christ 'took our place and acted for us, not merely as the Son of God who established God's right and our own [that is, justification] . . . but also as the Son of Man who was sanctified, who sanctified himself.'[6] It follows that it is 'the Holy One [that is, God, in Jesus Christ] who is the active Subject of sanctification, and who constitutes the saints in this action . . .'[7]

It is at this point that questions about the significance of the moral activity of human beings other than Jesus Christ arise. If our sanctification is accomplished

---

[3] CD II/2, 510 f./566.
[4] CD II/2, 740/827 (revised).
[5] CD IV/1, 101/109.
[6] CD IV/2, 516/584.
[7] CD IV/2, 513/580.

by Christ just as our justification is, what status does our moral activity have? Does it count for anything at all? If our holiness is constituted in Christ just as our righteousness before God is, what meaning does our moral activity have? Has not its purpose already been achieved before we act? While it is undoubtedly the case that the divine determination of human beings in the grace of election requires a genuinely human self-determination in correspondence to it, nothing seems to be at stake in this human self-determination insofar as it concerns human beings other than Jesus Christ. By taking our place, Christ seems to have deprived our place of any significance. Yet we have seen enough already in this study to know that Barth resists this implication. He has insisted that by taking responsibility for us, God has made us responsible. He has argued that in the command of God, what God has done for us confronts us as what God demands of us. As we saw in the previous chapter, Barth's entire moral theology rests on the claim that it is precisely what God has done in our place that constitutes us as genuine moral subjects. In all these respects, what God does for us establishes our own moral action. Nor should this surprise us; it would be strange, after all, if Christ's fulfillment of our determination as God's active covenant partners were in effect the nullification of this determination as it concerns us in our concrete, active existence.

The crucial point in all of this is that Barth rejects the zero-sum economy in which divine and human action compete with one another in favor of a very different economy in which it is what God does for us that puts human moral action on secure ground for the first time. In his eloquently blunt words, 'the formula "God everything and man nothing" as a description of grace . . . is complete nonsense. . . . God is indeed everything but only . . . in order that as such [man], too, may be everything in his own place, on his own level and within his own limits.'[8] This chapter can be read as an extended commentary on this remark.

Before turning to that commentary, and as a way of orienting ourselves, it is appropriate to recall the basic ontological and analogical structure of Barth's ethics. For Barth, God resolves on the good from eternity in the determination of human beings in Jesus Christ as active covenant partners of God, and God fulfills this good in time in the incarnation, life, death, resurrection, and ascension of Jesus Christ. It is as fulfilled in this way that the good addresses us as the summons to confirm it in our action. We will soon see that the confirmation of the good occurs in the analogy of our action to God's action in Jesus Christ. But at this point it is crucial to note the importance Barth attaches to this last move, from what Christ has done in our place to its confirmation in our action. 'If there are no human works which are praised by God, and praise him in return, and are thus good, in what sense can we speak of a real alteration of the human

---

[8] CD IV/1, 89/94 f.

situation effected in the death of Jesus Christ and revealed in the power of the resurrection by the Holy Spirit? And how can our attestation of it fail to be pointless and empty?'[9] Without genuinely good human action, the divine action of grace fails to accomplish the divine determination of grace, which elects human beings as active partners in covenant with God. Yet it is difficult to make clear how Barth can affirm both the completeness of God's action in our place and the necessity of our action. The success of his project will depend on whether his account of human action vindicates the claim that '[man], too, [is] everything in his own place, on his own level and within his own limits.'

Our examination of Barth's account of human moral action considers, in succession, the meaning of this action, its reality, and its limits.

1. THE MEANING OF HUMAN MORAL ACTION

It is difficult to exaggerate the point, emphasized by Barth himself, that in the *Church Dogmatics*, special ethics—which turns from examining how human beings are placed under God's command (general ethics) to examine human action as sanctified by God's command—begins with the command of God regarding the Sabbath.[10] The Sabbath commandment, he asserts, 'explains all the other commandments' and thus belongs at their head. 'By demanding man's abstention and resting from his own works, it explains that the commanding God who has created man and enabled and commissioned him to do his own work, is the God who is gracious to man in Jesus Christ. Thus it points him away from everything that he himself can will and achieve and back to what God is for him and will do for him.'[11] The point of the commandment is not that God's action replaces our action. The commandment regarding the Sabbath is, after all, a commandment and thus a demand for a specific action, albeit one that consists mainly in an abstention. More important, the point of this commandment, as Barth sees it, is not that God alone works while we do nothing but that the God who 'enable[s] and commission[s]' us to work is the one who is gracious to us in Jesus Christ so that the meaning of our work is found in what he is and does for us. The point of the Sabbath commandment, then, 'is simply that God has taken [man's] case into his own hands and therefore out of those of man.' The commandment therefore demands one's self-renunciation as one who, in one's works, would 'posit, affirm, and express himself, and as far as he is able, represent and help and justify himself.'[12] The Sabbath commandment, by directing human beings to abstain from their own work on the first day (as Christians

---

[9] CD IV/2, 585/662.
[10] CD III/4, 50/55.
[11] CD III/4, 53/58.
[12] CD III/4, 58/62 f.

mark it) and to celebrate God's work on our behalf in Jesus Christ, thus establishes the condition under which all our works are carried out, namely, the grace of God which accomplishes its work apart from ours and thereby establishes our own work. As Barth understands it, then, this commandment is ideally suited to convey the meaning of human moral action in light of the fact that Christ has accomplished the good in our place, and by situating this commandment, so understood, at the beginning of his special ethics, Barth underscores the centrality of this fact to his understanding of human moral action.

The emphasis on the self-renunciation of the self-positing subject in Barth's treatment of the Sabbath commandment recalls his emphasis in *Romans₂* on the effacement of perceptible, material action before its transcendent ground, as a sign or witness of a transcendent good that is never embodied in human actions themselves.[13] In the *Church Dogmatics*, Barth will continue to press the point that human moral action 'cannot and will not mean abolition of "the infinite qualitative difference" between God and man.' What this means concretely is that 'the action demanded of us . . . will be our action, a human action. It will have to attest and confirm the great acts of God; but it will not be able to continue or repeat them.'[14] What is new in relation to *Romans₂*, however, is Barth's insistence that Christ has accomplished the acts of God as a human being. 'The basic divine decision concerning man is embodied in Jesus. The determination in which man is directed to his promised future, and set in motion towards this future, is given in him.'[15] Whatever significance is ascribed to the moral action of other human beings in light of the fundamental fact of Christ's accomplishment of the good in our place, it cannot imply that what he has done for us is not definitive (so that it would be the task of our action to do again what he has already done) or is unfinished (so that it would be the task of our action to complete what his action has left unfinished). On these grounds, Barth denies that moral action should take the form of the *imitatio Christi*, at least to the extent that the latter involves taking Christ's life as a literal and comprehensive pattern for our lives to follow.[16] On the same grounds stands his controversial thesis that the work of Jesus Christ which culminates in his death and resurrection and is mediated to us by the Holy Spirit is the only true sacrament.[17] The point in both cases is that because Jesus Christ fulfills the divine determination of human beings for fellowship with God in our place it cannot be the task of human action to continue or complete his work.

---

[13] *Romans₂*, 197/216, 417/431, 417 f./432, 420/435.
[14] CD II/2, 577/641.
[15] CD II/2, 567/630.
[16] CD IV/2, 533/603.
[17] CD IV/4, 102/112, 128/140.

However, what Christ does in our place does not eliminate the necessity for our action in response to the divine determination. Far from leaving no place for human work, the completeness of what Christ has done for us ensures that our work, whatever it turns out to be, will not be caught up in competition with Christ's work. Because God's work in Christ is definitive and complete it is neither increased nor diminished by what we do or fail to do, and it is for this very reason that there is no rivalry between divine and human action.[18] At the same time, our action is not independent of God's action in Christ, as if the completeness of the latter had cut the former loose of any obligation with respect to itself. The question, therefore, is what does it mean to respond to that determination as one that has already been fulfilled by Christ? Barth's answer is that the goodness of our actions consists in their *correspondence* to what Christ has done on our behalf. 'An active life lived in obedience must obviously consist in a correspondence to divine action.' Affirming at the same time the complete-ness of what God has done, Barth immediately adds: 'We are careful not to say in a continuation or development of divine action.'[19] To state it clearly and concisely: 'Neither for ourselves nor for others can we do the good which God does for us. What we should and can do is correspond to this good. We can and should seek and find in it the pattern [*Vorbild*] of what we have to do. But what we do now will always be something different.... This action is a good action only in virtue of its correspondence with God's grace.'[20]

What exactly is the correspondence of our actions with the action of God's grace, and what significance do our actions have by virtue of this correspondence? The grace of God, Barth stresses, has an aim or a *telos*, and in light of Matthew 5: 48, Barth relates this *telos* to the perfection (*teleiotēs*) of God's grace. 'As the one Word of God which is the revelation and work of his grace reaches us, its aim is that our being and action should be conformed to his. "Be ye (literally, ye shall be) perfect (literally, directed to your objective) even as (i.e., corresponding to it in creaturely-human fashion) your Father which is in heaven is perfect (directed to his objective") (Mt. 5: 48).'[21] That we are to be perfect 'even as' God is perfect entails a certain *identity* of our action with God's. Thus, just as the perfection of the heavenly Father is said in Matthew 5: 43–7 to be manifested 'in the fact that he vouchsafes rain and sunshine to all men, and therefore loves even his enemies,' so 'the peculiarity of those who know and receive his grace ... must and will consist (*esesthe* [you shall be]) in the fact that they, too, love their enemies, and are therefore *teleioi* [perfect ones] like their Father in heaven.'[22] Here, correspon-dence to God's action takes the form of the *imitatio Dei* after all; our actions

18 CD I/2, 366/402.
19 CD III/4, 474/543.
20 CD II/2, 578/642 f.
21 CD II/2, 512/567.
22 CD II/2, 567/630.

towards others are to reflect the grace God has shown to all humankind. It is therefore in light of Matthew 5: 41–8, Barth writes, that we are to understand the particular commands in the New Testament enjoining us to forgive one another, to be compassionate, to bear one another's burdens, to show kindness even to persecutors, to look not to our own things but to the things of others, and to love our enemies. In all of these actions our aim corresponds to the aim of the gracious God 'who meets both the good and evil with the same beneficence.' Yet Barth immediately qualifies this *imitatio Dei* or *imitatio Christi* with a reminder of the fundamental *difference* between God's action and ours. 'The fulfillment of all these commands does not in any sense mean that he becomes a "gracious Lord" to his neighbor. Neither for himself nor for others can he or will he do what Jesus Christ did.' Nor does God expect of human beings this strict identity with God's own actions. 'The content of the divine demand on man is that he should do in *his* circle . . . that which God does by Christ in his circle.'[23] As Barth's 'targum' on Matthew 5: 48 (quoted above) makes clear, the human action which corresponds to the divine action is a 'creaturely human' action.[24]

The correspondence of our action to God's gracious action therefore involves a relation of identity in difference or difference in identity. The technical term for these relations of identity and difference is, of course, *analogy*; for Barth, our action is to be analogous to God's gracious action on our behalf.[25] Human moral action is an analogy of grace. Barth exploits the full semantic range of the German term *entsprechen* in its verbal and nominal forms to characterize this correspondence. Thus, human action in correspondence to God's action is the 'image and repetition and attestation and acknowledgement' of God's action; it involves 'correspondence, conformity, uniformity with God's action'; the required correspondence occurs as we 'accept as right what the gracious God does for us, and acquiesce in it.'[26] Correspondence thus combines in one concept the endorsement or affirmation of God's gracious action (our 'Yes' to grace),

---

[23] CD II/2, 578 f./642 f.

[24] One implication Barth will repeatedly draw from the difference between God's action in Christ and our action is that the specific commands given in the Sermon on the Mount and elsewhere will not necessarily be the command given to us in our circumstances. See CD II/2, 686–700/766–82; CD IV/2, 547/619. This way of handling particular scriptural commands is not without its problems, but this matter is beyond the scope of the present chapter and will be deferred to the following chapter.

[25] By the time of his 1928–9 lecture course on *Ethics*, Barth had relaxed some of the extraordinary caution that surrounded his muted appeals to the analogy of human to divine action in *Romans₂*, speaking explicitly of a 'correspondence, analogy, and conformity' of human action to the action of God and referring to the 'perfection that is analogous to that of the Father in heaven' asserted in Matthew 5: 48 (*Ethics*, 250/423 f.). However, these remarks all occur in a context that stresses the difference between human and divine action over their similarity. In this as in other related respects, the shadow of *Romans₂* still falls over *Ethics*. By contrast, the treatments of ethics in the *Church Dogmatics* exhibit an unambiguous intention to balance identity and difference in speaking of the analogy of divine and human action.

[26] CD II/2, 512/568, 575/639, 579/643.

imitation of it (in a creaturely manner), and witness to it. Without reducing the complexity of these various modes of correspondence, we can sum them up by saying that the *telos* of God's grace is realized when human beings in their action become the image of God.

What is involved is that man and man's action should become the image of God: the reflection [*Spiegel*] which represents [*darstellt*], although in itself it is completely different from, God and his action; the reflection in which God recognizes [*wiedererkennt*] himself and his action. . . . God's action is that he is gracious, and man in his action is committed to correspondence to this action. He is the image of God and his action when his own action reflects and to that extent copies the grace of God.[27]

We have come full circle. From eternity, God determined humankind for fellowship with God in the form of service to God. 'God elects himself to be gracious toward man, to be his lord and helper, and in so doing he elects man to be the witness to his glory. . . . He wills to take him into his service, to commission him for a share in his own work.'[28] In this commission to divine service we find the meaning of human moral action. 'The elect man is chosen in order to respond to the gracious God, to be his creaturely image, his imitator. . . . What else is the elect Jesus Christ but the original of this representation and illustration of the gracious God. . . . And what else can his community be but the people and assembly which, as they are created by the grace of God, declare this their creation. . . . So, too, it is with the elect individual. . . . His determination is to be its witness. . . .'[29] If the question of the meaning of human action is what does it mean to respond to the divine determination of humanity by grace given that this determination has already been fulfilled in our place by Jesus Christ, the answer is that God grants us a participation in God's own work by establishing us as witnesses to it, as those who become in their conduct the image of the gracious God and thereby glorify God in their creaturely life.

It is at this point that readers of Barth often feel disappointed. Are we only witnesses to God's work? On further reflection this immediate disappointment may run even deeper. It seems that human action as the analogy of divine grace has only a representational function with respect to grace. Human action seems to be 'merely' a wholly creaturely sign pointing to God's action. As such, Barth's account of human action seems grossly inferior to that of the pedagogical account, which understands human action as a gradual approximation, with the help of grace, to the divine goodness—in its most ambitious forms, as a process of deification. Barth quite explicitly rejects the notion of deification. In describing the correspondence of human action to God's grace as conformity (*Gleichförmigkeit*) with it, he denies that this involves a 'deification or

---

[27] CD II/2, 575 f./639.
[28] CD II/2, 510/565.
[29] CD II/2, 413 f./457 f.

Christification' of humanity. 'There will be no more Christs.' Indeed, 'even in the kingdom of perfection' the distance of God and humanity will remain intact.[30] It is easy to understand what prompts Barth's concerns with the notion of deification. In no small measure his entire conception of the relationship of Christology and anthropology is presented as an alternative to nineteenth-century German Protestant attempts to understand Christ as an ideal expression of humanity which is in principle attainable by every other human being. Yet in opposing this line of thought has Barth moved too far in the other direction, leaving a merely representational conformity of human beings to God? Is the movement by which God determines humankind as God's covenant partner from eternity and then fulfills this determination in time complete in itself, so that the only role for human action is to signify this movement by action which corresponds to it? If so, we might see little reason to exchange the pedagogical conception for this one. Or is human action, precisely in its correspondence, somehow caught up in this movement?

In answer to this question we may be certain from the start that for Barth human action is, by divine grace, genuinely caught up in the movement of God's own action—the movement by which God resolves on and brings about God's covenant with humankind.[31] It is therefore legitimate for Barth to describe the service of human witness as participation in God's very life (*Teilnahme an Gottes Leben*).[32] At the same time, the kind of participation involved must be appropriate to the divine nature and to the status of human beings as God's covenant partners. As Barth understands it, the God who chooses humankind from eternity as God's covenant partner is the gracious God, and God does not cease to be this God at any point in the history of the covenant. But if God really is the God of grace—the God who establishes and fulfills the covenant by God's gracious action in Jesus Christ from eternity and in time—then God's work cannot be in need of a supplement or a continuation in the work of human beings in order to complete the covenant. An economy of this kind is precisely what is ruled out by God's determination of human beings as God's covenant partners from eternity and Christ's fulfillment of this determination in our place. But how can human action genuinely participate in the movement of God's own action without implicating God and humankind in an economy which would dissolve the covenant as a covenant of grace?

Barth avoids this result by identifying the paradigmatic act of service to God as gratitude. 'This service, and therefore the blessedness of the elect, consists in

---

[30] CD II/2, 577 f./641 f. (revised).

[31] Explicit statements can be found in many places, including CD IV/2, 556 f./629 f. However, Barth's entire theological vision in the *Church Dogmatics*, from revelation as the movement by which God brings human beings into participation in the divine self-knowledge to reconciliation as the movement by which God goes into the far country and brings humankind back, is unintelligible except as a massive attestation of the divine *exitus et reditus*.

[32] CD II/2, 413/457 (see also 413/456).

gratitude for the self-offering of God. God chooses him in order that there may be gratitude in his life (and therefore life in and by grace).'[33] As the paradigmatic human action, gratitude is the participation of human action in the divine movement of grace. 'Hidden in thanksgiving, and therefore in the act of man, grace itself, which came from God in his Word, now returns to God, to its source of origin.'[34] Yet far from completing an economy, gratitude entails acknowledgment of the impossibility of closing the account. It is true that the recipient of grace has an obligation to be grateful. But 'i[f] the obligation of thanksgiving could be fully discharged in an attitude towards the benefactor, there would be no real gratitude, just as a benefit which could be cancelled by an attitude on the part of the recipient would certainly not have been a benefit. In such a case both the benefit and the gratitude would simply have been the two sides of a transaction based on mutual self-interest.'[35] Gratitude does not and cannot complete the movement of divine grace. To complete it would be to dissolve it. The benefit (grace) is complete in itself and does not depend on the gratitude of the recipient. If it were so dependent—if the recipient could repay it by her gratitude—it would no longer be a benefit but an economic exchange. Yet at the same time, the benefit calls for gratitude. The gratitude of the recipient is an obligation. How should we understand this obligation? Obviously, it cannot be understood as a condition of grace. It can only be understood as the acknowledgment of the benefit by the recipient. 'To be grateful is to recognize a benefit': not merely to receive it but 'to understand it as such, as a good which one could not take for oneself but has in fact received, as an action which one could not perform for oneself but which has nevertheless happened to one.'[36]

Gratitude is the paradigmatic human action because it is the action which corresponds to grace *as grace*. The movement of God's grace is complete in itself; it requires no human action to complete it. Indeed, human action could complete it only by dissolving it. Nevertheless, grace would not be grace—not the grace of *this* God, at any rate—if it did not take up human action into its own movement, making human beings genuine partners of the gracious God. Gratitude is the human action that participates in this movement. It is suited to this participation because it is the action that acknowledges the sufficiency of grace, and thus the completeness of the divine movement of grace. Yet precisely as such, it is the human action in which grace returns to its divine source—the human action which reflects grace, in which human action becomes the image of God, in which God recognizes God's own action of grace. This does not, of course, imply that the return act contributes to the movement as such. 'His thankfulness

---

[33] CD II/2, 413/457.
[34] CD III/2, 168/201.
[35] CD III/2, 167/199.
[36] CD III/2, 167/199.

cannot consist in his giving grace for grace.'[37] Gratitude would contradict itself if this return act were mistaken for the movement of grace itself—and it is precisely because this is so that gratitude genuinely *corresponds* to grace rather than competing with it or being confused with it. The movement of divine action, precisely as the movement of grace, is God's alone to make. The action of grace is proper to God alone while gratitude is a fully human action. Yet in the requirement of gratitude, God grants the recipient of grace genuine participation in the divine movement of grace.

It is as grateful recipients of God's gift of grace that we are to relate to others. As recipients of grace, we act graciously to others, as Barth's repeated references to the Sermon on the Mount and the apostolic exhortation (some of them quoted above) throughout his treatment of general ethics in *Church Dogmatics* II/2 make clear.[38] As we conduct ourselves toward others in analogy to God's grace, our actions bearing the image of God's gracious action, we acknowledge ourselves as the recipients of that grace. Whether it is by forgiving one another, bearing one another's burdens, or loving our enemies, we actively acknowledge that we are the beneficiaries of the divine grace which 'meets both the good and the evil with the same beneficence.' To act otherwise would be to fail to actively acknowledge ourselves as recipients of grace. Of course, not every action is a direct expression of gratitude. Our discussion of the meaning of human moral action has focused on Barth's general ethics where what is at issue is the correspondence of human to divine action in its most fundamental sense, as placed under God's command. Special ethics examines the correspondence of human action to the divine actions of creation, reconciliation, and redemption, and a full account of the meaning of human action in Barth's moral theology would have to consider each of these domains. Much has already been made by scholars of Barth's identification of freedom as the characteristic of human action that corresponds to God's work of creation and of invocation as the human act that corresponds to God's work of reconciliation. Each is a kind of synecdoche that indicates the nature or character of all human action in its domain. Just as important in determining the meaning of human action, however, are the mostly unnamed themes that persist in Barth's descriptions of human action in each domain. In the case of creation, we have in mind Barth's tenacious affirmation of human creatureliness in the face of ethical norms and practices that deny or denigrate instinct, eros, temporality, finitude, and bodily existence.[39] In the case of reconciliation, we have in mind Barth's refusal to acquiesce in the claims on our behavior made in the name of 'given factors,' that is, alleged requisites of

---

[37] CD III/2, 188/224.

[38] In addition to passages we have already quoted, see CD II/2, 693–7/774–8.

[39] Instances of this tendency are present throughout the entirety of volume III of the *Church Dogmatics*, but two of the most poignant examples, both mentioned earlier in this study, are Barth's discussions of eros and of the reverence due to human life. See, respectively, CD III/2, 274–85/ 329–44; CD III/4, 344–97/391–453.

natural and social existence.[40] The life of the reconciled is in no small part an ongoing revolt against the false authority of such claims.[41] An adequate examination of these matters is beyond the scope of this study, but enough has been said to indicate that the meaning of human action, like everything in Barth's dogmatics, takes its specific form from its particular dogmatic site.

2. THE REALITY OF HUMAN MORAL ACTION

Jesus Christ has done the good in our place, yet we have also seen how we are summoned to action that corresponds to this work of God's grace. What is accomplished by Christ is affirmed, imitated, and attested in our own conduct, which thus becomes the image or analogy of God's gracious action in which we acknowledge ourselves to be the recipients of grace. This is Barth's answer to the question of what meaning human moral life can have, given that Christ has accomplished the good in our place. We are now faced with a second question, namely, how is it that the sanctification that is real in Jesus Christ, who has accomplished the good for us, becomes effective for other human beings? How does it come about that action corresponding to God's action in Christ actually occurs in our lives, that genuine human moral action becomes a reality? 'How can that which he was and did *extra nos* become an event *in nobis*?'[42] Barth explains that the lives of all human beings are included in Christ's life by virtue of the incarnation, so that all human beings objectively participate, in a concealed form (our lives are 'hidden with Christ in God'), in what Christ is and has done in our place. In this objective sense we share in his sanctification. 'Our existence is enclosed by his, and therefore we ourselves are addressed and claimed as those who are already directed and obedient to God in him, as those who are already born again and converted, as those who are already Christians.'[43] But to leave the matter at this objective level will not do. Indeed, the very fact that we are addressed and claimed in this way indicates that the matter does not end with what is objectively the case. 'What we have said about the objective content of truth of the reality of Jesus Christ, which includes our own reality, presses in upon us, from its objectivity to our subjectivity, in order that there should be in us a correspondence.'[44] We are 'concretely seized,' Barth says, as the reality and

---

[40] Once again there are many examples, but see especially CD IV/2, 543–53/614–26; and CL, 213–33/363–99.

[41] John Webster did not distort Barth's ethics of reconciliation when he gave his essay on Barth's posthumously published *The Christian Life* the title 'The Christian in Revolt.' This essay appears in *Reckoning with Barth: Essays in Commemoration of the Centenary of Karl Barth's Birth*, ed. Nigel Biggar (London: Mowbray, 1988), 119–44.

[42] CD IV/4, 18/20.

[43] CD IV/2, 273/302.

[44] CD IV/2, 303/338.

truth of God's Word and work in Jesus Christ summons us to this correspondence in our own action. But '[h]ow does it come about that [human beings] are actually reached by this call in such a way that they render obedience...?'[45]

This question has to do with the divine empowerment of human moral action, and Barth's answer brings us to a topic we have thus far neglected: the role of the Holy Spirit in the moral life. The Holy Spirit as the agent of this transition from objective to subjective has been treated insightfully by John Webster and others, and it is tempting simply to refer the reader to their accounts.[46] However, the last word on this matter has yet to be said, and it will be clear from what is said below that certain features of Barth's account become more visible when that account is viewed from the angle of Christ's completed work in our place. From that angle, the question of the reality of human action has to do with the completion of the divine determination of humankind from eternity. What is ultimately at issue in the reality of human moral action is whether that on which God has resolved from eternity truly does become actual 'in time and on earth,' that is, as a creaturely reality.[47] The stake in this issue is high, for 'the reality of God stands or falls with the reality of this event' of the sanctification of human beings other than Jesus Christ.[48] Why? Because if this event does not take place, God turns out not to be the God of the covenant with humankind, and thus (on Barth's terms) is not God at all.

Barth's treatment of the operation of the Holy Spirit in effecting this transition from what Christ accomplishes in our place to our correspondence to it indicates a determination to avoid what he sees as two errors. The first error is to treat the work of the Holy Spirit in isolation from human action, whether by abstracting it from its Christological context or by conceiving it as a replacement for human action. In the latter form, Barth attributes this error to Peter Lombard, who held that the love with which we love God and the neighbor is the Holy Spirit himself.[49] Human action is altogether displaced by the work of the Spirit. In the former form the error is associated with a tendency to reduce ourselves to silence before the Spirit's work, regarding it as something utterly beyond human comprehension. Against this tendency, Barth opposes 'the fact that in the Holy Spirit, although we have to do with God, we do not have to do with him in his direct being in himself, which might well reduce us to silence or allow us only to stutter and stammer, but with God (directly) in the form of the power and lordship of the man Jesus.'[50] If this is so, then the operation of the Holy Spirit is inseparable from the human action of Jesus, and this means that it is intelligible—a point that will be fundamental to Barth's account of the work of

---

[45] CD IV/2, 554/626.
[46] Webster, *Barth's Ethics of Reconciliation*, 132–47. Webster deals mostly with the baptism fragment of CD IV/4, but most of his analysis would also apply to CD IV/2 and IV/3.
[47] CD IV/2, 554/626, 556/630.
[48] CD IV/2, 558/631.
[49] CD I/2, 374/411.
[50] CD IV/2, 360 f./403.

the Spirit. 'His operation is neither anonymous, amorphous, nor, as we have already maintained, irrational. It is an operation from man to man. It is divine because the man from whom it proceeds is the eternal Son of God. But it is also human, and can therefore be defined and more clearly described, because the eternal Son of God who is its origin is a man.'[51] In accordance with Barth's theology of the Trinity more generally, the *filioque* of the Nicene Creed in its Western version, wherein the Spirit proceeds from the Son as well as from the Father, characterizes the economic as well as the immanent Trinity.

We may wonder whether Barth has done equal justice to the procession of the Spirit from the Father, but what is immediately relevant to our concern is his claim that the operation of the Spirit understood in this Christological context takes the form of direction (*Weisung*). 'The sanctification of the saints by *the* Holy One takes place in the mode appropriate to the being of the Son of God who is the eternal Logos, and to the relationship of the Son of Man to other men. He speaks. . . . And others hear him. . . . Hence the sanctification of man as the work of the Holy Spirit has to be described as the giving and receiving of direction.'[52] With this move, Barth unambiguously characterizes the operation of the Holy Spirit in ethical terms, which he explicitly contrasts to a mode of operation conceived in nonmoral terms, along the lines of a natural force. 'We have to distinguish the sense in which we use [the term power in relation to the Holy Spirit] from the idea of a power which either mechanically pushes, propels, thrusts, or draws, or organically produces; from a higher force of nature . . .'[53] Barth seems to object to all such notions of the Spirit's power on the grounds that they are incompatible with the reality of human action. In relation to such a force, 'man can only be an object, an alien body which is either carried or impelled, like a spar of wood carried relentlessly downstream by a great river.'[54] Against such conceptions, Barth insists that '[t]o receive and have the Holy Spirit . . . is simply to receive and have direction.'[55] In Barth's doctrine of reconciliation, 'direction' is an explicitly ethical term; it stands in for the term 'command' as the synonym of the latter that is most appropriate to the reality of reconciliation in Christ. Of course, to characterize the operation of the Spirit as ethical is not to deny that it lacks genuine effective power. Barth is clear that 'unlike any direction which one man may give to others, [the direction of the Spirit] falls, as it were, vertically into the lives of those to whom it is given. It is thus effective with divine power. . . . It constitutes itself the ruling and determinative factor in the whole being of those to whom it is given.'[56]

---

51 CD IV/2, 361/404.
52 CD IV/2, 523/592.
53 CD IV/2, 309/345.
54 CD IV/2, 578/654.
55 CD IV/4, 362/404.
56 CD IV/2, 523/592.

In what does this divine power of direction consist? It is not surprising that Barth is mostly silent on this question or simply avoids it with seemingly indiscriminate references to how God's action 'awakens and demands' corresponding human action or 'awaken[s], summon[s], and empower[s]' it.[57] Yet he does offer a distinct answer to the question, and it is an answer that is fully consistent with the ethical character of direction. What Barth says is that the Holy Spirit operates on us and in us by setting us free to do the action that corresponds to God's grace, and that this freedom comes to us through direction. This, of course, brings us back to the theme of gospel and law, and more specifically to the point, made at the end of the previous chapter, that it is the command of God itself, as the form of grace, that sets us free to do what it demands. 'In short, it is unequivocally and exclusively by the Gospel, the revealed grace of God, that conversion is effectively commanded as a radical termination and a radical recommencement. But effectively means as a gift of freedom, and therefore as the law of his own free act apart from which he has no freedom to choose any other.'[58] To be sure, the power of the Spirit in direction does involve a kind of compulsion. The direction of the Spirit does not simply set the hearer under the demand to correspond to God's grace and leave her to her own choice whether to obey or not. That conclusion is already ruled out by the denial that freedom (in the proper sense) can choose any other. But neither is this compulsion that of the driftwood carried downstream. 'It is the compulsion of a permission and ability which have been granted. It is that of the free man who as such can only exercise his freedom.'[59] In the end, Barth can answer the question of the effectiveness of the operation of the Holy Spirit in direction only by pointing us yet again to the command of God itself, which never sets before us a naked demand but always confronts us with the reality of all that Christ has done in our place and thus speaks to us by saying 'you may' rather than 'you must.' Here, as elsewhere, moral theology can only speak from the position of the addressee of this command rather than attempting to step outside of its address to explain it.

The second error Barth is determined to avoid is the notion that the work of the Holy Spirit extends human moral capacities beyond their natural possibilities and limitations. Just as he accused Peter Lombard of committing the first error, Barth charges Thomas Aquinas with committing the second in his notion that the operation of the Holy Spirit can be understood in terms of a *forma habitualis superaddita* which gives our own capacities a power they lack on their own. For Barth, 'the miracle of the outpouring of the Holy Spirit consists in the fact that this man with his natural capacity [*Vermögen*], which in itself is utter incapacity [*Unvermögen*], does in faith participate in the promise and in faith begin to

---

[57] CD IV/4, 106/116, 143/157.
[58] CD IV/2, 580/656.
[59] CD IV/2, 578/654.

love. . . .'[60] God's commands, Barth says in another context, 'do not actually exceed the measure of human power. On the contrary, they stir human power to action—only human power, but really to action.'[61] (It is in this sense that Barth understands, and frequently refers to, Matthew 11: 30: 'My yoke is easy, my burden is light.') There are two closely related points here. One is that the work of the Holy Spirit preserves the full natural integrity of our own action. 'The work of this power is not to destroy our earthliness [*Diesseitigkeit*] but to give it a new determination.'[62] What holds for the meaning of human moral action holds also for its reality; in both cases, Barth is strongly committed to our natural human action as the material of sanctification. 'Taking place wholly and utterly on the earthly and creaturely level, it does not merely have an aspect which is wholly and utterly creaturely, but it is itself wholly and utterly creaturely by nature.'[63] The other point is that the Holy Spirit effects sanctification in our lives by activating our natural capacities, supplying them with effective power which they lack in themselves. For Barth 'man himself is the free subject of this event on the basis of a possibility which is present only with God.'[64] While sanctification involves our natural, creaturely action, it is not a matter of our capability (*Können*). What happens here is 'a human act without the corresponding human potency.'[65] It follows for the one whose action corresponds to grace that the 'initiative on which he does it, the spontaneity in which he expresses himself in it' has its origin in the power of the Spirit's direction.[66] '[T]he initial shock comes from God.'[67] All of this is quite clearly compatible with the notion that the operation of the Spirit consists in setting our action free. But for our present purposes the major point is that the work of the Holy Spirit involves our capacities yet is by no means a work of which we are capable. For Barth, sanctification does not consist in extending natural capacities so that they become capable of acts that exceed the limits of creaturely nature. Rather, it consists in empowering creaturely nature to exercise natural capacities.

The upshot of these two points is that the transition, effected by the Holy Spirit, from what is objectively the case for us in Christ to our subjective correspondence to it involves a relationship of divine and human action in which both maintain their own integrity yet cooperate with each other. Our awakening to new life is 'both wholly creaturely and wholly divine.'[68] This does not, of course, imply that divine and creaturely action enjoy the same status.

---

[60] CD I/2, 375/412.
[61] CD II/2, 579/643.
[62] CD IV/2, 318 f./356.
[63] CD IV/2, 557/630.
[64] CD IV/4, 5/5.
[65] CD IV/2, 309/345.
[66] CD IV/2, 528/598.
[67] CD IV/2, 557/630.
[68] CD IV/2, 557/630.

Divine action clearly enjoys primacy. 'The creaturely is made serviceable to the divine and does actually serve it. It is used by God as his organ or instrument.' Creaturely action remains intact, but 'it cooperates in such a way that the whole is still an action which is specifically divine.'[69] Barth thus speaks of 'a conscription and cooperation' of the whole of our natural capacities.[70] The reality of human action ultimately rests on the fact that, by the power of the Holy Spirit, human action is taken up into God's own action, yet without ceasing to be human.

It should be clear from all we have seen that Barth affirms the reality of human moral action in response to God's action on our behalf. We have also seen that far from denigrating the role of the Holy Spirit in the moral life, as he is often accused of doing, the Holy Spirit is given the crucial role of effecting the transition from the sanctification accomplished in and by Christ and our own sanctification. Without this transition, all that Barth has said about the command of God setting before us the reality in which we stand is illusory. The command of God would have been actualized in Jesus Christ but in him alone. Other human beings would still share in Christ's accomplishment of the good, but only objectively, and thus not in their existence as active subjects. The Holy Spirit is thus essential to Barth's moral theology. If Barth conceives the Spirit too narrowly as the Spirit of Christ—we raise this as a possibility, not as a conclusion—this would be the fault of the role played by Christology in his theology more generally and not of any defect in his pneumatology as such. However, one criticism of Barth that is relevant to this section cannot be easily dismissed. We may phrase it in terms of the role of sacramental mystery in the transition Barth discusses. The best way to get at this matter is through Barth's distinction between Christ's action and ours. On the one hand, the good which Christ accomplished in our place is a good which we are utterly incapable of achieving and is in effect not even demanded of us. On the other hand, our ability to do the good that *is* demanded of us—to act in a way that corresponds to Christ's action in our place—is given to us in the form of ethical direction and involves an entirely natural exercise of our moral capacities, albeit empowered by the Holy Spirit. The conception of the operation of the Holy Spirit in ethical terms and the insistence that the work of the Spirit does not extend our moral capacities to make them capable of achieving something that exceeds their nature but rather makes them capable of achieving something that remains a fully human work both seem to demystify the transition from what is objectively the case for us in Christ and our subjective correspondence to it.

Yet in spite of this impression of demystification—or more likely because of it—Barth is determined to instill in us a sense of amazement at the reality of the

---

[69] CD IV/2, 557/630.
[70] CD IV/2, 556/629.

transition. 'Could anything be more astonishing?' he asks at one point.[71] Indeed, we have not truly understood what is involved in the transition at all if we lack this sense of amazement at it. 'The compass of what it means for a man to become faithful to the faithful God is not merely underestimated but completely missed if one does not ultimately stand before this fact with helpless astonishment.'[72] In the end, he insists, we must acknowledge that the transition is 'a mystery and a miracle.'[73] There is no reason to suppose that Barth is not serious or sincere in insisting on the mysterious and miraculous nature of the Holy Spirit's work. And it is true that the power of direction to liberate us for the action it requires involves 'a very definite power which is more extensive than appears in the demand as such.'[74] If the operation of the Spirit is ethical, at work in the event of the command addressed to us, this does not mean that its operation is reducible to an ordinary mechanism such as the psychological force of the imperative. Nevertheless, the appeals to mystery and miracle and the attempts to evoke our astonishment appear as efforts to compensate for the absence of a sacramental mystery—a mystery which is necessarily excluded by the sharp distinction between the action Christ performs on our behalf, entirely apart from our activity, and the action we perform in correspondence to it. The reasons for Barth's denial that sacraments play a role in effecting the transition from objective to subjective have been explored at length by others.[75] But we rightly wonder whether this denial ironically contributes to the very scenario he wishes to avoid at all costs: one in which the reality of human moral action becomes intelligible on its own terms, as an exclusively human response to what Christ has done in our place and apart from us. Everything Barth explicitly says about the reality of human action presses against this conclusion. But to the extent that he is determined to reject a role for sacramental mediation in effecting the transition, this conclusion will keep pressing back against him.

3. THE LIMITS OF HUMAN MORAL ACTION

The transition from the objective to the subjective is a real one, and the result is that there is such a thing as human moral action in correlation to the action of God's grace. But everyone who knows Barth's dialectical strategy as well as the substance of his theology knows that we cannot stop with this claim. While it is now clear that Jesus Christ has made the good visible in the human realm, Barth is no more prepared in the doctrine of reconciliation of his *Church Dogmatics*

---

[71] CD IV/2, 307/343.
[72] CD IV/4, 3/3.
[73] CD IV/2, 557/630; IV/4, 5/5.
[74] CD IV/2, 304/339.
[75] See especially Webster, *Barth's Ethics of Reconciliation*, 118–32; and Hütter, *Evangelische Ethik als kirchliches Zeugnis*, 33–109.

than he was three decades earlier in *Romans₂* to admit that our actions amount to a genuine visibility of the good on the grounds of which we can construct a moral theology. The whole of human moral action continues to stand under the proviso of Colossians 3: 3: 'for you have died, and your life is hidden with Christ in God.'

There can be no doubt that the work of the Holy Spirit does not, at least in this life, produce human beings who perfectly and consistently correspond to God's grace in their actions. 'They are still sinners—these saints, these recipients of the direction of the exalted man, of the Son of Man who is also the Son of God. They are still below. The direction given and received is one thing; they themselves in comparison with it are quite another.'[76] At various points in this study, we have drawn attention to Barth's determination to treat sanctification on the same terms as justification (and election), concerned as he is to rule out the notion that human moral action falls under different terms with respect to God's grace than the terms that govern the rest of the creature's status before God. This determination is central to the problem of ethics, and Barth's entire moral theology should be read, as we have read it here, as an attempt to show how ethics under these terms is possible and even necessary. We have now arrived at the point where an emphasis on the reality of human moral action as described in the previous section could once again betray grace by treating the transition from objective to subjective as one which can in principle be completed, producing at long last a moral subject who stands on her own accomplishment, even if she got to that point only by the power of the Holy Spirit and even if her accomplishment only corresponds to, and therefore cannot replace, the real accomplishment in and by Jesus Christ. In fact, the reality of human action in Barth's moral theology cannot be misunderstood in that way. The reason is that Barth assimilates sanctification to justification in a way that rules out any such misunderstanding. However, this raises the question whether this assimilation distorts sanctification. There are certainly grounds for thinking that the answer is affirmative. But if the answer is negative, it is because Barth understands justification in a way that already provides an opening to sanctification. This, at least, is what we will try to show in this section. Once again, however, we are in the position of being tempted to refer the reader to a discussion of these issues by another scholar, in this case George Hunsinger.[77] Yet once again, we may justify our own inquiry to the extent that from our angle of vision something new becomes visible.

We have already gestured to the first sense in which Barth assimilates sanctification to justification by referring to his conviction that the saints remain sinners.

---

[76] CD IV/2, 524/592 f.

[77] George Hunsinger, 'A Tale of Two Simultaneities: Justification and Sanctification in Calvin and Barth,' in *Conversing with Barth*, ed. John C. McDowell and Mike Higton (Aldershot: Ashgate, 2004), 68–89.

This conviction is underscored by Barth's ascription to sanctification of the famous Lutheran formula of justification. It is not the case, Barth argues, that in sanctification a complete and entire 'new man' coexists with a mere shadow of the 'old man' of sin. 'If we are just a little honest with ourselves,' he suggests, we must admit that 'we have to do with two total men' who are in irreconcilable conflict. 'Luther's "*simul (totus) justus, simul (totus) peccator*" has thus to be applied strictly to sanctification. . . . For the new man is the whole man; and so too is the old. And conversion is the transition, the movement, in which man is still, in fact, wholly the old and already wholly the new man.'[78] This, of course, is precisely how Barth describes justification. In parallel with sanctification, justification involves 'the turning, the movement, the transition of the existence of man without God and dead into the existence of man living for God and therefore before him and with him and for him.'[79] And while the doctrine of justification cannot abstract from this movement by treating justification in static terms, it is nevertheless the case for the one justified that 'as long as he lives in time and considers his own person, he is both together: *simul peccator et justus*, yet not half *peccator* and half *justus*, but both altogether.'[80]

Sanctification is further assimilated to justification inasmuch as it is constituted not by anything that occurs or is achieved on the subjective side, within the life or activity of the sanctified, but entirely by its objective side. 'They are saints only in virtue of the sanctity of the one who calls them and on whom their gaze is not very well directed.'[81] We have already seen that the sanctification of other human beings is originally and properly the sanctification of the human being Jesus Christ. In this sense sanctification, like justification, is alien; it is ours only as we are in Christ.[82] Barth continues this point along the line set out by the doctrine of justification, arguing that even our good action falls short of God's demand and is thus in constant need of the grace of justification. 'We speak of men who are always sinners like others; who at every moment and in every respect need forgiveness, the justification before God which is sheer mercy. Their sanctification takes place here below where there is no action that does not have the marks of sloth or can be anything but displeasing to God. . . . He alone sanctifies it by accepting it as perfect, and therefore by continually justifying it.'[83] The point is not that Barth is a dour realist or a pessimist about sanctification. He continually directs our attention to the change God has effected and to the power of the Holy Spirit in effecting the transition in which we stand. If it is true that the sanctified are merely 'disturbed sinners' who have a limit set against their sin, it is also true that the disturbance issues from a call that has set

[78] CD IV/2, 571 f./646 f.
[79] CD IV/1, 520/580.
[80] CD IV/1, 596/664.
[81] CD IV/2, 528/597.
[82] On *justitia aliena* see CD IV/1, 549/613, 631/705, 633/707.
[83] CD IV/2, 527 f./597.

them in a new reality while the limit is set by the actuality of freedom in which they now stand.[84] This positive aspect can even be said to be the controlling factor in Barth's description of sanctification. However, it is significant that both the call and the freedom come to us from outside ourselves; they do not well up within us in a gradual progress towards holiness. Our sanctification is effected on the same terms as our justification. In both cases, it is constituted in Christ and is ours only in relation to him, and in both cases, our action falls ever short of what pleases God.

If sanctification is alien and in constant need of forgiveness in the face of its shortcomings, and if the sanctified like the justified are *simul (totus) justus et simul (totus) peccator*, it is no surprise that obedience, the human response to God's sanctification of human beings in Christ, is assimilated by Barth to faith, the human response to justification. Faith is paradigmatic in both cases because it is the human act which exhibits in its very structure the status of human action in light of divine action on our behalf. (In this sense it is itself assimilated to gratitude, as described above.) As Barth describes it, faith entails the acknowledgment that no human work, including faith itself, is sufficient, that it itself, along with all other works, stands in constant need of justification. Yet faith also entails the acknowledgment that the fact that we live by grace apart from our own works must itself be expressed in works.[85] It is clear from what we have said about sanctification that Barth understands obedience in precisely these terms. And it is on these grounds that Barth understands faith as a necessary condition for genuinely obedient action. 'Faith and faith alone already does the good simply because it is also the acknowledgement that only one is originally, intrinsically, and eternally good.'[86]

Barth assimilates sanctification to justification in order to limit the claims that might be made regarding the reality of sanctification—claims that could amount to a betrayal of grace by moral theology. Does he thereby distort sanctification, diminishing the significance for moral theology of the new life in Christ? And if so, must we not conclude that the reality of good human action is in jeopardy, and with it Barth's entire solution to the problem of ethics? We would likely be forced to draw this conclusion if Barth had not also assimilated justification to sanctification (or more accurately, described justification in a way that affirms the reality of sanctification) and explicitly made room for a genuine if highly qualified visibility of goodness in human beings other than Christ. With regard to justification, Barth repeatedly emphasizes that the coexistence of the 'old man' of sin and the 'new man' of righteousness is not a static dualism but a dynamic history. 'I was and still am the former man . . . But I am already and will be the latter man.'[87] Justification is not merely forensic but sets us in motion from one

---

84 CD IV/2, 526 f./595–7, 530 f./600 f.
85 CD IV/1, 618–28/690–701.
86 *Ethics*, 250/424 f.
87 CD IV/1, 544/606 f.

state to another. 'It is our wrong and death which is behind us, our right and life which is before us.'[88] This direction is irreversible, and it is therefore where we are going and not where we have been that takes priority as we understand ourselves as those justified by God. 'The new thing which comes from God has as such precedence over the old of man. The right which is ascribed to him by God has as such precedence over his own wrong. His life has precedence over his death. The goal, the *terminus ad quem* of his way, has precedence over its *terminus a quo* and beginning.'[89] Remarkably, Barth also says all of this about conversion, which is the event that constitutes sanctification as a human phenomenon. In conversion, too, there is 'a coincidence of the "still" and the "already"' but only in a direction from the former to the latter. The 'old man' and 'new man' are related by 'a *terminus a quo* and a *terminus ad quem*,' but the one caught up in the movement of conversion 'can be the two only in the whole turning from the one to the other,' which is precisely what conversion is.[90] The point here is not that Barth identifies justification and sanctification or confuses the two. Rather, the point is that just as he holds sanctification to the same terms that govern justification, the terms that govern justification also prepare the way for sanctification. Here as in the whole of Barth's account, justification is the basis and presupposition of sanctification while sanctification is the goal and consequence of justification.[91]

Finally, despite all of the qualifications with which he surrounds it, and which we have already considered in this section, Barth does believe in the reality of human action that corresponds to the divine action of grace. 'What remains, then, for us? Jesus Christ remains. . . . And the knowledge of faith remains. . . . And there remain the little movements of our own inner and outer life . . . in which the great critical and positive movement which he has made for us and with us must and will be reflected, but in which we can only attest this (in the measure of seriousness and fidelity which we are given and which we have to exercise).'[92] This qualified assertion from the later part of Barth's career may not seem to reveal much of an advance from the qualified assertions about the reflection of divine action in human action from the earlier part of his career, in *Romans₂*. Yet advance there is. It can now be stated explicitly and without reservation that 'the great critical movement' is 'made for us and in us' and that this divine movement 'must and will be reflected' in our actions. There is no great evidence here that Barth thinks that we can now make out the visibility of the good on the horizontal line. But there is a great deal more confidence that God is effecting in us a secondary visibility which reflects the primary visibility of

---

88 CD IV/1, 547/610.
89 CD IV/1, 591/659.
90 CD IV/2, 572 f./647 f.
91 CD IV/2, 508/575.
92 CD IV/2, 584/660.

the good in Jesus Christ, and that while this divine work gives us no grounds for moral confidence in ourselves, it does give us grounds for confidence in the work of the Holy Spirit. And as Barth saw it, that confidence was sufficient.

4. CONCLUSION

Our final verdict is an ambivalent one. We conclude that Barth did indeed vindicate his claim that God is everything only in order to make human beings everything on their level but that he did not do so without incurring significant liabilities. Among these liabilities are his denial of sacramental mystery and the extraordinarily qualified affirmation he gives to visible human goodness. Both liabilities indicate features of Barth's theology that can be traced to the period of *Romans$_2$*. On the one hand there is the denial, mitigated to be sure, but still in effect, that we can find the good in our visible moral achievements, whether individual or collective. On the other hand, there is the affirmation, now more resounding, of the integrity of our moral capacities in their natural exercise. We may legitimately question whether the denial does justice to the work of the Holy Spirit in our lives and whether the affirmation, with its blanket rejection of deification, can make sense of the participation of our action in God's action or of the way in which the Holy Spirit accomplishes this participation. Far from ignoring or denying the reality of our natural human capacities and limits, as he is so often accused of doing, we may wonder whether Barth's moral theology concedes too much to the latter, thus failing to do full justice to the power of grace to transform us. Nevertheless, we must confirm the growing consensus that Barth recognizes the necessity of real human moral action in the movement of divine grace. Without human action, the movement of grace would not accomplish its own eternal aim, which is to make human beings into genuine covenant partners with God. The fact that this movement is accomplished by God's grace alone does not exclude human action but entails that the latter will take the form of gratitude, which in the context of God's reconciling work, also means faith.

We conclude this chapter with a brief remark on the general type of moral action exhibited by Barth's moral theology. We may think of moral action in several ways: as oriented to an end to which it is naturally yet imperfectly inclined (teleology), as productive of states of affairs that can be measured and judged as more and less good and evil (consequentialism), as conformity to a moral law or command (deontology), etc. We noted above that a view often attributed to Barth is that moral action is representational, serving as a sign of what divine action has accomplished. A more accurate description of Barth's position is that moral action for him is *expressive*. In our action we express who we are: not, as in nineteenth-century Romanticism, our authentic nature or self but our being as those created, reconciled, and to be redeemed, that is, our being in Christ. As we noted at length in the previous chapter, because the good has already been accomplished by Christ in our place, it confronts us as a reality in which we already stand, in which we are already placed. It is precisely for this reason that it takes the form of permission, confronting us with what we may be and do, what we are now, in Christ, free to be and do. Thus 'its imperative amounts to a simple: "Be what thou art! [*Sei, was du bist!*]."'[93]

But what is the action that genuinely expresses what we are? How is that action recognized among the various actions and courses of action that recommend themselves to us at any given time? With this question we confront the last temptation of ethics as the expression of our being for ourselves.

[93] CD IV/2, 363/406.

6

Ethical Reflection and Instruction

The command of God, as we saw in Chapter 4, claims human beings, demanding that they bear witness in their actions to the grace of God. As claimed by God, those actions, as we saw in Chapter 5, have a certain character whose general features we sketched. But how do we get from the general characteristics of human action as claimed by God to judgments about whether or not a particular action fulfills the divine claim? How, and by whom, is it determined that one or another particular action does or does not genuinely correspond to the grace of God? Since it is its correspondence or lack thereof to the grace of God that makes any such action right or wrong, good or evil, this question concerns the concrete rightness or wrongness, good or evil, of our actions claimed by God. It is the ethical question—'What should we do?'—in its most concrete sense.

This question provokes some of the liveliest controversies over Barth's ethics in the English-speaking world. Some critics, mostly of an earlier generation, have charged that Barth's moral theology comes to ruin on the question of particular ethical judgments. For these critics, Barth's emphasis on God as the one who determines the rightness and wrongness of human actions is inimical to or at least in tension with responsible human deliberation and choice.[1] Some recent

---

[1] Reinhold Niebuhr argued, variously, that Barth's theological absolutism, religious perfectionism, eschatology, or emphasis on human sinfulness makes relative moral judgments in history impossible, irrelevant, or suspect. Niebuhr, 'Barthianism and the Kingdom,' *The Christian Century*, July 15, 1931, reprinted in Niebuhr, *Essays in Applied Christianity: The Church and the New World*, ed. D. B. Robertson (New York: Meridian Books, 1959), 148 f.; idem, *The Nature and Destiny of Man*, i: *Human Nature* (New York: Scribner's, 1941), 220; idem, 'We Are Men and Not God,' *The Christian Century*, October 27, 1948, reprinted in *Essays in Applied Christianity*, 171, 174 f. While these comments predate the publication of Barth's 'special ethics' (CD III/4) in 1951, Niebuhr sees the problem of concrete moral judgments as part of a broader inability of Barth's theology to address concrete problems of political, social and cultural life, an inability which Niebuhr continued to find in Barth after 1951. James Gustafson and Stanley Hauerwas have, with qualifications, criticized Barth for an occasionalism that allows for no continuity in the divine command and/or for an intuitionism for which all rational deliberation is futile and even sinful. Gustafson, *Can Ethics Be Christian?* (Chicago: University of Chicago Press, 1975), 160; idem, *Ethics from a Theocentric Perspective*, ii: *Ethics and Theology* (Chicago: University of Chicago Press, 1984), 30–2; Hauerwas, *Character and the Christian Life: A Study in Theological Ethics* (San Antonio, Tex.: Trinity University Press, 1975), 142, 142 n. 44, 172. Robin Lovin offers a similar criticism, though his description of Barth as an act-deontologist concerns the form of moral judgments rather than their epistemology (intuitionism) or the metaphysics they presuppose (occasionalism). Lovin, *Christian Faith and Political Choices: The Social Ethics of Barth*,

scholars reject this conclusion. They find in Barth variations on familiar methods of practical moral reasoning that allow for concrete human judgments.[2] The latter assessment does more justice to Barth's actual practice of concrete moral inquiry, but both sides of this controversy err in ignoring the kind of activity concrete moral inquiry is for Barth and the relation of human choice or decision to the divine decision of election.

From early on, Barth held that it is not the task of moral theology or any other kind of ethical inquiry to make concrete determinations of the rightness or wrongness or the good or evil of our actions.[3] But what is unique to Barth is not the notion that ethical inquiry cannot itself get us from a general characterization of the right or the good to the determination in a particular case whether a specific act is right or good. Most theories of ethical inquiry make modest claims about the capacity of inquiry to determine particular actions.[4] What is unique, and indeed notorious, is Barth's insistence that it is not human judgment at all but rather the command of God itself that makes these determinations. In Barth's terms, the command of God does not only claim our actions but also *decides* concerning them. It interrogates, measures, and judges our choice of an action or course of conduct with respect to its witness to grace. As such, it is the criterion of the good or evil of our conduct. And not only of our conduct: According to Barth we realize ourselves in our conduct—in a continuous series in which present decisions are connected with past and future decisions—so that God's decision on an action at any moment is inseparable from God's decision on our life as a whole.[5]

Brunner, and Bonhoeffer (Philadelphia: Fortress Press, 1984), 27–8. Robert Willis argues that Barth does allow a genuine place for moral deliberation but only at the price of an inconsistency between a stress on response to an already determinate command of God in CD II/2 and a stress on human deliberation over the command of God in CD III/4. Willis, *The Ethics of Karl Barth*, 440 f.; Willis, 'Some Difficulties in Barth's Development of Special Ethics,' *Religious Studies* 6 (1970): 152–5.

[2] For Nigel Biggar and William Werpehowski, Barth exemplifies, respectively, a nondeductive form of casuistry and a certain kind of narrative. See Biggar, *The Hastening that Waits*; Werpehowski, 'Command and History in the Ethics of Karl Barth,' *Journal of Religious Ethics* 9 (1981): 298–321; and idem, 'Narrative and Ethics in Barth,' *Theology Today* 43 (1986): 334–53.

[3] At various points Barth explicitly states that the task of moral theology is not to determine the concrete action God commands but rather to describe the condition of humanity as addressed by the Word of God. See *Ethics*, 118/194, *The Holy Spirit and the Christian Life*, 9 f., 'The Gift of Freedom,' 85–8.

[4] For Aristotle, as for most ancient theorists of eudaemonia, the determination of what counts as a genuine specific instance of a good in a particular situation of choice is a matter for trained perception rather than for theoretical inquiry. Aquinas held that the certainty of moral judgment diminishes in proportion with the degree of particularity of circumstances such a judgment must consider. Finally, Kant held that the capacity to bring a case under a principle belongs to 'mother wit' rather than to discursive rationality. We owe above all to utilitarian theories the notion that rational calculation can identify the specific actions or policies to be chosen or avoided.

[5] CD II/2, 634/705. It will be necessary to keep in mind this notion of conduct as unfolding in a continuous temporal sequence of choices in order to avoid misunderstanding the encounter with God's decision in the present moment of choice as one in a series of isolated events.

Why does Barth understand the concrete measure or criterion of human conduct in terms of a divine decision? There are two questions here. The first question is why does Barth insist that it is *God* who decides concerning particular human actions? The answer to this question is clear: If God were merely to claim our actions but not to make specific determinations as to whether or not the actions we in fact choose genuinely correspond to the grace of God and thus fulfill the claim made on them, we would be the ones who make concrete judgments of the good or evil, rightness or wrongness of our actions. We would thereby assert ourselves as knowers and judges of concrete good and evil, and ethics would at this point come under human control, notwithstanding the divine claim. At the point of the concrete judgment we pronounce on an action or a course of action—whether our own action or that of another—we would put ourselves in the place of the judge, repeating the sin of Adam and Eve with all of the implications we discussed in Chapter 2. The second question is why does Barth insist on understanding God's judgment concerning particular actions as a *decision*? This question is especially pertinent insofar as the emphasis on decision evokes existentialism (from which Barth explicitly distanced himself) and voluntarism (most implications of which he wished to avoid). The answer is that the theme of God's decision brings the situation of choice, of decision on a particular action, and therefore we ourselves in our action, into proper connection with election. Our concrete righteousness or unrighteousness 'is a matter of the prior decision [*Vorentscheidung*] made and expressed in the will of God from eternity and in the act of God in the midst of time, and continually made and expressed at every moment of our life in time.'[6] This connection means that the divine decision as the criterion or measure of our present actions—that which distinguishes them as good or evil—is the expression of God's decision from eternity, fulfilled in time, to be gracious to us in Jesus Christ. The command of God given moment by moment in the course of our temporal lives is the concrete expression of that decision of the eternal will and historical act of God. What God commands at every moment of our temporal lives is the action which, according to the divine wisdom, expresses the purpose of election at that moment in its relation to all other moments in the course of our lives.

But God's decision is not the only decision moral theology has to investigate. Just as the command of God summons us to a free confirmation of election, so that the latter involves us in ethical action rather than mechanical conformity, so it is our free decision that God decides on, judging it as to its witness to the grace of election. 'It is our own free decisions whose character God decides even as we ourselves make them . . . It is the use of our freedom which is subjected to the

---

[6] CD II/2, 633/703 (revised). With this connection between the eternal decision and its moment-by-moment expression in time Barth does justice both to his more recent emphasis on election as from eternity and to his earlier emphasis, evident in *Ethics*, on election as decided in each moment of human action.

prior divine decision—the decision of the question whether it is right or not, whether it consists or not in the witness required of us.'[7] Once again, then, electing grace itself requires ethics—in this case a human decision or choice of a particular action. Yet once again, as we will see, it is in terms of ethics that human beings express and carry out their desire to be like God, to be their own lawgiver and judge—in this case by presuming to determine for themselves, and thus apart from electing grace, the rightness or goodness of particular actions. And, finally, once again it is the task of moral theology to articulate electing grace as ethics while precluding ethics as the expression of the determination of human beings to be for themselves—to pronounce the concrete judgment of good and evil on themselves and others.

We thus arrive at the problem of ethics in its most concrete manifestation, namely, the decision or choice for a particular action or course of action. There is no moral life without such decisions or choices. Yet how can we say of an action or a course of action 'this is right' or 'this is wrong' without asserting ourselves as judges of good and evil? We recall Barth's conviction that '[a]ll sin has its being and origin in the fact that man wants to be his own judge.'[8] In Chapter 4 we described the workings of this desire—how in seeking to establish our moral worth we subject ourselves and others to moral demands that commend themselves to us in our effort to justify ourselves. Yet in Chapter 2 we noted that Barth does not simply reassert the divine right to judge good and evil against human usurpation of this office but instead claims that human ethical decisions participate in the divine decision. The central claim of this chapter is that Barth's treatment of concrete ethical inquiry and decision attempts to solve the problem of ethics at this, its most concrete level—the level at which the moral subject realizes itself in its concrete actions—by showing how the human and divine decisions relate to one another. We may state the problem of ethics as it now concerns us in this way: Ethics is impossible without concrete human judgments, choices, or decisions. How, then, can ethics involve the participation of human beings in the divine judgment, choice, or decision regarding good and evil instead of expressing the determination of human beings to be their own judges?

Barth's attempt to solve this problem stresses the encounter of our decision with the decision of God. Both the earlier and the more recent interpretations of Barth's practical ethics fall short precisely to the extent that they shift the focus away from this encounter, whether to the divine decision alone (arguing that Barth leaves no room for human deliberation and choice) or to the human decision (arguing that Barth offers a variation on a standard form of moral reasoning). For Barth, however, the focus of ethics must be on the encounter itself. 'Ethics has to make clear that every single step man takes involves a specific and direct responsibility toward God, who reached out for man in specific and

---

[7] CD II/2, 633 f./704.
[8] CD IV/1, 220/241.

direct encounter. . . . Ethics exists to remind man of his confrontation with God, who is the light illuminating all his actions.'[9] The task of moral theology is not to try to determine the particular actions God commands but to explicate this encounter of our free human decision with the free decision of God. Where other theories of ethics speak of moral reasoning, deliberation, or discernment, Barth speaks of *ethical reflection* as the attitude and practice in which we encounter God and of *ethical instruction* as the moral knowledge we pursue in order to prepare ourselves for this encounter. Our effort to keep this encounter before us begins with two questions. First, what exactly is the relation of our choice or decision to the decision of God? Second, how is our choosing or deciding to be carried out given that God decides on our choice or decision? These questions are answered in the notion of ethical reflection.

1. ETHICAL REFLECTION

Because God decides on our conduct, measuring it by the criterion of the actualization in Christ of electing grace and questioning it as to its fulfillment of this criterion, our conduct, and we in our conduct, constitute a continuous reply (*Antwort*) to the Word of God as command. Barth can therefore refer to the notion of responsiveness (*Verantwortlichkeit*) as 'the most precise description of the human situation in the face of the sovereign decision of God.'[10] The decision of God on our conduct gives our conduct the character of a reply or response to the question posed to us by and in the command of God as the witness to or expression of God's decision on us and our conduct. In this responsiveness consists our accountability (*Verantwortung*) to God: the command of God places us in the position of having to render an account (*Rechenschaft*) to God.[11] Accountability is the objective situation of human beings before God; it pertains whether we are conscious of it or not, whether we affirm or deny it. It is in Christian ethics, Barth insists, that our accountability before God is known as such and becomes a matter of conscious awareness.[12] This conscious awareness Barth calls ethical reflection (*ethische Besinnung*).

To reflect ethically is to ask the ethical question 'What should we do?' But now this question is posed not with regard to the standard of conduct itself but with

---

[9] Barth, 'The Gift of Freedom,' 86.

[10] CD II/2, 641/713 (revised).

[11] CD II/2, 641/713 f.

[12] CD II/2, 642–4/714–16. As is usually the case when Barth makes exclusivist claims for Christian ethics, the comparison is less between Christian ethics and other kinds of religious ethics than between Christian ethics and a general conception of moral philosophy which is treated more in terms of what it lacks as a purely formal enterprise than as a rival substantive ethic. Even as applied to moral philosophy, however, the claim is doubtful in the unqualified version stated here. Presumably, Barth means here what he says elsewhere: that apart from a Christological determination, accountability to God remains obscure or abstract in moral philosophy.

regard to the specification of this standard in a concrete situation. 'Formally,' Barth notes, 'it is a question of the rightness and goodness of our choice between the various possibilities of our existence . . . in the light of the command and decision of God . . .'[13] This, of course, is the question of choice and deliberation. But to pose this question is not merely or even primarily to practice ethical deliberation in the strict sense, that is, to consider the reasons for and against different possible actions or courses of action. Most fundamentally, ethical reflection is not a formal or informal method of reasoning but an attitude (*Stellungnahme*)—the attitude proper to a conscious awareness (as the term *Besinnung* implies) of the human condition of accountability. 'How, then, should we and will we encounter his decision? In what understanding of the command of God given to us? In what readiness for his judgment, for his distinction between good and evil? In what position in view of the standard by which we will be measured?'[14] These are the questions to which ethical reflection is the answer. To be properly aware of our accountability to God is to be ready to encounter God as the one who judges our conduct as good or evil and to go forth, in every situation of choice, to this encounter.

Testing our Actions

This readiness to encounter the divine decision on our conduct (and on ourselves in our conduct) is exercised in a moral practice, namely the examination (*Prüfung*) of how we and our conduct stand in light of the command of God. We approach our own decision with the knowledge that the command of God awaits it and judges it and with a readiness to receive this judgment. It is therefore necessary that we test it in light of this divine decision. 'Our submission to this decision, and therefore our obedience to God's command, begins always with the fact that we look towards [*entgegensehen*] it as those who know that it is our own free decision [*Entscheidung*] which will there be judged [*entscheiden*]. From the very outset, then, this, our own free decision is there called in question, and therefore in need of preparatory testing [*vorlaufenden Prüfung*] as we approach [*entgegengehen*] it.'[15] Rather than deliberation, then, Barth speaks of this practice of examining or testing our conduct, for this notion is better suited than is the notion of deliberation to express the claim that we properly raise the question of the rightness and goodness of our choice in an encounter with the decision of God: that our actions are put to the test by this decision which determines the rightness and goodness of our choice.

Barth clarifies the nature and limits of this testing of our actions and its similarities and differences with respect to deliberation in an exegetical study of

---

[13] CD II/2, 644/716 f.
[14] CD II/2, 634/705 (revised).
[15] CD II/2, 634 f./705 f.

New Testament instances of the term *dokimazein* (to test, examine, prove, approve) and its cognates—the source for his conception of *Prüfung*. At one level, *Prüfung* clearly is a form of ethical deliberation; it is a process of testing the various possibilities (in Greek, *ta diapheronta*, roughly, what matters or is relevant) open to us in a situation of choice. But *Prüfung* is a special kind of inquiry; it asks in what relation the command of God stands to our prospective act and our prospective act to the command of God.[16]

The sovereign decision of God in his command stands absolutely supreme above the existing situation, although absolutely related to it. And the point at issue [*das ist zu prüfen*] is the mutual relationship between this, that or the other possible line of action in this situation and the divine command. *Ta diapheronta* are, then, the various possibilities of action open to us in the existing situation, and the relevant question is whether we can (and so should) adopt this or that particular possibility in the confidence that the relation between it and the divine command will be positive and therefore the action will be 'good, and acceptable, and according to the purpose of God' (Rom. 12: 2).[17]

Given its orientation, *Prüfung* must go beyond efforts to determine the relative value or disvalue internal to alternative actions or courses of action, whether these efforts involve a nondiscursive grasp of an alleged moral necessity inherent in the situation (a 'command of the hour') or a rational evaluation of the arguments for or against each alternative.

This inquiry [*Prüfung*] cannot be replaced by even the most penetrating systematic or intuitive analysis of the situation as such and the objective and subjective factors which condition it. For, obviously, this enquiry only begins where an analysis of that kind leaves off. It presupposes that the *diapheronta* are spread out before us in their immanent value or lack of value. . . . Only then, in contradistinction to every mere analysis of the situation, does the enquiry [*Prüfung*] begin in which it is a question of the will of God (whose judgment is not discoverable in the various possibilities open to us, but stands in sovereign transcendence over them).[18]

Barth's central concern is obvious: he wants to point out the transcendence of the divine judgment over all determinations of the ethically relevant features internal to the *diapheronta*, that is, the possible courses of action that comprise the situation. However, this does not mean that those determinations have no place in the testing of our actions. *Prüfung* does, after all, presuppose that the immanent value and disvalue of alternative courses of action has already been determined. Ethical reflection, then, is twofold. It involves, first, the determination of the immanent value and disvalue of possible courses of action. And,

---

[16] CD II/2, 639/711.
[17] CD II/2, 639/711.
[18] CD II/2, 640/711 f.

second, it involves inquiry (*Prüfung*) into the mutual relation of these immanent possibilities of action to the will of God.[19]

This account of ethical reflection raises some serious questions. But before turning to them we will show how the twofold process of testing actions is exhibited in several of Barth's discussions of concrete ethical issues. Considering various cases in which one might think oneself justified in taking one's life Barth remarks: 'It is not the greater or lesser weight of human reasons that decides in this matter... but solely the judgment of God, which in the last analysis each person must hear in every real or conceivable situation after considering all of the human arguments on each side. [The judgment of God] can decide against taking one's life in spite of strong human reasons for it, and it can decide for taking one's life in spite of strong human reasons against it.'[20] In the case of abortion, where he argues that any commanded instance would involve a conflict of life against life and that no prior definitions, whether broad or narrow, of what would constitute such a conflict can determine in advance what God will command, Barth speaks of a 'required calculation and risk [*gebotene Wägen und Wagen*]' both of which 'must take place before God and in responsibility to him'; otherwise there is no good or right or obedience in the decision 'even though human reason and justification appear to favor one side or the other.'[21] Finally, in a normative analysis of political decision prompted by the controversy certain German theologians sparked when they publicly opposed the remilitarization of Germany in the early 1950s, Barth put forth a general account of how a Christian ought to make such decisions, namely by thoroughly and conscientiously considering all of the arguments and counter-arguments on each side of the issue in order to determine their relative value and weight just as any conscientious fellow citizen would do—but doing all of this before God. 'In the midst of questions of rational evaluation he [the Christian] is faced with the question of obedience.' Here the Christian differs from his or her fellow citizens just as the question of the will of God in relation to the alternatives differs from the rational determination of their relative value and weight. 'He will inquire after a decision not in arbitrariness nor even in human prudence but in the freedom of obedience to the command of God.'[22] In each of these cases, Barth affirms the necessity of a rational analysis of possible courses of action. Yet he continued to insist that the question of the relation of God's will to alternative possibilities of action is

---

[19] A shortcoming of John Howard Yoder's account is its failure to distinguish these two aspects or stages. See Yoder, *Karl Barth and the Problem of War and Other Essays on Barth*, ed. Mark Thiessen Nation (Eugene, Ore.: Cascade Books, 2003).

[20] CD III/4, 412/470 (revised).

[21] CD III/4, 422 f./482 (revised).

[22] Barth 'Politische Entscheidung in der Einheit des Glaubens,' in *Theologische Existenz heute* (Munich: Christian Kaiser Verlag, 1952), 8, 7 (translation 'Political Decisions in the Unity of the Faith,' in Barth, *Against the Stream: Shorter Post-War Writings, 1946–52*, ed. Ronald Gregor Smith (London: SCM Press, 1954), 154, 152).

distinct from the question of the immanent value and disvalue of these possibilities as determined by that rational analysis.

The process of testing the possibilities before us culminates in a decision, the choice of an action or course of action. This, of course, is not the last word in the matter; it is precisely this human decision on which God decides. In Barth's terms, we test our actions 'in the presence of God and in the light of God's own examination of them.'[23] This is precisely what it means to test our actions in readiness to encounter the divine decision. This is why Barth can speak of the decision resulting from our testing as penultimate in relation to God's decision, that is, as a 'prior decision [*Vorentscheidung*] from which I proceed toward the divine decision.'[24] As we have said, Barth's account of the testing or examining of our prospective actions raises serious questions. The first has to do with whether the scriptural instances of *dokimazein* to which Barth appeals support his view. The texts Barth cites (Rom. 12: 2; Phil. 1: 10; Eph. 5: 8–10; 1 Thess. 5: 21) show no indication of Barth's distinction between an inquiry that considers only the *diapheronta* in themselves and an inquiry that considers them in light of the will of God. Nor is there any indication in these texts that God tests human actions. We must conclude that the exegetical basis for Barth's account of ethical reflection is weak, and it is weak at precisely the point that is most critical for his enterprise, namely where it is a question of whether it is God, and not we, who knows and judges good and evil.

The second question concerns Barth's use of New Testament portrayals of the Jew or the Pharisee as instances of an inadequate or incomplete *Prüfung*. Quoting Romans 2: 18 and Luke 12: 56, Barth ascribes to the Jew or the Pharisee the ability 'to test [*prüfen*] the possibilities lying before him' so that he is 'adept in the analysis of every kind of situation.' But because the Jew or Pharisee fails to recognize Christ as the *telos* of the law according to Rom. 10: 4, he does not carry the test to the point where the question is the will of God; he therefore does not practice a genuine *dokimazein*.[25] His *Prüfung* stops with the first activity, namely the rational analysis of alternative possibilities of action and thus remains within the realm of immanence. And it stops here precisely because of the rejection (Barth exploits the Greek term *apodokimazein* in several passages in the synoptic gospels) of Christ as the *telos* of the law. We will see that Barth will continue to contrast the Judaic and the Christian along these lines of immanence and transcendence in ethical inquiry. This, to say the least, is a deeply disturbing contrast, one which we will examine below.

Third, we have seen that for Barth the testing of the possibilities before us with respect to the will of God, the second activity, begins only after the determination of the value or disvalue immanent in these possibilities. But how is that value or disvalue determined, and what status does its determination have in relation to

---

[23] CD II/2, 638 f./710. See also CD II/2, 636/707.
[24] CD II/2, 655/729 f. (revised). See also CD II/2, 644/717.
[25] CD II/2, 639/711, 640/712 (revised).

the will of God? With regard to the first question, Barth's talk of calculation implies a technical procedure and a quantitative notion of value. However, in his most explicit treatment of the matter, in his essay on 'Political Decision in the Unity of Faith,' Barth describes a very ordinary, nonformal process of reasoning, namely the careful consideration of the reasons for or against an action or course of action and the weighing or balancing of these reasons in favor of one alternative or another. In the absence of any evidence to the contrary, we should assume that in spite of his talk of calculation he has in mind this ordinary, nontechnical form of moral reasoning rather than the technical and quantitative forms of reasoning exhibited by many consequentialist theories.[26] This brings us to the second question, regarding the status of this process of deliberation. The question here is how this or any process of moral reasoning can ultimately count for Barth. The problem is especially acute in the instances, cited above, of suicide and abortion, where he explicitly declares that God's judgment may go against a balance of human reasons in favor of one alternative or another. But if God's judgment as to the mutual relation between one of these possibilities and the command of God so radically transcends all human determinations of the immanent value or disvalue of those possibilities, why make those determinations in the first place? Why weigh reasons at all if the weight human deliberation assigns them can be overruled by a divine judgment? Despite asserting the necessity of rational deliberation, Barth seems to leave us with a divine voluntarism in the face of which all human deliberation is ultimately futile.

The final question is closely related to the previous one. How, on Barth's account, is our activity of weighing various possible courses of action to determine their relative value or disvalue related to our activity of testing these possibilities with respect to the will of God? Unfortunately, Barth does not answer this question.[27] There are, however, at least two plausible interpretations of his position. On one interpretation, Barth holds that we should act in accordance with our rational evaluation of the possibilities of choice while keeping in mind that God's judgment may differ from the conclusion of our rational evaluation. In this case, we should always act according to human reason but should never presume that human reason coincides with God's will. On the other interpretation, Barth

---

[26] To determine the weight or value of competing arguments is closer to the informal process of practical reasoning described by Stuart Hampshire than it is to utilitarianism (See Hampshire, *Innocence and Experience* (Cambridge, Mass.: Harvard University Press). Yoder's account (*Karl Barth and the Problem of War*, 32–4) therefore misleads when it uses terms like 'pragmatic calculation' and 'the best, or the least evil' with reference to Barth. Barth makes no reference at all to any method or process of calculation, nor to any quantification and tallying up of goods and evils.

[27] At one point, Barth speaks cryptically of an agent discerning the spirits in the various arguments for and against a proposed action or policy in accordance with the standard of the Word of God and of confronting in them 'the mystery of history and of his own life' (Barth, 'Politische Entscheidung,' 8/154). This seems to point to some nondiscursive (though not necessarily nonrational) process, but it raises many more questions than it answers.

holds the more controversial view that on some occasions we may be obligated to decide on a course of action other than the one favored by a rational evaluation. That this interpretation is the correct one is strongly suggested by Barth's remarks on suicide and abortion noted above. If so, then it is Barth's view that there are at least some occasions (almost certainly extremely rare) in which we should act against what reason prescribes—or at least against what is prescribed by the discursive weighing of reasons to determine immanent value and disvalue. This last qualification raises the question of what rational ground there could possibly be for such a decision and whether it might involve some nondiscursive yet still rational activity. What kind of cognitive procedure, if any, is involved in testing possible courses of action with respect to the will of God? It is typical of Barth not to say. Rather than describing the form *Prüfung* should take, he is content to stress the negative point that in its proper and required sense it is not conducted simply by carrying out ordinary practices of rational evaluation. Rational evaluation is therefore necessary (the decision of God is related to the situation of choice) but not sufficient (the decision of God transcends the situation of choice). Ethical reflection must be practiced with the awareness that there is something more at stake in any situation of choice than the value or disvalue that can be determined by common rational insight, and it must exercise this awareness by remaining open to the possibility that an action which goes against common rational insight may be required. This position is undoubtedly problematic. Its problematic character is partially but not entirely mitigated by the fact that (as we will see) ethical reflection occurs in the context of extensive rational instruction about what God commands.

Self-examination

The second, third, and fourth questions remain at least partially unanswered and will have to be deferred to the last substantive section of this chapter. Meanwhile, there is one important thing left to say about *Prüfung* as the testing of our prospective actions, namely that such testing is not merely the examination of our conduct but also of ourselves in our conduct. Barth consistently rejects moral theories that treat actions (and their evaluation) apart from the subject who realizes herself in her actions, that is, in the continuous series of decisions that comprises her temporal existence. In this spirit he connects the Pauline *dokimazein diapheronta* with the Pauline *dokimazein eauton* ('to examine oneself'). 'It is not a matter of an essentially different testing [*Prüfung*] . . . if the reference is now specifically to a self-examination [*Selbstprüfung*]. The *diapheronta* themselves are the various courses of action open to man in existing situations, and the object of the inquiry [*Prüfung*] is to fix the mutual relationship between one or another of them, *between the man himself in their realization*, and the will of God.'[28]

---

[28] CD II/2, 640/712 (emphasis added).

Self-examination is included in the examination of our actions—or rather, as we will soon see, the examination of our actions is an extension of our self-examination, which will turn out to be theologically prior.

The grounding of the examination of our prospective actions in the examination of ourselves takes *Prüfung* even further beyond deliberation as it is usually conceived. There is, of course, a long history of practices of self-examination in the history of Western morals, but we should not be too quick to assimilate Barth to this history, and especially not to the discernment or inspection of internal states that has been prominent since the early modern period.[29] In his case, self-examination has to do with the decision of God, which is of course external to the self. Once again, then, the readiness to encounter God is determinative of *Prüfung*. 'To examine ourselves means . . . to prepare ourselves for the encounter with our Judge.'[30] Notably, for Barth the paradigm instance of this readiness to encounter God is the self-examination to be carried out in relation to the Lord's Supper according to 1 Corinthians 11: 28. Ethical reflection thus has a eucharistic meaning. What exactly is this meaning? Barth does not articulate it in detail, and it is uncertain whether the unwritten treatment of the Lord's Supper projected for the part-volume of the *Church Dogmatics* on the ethics of reconciliation would have continued this line of thought or moved in a different direction. Nevertheless, a rough picture emerges from what he does say. For Barth, the Lord's Supper (the common name for the Eucharist in the Reformed tradition) is our communion (*Gemeinschaft*) of the body and blood of Christ. In eucharistic self-examination, then, 'we ask ourselves how it stands between Jesus Christ and us' or, in the words of 2 Corinthians 13: 5 through which Barth construes eucharistic self-examination, 'whether we are "in the faith."' This question is 'the true theme of all ethical inquiry [*Prüfung*].' It follows that readiness for the encounter with God in the Lord's Supper is the prototype of all readiness to encounter the judge of our actions, the prototype of all testing whatsoever. All other testing is only 'a repetition and modification' of this testing.[31] The goal of all testing is therefore this self-knowledge (*Selbsterkenntnis*), which corresponds to the divine action in the Lord's Supper, which is the invitation to the eucharistic table.[32]

---

[29] For treatments of Christian and pagan forms of ethical and spiritual practice in antiquity and their implications for modern ethics and culture, see Pierre Hadot, *Philosophy as a Way of Life: Spiritual Exercises from Socrates to Foucault*, ed. with introd. by Arnold I. Davidson (New York: Blackwell, 1995), and Michel Foucault, *Ethics*, ed. Paul Rabinow (New York: The New Press, 1992).

[30] CD II/2, 640/712.

[31] CD II/2, 641/713.

[32] CD II/2, 640 f./712 f.

Conclusion

This analysis of ethical reflection answers the two questions raised by Barth's claim that the decision of God determines the rightness or wrongness, the good or evil of our own decision: Despite the questions that remain unanswered, we now know something about (1) the relation of our choice or decision to the decision of God, and (2) how our choosing or deciding is to be carried out given that it is God who decides on our choice or decision. For Barth, what is at stake in ethical reflection is whether to ask the ethical question in the situation of choice is once again to claim to be like God, deciding and judging good and evil, or whether it is to encounter the divine decision and judgment and thus to be, in one's conduct, the covenant partner of God, the recipient of divine grace. To ask the ethical question in a situation of choice is, of course, to deliberate.[33] Ethical reflection as Barth describes it ensures that the asking of the ethical question does not become, as a process of deliberation culminating in a human judgment about a prospective act, an autonomous human exercise but instead remains within the accountability to God that defines the human situation in the face of the divine decision. 'When we seriously ask this question . . . we take up the stance appropriate to our responsiveness and our concretely realized accountability.'[34] Ethical reflection is therefore not a technique or an insight by which human beings make judgments regarding particular actions, and those who think Barth is clumsily attempting to describe such a thing or carelessly neglecting it fail to understand him. Rather, ethical reflection describes how we should approach prospective actions in anticipation of God's judgment on them, and on us. It is to deliberate in what for Barth is the only possible position in view of the command of God: the position of the addressee of the command of God.

As an attitude of readiness to approach God, as a twofold process of testing our actions before God, as the awaiting of the divine decision on our choice, as a repetition or extension of eucharistic self-examination—in all of these respects ethical reflection seems best characterized as a form of prayer. For Barth, the characteristic ethical question—'What should we do?'—is a question asked of God in prayer. Barth thus transforms ethical deliberation into a spiritual practice—not in the sense of a technique of self-formation but rather an encounter

---

[33] By describing ethical reflection in these terms Barth takes the side of those for whom the question of the rightness or wrongness of actions is most properly posed from the standpoint of the deliberating agent rather than from a neutral standpoint of evaluation. See Stuart Hampshire, 'Fallacies in Moral Philosophy,' *Mind* 58 (1949): 466–82, reprinted in *Revisions: Changing Perspectives in Moral Philosophy*, ed. Stanley Hauerwas and Alasdair MacIntyre (Notre Dame, Ind.: University of Notre Dame Press, 1983), 51–67. However, for Barth this position is demanded not by a view of the proper logic of moral discourse but by the fact that God requires our decision corresponding to electing grace and decides concerning that decision. There is no time for a neutral, theoretical evaluation because we are involved in a continuous responsibility: at each moment we are answerable to the divine decision.

[34] CD II/2, 645/718 (revised).

with God. In this as in other respects, he returns ethics to the spiritual life—specifically, to the practice of self-examination before God—from which modern ethics extricated it.

Barth is well aware, however, that ethical reflection alone, as described here, does not tell us anything specific about what God decides with regard to particular actions and therefore does not give us much guidance as to what decision we should make in anticipation of God's decision. His first concern has been to establish the position of ethical reflection in accountability to the decision of God. But the question of ethical guidance cannot be avoided. Can moral theology, as a form of inquiry, tell us anything substantive about that decision, anything more than the general point that it expresses the eternal resolve on, and historical actualization of, election? Much is at stake in this question. If the answer is affirmative, how can Barth avoid the implication that human beings are capable in the end of ascertaining what God commands, of knowing and judging good and evil? In this case ethical reflection will have been only a deferral of an inevitable human usurpation of the command of God. Those who argue that Barth's ethics is business as usual will have been right. On the other hand, if the answer is negative, how can Barth avoid the implication that his ethics of the command of God involves a radical voluntarism in which, so far as human beings can determine, the command of God is arbitrary? In this case those who accuse Barth of denigrating human ethical inquiry will have been right. Barth will answer this question by arguing that the Word of God prepares us for the encounter with God by instructing us concerning it. Ethical reflection, if it is to be genuine, presupposes ethical instruction, that is, approximate though not definitive knowledge of what God commands. Almost all of what Barth offers in his treatments of moral issues in the *Church Dogmatics* is this ethical instruction which prepares us for the encounter he has described under the heading of ethical reflection.[35] But before we turn to his description of ethical instruction we must examine Barth's confrontation with casuistry, for casuistry attempts to provide concrete moral guidance, and we must understand why he rejected it (insofar as he did) in favor of ethical instruction.

2. CASUISTRY

Let us begin with what the ethics of the command of God has in common with casuistry: In both cases a person faced with a choice is confronted in the particularity of her situation with the specification of a general norm. To specify a norm is to articulate its concrete content or expression in a particular case.

---

[35] Failure to distinguish ethical reflection and instruction is fatal to interpretations of Barth's special ethics. Unlike many interpreters, Paul Nimmo grasps the distinction, but not in its full complexity, as we will see below.

Moreover, in both cases this specification is spoken from one person to another. Ethics in both cases is an intersubjective practice—a point that is lost in the common caricature of Barth's ethics as placing the individual alone before a commanding God. However, there is fundamental difference between casuistry and the ethics of the command of God, and it has to do with the question of *how* in each of them a general norm is related to a particular action. (For Barth, of course, this is the question of how the standard of ethics—the fulfillment of electing grace in Jesus Christ—is expressed in one of the possibilities of action in a situation of choice.) This difference entails a further difference in the precise form of intersubjectivity ethics involves—a point that is touched on here but treated more fully below.

For Barth, the most crucial feature of casuistry is that it takes the command of God as a general law which must then be specified by the casuist. Casuistry begins with the codification of the command of God as a set of general laws (*Gesetzetext*). It matters little to Barth whether biblical, natural law or traditional precepts predominate in this text; it is the feature of legality itself that concerns him, and whether it takes the 'Protestant' form of biblical legality or the 'Catholic' form of legality of natural law or tradition is, at this point, immaterial. Having fixed the command of God in one or another kind of legal text, the task of casuistry is one of interpretation (to determine the implications of general laws for the various conditions and possibilities of human action) and application (to make retrospective or prospective judgments regarding particular actions).[36]

Contrast this with what Barth says is properly the case with the command of God: 'The command of God is therefore not comparable with any human law because it is, for each particular case, both the norm and its specification [*bestimmte Vorschrift*] and is therefore both the law and the judge who applies it.'[37] The problem with identifying the command of God with a general law or a set of such laws is that in such a form it is not really a command at all but must be interpreted and specified in order to become a command.

A general formal and abstract command is, strictly speaking, no command at all. First it must in all cases be heard, understood and acknowledged in itself; only on the basis of this apprehension and acknowledgment can it become a command. Even then, interpretation and application to a particular case—which is again left for us to carry out—are necessary so that something like a command can occur. . . . A command whose truth is conditioned in this way is no command at all. A command—the command in its strongest sense, the command of God—is a demand that confronts us totally, over whose content we have no disposal and which therefore is in no need of filling out according to our own judgment.[38]

---

[36] CD III/4, 6/5, 9 f./9.

[37] CD II/2, 663/739 (revised).

[38] CD II/2, 665/741 (revised). Barth distinguishes between what he sees as Kant's understanding of the categorical imperative (he considers only the first formulation) as purely formal and the understanding of (unnamed) Kantians who have argued (Barth thinks successfully) that the categorical imperative entails some material content. In either case, Barth argues, the categorical

Of course, to fill out the content of the demand according to our own judgment is exactly what casuistry does. We thus face two problems. First, because it is only through casuistical interpretation and application that the command of God becomes a command in the proper sense, the casuist in effect becomes the commander, usurping the place of God by presuming to be 'able to speak as law.' By thus taking the position of the addressor rather than that of the addressee, the casuist violates the most fundamental condition of human beings in the face of the command of God. Instead of deciding in the face of the divine decision, terrified and consoled in the face of its judgment on one's decision, the casuist presumes an expertise, an administrative authority over the command of God.[39] The second problem follows from Barth's claim that the command of God demands not only our actions but ourselves. The command of God demands not only the conformity of will or deed to what God requires but also the one who wills and acts; to obey the command of God is to offer oneself to God in one's willing and acting. In casuistry, by contrast, one is not confronted with any such demand but only with a concrete judgment by which one measures one's conduct.[40] The point here is not that the command of God demands something in addition to one's action, namely oneself, but rather that the command of God addresses its demand to the person, who is to offer herself to God in her action (in which, as we have pointed out, she realizes herself), whereas casuistry, involving as it does a human specification of a law, is in no position to make such a demand and thus requires only that one measure one's

---

imperative is not itself an imperative; it becomes such only when we receive a concrete imperative that corresponds to the formula (in Kant's case) or specifies it (in the case of the Kantians). Barth also holds that Kant understood 'categorical' as distinguishing the imperative as such from desires, aspirations, and supposed demands while the unnamed Kantians understand it as confronting human beings with an absolutely obligatory demand. As a result, Barth argues, these Kantians erroneously treat the categorical imperative as itself an imperative rather than simply the formula for concrete imperatives while Kant rightly treats it as merely indicating what is involved in an imperative, which must always be concrete. Hence, Kant 'was far less inclined than those who thought they could improve on him to imagine that one of his formulae could take the place of the genuine moral imperative, of the command which is actually addressed to man and claims and judges him' (CD II/2, 667/743). In other words, Barth thinks that these Kantians treat the categorical imperative as a genuine imperative but fail to recognize that because it still requires human specification it is not truly an imperative at all, while Kant treated it as merely the form of genuine concrete imperatives and therefore understood that it comes into force only with the concrete imperatives that supply its content. Kant would therefore be on the side of Barth against the casuists, for Kant thus expresses philosophically, and therefore formally, what the command of God involves. However, Barth is wrong to enlist Kant as an ally here. For whatever one concludes regarding the formalism or nonformalism of the categorical imperative, for Kant the latter is not a formula of concrete imperatives. It is a test of maxims, that is, of general rules, not of individual imperatives. It follows that even if Barth is right that for Kant the categorical imperative is purely formal, it would still express the form taken not by concrete imperatives but by maxims. Kant therefore fails to express philosophically the concrete specification of the command of God as Barth understands the latter.

[39] CD III/4, 10 f./9 f.
[40] CD III/4, 13 f./13 f.

conduct by the relevant specification. In both of these respects, casuistry violates ethical reflection insofar as 'something other and alien' intervenes into the encounter with God, namely the casuistical interpretation and application, which constitute a 'law that [the casuist] has set between the divine decision and his own or that of others.'[41] In effect, the casuist dissolves the encounter of our decision with the divine decision by identifying the command of God with a general law and then mediating between the command, so understood, and our decision with a human judgment through which alone the command comes into force as an imperative.[42] Casuistry thus removes us from the fundamental position of ethical reflection described in the previous section.

It is legitimate to ask what forms of moral reasoning fall under this description of casuistry. Barth himself cast a wide net, including rabbinic Judaism and virtually all of Christian ethics, excluding only first-century apostolic exhortation, sixteenth-century Protestantism (presumably, Barth means the Lutherans and the Reformed), and, surprisingly, though not without ambivalence, eighteenth- and nineteenth-century Protestantism.[43] The case of rabbinic Judaism is dubious: the latter does not, as Barth seems to think, treat biblical command-ments as general, abstract laws awaiting halakhic specification. As for Christian ethics, Barth simply mentions Tertullian, Ambrose's *De officiis*, medieval peni-tentiaries (to which category he assigns the *Secunda secundae* of Aquinas' *Summa theologiae*), and Jesuit casuistry, without indicating in what senses these disparate texts exhibit the problematic features of casuistry. No one, then, will mistake this drift-net approach for a nuanced discrimination of forms of casuistical ethics. However, our doubts about whether Barth has done justice to casuistry histori-cally or conceptually should not distract us from understanding his aim here. The fundamental question for him is whether in our moral decisions, in which we realize ourselves, we genuinely encounter God or not. For this reason, the validity of Barth's analysis rests less on whether or not his characterization of casuistry is sufficiently nuanced to account for the various forms of practical reasoning in Christian ethics than on whether these forms adhere to a general pattern in which the will of God is identified with general laws, rules, or principles which it is the task of human ethical inquiry to interpret and specify in order to arrive at a concrete imperative. His focus is therefore on the question of whether the command of God must be treated as a general law requiring human specification or whether it comes to us already specified by God.[44]

---

[41] CD III/4, 13/13, 11/10.

[42] Nimmo correctly identifies Barth's emphasis on the encounter over against mediation, but he largely fails to see that Barth executes a casuistry that operates without general principles and without forming a system. See Nimmo, *Being in Action*, 55–60.

[43] CD III/4, 7 f./6 f.

[44] John Howard Yoder and Nigel Biggar both seek to reduce the range of what falls under Barth's rejection of casuistry. Yoder argues that Barth treated casuistry only as a means by which to secure a clear conscience and ignored casuistry as a way of asking what is commanded. This second use Yoder

The Command of God Specified

In order to rule casuistry out of moral theology, Barth must show that the command of God is already specified: that it encounters our decision concretely and thus without the mediation of casuistry.[45] He attempts to do this by appealing to scripture. It seriously distorts scripture, Barth argues, to think of biblical ethics exclusively or even primarily in terms of what appear to be lists of general laws in texts such as the Decalogue and the Sermon on the Mount. Here, Barth offers an early version of what has now become a common critique of a once-dominant model of biblical ethics. According to this critique, moral theology has long been under the influence of extrabiblical moral theories in which ethics consists of abstract rules or principles which must be interpreted and applied. Since the Bible appears to contain lists of laws of this type, the assumption is that these lists of laws comprise the content of biblical ethics. Biblical ethics accordingly takes the form of casuistry, that is, of interpreting and specifying these general laws. For Barth, however, this approach is fundamentally mistaken. A Jewish critique of this kind of biblical ethics would likely point to the entirety of the 613 commandments in order to challenge the privileged status of a set of general moral laws allegedly distinguishable from nonmoral cultic or judicial laws. Barth shares with this critique the refusal to distinguish moral law from nonmoral law and to privilege the former over the latter. But instead of the commandments in all their variety, he identifies the command of God with the innumerable highly specific orders and directions (*Befehlen und Anweisungen*) concerning particular deeds, performances, and modes of conduct (*Taten, Verrichtungen und Verhaltungsweisen*) given by God to Israel, by Jesus to his disciples, or by the Holy Spirit through the apostles—orders and directions belonging not to the domain of the abstract and general but rather to a particular history in all of its specificity and uniqueness. These orders and directions range

thinks Barth would consider legitimate on his own grounds (*Karl Barth and the Problem of War*, 42 f). But in fact, Barth deals extensively with casuistry as a way in which human beings try to determine what is commanded—and he rejects precisely this use of casuistry. Biggar argues that, properly understood, Barth's quarrel is only with a certain kind of casuistry, namely deductive, rationalistic versions (*The Hastening that Waits*, 7–45). Biggar insightfully shows how Barth in fact practices a kind of nondeductive casuistry, as we will see below. However, he largely ignores the sharp distinction Barth draws between the casuistry involved in inquiry into the domains in which God commands and the command of God itself—a distinction discussed in the following section of this chapter. He is therefore mistaken in thinking that Barth's primary distinction is between deductive forms of casuistry that leave no room for the divine freedom and nondeductive forms of casuistry that recognize limits to judgment of particular actions and therefore leave room for the divine freedom. Barth's primary distinction, as we will soon see, is between a kind of casuistry that leads one to the encounter with God and a kind of casuistry that substitutes itself for this encounter.

[45] Barth's characterization of the command of God as fully specified is coterminous with his notion of the command of God itself; it is a major point made in the first section of his first extended treatment of the command of God. See Barth, 'Das Halten der Gebote,' in *Vorträge und kleinere Arbeiten, 1925–1930*, 100.

from the momentous, such as God's call to Abraham to leave his country of origin and his kin, to the seemingly trivial, such as the command of Jesus to two of his disciples to bring the ass and colt to him.[46] Whether momentous or seemingly trivial, in all of these instances the command of God comes fully specified.

The specificity of these orders and directions may seem to make the command of God entirely arbitrary, but Barth denies that this is so. However contingent and ad hoc it appears, 'the divine commanding and forbidding follows a distinct thread—that of the history of the divine covenant of grace.'[47] Rather than general laws that can be lifted out of scripture and treated as abstract norms, biblical ethics consists of highly specific orders and directions along the lines of which we can trace the narrative of the actualization of the covenant of electing grace. We now recall what we noted above, namely, that for Barth, God's decision on a particular action is a concrete instance of the divine decision made from eternity and fulfilled in the life-work of Jesus Christ; that the action commanded by God in any situation is the action that expresses the reality of electing grace in that situation. These historically specific orders and directions, then, are the particular decisions by which God actualizes that primary decision, that is, they are the specifications of that decision. 'If God wills this or that from these men according to the texts, commanding and forbidding so particularly, it is because and to the extent that he wills supremely and uniquely this particular thing—the actualization of his election of grace. . . .'[48] If it is, as Barth believes he has shown, 'a decisive principle of biblical ethics' that God commands in the form of these orders and directions rather than in the form of general laws, then it follows that the ethics of the command of God cannot take the form of casuistry—that 'human beings are in no way required to appropriate general rules so that they themselves decide in applying them what is good and evil, but rather to keep continually before them the particular and specific thing that is prescribed or proscribed by God.'[49]

The decision of God towards which we move in ethical reflection is therefore a concrete, fully specified decision.[50] If the alternative were true—if the command of God were a general law in need of specification by human beings in order to become an actual command—there would be no genuine encounter with the decision of God at all. Human beings would in fact decide the good and evil, rightness and wrongness of particular actions. This is precisely what Barth seeks

---

[46] CD II/2, 672–6/749–54.
[47] CD II/2, 678 f./757.
[48] CD II/2, 678/756.
[49] CD II/2, 675/753 (revised).
[50] As such, what holds for the command of God is simply what holds for the Word of God more generally: the specificity of the command of God is that of the Word of God as such, the content of which cannot 'be construed and reproduced by us as a general truth' (CD I/1, 141/145; see also 136 f./141).

to exclude and what he believes in fact happens in casuistry. By identifying the command of God with a general law which then requires the casuist's specification in order to address us with the force of the imperative, casuistry evades the encounter of our decision with the decision of God—or rather it dissolves this encounter by mediating it. By contrast, this encounter remains in the ethics of the command of God. In this ethic the command of God is already interpreted and applied; what is required of us is not to articulate and specify it but only to obey it.[51] And with this last distinction we arrive once more at the fundamental contrast between ethics as the human effort to determine the good and ethics as the question of how human beings stand with respect to the good already given.

The Casuistry of the Prophetic Ethos versus Casuistical Ethics

Thus far, Barth's critique of casuistry is likely to strike many readers as neither plausible nor attractive. It seems to offer fodder to those critics who accuse him of exalting divine action at the expense of human action. It also seems to present, as polar opposites, a rationalistic morality of divine absence in which human moral reasoning replaces God and a nonrational morality of divine presence in which the command is given in the immediacy of an encounter with God. Finally, it seems to ignore what seem to be general moral laws in scripture. We will eventually see that these impressions are not quite accurate, but at this point it is necessary to introduce an important distinction Barth makes. Thus far we have spoken of a contrast between casuistry and the ethics of the command of God. While this is legitimate shorthand, the contrast is actually between two opposed understandings of casuistry and of the command of God. These opposed understandings emerge against the background of the two similarities between casuistry and the ethics of the command of God noted at the beginning of this section. First, both are case oriented, sharing a focus on the situation of choice or decision. In the case of the ethics of the command of God, 'God's general command for all human beings in every situation is as such also the fully particular, concrete, special command for this or that human being in the "case of conscience" of her particular situation.'[52] But as we have seen, they differ in their accounts of specification. In one case the command of God is both the general norm and its specification: God—not the casuist—specifies the norm, and it comes to human beings already fully specified. In the other case the command of God is identified with a general law—be it biblical, natural, traditional, or some combination of these—and is then left to the casuist to interpret and to specify. Second, in both cases ethical direction is given from one person to another. In Barth's terms again, 'the individual human being with his conduct is no atom in empty space but a human being among his fellows, not left

---

[51] CD II/2 667/744. See also CD III/4, 12/11.
[52] CD III/4, 9/8 (revised).

to himself in cases of conscience nor in a position to leave others to themselves.'[53] But in the case of the ethics of the command of God the person through whom the command of God is given does not mediate the command of God and thereby dissolve the encounter to which those who hear her must still proceed. Rather, the decision proclaimed by one person is a prophetic word which prompts those to whom it is spoken to undertake their own *Prüfung* in which they carry out their accountability to God.[54]

Barth refers to these two opposed understandings, respectively, as casuistic ethics and the casuistry of the prophetic ethos.

[The casuistry of the prophetic *ethos*] consists in the unavoidable venture [*Wagnis*]—the final judgment on this venture belongs to God [because, of course, it is God who specifies the command]—of understanding God's concrete, specific command here and now in this particular way, of making a concrete and specific decision corresponding to it and summoning others to such a decision. But there is no casuistical *ethics*, i.e., no fixing of the divine command in a large or small text of ethical law, no method or technique of applying this text to the many conditions and possibilities of the action of all human beings, no deduction of the good or evil of human action in a particular case from the truth of this text presupposed as a general rule and identified with the command of God.[55]

This distinction between the two types of casuistry has multiple dimensions. There is, first, the distinction between 'ethos' and 'ethics,' that is, between an event of encounter and a rational technique.[56] This distinction is connected with two types of intersubjectivity, one involving the speaking and hearing of a prophetic utterance, the other involving the mediation of a command. We will see below that these forms of intersubjectivity entail two types of ecclesial moral authority. In any case, the casuistry of the prophetic ethos treats the ethical encounter as one in which we risk a concrete decision in correspondence to a fully specified concrete command of God which confronts us as a decision, a judgment, on the rightness or wrongness, the good or evil of our own decision. However, the rejection of casuistic ethics in favor of the casuistry of the prophetic ethos seems to leave us with no way to reduce the risk involved in understanding and deciding. Under these terms can moral theology give us any concrete

---

[53] CD III/4, 9/8 (revised).

[54] CD III/4, 9/8; 'Politische Entscheidung,' 12 f./157 f.

[55] CD III/4, 9 f./8 f. (revised).

[56] Barth's distinction invites comparison with a similar distinction made by Martin Heidegger. Interpreting the fragment of Heraclitus, *ēthos anthrōpō daimōn*, Heidegger sought to recover an 'originary ethics' by understanding *ēthos* as a concern with 'dwelling' rather than character, in which Heidegger finds an understanding of ethics 'older than that of Aristotle.' Heidegger apparently means to distinguish a way of being that lets things be from a way of being that forms or shapes a character as the result of willed activity, what we might call an 'ethos without ethics.' This is not identical to but also not entirely different from Barth's distinction between hearing a command and employing a technique to make a specification from a general law. See Heidegger, 'Letter on Humanism,' in *Pathmarks*, edited by William McNeill (Cambridge: Cambridge University Press, 1998), 268–71.

ethical guidance? To answer this question we now turn to the topic of ethical instruction.

3. ETHICAL INSTRUCTION

On the one hand, Barth's moral theology seems to be in no position to give any concrete guidance at all. We now know that the divine decision is a fully specified decision. We also know that ethical inquiry therefore involves the question of whether our decision corresponds to and thus obeys this specific divine decision—not the question of how to specify a general norm. But we still have no substantive guidance about what God might or might not decide in a given instance. It seems that with the rejection of casuistical ethics, moral theology can only gesture to the encounter of our decision with the divine decision, that it can make only a 'formless reference' to it. This would mean that for Barth there is no substantive human ethical inquiry whatsoever. The command of God would be, so far as we can tell, thoroughly arbitrary, and in practice this could, as Barth recognizes, leave the door open to some kind of nonrational means of discerning it.[57] In principle, Barth would be endorsing the crude, anti-intellectual type of moral pronouncement that is often practiced in Protestant ethics today (though not only there) under the heading of being 'prophetic.'[58] The task for Barth is to identify a form of ethical inquiry that does not substitute a human decision on the rightness or wrongness of an action for the decision of God, as he claims casuistical ethics does, and yet does more than simply point to the encounter.

On the other hand, we have already begun to see how Barth addresses this problem. For we have seen that specific commands of God are not ad hoc, arbitrary events but rather are specifications of God's eternal decision and moments in the history through which God executes this eternal decision. They are expressions of God's one, eternal purpose carried out in history, in the covenant between God and humankind fulfilled in Christ and attested in scripture. There is therefore no ground to the accusation that for Barth the command of God is occasionalistic, for in such a case there would be no unity of

---

[57] CD III/4, 15/15.

[58] The pronouncements on ethical issues found in much Protestant denominational literature exhibit a form of theological ethics that was accurately characterized by Ernst Troeltsch as a series of 'catchwords and general suggestions of principles.' See Troeltsch, 'The Social Philosophy of Christianity,' in *Religion in History*, 212. The current Catholic counterpart of this Protestant anti-intellectualism is the growing tendency to treat the moral pronouncements of the magisterium as commands which should be simply accepted on faith. This attitude is in direct conflict with another which assumes that the same pronouncements are to be subjected to reason and experience as the latter operate as sources in secular moral reasoning. There is obviously a position in between these extremes, and a major task of current Catholic moral theology is to reflect on its rich moral tradition in a way that neither abandons this task entirely to the magisterium nor subjects this tradition to secular forms of reason and experience that may distort it.

the divine purpose and its execution but only a disconnected multiplicity. Correlatively, human decisions are not atomistic events; rather, a human subject is actualized in these decisions in subordination to the command of God, whose decision is determinative of this human subject.[59] The specific command of God given here and now in one's encounter with God is thus inseparable from the historical covenant of grace. Their connection raises three questions: First, what exactly is the relationship between this history and the event of encounter with the divine decision? Second, what can we know about this history and how do we know it? Third, what status does this knowledge have with respect to the specific command of God itself? As the last two questions imply, the viability of Barth's position will turn largely on whether he can affirm genuine moral knowledge through inquiry into the covenant of grace while preventing this knowledge from dissolving the encounter with the fully specified command of God. To antici-pate, Barth will argue that ethical inquiry gives us instruction by which we can arrive at a close approximation to what God will command, but that the role of this instruction is not to determine the command of God itself but to prepare us to go forth to the prayerful encounter described above, under the heading of ethical reflection.

History and Encounter

The first question can be answered rather quickly. We now know that for Barth, the encounter is never an isolated event but is always related to the history of the covenant of grace in which God and human beings encounter one another, and we know from Barth's theology generally that they encounter one another, respectively, as creator and creature, reconciler and reconciled, redeemer and redeemed. The encounter occurs within this history, but not in such a way that the history is prior to, or the condition of, the encounter. Rather, this history is the self-unfolding of the encounter itself, its 'articulation and differentiation.'[60] Barth must insist on this point in order to avoid the notion that this history or its characterization is a norm from which the decision or judgment issued in the encounter can be inferred, such that one who knew the history in all its detail (a counterfactual possibility) would know what God commands without having to encounter the divine decision in a situation of choice. The concrete norm is always the eternal decision of God specified; it follows that the latter must always be the norm of the history, not vice versa. If this were not the case, the history would determine what God decides in the encounter. But, God is not bound by

---

[59] It follows from this that Barth's claims that human beings realize themselves in decisions and that present decisions occur in a continuous narrative which links them with past and future decisions do not represent the intrusion of an independent (and perhaps controversial) anthropology into theology but simply the counterpart of the reality of the divine decision.

[60] CD III/4, 28 f./30 f.

this history (even though God freely binds himself to it)—rather, this history is bound by God.[61] However, with these qualifications in place, we can affirm that this history provides the context in which substantive moral guidance can be found.

That the history of the covenant of grace unfolds in this encounter of creator and creature, etc., has major implications. Perhaps the most significant and controversial implication is that creation does not stand apart from the covenant of grace but is folded into the latter as its presupposition.[62] Meanwhile, in his analyses of pride and sloth Barth shows how sin disrupts every feature that constitutes the creaturely life of human beings (though it is powerless to destroy the latter).[63] In practice these points mean that the ethics of creation cannot be articulated independently of the ethics of reconciliation. God created human beings for fellowship with God, and the meaning of the life of the creature is therefore its determination by and for the covenant of grace. The ethical evaluation of each aspect of creaturely life must be made in light of this determination.[64] At the same time, the creature God brought into being for this purpose is a certain kind of creature—this kind and not another—so that the task of the ethics of creaturely life is to show how the life of the creature ought to reflect in all of its aspects its determination for fellowship with God actualized in Christ. In his posthumously published work on the ethics of reconciliation, Barth expressed this point by characterizing reconciliation as the body of the text of ethics of which creation and redemption form the prologue and epilogue, respectively.[65] This seems to be an expression in narrative terms of his earlier claim that creation is the presupposition of the covenant, the set of conditions God has brought into being in order to realize electing grace. In any case, it is clear that to relate the encounter with the command of God here and now to the history of the covenant of grace is not simply a matter of narrating a history that runs in linear fashion from creation to reconciliation to redemption.

---

[61] In relation to some of his nineteenth- and early twentieth-century predecessors, Barth's position marks a double displacement of history in theological ethics. Both Schleiermacher and Troeltsch had sought to locate Christian ethics in the horizon of a philosophy of history; in Troeltsch's case this meant that the content of Christian ethics as well as the evaluation of its achievements or lack thereof must be understood in historicist terms. Barth departs from this by treating history as the unfolding of the relation of God and humankind in creation, reconciliation, and redemption, rather than by locating these in an allegedly universal history. But Barth also displaces history by refusing to make even the history constituted by creation, etc. a direct normative ground. One cannot determine what God commands by narrating this history even if one narrates it rightly. The command of God is inseparable from this history but is not deducible from it.

[62] This point is made at length in CD III/1. See especially § 41 (pp. 42–329/44–377).

[63] See CD IV/1, 413–78/458/531; CD IV/2, 403–83/452–546.

[64] The implications of this determination of the creature by the covenant of grace are apparent throughout Barth's ethics of creation. Barth's ethical analyses of such fundamental aspects of creaturely life as preservation of life, procreation, and human fellowship are governed by the Christological and soteriological considerations which for him are the normative meaning of the biological and social aspects of creaturely existence.

[65] The clearest statement of this point is CL, 9–12/12–16.

Moral Knowledge: The Domains in which God Commands

We now turn to the second question: What can we know about this history and how can we know it? The answer will bring us to some of the most difficult and complex matters in Barth's ethics, and it will take some effort to clarify them. For the sake of clarity, we will treat this question in two subsections. In this subsection we will show how for Barth the continuities in the history of the covenant of grace take the form of certain 'spheres' (or 'domains,' as we will call them) in which God commands, which we can know from the Word of God. In the next subsection we will show how such knowledge actually proceeds and what its limits are.

Christians have historically derived moral knowledge from three major sources: scripture, tradition, and natural law. Most traditions of twentieth-century Protestant ethics allotted tradition a subordinate role while attempting to reconcile a biblical principle that tries to derive moral guidance from scripture and another principle that acknowledges some sort of moral order to the world, the equivalent of a notion of natural law. From what we have seen thus far, Barth appears to resist this trend, holding exclusively to the biblical principle. While he clearly rejects any version of this principle that treats scripture as a collection of general rules or principles, we would expect that for him moral knowledge would be found by tracing the lines of the specific orders and directions described above and inscribing our present situations of choice into this narrative. Barth himself supplies what appears to be a sufficient ground for an intratextual practice of this kind. The biblical commands in all their specificity, we have seen, follow the lines of the covenant of grace, and it is along these same lines that God continues to command today. Barth thus denies that the biblical testimony to the concrete orders and directions given by God is a mere record of past encounters with God's command. 'The Bible speaks of God's command in order to call our attention not merely to what the will and work and self-revelation were there and then, but to what they are here and now for us ourselves.'[66] We are contemporaries with the biblical recipients of God's commands. The biblical commands 'demand that in our own very different external circumstances we should not only act *like*' the biblical recipients 'but again act *as* those who then and there were addressed by God, allowing the command given to them to be again, in our very different time and situation, the command given here and now to us . . . and in their divinely addressed person taking our place in the history and sequel of the covenant of grace . . .'[67] On these grounds it would seem that ethical inquiry

---

[66] CD II/2, 701/783.

[67] CD II/2, 706/788 f. (second emphasis retained from German original). Barth's point here is not that the commands given to biblical figures are timeless or that there is some mysterious relation between these commands and our own situation. 'They and we are not identical, nor is their time or situation ours' (CD II/2, 706/788; see also 704/786 f.). The point is rather that the unity of the divine command is not found in a general rule by means of which we may draw inferences from

should be able to proceed by tracing the lines of these highly specific orders and directions in the biblical narrative, folding our world—our situation of choice—into the biblical world, to borrow George Lindbeck's formula of intratextuality.[68]

The problem, however, is that many of the orders and directions Barth identifies are too specific to allow for much guidance from such an approach. It is not clear how this approach could illuminate for us how a command given to us in our situation of choice is identical with the command Jesus gave to his two disciples to fetch the ass and colt. It may be for this reason that in fact Barth takes a very different approach, one that brings him closer to those who combine the biblical principle with a principle of moral order. In place of a scriptural narrative that would trace the lines of the divine commanding to inscribe the present into it, he argues that in this history of the covenant of grace certain 'domains and relationships' in which God and human beings encounter one another come into view. This notion of the domain (*Bereich*) is critical to Barth's enterprise.[69] It refers, first, to the fact that the encounter between God and humanity unfolds in the relationships of creator and creature, reconciler and reconciled, and redeemer

---

biblical commands to what is commanded in our own situation but rather in an identity of the divine will and purpose in the highly specific orders and directions given to them and those given to us.

[68] See Lindbeck, *The Nature of Doctrine*, 113–24. For Lindbeck, intratextuality means that 'the text, so to speak . . . absorbs the world, rather than the world the text' (118). One problem with this formula is that it is unclear how we can know in a given case that the former has occurred and not the latter. In Lindbeck's own example (117), when Carolingians treated King David as a type for Charlemagne the Old Testament text was apparently absorbing the early ninth-century world, but unless these Carolingians set themselves the task of turning Charlemagne's kingdom into a replica of the kingdom depicted in 2 Samuel, they were also absorbing the text into their world. Of course, Lindbeck is well aware that the hermeneutical process works both ways; a few pages later, he concedes that catacomb dwellers and astronauts might emphasize diverse aspects of the biblical world in describing their respective situations (121). But, this is tantamount to saying that features of the text are selected in light of features of the world—in effect, the world decides exactly what text it is that absorbs the world. Again, Lindbeck is aware of this; he never claims that a sharp line can be drawn between intratextuality and extratextuality, and he points out that a shift from the former to the latter can occur, as it did, he suggests, in the case of Gnosticism (118). But, if Lindbeck is only saying that intratextuality and extratextuality are the two poles of a common hermeneutical field, then it is difficult to see how he differs from a correlationist, who is also quite capable of tracking shifts of emphasis in particular correlations between the two poles of the biblical text and the cultural world in which the interpreter is situated. 'Postliberalism' turns out to be an attractive name for a form of correlationism that wants to make sure the former pole retains a stronger pull than the latter pole.

[69] The translators of the *Church Dogmatics* have rendered *Bereich* as 'sphere.' The geometrical image is consistent with other terms Barth uses, such as 'lines' and 'dimensions.' However, the importance of the notion of 'boundary' (*Grenze*) suggests the political and geographical resonances of 'domain' rather than the geometrical resonance of 'sphere.' Moreover, 'domain' is more consistent with the notion of a place where the encounter with God's command occurs; it is difficult to visualize an event of personal encounter such as this occurring in a 'sphere.' For these reasons, *Bereich* will be translated as 'domain' in all that follows.

and redeemed.[70] But it also refers to certain relationships and forms of activity that appear within these broader modes of encounter. For example, Barth identifies worship of God, the relationships of husband and wife and of parents and children, and vocation as some of the specific domains that constitute the encounter of creator and creature. The following exposition treats domains in this latter sense, for which Barth also uses terms such as 'dimensions' or 'lines' of continuity of the command. Barth's position, then, is that the historical covenant of grace sketched above unfolds in the form of these domains, and the more we know about these domains the more we will know about what God actually commands.

By elucidating the history of the covenant of grace in terms of these domains, Barth seems to be shifting away from the biblical principle and towards the other pole in the tension, namely, to a notion of moral order akin to natural law. His domains are similar to other concepts articulated by Protestant theologians in the first half of the twentieth century to give content to an ethic whose focus is the command of God. The most common of these concepts was that of orders (*Ordnungen*) of creation, which like natural law refer to a moral order created by God, although in this case what was taken to be natural was the givenness of a general form of social or institutional structure such as work, marriage, family, and the state rather than a form of practical reason or a set of inclinations rooted in human nature. However, domains as Barth understands them are characterized by two features that distinguish them from these orders. First, he claims that the domains are located in the history of the covenant of grace and are thus knowable from the Word of God. Contra Emil Brunner, they do not exist in a nature or history independent of this history and thus are not knowable through an independent investigation of any such nature or history.[71] This feature also distinguishes domains from natural law. Their relation to the Word of God determines the identity of these domains, their precise location in the historical outworking of creation, reconciliation, and redemption, and the content ascribed to them. It is from the Word of God, for example, that we know, according to Barth, that the relationships of man and woman and of parent and child are distinct from one another and not aspects of any common domain of family, and that one's orientation to oneself as a living creature is the presupposition of one's ontologically prior orientation to God and to one's fellow human being.[72] Thus, in Barth's case, talk about domains is not a departure from the biblical principle; it simply implies that the biblical principle does not take the form of specifications of general biblical laws or the form of intratextual interpretation, but rather involves the identification and description of these domains within which specific

---

[70] The remainder of this paragraph is indebted to Matthew Loverin's critical comments on an earlier effort to clarify Barth's complex and perhaps not entirely consistent use of the term *Bereich*.

[71] CD III/4, 19–22/20–3.

[72] CD III/4, 241 f./270 f., 324 f./367.

commands will fall. Second, because what is normative for human action is the divine decision which confronts one in the encounter with God and not the history of that encounter, Barth rejects the notion that the domains are themselves commands. God does not command acts that fall outside of these domains, but what God commands cannot be derived from a description of the domains. 'They are domains *in which* God commands and *in which* human beings obey or disobey, but they are not laws *according to which* God commands and human beings do good or evil.'[73] With this distinction, Barth distances his domains from Dietrich Bonhoeffer's 'mandates.'

Both of these features by which Barth distinguishes domains from orders or mandates reflect his deep unease with categories that could be, and were, used to legitimize existing social and political arrangements. Because of their institutional form and their historical nature it was all too easy to identify orders of creation with current forms of social and political life. When these orders are then taken as the command of God itself, obedience to them is equated with obedience to God—a monstrous equation to make, as some Protestant theologians did, in Germany in the 1930s. Of course, not all proponents of orders of creation made such an equation then or do so now, and not all formulations of these orders are susceptible to such an equation or to the criticisms Barth makes of Brunner and Bonhoeffer.[74] But it is important to observe that these two features distinguish Barth's mature ethics of the command of God not only from Brunner and Bonhoeffer but also from his own earlier versions. Tracing the major lines of this development will give us a clearer picture of what domains actually are for Barth. The development of Barth's ethical thought leading up to the *Church Dogmatics* exhibits a struggle to find a place for substantive moral guidance while preserving the critical eschatological thrust of his ethics. We saw in Chapter 1 that in the wake of *Romans₂*, in the early 1920s, Barth rejected the notion that participation in the orders of creation could secure a relative justification in place of the justification that comes only in and through the negation, by the good itself, of all human efforts to realize the good this side of the eschatological gulf. He did not deny that the orders are the substance of a relative obedience; in fact he claimed that, rightly understood, the negation by the good of all this-sided attempts to realize the good establishes the orders in their relative, profane reality so that the ascription of sacred status to them is superfluous as well as

---

[73] CD III/4, 29 f./31 (revised). This is in direct contrast to Emil Brunner. See *The Divine Imperative: A Study in Christian Ethics*, trans. Olive Wyon (Cambridge: Lutterworth Press, 2002), 291.

[74] Robin Lovin's *Christian Faith and Public Choices* argues successfully that an ethics of orders of creation can avoid identifying these orders with current social and political arrangements while Oliver O'Donovan's *Resurrection and Moral Order* splits the difference between Barth and Brunner by defending the reality of a created moral order but arguing that it can be known properly only through scripture.

theologically mistaken.[75] Barth's concern at this stage was to strip the orders of any presumed sacrality, but in so doing he paradoxically legitimized them in their secular content. In his 1928–9 *Ethics*, Barth's attempt to combine a robust notion of the command of God with a more substantive doctrine of creation led to a stronger, if still cautious theological endorsement of orders of creation. Barth's overall strategy in his ethics of creation during this period was to acknowledge the givenness of certain features of human existence as created by God—life itself, the particularity of human lives, the orders which give constancy and continuity to human life—while arguing that the normative force of these features is not intrinsic to them but lies entirely in their relation to the command of God.[76] By this strategy he sought to do justice to the moral significance of created reality while foreclosing the possibility of extending to it an independent normative status. It followed that the orders of creation are not normatively binding in the givenness with which we may experience them. God will always command the actualization of a possibility of our creaturely being, but which possibility is to be actualized in a situation of choice is for God to determine. Orders of creation are therefore normatively binding only as representatives of *the* order, which is God himself in the necessity and unity of the divine command. 'The one who binds me is God, no one and nothing else.'[77] Moreover, we can no more identify and analyze these orders in their concrete form as representative of divine order than we can identify and analyze the actual command of God itself.

In principle at least, if still somewhat ambiguously, Barth's *Ethics* already expresses the two critical points which he will later urge with more clarity against the formulations of Bonhoeffer and Brunner, respectively: The orders are not themselves commands, and any natural knowledge we might claim to have of these orders in their givenness is not itself knowledge of them in their relation to the command of God. However, what distinguishes Barth's position in *Ethics* from his later position is the view that the orders are aspects of creation apart from and prior to grace. 'The divine order does not first encounter us in the divine institutions of the kingdom of grace [*Gnadenreiches*], but truly meets us already in the kingdom of nature [*in regno naturae*].'[78] Barth, of course, will go on to reject the notion of a natural order apart from and prior to grace. Creation for the later Barth is inextricable from the covenant of grace, and with regard to its theological significance it is knowable only through the Word of God,

---

[75] 'Das Problem der Ethik in der Gegenwart,' 130–6. Holger Finze, the editor of the German edition of Barth's lectures and essays of this period, points out that in a letter to Thurneysen, Barth stated that his criticism of the orders of creation in this lecture was directed against Gogarten who, in a meeting with Barth earlier that year (1922), had urged against Barth's position in *Romans₂* a place on this side of the 'great disturbance' for the establishment and justification of orders of family, vocation, and the state. See 'Das Problem der Ethik in der Gegenwart,' 133 n. 79.

[76] See especially *Ethics*, 117–20/193–7, 173–6/292–7, 213–16/362–7.

[77] *Ethics*, 214/364. See also Barth, *The Holy Spirit and the Christian Life*, 8–10.

[78] *Ethics*, 215 f./366.

however necessary and useful other forms of knowledge will turn out to be for the articulation of that significance. To speak of orders of creation in this later context can only mislead. What is needed instead is a concept that indicates the continuities in the history of the covenant of grace, in which creation is included along with reconciliation and redemption. These continuities will be knowable only through the Word of God, which in its Christological form constitutes the covenant of grace and in its scriptural form attests the latter.

We are now in a position to understand the relation between the domains and the biblical principle as Barth develops it. If these domains are derived from the Word of God, scripture will play a fundamental role in their identification and description. It is here that the apparently general biblical laws found in the Decalogue, the Sermon on the Mount, and similar texts enter in. We recall that Barth denies that these are general laws awaiting casuistic elaboration and interpretation, yet he was well aware that they appear to be such, and that in any case they are by no means the fully specified orders and directions in which the command of God is given. Rather, they are 'programs or summaries' of the history of the covenant between God and the people of God. As such, these general laws or commandments mark out at least some of the domains in which the command of God will be given. 'In these texts . . . the space is marked out in which the concrete divine requiring and prohibiting occur. What these people should do or not do in particular is not told them in the Ten Commandments, or the Sermon on the Mount, or in other biblical texts of this kind. . . . What is given in these texts is the place where this direction is issued, is audible and is effective.'[79] There is more. Negatively, these general laws or commandments establish the boundaries of these domains, indicating, in their form as prohibitions, what can never be permitted in the relevant domain. Thus the sixth commandment not only denotes a domain in which specific commands concerning life are given, both in scripture itself and throughout the longer history of the covenant of grace. In its negative form, as a prohibition, it marks the boundary of this domain by indicating what God will never command, namely, murder. Finally, these general laws also have a positive function. In the manner of Luther in the first part of *The Large Catechism* and Calvin in *Institutes* II. 8, Barth finds in the negative form of the commandment a positive admonition, contained in it but not explicitly expressed. In the case of the sixth commandment, the admonition is to live a genuinely human life.[80] If the negative form of the commandment identifies a domain by demarcating its

---

[79] CD III/4, 12/12 (revised). See CD II/2, 681–4/760–4 for the various ways, most of them implausible, in which Barth struggles to account for these texts as something other than general laws requiring casuistry. The strength of Barth's determination to preclude casuistical treatment of these texts clearly exceeds the strength of his arguments.

[80] CD III/4, 344/391. In their fascination with what Barth says about the taking of life, scholars have almost entirely neglected his positive account of what the required will to life entails in this domain.

boundary, its positive form, though it is only implicit in the prohibition, illuminates its interior.

This demarcation by biblical commandments nevertheless plays a limited role in the identification and description of the domains, and this for two reasons. First, their negative form as prohibitions makes many of these commandments more suited to indicating the boundary of its domain—denoting what must never occur in that domain—than to stating positively what should occur in that domain.[81] This means that the positive content itself—indicated but not explicitly stated by the commandment—must be supplied by a broader theological inquiry into these domains as the Word of God represents them apart from the commandments themselves. This latter kind of inquiry—the positive articulation of what God commands in a given domain—occupies the greatest portion of Barth's moral theology. Second, the domains Barth identifies are not all derived from lists of commandments such as the Decalogue, nor do all of the commandments found in these lists give rise to domains. In itself, this is not a problem since knowledge of the domains is derived from the Word of God in the broadest sense rather than from any particular passage of scripture. Still, it cannot be denied that Barth's descriptions of the domains of creaturely life in *Church Dogmatics* III/4 reflect the conventions of mid-twentieth-century bourgeois society, and this raises the question of how decisive scripture has been in their identification and formulation.

Moral Knowledge: Procedures and Limits

We now have a preliminary answer to the question of what we can know about the history of the covenant of grace and how we can know it. The fully specified command of God falls within various domains, many of them identified by the general laws or commandments such as those that comprise the Decalogue. It may come as a surprise to realize that in reconstructing Barth's answer to this question we have in fact been tracing a casuistical argument. We began by showing the inseparability of the command of God from the historical covenant of grace with its three modes of relationship between God and human beings (creation, reconciliation, redemption). We then showed how this history is specified by its unfolding in certain domains (for example, in the case of creation, various domains in which human beings are related to God, to other human beings, and to themselves as living creatures). Barth completed only the mode in which God and human beings encounter each other as creator and creature, and in the conclusion to this section we will have to raise the question of the extent to which what he has to say about knowledge through these domains is limited to the encounter of creator and creature. But in any case, the domains that constitute the encounter of creator and creature fall under a general characterization of

---

[81] CD II/2, 684 f./764.

creation in terms of freedom. One of those domains is freedom for life, namely, the orientation of human beings to themselves as living creatures, and in this subsection we will take this domain as an example to show how knowledge of the domains proceeds and what limits such knowledge must finally acknowledge.[82] The domain of life is ideal for our purposes because Barth's description of it is a paradigmatic form of casuistry that is approximated to different degrees in his descriptions of the other domains. From the description of this domain we will see how Barth assigns to something like (though not identical to) casuistical ethics a necessary instructional role in preparing one for the encounter with the already specified divine command—even as he denies (as we have seen) that it is casuistical ethics that gives us the actual, fully specified command of God.

That life is a domain in which God commands is indicated by the sixth commandment of the Decalogue, 'Thou shalt not kill.' Knowledge of the domain of life, as with all the domains, must be derived from the Word of God, and for Barth, knowledge of ourselves as living beings begins with the fact that God addresses us. As recipients of this address we know ourselves as existing in distinction from God and we know that our life belongs to God. Our life 'is not [our] property; it is a loan.'[83] Ethical inquiry into the domain of life therefore rests on a fundamental principle which Barth formulates as follows: 'The freedom for life to which man is summoned by the command of God is the freedom to treat as a loan both the life of all men with his own and his own with the life of all men.'[84] This principle is abstract, however, and must be specified in accordance with what the Word of God instructs. The first specification is straightforward: As divine property, received on loan, human life is the object of reverence (*Ehrfurcht*). Reverence is an attitude of 'astonishment, humility and awe of a human being before a fact in which something superior encounters him: majesty, dignity, holiness, a mystery that compels him to establish and maintain a distance, to deal with it modestly, circumspectly and carefully.'[85] This attitude

---

[82] What follows both corrects and expands Biggar's pathbreaking account (see *The Hastening that Waits*, 31). This account is indebted to Biggar's account, though the latter displays less the casuistry of the domain of life than its architectonic structure.

[83] CD III/4, 327/370 f. (revised).

[84] CD III/4, 335/380.

[85] CD III/4, 339/384 (revised). The insistence of Henry A. Kennedy, the translator of this section of CD III/4, on using 'respect' to render *Ehrfurcht* effaces the language of the sacred that governs Barth's understanding of life: from his conception of life in terms of divine property to his conviction that in the divine acts of creation, preservation, and, above all, incarnation God has exalted human life and separated it from all nonhuman life (See CD III/4, 339/384 f.). 'Respect' moralizes and secularizes Barth's conception of the proper attitude to life and thus distorts it. It is true that in using the phrase *die Ehrfurcht vor dem Leben* Barth distinguished his position from that of Albert Schweitzer's essay of the same title. However, what Barth objected to was the status Schweitzer gave life as a first principle of ethics rather than a domain and the confidence with which Schweitzer extended reverence to all living things (CD III/4, 324/366 f., 349 f./397 f.). He did not object to but rather affirmed the concept of reverence for life itself and what he saw as Schweitzer's basic insight into it.

of reverence, however, is a kind of theoretical-aesthetic awe; it is not yet practical. The principle that life is a loan from God must therefore undergo a second specification in the requirement that one *will* one's life together with that of others. By the will to life Barth means an affirmation of life as a divine loan and a resolution (*Entschlossenheit*) and readiness for action (*Tatbereitschaft*)—the disposition to preserve, maintain, and promote both one's own life and that of others.[86] It is notable, especially in light of the frequent complaint that Barth's ethics is exclusively act-oriented, that in these two specifications we have to do, respectively, with an attitude and a disposition.

We have pointed out that the domain of life is indicated by the sixth commandment of the Decalogue, the proscription of murder. In its literal, negative form, of course, the sixth commandment indicates the boundary that tells what is morally impossible in this domain, namely to murder. The will to life is therefore expressed in the defense of life against its destruction (protection of life).[87] Yet, as we noted above, Barth also finds in this commandment a positive admonition to live a genuinely human life (affirmation of life). We briefly described this positive requirement to live a genuinely human life, which is routinely neglected by commentators on Barth's ethics of life, in Chapter 3, pointing out Barth's theological biopsychology in which the affirmation of instinct, the pursuit of health, the will to joy, self-affirmation, and the will to power all constitute the affirmation of human life required by the commandment in its positive form.[88] In the protection and affirmation of life, then, we find a third level of specification of the principle that life is a loan from God, as the will to life (the second-level specification) undergoes further elaboration in the requirements, given in the sixth commandment, to protect life (negative) and affirm life (positive).

Up to this point all has gone smoothly, but there is more to say about the life that is loaned by God, and this will complicate Barth's position. From the Word of God we know, according to Barth, that the life we receive on loan from God is limited in two respects: First, it is created and is thus subject to the will and purpose of the one who created it; second, it is temporal life, not the eternal life that is given to human beings as a permanent and inalienable possession.[89] Hence 'the required protection of life must take into account its limitation in relation to that which is to be protected,' that is, the twofold limitation of life as created and therefore subject to the will of God, and as temporal rather than eternal and therefore not the inalienable possession of a human being.[90] This creaturely determination of life for the service of God and eschatological

---

[86] CD III/4, 341/386 f.
[87] CD III/4, 397 f./453.
[88] CD III/4, 344–97/391–453.
[89] CD III/4, 337 f./382 f.
[90] CD III/4, 398/454.

limitation of life as temporal require us to qualify the fundamental principle itself and its specifications. The life which is loaned to us and which we are to revere, will, affirm, and protect is precisely *this* life, characterized by this creaturely determination and eschatological limitation. It must be said, however, that Barth's attempts to qualify the specifications of the principle are crude and vulnerable to misunderstanding. The crucial question is whether God may command the surrender or sacrifice of the life God has loaned for the service of God, and if so, whether such a command is an exception to the required reverence, will, and protection due to human life or is, on the contrary, an unusual expression of the latter. This brings us to the well-known 'boundary case' (*Grenzfall*) in Barth's special ethics.

At first glance, Barth seems to think that obedience to a command to surrender or sacrifice life entails suspension or abrogation of the required attitudes, dispositions, and practical commitments involved in reverence for life. Thus he writes that reverence for life 'will not consist in an absolute will to life, but in a will to life which by God's decree and command, and by *meditatio futurae vitae*, may perhaps in many ways be weakened, broken, relativized and finally destroyed.'[91] Along the same lines he asks, rhetorically, 'Does it hold absolutely that the command of God in all cases and under all circumstances must contain the imperative that a human being should will to live?'[92] In these instances, Barth implies that God may command exceptions to the otherwise required reverence for life and will to life. However, a close reading of the relevant passages indicates that Barth generally understands the boundary case not as an exception but as a strange or paradoxical instance of the required reverence, will, and protection. Barth points out that the qualification of reverence for life 'will always have the character of an *ultima ratio*, a boundary case [*Grenzfalles*]. It concerns the boundaries [*Grenzen*] of life and therefore the reverence owed to it—and only that. It is therefore not the case that reverence for life is alternately commanded and not commanded us.'[93] Thus, while reverence for life is relativized by the twofold limitation of human life—life as a loan subject to the will of God and as temporal, not eternal—'this relativization never means that we are released from this reverence. . . . Indifference, wantonness, arbitrariness or anything else opposed to reverence cannot even be considered as a required or even a permitted attitude.'[94] The case of the will to life is less clear; Barth seems undecided whether it is 'the opposite imperative' of the imperative to will one's life and that of others, or 'this imperative in its most paradoxical formulation' that is

[91] CD III/4, 342/389 (revised).
[92] CD III/4, 334/379 (revised).
[93] CD III/4, 343/ 389 (revised). Yoder rightly points out that for Barth *Grenzfall* also means 'limit case,' in the twofold sense that because life is not an absolute good there are limits to what is required of human beings with respect to it and that there is a limit to what human beings can determine with respect to what God commands (*Karl Barth and the Problem of War*, 23 f.).
[94] CD III/4, 343/389 (revised).

entailed by God's command to surrender or sacrifice life. Most likely, both interpretations are needed to account for a range of possibilities in which the will to life might legitimately be 'relativized, weakened, broken, and even destroyed.'[95] However, no such ambiguity attaches to the requirement to protect life. Here it is clear that the boundary case is an unusual or paradoxical instance of the defense of life rather than an exception to it. '[T]he required protection of life must take into account its [creaturely and eschatological] limitation in relation to that which is to be protected.' As such, this protection 'is simply the protection which God wills to demand of man as the creator of this life and the giver of the future eternal life. With this self-evident modification [protection of life] is commanded absolutely.'[96]

We are now in a position to make three claims about the nature of the boundary case in Barth's special ethics. First, neither the fundamental principle nor its specifications entail an absolute or exceptionless rule against taking human life. The fundamental principle that life is to be treated as a loan from God is qualified from the outset by the creaturely determination of life for the service of God and by the eschatological limitation of life as temporal rather than eternal. It is precisely *this* life, and not some other life with different characteristics, which is the proper object of our reverence, will, and protection. In accordance with this determination and limitation of human life, God may command the surrender or sacrifice of life. It follows, then, that reverence, will, and protection cannot legitimately take the form of an absolute or exceptionless rule against the surrender or sacrifice of life.

Second, boundary cases are properly understood not as exceptions to the fundamental principle and its specifications but rather as highly unusual instances of the latter. They are cases that belong to a domain but fall on its boundary, on the edge of it yet still part of it. Nor do boundary cases mark the point at which the principle and its specifications fail, that is, cease to apply in a given set of circumstances. Rather, they are strange or paradoxical instances of reverence for and protection of life (and in many though apparently not all cases, also of will to life). We may rightly think of them, along with 'normal' cases of commands falling within the interior of a domain, as constituting a fourth level of specification of the fundamental principle.

Third, to be considered a boundary case the surrender or sacrifice of life bears a very strong burden of proof. It must be treated as a last resort, to be carried out only after all other possibilities are exhausted.[97] 'Even the way to these boundaries ... must in all cases be a long way, to be traveled carefully and conscientiously, always asking and testing [*prüfend*] whether that *ultima ratio* really may

---

[95] CD III/4, 334/379, 343/389.
[96] CD III/4, 398/454, 398/453.
[97] CD III/4, 398/454. This point is repeated at various points where Barth discusses particular forms of surrender or sacrifice of life.

and must be in force.'[98] We may therefore say that Barth recognizes a strong presumption against the destruction of human life so long as we (1) understand the presumption not as a prima facie rule that may be overridden under certain circumstances but as the normal form of a command which may, on very rare occasions, take a highly paradoxical form, and (2) remain open to the possible occurrence of the paradoxical form in every relevant situation, though only under the condition that all alternatives must first be ruled out.[99]

If the boundary case is a paradoxical specification of a norm rather than an exception to it, then the widespread impression that Barth endorses a radical voluntarism in which God might at any time command anything is false. In the last substantive section of this chapter we will question whether he consistently observes the conditions of the boundary case set out here. Yet in principle, at least, Barth is far from any form of voluntarism that denies the generic consistency of God's command. In any case, we have now seen that with each level of specification, Barth's casuistical exposition of the domain of life yields more detailed moral knowledge of the command of God. Having set up this general topography of the domain of life, Barth takes this process of specification even further, engaging in extensive discussions of concrete forms that the surrender or sacrifice of life in the service of God might take in what we might call 'microdomains'—regions of the more general domain of life in which the boundary between murder and the surrender or sacrifice of life is at stake in particular ways (for example, in suicide, abortion, capital punishment, and war). The least problematic application of the boundary case occurs in the first of these microdomains, where Barth treats the risking and taking of one's own life. (We will point out problems of application in some of the other microdomains below.) Here Barth further specifies what is required in terms of both the attitude of reverence for life and the determination of life for the service of God which may qualify that reverence. For example, he argues that reverence for life requires a proper fear of death that must be present even if God commands one to put one's life at risk, and he points out several reasons for committing suicide that cannot legitimately count as instances of service to God.[100] However, in each case, specification stops at precisely the point where further specification would involve the classification of specific cases of risking or taking one's life as positive or negative instances of the required fear of death and service to God. Barth does identify various acts of risking life and various

---

[98] CD III/4, 343/389 f. (revised).

[99] Failure to understand how these three points govern Barth's treatment of the boundary case has often led readers to think that the boundary case is Barth's effort to protect an arbitrary divine freedom, out of which God commands something that contradicts what we otherwise know to be right. This kind of reading can sound plausible only if one ignores the casuistical context of Barth's discussion of the boundary case as we have been describing it here. An early case of such a misreading of Barth is found in Hendrik van Oyen, 'Gibt es eine evangelische Ethik der Grenzfälle?,' *Evangelische Ethik* 1 (1957): 2–17 (see especially 5–7).

[100] CD III/4, 401/457, 412/470.

circumstances in which suicide has sometimes been considered permissible.[101] But he denies that one can determine in advance whether under these or any similar circumstances suicide will in fact be commanded by God. To classify cases in this way would be to presume to know what God commands prior to hearing the command. This presumption is illegitimate; the boundary case is God's possibility, not ours.[102] To rely on a classification of permissible and impermissible instances codified in advance would inevitably involve risking and taking one's life in situations where God has not commanded it and refusing to risk or take one's life in situations where God commands it. One would evade the encounter with the divine decision, delivering into human hands a judgment that belongs to God alone. At this point, then, ethical inquiry breaks off and specification comes to a halt. One who believes that she is faced with a boundary case can only make certain that she has examined (*geprüft*) all alternatives with the high burden of proof demanded in such cases.[103]

We are finally in a position to complete our answer to the question of what we may know of the history with which the ethical encounter is connected, how we may know it, and what limits to this knowledge must be conceded. Through inquiry into the domains that constitute this history, moral theology can investigate and represent with increasing specificity the character human action must exhibit and the standards or criteria by which God will decide, in any situation of decision, the good and evil of human actions.[104] However, moral theology cannot determine which among the possibilities of action that in principle embody this character and meet these standards is the action that God commands. This kind of ethical inquiry can determine whether an act is a normal act that falls in the interior of a domain or a paradoxical act that falls on the boundary. But, it cannot determine whether, in a situation of decision, God will command a normal act or a paradoxical one. To return to our example, in the domain of life the command of God decides, and must decide, which act will fulfill the required reverence and service—whether the fulfillment will take a normal or a paradoxical form.[105] Even where there is no question of a paradoxical form, as in some of the other domains Barth considers or in the routine choices people face in any domain, the command of God still decides which among possible normal forms counts as fulfillment of what God requires in that domain.[106]

---

[101] CD III/4, 402/458 f., 411 f./469 f.
[102] CD III/4, 411/469, 413/470.
[103] CD III/4, 411/469.
[104] CD III/4, 18/18.
[105] See CD III/4, 402/458, 402 f./458 f., 404/460 f., 412/470. In all of these places Barth discusses either a form of the attitude of reverence or an instance in which the latter might or might not be expressed, or a general or particular expression of the service of God, yet refuses, implicitly or explicitly (see 411/469 for the explicit rejection), to construct a classification but rather explicitly refers the concrete specification to the command of God.
[106] For example, the honor one owes to one's parents can take a wide variety of 'ordinary' forms; which one God commands is not simply left to one's own choice but must be heard as one attends to the will of God in a situation of choice. See CD III/4, 252 f./282 f.

What is striking about Barth's analysis is how his inquiry into the domains in which God commands exhibits the very features of casuistry which he finds problematic when casuistry is used to attempt to determine the command of God itself. Thus we are told that in these domains ethical inquiry 'has a text which it is its task to understand and interpret' in relation to the encounter.[107] The very features that make casuistical ethics suspect—its textuality, its hermeneutical practice, its progressive specification of a general norm—are legitimate and necessary in the case of inquiry into the domains where, if the inquiry sticks to its theme and its limits, there can be no question of dissolving the encounter with the divine decision. For the determination of the character and standards that hold sway in a domain does not determine what God specifically commands in that domain. The precise sense in which God commands reverence for life, or whatever is required at this level in another domain, will be decided 'not by the moralist and his ethics, but by God the commander.'[108]

Instructional Preparation

We have now seen how the giving of the fully specified command in the event of encounter relates to the history of the covenant of grace which the command actualizes. We have also discussed at length, through a consideration of the domains, what can (and cannot) be known about that history and thus about the command of God. We now turn at last to our third question: What is the status of knowledge of the domains in relation to the actual command of God itself? On the one hand, we have seen that knowledge of the domains does yield genuine ethical guidance. Not only is the guidance substantial in the sense that the moral topography of the interior of the domains as well as their boundaries is mapped in enough detail to cover hundreds of pages of the third volume of the *Church Dogmatics*; it is also specific in the sense that it brings us very close to the command of God itself: Barth speaks of inquiry into these domains resulting in a progressive approximation of our knowledge to the fully specified command of God, and he speaks of an increasing urgency and compulsion attaching to the findings of this inquiry in correlation with our increasing knowledge of these domains. As our knowledge of these domains increases, we can be increasingly confident that our own decision, made in accordance with this knowledge, is in line with the divine decision. On the other hand, between human ethical inquiry and the actual command of God there remains an unbridgeable gap. Progressive approximation does not end in a point of convergence between human ethical inquiry and the command of God. Even in the ideal case of complete knowledge of the domains—a counterfactual case, since in fact this knowledge is never complete—'the most concrete sphere of the individual ethical case to which an

---

[107] CD III/4, 27/28 (revised).
[108] CD III/4, 18/18.

answer [to the ethical question] must always relate will still have escaped ethics [as inquiry]. Ethics will still have to leave the final judgment to God.'[109] Even with the greater urgency and compulsion attaching to directives that accompany a more thorough knowledge of the domains, ethical inquiry cannot spare one the demand 'to dare to make for himself the leap of choice, decision and action, which he must make for himself and on his own responsibility,' that is, the risk of a decision in correspondence to the divine decision.[110]

It follows that ethical instruction does not replace ethical reflection or dissolve the encounter between the divine decision and ours.[111] It does not obviate the necessity of moving toward the encounter with the divine decision, nor does it eliminate the risk with which we venture a decision in correspondence to the divine decision. We have already seen that Barth rejects the attempt to bring ethical inquiry to the point of classifying acts and circumstances so that judgments of the rightness or wrongness of particular choices could be made in advance. This kind of attempt is not the proper role of ethical inquiry. Unlike casuistry, '[i]ts function or service . . . is not to pronounce an anticipatory judgment on the good or evil of human action in encounter with the command of God, but to give definite instruction with regard to this event.'[112] As the last clause indicates, ethical inquiry for Barth does not play the role that it plays in most theories of ethics. It is not itself an effort to reason or discern what is right or good—an effort to which Barth calls a halt just before it reaches its goal. It belongs instead to the very different category of moral pedagogy. In Barth's terms, it offers 'instructional preparation' for our encounter with the divine

[109] CD III/4, 31/33.

[110] CD III/4, 16/16.

[111] The major shortcoming in Biggar's generally excellent account of Barth's casuistry is the way he allows the notion of vocation to substitute itself for the encounter with God. Biggar begins with the correct insight that for Barth the specific command of God cannot be reduced to a moral rule. He then proposes that 'what is actually commanded is finally determined not by moral rules, but by personal vocation' (*The Hastening that Waits*, 44). This is unobjectionable if personal vocation is simply shorthand for whatever expresses the grace of election at this point in the continuous series of decisions that for Barth comprises one's moral identity. At first, this seems to be how Biggar understands it, referring to one's decision as 'a response to a definite vocation to play a particular part in this moment of the redemptive history of the covenant between God and humankind' (ibid.). However, in a later chapter when Biggar reaffirms this identification of the command of God with personal vocation, he understands personal vocation in a way that is incompatible with the emphasis Barth puts on the encounter of one's own decision with the decision of God. Here, in accordance with CD III/4 385–90/439–45, vocation is connected with character; it involves a form or pattern of life (*The Hastening that Waits*, 133–5). This emphasis on vocation and character is appropriate in the context of CD III/4, but Biggar takes what Barth presents as only one of several aspects of the reverence for life (that is, vocation as a subdomain in the domain of life) as the paradigm for what God commands generally, and this is questionable. The identification of the command of God with a form or pattern of life seems to dissolve the encounter with God in precisely the same sense rejected by Barth in the case of casuistical ethics. In general, Biggar is reluctant to stress to the extent that Barth does the radical confrontation of our decision, whether we understand the latter in terms of a personal vocation or not, with the decision of God.

[112] CD III/4, 18/18 f. See also CD III/4, 16/16.

decision and 'encouragement to go meet this event.' As pedagogy in this twofold sense of instruction and encouragement to face the divine decision, ethical inquiry is characterized by the same readiness to encounter the divine decision that constitutes ethical reflection. This suggests that for Barth, ethical instruction is a preliminary stage of ethical reflection itself, and his extensive treatment of the former is designed to show how it can play its proper role in relation to the latter without substituting itself for the latter as the form of inquiry involved in casuistical ethics does.

Conclusion

We close this section by returning to the question we posed at the end of the section on ethical reflection. The question was whether moral theology can offer any substantive guidance to ethical reflection. An affirmative answer seemed to reinstall human beings as knowers and judges of good and evil while a negative answer seemed to entail a radical voluntarism. In contrast to casuistical ethics, Barth's ethical inquiry shows how he was able to answer the question affirmatively without authorizing the usurpation of the divine office of lawgiver and judge. On the one hand, the moral guidance ethical instruction offers is genuine. It gives us a significant approximation to the command of God. Thanks to ethical instruction, we have a high-resolution map of the domains in which God commands so that we know, for example, which criteria hold sway in a domain and which possibilities of choice fall within the interior and which (if any) on the boundaries of these domains. We therefore know which of these possibilities (if any) will have to pass through the most thorough and rigorous scrutiny before we can venture it as a decision corresponding to the divine decision. On the other hand, ethical instruction, as a preliminary stage of ethical reflection, is carried out in the position of the addressee of the command of God. It does not substitute itself for the divine act of specifying the command. It leaves to God what God does as lawgiver and judge and instead prepares human beings for the encounter with the divine lawgiver and judge. The result is that Barth retains the features of voluntarism that enable him to preserve the sovereignty of the divine decision without incurring other features, such as divine arbitrariness and the futility of human inquiry, that are inimical to ethics.

For Barth, ethical inquiry is instructional preparation for the encounter with God's command. Unlike casuistical ethics, this inquiry and encouragement do not dissolve this encounter but rather preserve its necessity. How so? Inquiry into the domains in which God commands leaves a gap between the command of God itself and what ethical inquiry can determine with respect to it. This gap is the site of the encounter with God where ethical reflection takes place. What happens in this encounter? Instructed by ethical inquiry into the domains, we rationally test the possibilities before us in readiness for the divine decision, making a decision of our own in the risk of an understanding of the divine decision, and wait to hear the divine decision on our decision.[113] The name for this practice of testing and waiting for which ethical inquiry prepares us and to which it directs us is prayer.

Barth never completed his ethics of reconciliation and never even began his ethics of redemption. The analysis of moral knowledge carried out here is drawn from material Barth clearly intended to apply to special ethics generally, that is, to the ethics of creation, reconciliation, and redemption, but because this material appears only in connection with the ethics of creation there is reason to question whether it, and thus also our analysis, pertains in the same way to reconciliation and redemption. There are two reasons for hesitation here. One is that in the section of his posthumously published draft of the ethics of reconciliation where he introduces the latter Barth does not refer at all to the 'domains and relationships' that played such a major role in his discussion of special ethics generally and in his introductory remarks on the ethics of creation.[114] Nor does the structure of the ethics of reconciliation, with its orientation around the practices of baptism, prayer, and the Lord's Supper, exhibit the kind of moral topography involved with the domains in the ethics of creation. There is reason, then, to think that Barth either came to reject the notion of domains altogether or (more likely, since there is no explicit retraction) envisioned the ethics of reconciliation, and thus the moral knowledge associated with it, along different lines. In either case, we have a reason for caution in extending the account of moral knowledge we have given in this section beyond Barth's ethics of creation.

This brings us to the second reason for hesitation, which is that the centrality and priority Barth ascribed to the ethics of reconciliation as the body of the text requires that we consider the relation of the moral knowledge given in the ethics of creation to that given in the ethics of reconciliation. Barth consistently held

---

[113] While Nimmo grasps the distinction between instruction and reflection we have described here, he treats it as a simple distinction between ethical inquiry and the event of encounter with God, i.e., between knowledge of the domains as the formed reference to the event and the actual event of hearing the command of God. See Nimmo, *Being in Action*, 41–61. The account presented here is more complex than Nimmo's account. It distinguishes between preparatory knowledge that is accrued in advance (as it were) of the encounter and the situation-specific rational weighing of reasons in the very moment (as it were) of the encounter. The failure to make the distinction in this way leads to misplaced criticisms of Barth for an alleged failure to do actual moral reasoning in the *Church Dogmatics* or to a tendency to understand what Barth says in the *Church Dogmatics* under the heading of ethical instruction as an incomplete or bungled attempt to do concrete moral reasoning. As the account given here makes clear, Barth does not attempt to do concrete moral reasoning in the *Church Dogmatics* because any such reasoning is situation-specific; in responsibility before God one must 'test the *diapheronta*' by weighing the reasons for or against a concrete action or course of action presently before one. This kind of reasoning cannot be done in a dogmatic treatise, and Barth's ethical instruction in the *Church Dogmatics* does not clumsily attempt it. Rather, that instruction gives the agent what she needs to encounter God in a concrete situation of moral decision. It equips her with the knowledge of the general issue that will enable her to weigh situation-specific reasons responsibly. Much confusion about what Barth does and does not offer in his special ethics would be avoided if this distinction were widely recognized.

[114] CD III/4, 1–46/1–50.

that in fact there is only one command of God, not three, and that while finite human knowledge is unable to grasp the command as God does, in its unity, and must therefore proceed by treating the three modes distinctly and in succession, the three modes nevertheless interpenetrate each other (reflecting the Trinitarian perichoresis) so that, for example, the ethics of creation is already determined in many respects by the ethics of reconciliation and vice versa.[115] Since Barth held this view while writing his ethics of creation we can be sure that the descriptions of the domains given there reflect the relation of creation to reconciliation. However, in introducing his ethics of reconciliation, Barth makes the strong claim, which is not made explicitly in the introductory remarks to the ethics of creation, about the primacy and centrality of the ethics of reconciliation over those of creation and redemption. Hence, while the descriptions of the domains under the ethics of creation reflect the significance of reconciliation for our understanding of creation, they *may* not reflect the exact sense in which the *priority* of reconciliation over creation is articulated in Barth's late work. If they do not, then we have reason to ask whether the account of moral knowledge given here might have to be qualified even in the case of the ethics of creation.

Against these legitimate suspicions, however, stands the fact that nowhere in his doctrine of reconciliation does Barth claim or imply that any significant reconsideration of his ethics of creation is necessary. The Christian, who is aware of her reconciliation in Jesus Christ, is still the creature Barth describes so extensively in the doctrine of creation. We should therefore expect the expositions of baptism, prayer, and the Lord's Supper to deepen our moral knowledge, to supplement it, and to place our creaturely life in its true and proper context, but not to alter this knowledge substantially.

4. OBSERVATIONS AND CRITICISMS

We began this chapter by asserting that neither the earlier critics nor the more recent defenders of Barth have properly understood his approach to concrete ethical choice. While we have raised some questions about Barth's position, most of the effort in this chapter has gone toward establishing the centrality of ethical reflection as the site of the encounter with God's command and showing how ethical inquiry is related to ethical reflection as instructional preparation for this encounter. It should now be clear that with its elaborate descriptions of the history of the covenant of grace, Barth's position offers far more concrete ethical guidance than many of his critics have alleged and that with its orientation to the encounter with God, it is less familiar than some of his defenders have claimed. Is it, in the end, a plausible position? Barth clearly succeeds in carving out a

---

[115] See *Ethics*, 53 f., 262; CD III/4, 32–5/34–8; CL, 7–12.

position between notions of divine commands as a random series of discontinuous events into which human beings have no reliable insight, on the one hand, and the dissolution of the prayerful encounter with God into a technique of moral reasoning, on the other hand. He neither commits the crude errors his detractors attribute to him nor conforms to the business-as-usual familiarity his defenders attribute to him. Still, his position seems to raise almost as many questions as it answers. We now turn to several actual or possible objections to that position which raise questions about its viability while also providing the occasion for further elaboration and criticism of Barth's conceptions of ethical reflection and instruction.

Rationalism and Voluntarism

Several times in this study we have confronted the charge that Barth is a voluntarist. It is now time to address that charge directly. Accusers might press their case by pointing out how Barth makes at least three claims that could be construed as denials of rationalist claims made by Kant. He denies that obedience to the command of God is identical with or included in obedience to a rational moral law that is knowable in principle apart from historical revelation; he denies that the rational moral law is authorized to judge the validity of revealed commands; and he denies that biblical representations of God are properly understood as figures of a rational morality.[116] With these denials, Barth takes a position on the relation of God to morality which conflicts with the rationalist position with which Kant identified, holding against the latter that knowing that something is commanded by God is the necessary and sufficient condition for knowing that it is our duty. Yet an anti-rationalist is not necessarily a voluntarist. Barth explicitly rejects the notion of divine commands as decrees of a God conceived abstractly as a sovereign authority or power, and he strongly denies that God's command is arbitrary or capricious. His formulation of the command of God in Christological terms restates the fundamental concern of voluntarist divine command ethics in a way that enables moral theology to resist transformation into rationalism while also rejecting the problematic features of voluntarism.

However, this conclusion answers the charge only, as it were, from God's side. Is the decision of God still ultimately arbitrary from our side, that is, with respect to human ethical inquiry? As Barth describes it, the decision of God regarding the rightness or wrongness or the good or evil of human actions radically transcends rational deliberation; God may decide against the balance of human reasons for or against an action. This seems to put Barth squarely in the voluntarist camp. However, we have seen that the scope of arbitrariness with

---

[116] CD II/2, 523/580, 540/600; CD III/1, 261/297; CD IV/1, 371/410.

respect to human inquiry is very narrow. The command of God always actualizes the covenant of grace, and ethical inquiry can know a great deal about the covenant of grace, and thus about what God commands, from the Word of God. It is true that ethical inquiry cannot determine the specific action through which God wills to actualize the covenant of grace in a particular situation. But this means only that, given the ideal case of full knowledge of the domains in which God commands, ethical inquiry cannot determine which of various possible actions that (in some cases) meet or (in other cases) do not violate the standards or criteria that hold sway in a domain is the action God will command—whether, for example, God will command a normal or a paradoxical act or which act God will command among multiple normal acts. Even here, the agent knows that boundary cases are rare and require extraordinary caution. Thus far, the ethics of the command of God does not appear to be any more arbitrary than any theory of ethics for which ethical inquiry can establish strong criteria but relatively few absolute prohibitions and requirements. It is more arbitrary than other such theories only if the covenant of grace itself is arbitrary, if what the Word of God tells us about the covenant of grace is arbitrary, or if it is arbitrary for God rather than human judgment to make the ultimate concrete determination of what fulfils the covenant of grace.[117]

However, Barth still faces the question, raised above, of the status of rational deliberation—the weighing of reasons for and against alternative possibilities of action—given that the command of God may go against it. What purpose does rational deliberation serve if it is not decisive? One answer to this question is somewhat speculative but may be implicit in Barth's treatments of boundary cases. He tells us that all possible alternative courses of action must be exhaustively considered before one can venture a conclusion that God commands an act that falls on the boundary of a domain. This implies that rational deliberation may rule out the boundary case as a possibility in some situations of choice. How so? In weighing the reasons for and against possibilities of action one must consider the standards or criteria derived from knowledge of the domains in which God commands. For example, Barth thinks that the rare case in which God commands an abortion will be a case in which there is, in some respect, a conflict between the life of the mother and the life of the unborn.[118] We will revisit Barth's treatment of the morality of abortion shortly, but the point here is that the reasons a woman will give for an abortion must include reasons for preferring her life in a genuine conflict with that of the unborn. It is true that the

---

[117] The covenant of grace is indeed arbitrary in the sense that it originates in the divine freedom; God did not elect human beings out of any necessity, not even out of a necessity of the divine nature. But originary freedom of this kind raises no theological problems, and the point of this paragraph is that while the decision of God transcends rational deliberation, there are standards or criteria according to which God always commands and these are publicly available via the Word of God, even if they are revealed.

[118] CD III/4, 421/480 f.

command of God may go against the balance of her reasons: God may command an abortion when the balance of her reasons indicates otherwise or vice versa. But reasons are still necessary to determine that the condition for the boundary case is there at all. If in the course of her deliberation in a particular situation she comes to see that her reasons fail to show that there is indeed a genuine conflict of life against life (and given the strong presumption against the boundary case she will consider every possibility of interpreting her situation in these terms) then there will be no question of a boundary case at all; she can be sure that God will not command an abortion in that situation. Similar considerations hold with respect to domains where no boundary case is at stake. In these domains there are still criteria to consider in deciding for one action over another. For example, one criterion that must be met in order to venture a decision to defend one's honor requires that the dishonor one suffers involve a matter related to one's call or vocation and not merely a personal irritation. Presumably, the reasons one offers for defending one's honor will lean in one direction or another, and presumably, the command of God may support or oppose the preponderance of human reasons.[119] But the reasons one gives for defending one's honor must indicate that the dishonor targets one's call or vocation in order for there to be any question at all of a command of God to defend one's honor in a particular situation; if that condition is unmet, then one can be sure that no such command will be given.

If this answer is correct, Barth has succeeded both in establishing the necessity of rational deliberation and in showing why such deliberation is not sufficient. However, it leaves unclear why deliberation must involve the weighing and balancing of human reasons rather than simply the identification of all the relevant reasons. It also ignores the two most pressing questions, which are how a human decision can justifiably go against the balance of reasons in favor of a course of action and what determines the decision for a course of action that goes against the balance of reasons. What we need from Barth is a full description of the cognitive processes in the testing of our actions. Barth refuses to provide one, perhaps out of the fear that any such description would make of this testing yet another technique by which to dissolve the encounter with the divine decision and reinstall human beings as judges. Yet without such a description, Barth is unable to allay legitimate suspicions that there is an irreducibly arbitrary aspect to hearing the command of God. And as long as that is the case, he cannot finally distinguish his position from the features of voluntarism he wishes to avoid.

---

[119] We must presume this since Barth does not explicitly say it in the context of honor, nor does he explicitly say it in many other places where it seems warranted. This problem is treated below in the discussion of alleged inconsistencies in Barth's ethical instruction.

Inconsistencies in Ethical Instruction

Is Barth consistent in his ethical instruction? There are three points at which inconsistency may be or has been alleged. The first is that in his actual ethical instruction, Barth violates the strict prior conditions he has set for such instruction. One of these conditions, we recall, is that knowledge of the domains in which God commands must be derived primarily from the Word of God. This does not mean that its content must be drawn exclusively from the Word of God—in Chapter 3 we discussed how Barth's moral theology engages in a critical appropriation of content from other sources as directed by the Word of God. A thorough investigation of Barth's descriptions of the domains is likely to raise numerous objections to his actual use of these other sources—what he selects and does not select, whether he is too critical of some sources (for example, in virtually denying the normative significance of the natural bonds of parents and children) or not critical enough of other sources (for example, in his de facto acceptance of the patriarchal family and the bourgeois state)—but there is nothing inconsistent in the extensive use he makes of outside sources as such. The charge of inconsistency rings clearer, however, in relation to another condition of ethical instruction, namely that the latter does not give us the actual command of God itself. In much of his ethical instruction, Barth fails to make explicit what he says in his introductory remarks on special ethics, namely that knowledge of the standards or criteria that are always valid in a domain does not guarantee that a decision made in conformity with those standards will correspond to the decision of God—that there is an unbridgeable gap between such criteria and the actual command of God and therefore a risk, a leap in any such decision. Failing to make this explicit, Barth frequently identifies human decisions made in accordance with these standards or criteria with the command of God itself.[120] These identifications are clearly due to a lapse in vigilance. If one could determine what God commands in a domain simply by deciding in accordance with the standards or criteria appropriate to it, then all Barth says about ethical reflection and the necessity of an encounter with God would be moot; ethical instruction would be sufficient of itself for knowledge of the will of God; and special ethics would be a form of casuistical ethics.

A more serious instance of inconsistency involves the boundary case. We pointed out how, at his best, Barth presents the boundary case not as an

---

[120] The most notorious example is Barth's remark that he would consider an attack on the Swiss Confederation to be a boundary case (CD III/4, 462/529). Here Barth decides what God will command in advance of God's actual command. Yoder reports that in a later conversation Barth acknowledged that an affirmation of the boundary case cannot be made in advance. See *Karl Barth and the Problem of War*, 47 n. 1. Other examples in which Barth presents the criteria for a decision in correspondence with God's will as not only necessary but sufficient for a human decision include the defense of one's honor, mentioned above, and the discussions of opportunity and vocation that accompany the discussion of honor.

exception to a moral principle but rather as a paradoxical expression of the latter. He is thereby able to avoid the impression that the boundary case is either arbitrary or masks consequentialist or pragmatic considerations that in fact determine ethical judgments at these points. The clearest example of the boundary case as an expression of a rule rather than an exception to it is the one we briefly examined above, namely suicide. Barth's analysis of suicide includes his most extensive treatment of the boundary case and is also the least controversial version of it. It is not unfair to him, then, if we take the boundary case as it arises there as the paradigm. Once we do so, we find that other appeals to the boundary case depart from this paradigm to different degrees and in different ways. Significant departures occur in domains other than life. In the case of parents and children, Barth, relying on various sayings and commands of Jesus in the Gospels, acknowledges the possibility of a special calling in which children may be commanded to disregard their parents.[121] The paradigm would seem to require that he show, positively, how such a calling, if valid, would amount to a paradoxical expression of the requirement of children to honor their parents. Instead, he argues, negatively, that such a calling does not violate that requirement. The reason is that the requirement itself is a limited one; the fifth commandment of the Decalogue (which requires one to honor one's parents), Barth argues, is qualified by the first (which requires one to have no other gods before God), and such a calling, if genuinely commanded by God, expresses in a direct way—not paradoxically—this qualification or limit of the requirement to honor one's parents. That is, it constitutes a rare instance in which the qualification of the fifth commandment by the first—a qualification that is always in effect—is directly expressed. This kind of boundary case clearly differs from the paradigm, but it is not inconsistent with it.

Two boundary cases arise in the domain of marriage. In the context of the injunction against putting asunder what God has joined together found in Mark 10: 9 and Matthew 19: 6, Barth considers the possibility of the legal dissolution of marriage.[122] He does not argue, as the paradigm would require, that some instances of divorce might fulfill the injunction, or a moral requirement indicated by the injunction, in a paradoxical way, so that when God commands it, divorce paradoxically expresses a moral commitment on which marriage is based. Rather, he argues that a command to dissolve a marriage may occur in cases when the marriage is not truly constituted by God—when God has not in fact 'joined together.' Here the principle or rule—do not put asunder what God has joined together—simply fails to apply because the condition for its applicability—that God has indeed joined together—is lacking.[123] The other boundary case in this

---

[121] CD III/4, 260–5/291–7.

[122] CD III/4, 211–13/236–9.

[123] In other words, what Barth refers to here is not divorce as a possible boundary case but rather annulment as a case in which the rule about putting asunder simply does not apply.

domain involves the failure of a couple to institutionalize their marriage by civil or ecclesiastical recognition of it. Here, the boundary case seems to involve exceptions: either to a requirement that is not rigorously binding (in the case of failure to have an ecclesiastical ceremony, which Barth does not consider essential to the validity of a marriage) or to a requirement that is binding (in the case of recognition of the marriage by the state, which Barth does consider essential) but which the couple is practically unable to fulfill due to circumstances beyond their control.[124] In both of these instances the boundary case is an exception to a requirement rather than a paradoxical instance of it. However, the issues involved are marginal, so there is no serious inconsistency here.

The case is otherwise when Barth turns, in the domain of life, from suicide to abortion, self-defense, and war. The case of suicide is paradigmatic because Barth is able to show how in risking or taking one's life, one might be (albeit paradoxically) revering and protecting life in its twofold limitation, that is, its temporal nature and its orientation to the service of God. In the case of abortion, however, it is not clear how the death of the unborn might count as an act of service to God such that one who takes the life of the unborn might thereby express the proper reverence for its life. Barth simply asserts that God might will the death of germinating life and might will human participation in this death; unlike his discussion of suicide, he gives no examples which show how God might be served by such a death. There is merely a bald appeal to God's will. Moreover, the substantive criterion Barth identifies for cases in which God might will the death of the unborn is, as we have pointed out, a conflict of life against life—more precisely, the life of the unborn against the life or health of the mother. In such cases, Barth insists, one may not simply assume that God will give priority to the life of the unborn; one must prepare to hear a specific command.[125] But the nature of the boundary case seems to have shifted here: It is no longer a paradoxical expression of the required reverence for life but has become instead one solution to a conflict of lives, both of which must be revered in the normal way. The question is no longer whether killing the unborn in this instance is a paradoxical expression of reverence for life in its orientation to service of God but rather which of two lives God commands to be sacrificed for the other when both of these lives are (in some way) at stake.[126] The boundary case is now an exception, under tragic circumstances, to the required reverence for and protection of life rather than a paradoxical expression of that reverence and protection. But nothing in Barth's description of reverence for and protection of life allows for the possibility of genuine exceptions or even for this kind of tragedy. Here, the charge of inconsistency sticks.

---

[124] CD III/4, 229/257.
[125] CD III/4, 420–3/479–82.
[126] CD III/4, 421/480 f.

In the case of self-defense, Barth does not attempt to assert that the killing of an assailant expresses reverence for the latter's life in a paradoxical form. He does not argue that the death of the assailant fulfills an act of service to God that is the object of reverence for life on the part of the killer. Rather, he derives the command of God to take the life of the assailant from a divine resistance to evil which, Barth asserts, God may entrust to human beings. When one kills the assailant in such cases, one is carrying out a divine commission to resist evil. Here the boundary case does not express the required reverence for and protection of life in a paradoxical form but overrides them with a different command, namely, the command to carry out the divine resistance to evil.[127] Likewise in the case of war: Barth does not argue that in killing enemy soldiers one expresses reverence for and protection of their lives in a paradoxical form. Rather, he argues that the responsibility to preserve a different value, namely the physical, intellectual, and spiritual life of a people or the just order of a state, overrides the requirement to protect the life of those who attack such values.[128] Let us assume with Barth that the life of a people or the state can be identified with the service of God. Under this assumption it is plausible to argue that to risk or surrender one's life in defense of a people or a state might be a paradoxical form of the required reverence for and protection of life. On the same grounds, it is plausible to argue that one can revere and respect the lives of the young men and women one sends off to sacrifice their lives in battle. In both cases, one reveres and protects life in its orientation to the service of God. But it is not clear how one reveres or protects the life of the attacker whom one kills in defense of the life of the people or the state. As in the case of self-defense, the life of the attacker is not sacrificed in his or her service of God; rather, he or she is punished or resisted in the act of attacking forms and institutions in which God is served.

In the context of taking life, Barth initially presented the boundary case with the assurance that reverence for and protection of life are always commanded, that the boundary case does not abrogate these requirements but fulfills them in a paradoxical yet intelligible way.[129] However, in the examples of abortion, self-defense, and war the boundary case in effect functions as an exception to the required reverence for and protection of life rather than, as Barth initially advertised, an unusual or paradoxical expression of the latter. In these cases, Barth shifts from specifying the absolute requirement of reverence and protection to balancing conflicting demands or goods. The careful way in which he initially made sure that any legitimate appeal to the boundary case expressed the required reverence for and protection of life contrasts with the ad hoc way in which he invokes these demands or goods in order, one suspects, to avoid implications of his initial formulations that sit uneasily with his own moral intuitions about

---

[127] CD III/4, 434–6/496–8.
[128] CD III/4, 462/528 f.
[129] CD III/4, 342–4/388–90.

justifiable killing. In order to argue consistently that God might command killing in these instances, Barth must either show how such killings fulfill the proper criteria of a boundary case or he must build into his description of the domain of life a theory of moral conflict situations. The former solution would require less revision of his position than the latter. In the cases of war and self-defense, at least, Barth could attempt to reformulate the Augustinian and Thomist authorization of justifiable killing as an act of love to show how some acts of killing paradoxically express reverence for and protection of life. If successful in this effort, he will have shown how in such cases killing reveres and protects the life that God has loaned. By contrast, a theory of moral conflict would involve an extensive reworking of his position—not only to work out procedures for resolving such conflicts but also to account for why they occur in the first place.

Singularity and Solidarity

Is Barth's position ultimately individualistic? Some of his descriptions of ethical reflection evoke the caricature of the Protestant standing in solitariness before God. In one sense this caricature is obviously false in Barth's case. The command of God, we have seen, is always given from one person to another. It never simply takes place between God and the individual human being. It is a public, not a private occurrence. However, for Barth the prophetic word, heard in this intersubjective context, is only conditionally to be taken as the command of God.[130] As such it is always a summons to those who hear it to engage in their own process of testing. 'No one can believe in another's place or allow anyone else to do his believing for him. Therefore no choice and decision made in obedience to the faith can be taken over unexamined [*ungeprüft*] by anyone else and turned into his own choice or decision.'[131] Here, individuality reappears in the form of ethical singularity, which expresses the accountability of each person to God. The command of God addresses one as singular, that is, as irreplaceable in one's accountability to God. 'No one can take our place in this matter. We ourselves are summoned. . . . We ourselves must give an account.'[132] Singularity clearly involves a certain kind of individuality. However, to be *irreplaceable* in one's accountability is not necessarily to be *alone* in one's accountability. Barth appeals to the universality of the command of God in order to establish one's solidarity with all who are addressed by it. 'I may and must hear his command, but his command applies to us all. . . . Even in the necessary testing [*Prüfung*] of my conduct I cannot overlook or forget the fact that I am never alone and never

---

[130] Barth, 'The Gift of Freedom,' 86 f.
[131] Barth, 'Political Decisions,' 158/13.
[132] CD II/2, 654/729.

will be.'[133] This solidarity is 'from the beginning a constitutive element' of ethical reflection, which is therefore by no means a purely private exercise even though it is carried out by individuals. Indeed, the eucharistic context of ethical reflection in its most primary form assures this solidarity. Because it is not private, one's testing must itself be open to a possible summons to make its result public. '[N]o one can consider himself exempt from the duty of testifying . . . to his faith and the choices and decisions made in accordance with that faith, nor can anyone consider himself exempt from the duty of listening . . . to the testimony of a fellow Christian.'[134]

For Barth, then, the ethics of the prophetic ethos unfolds as an ecclesiastical practice of proclaiming, hearing, and testing of the prophetic word. From this perspective, casuistic ethics and the ethics of the prophetic word presuppose (and help to form) alternative forms of ecclesial moral authority, one based on office or expertise, the other on the dynamics of risk, proclamation, and summons in which the roles are reversible—that is, in which one may proclaim today and be summoned to hear the proclamation of another tomorrow. This question of moral authority in the church is a more adequate issue to press in relation to Barth than is the contrast between individualistic and communal forms of ethics. In fact, Barth's position can only be distorted when approached in terms of the latter contrast because his insistence on expounding ethical reflection in terms of singularity and solidarity and the complex relation between them is a refusal of the terms of the debate that would force Christian ethics to choose between individualistic and communal forms. With respect to the question of ecclesial moral authority, however, we may well wonder whether we are finally forced to choose between the bureaucratic authority of expertise and the ever-shifting and ever-tentative authority of prophetic utterance. These alternatives appear to be aberrant exaggerations of a more adequate notion of ecclesial moral authority which awaits an articulation Barth fails to provide. Given the importance of ethical instruction in preparing one to encounter God's decision, one wonders whether Barth could have found the proper middle ground in the practice of moral pedagogy in the church, locating the principal human moral authority in the office of the teacher rather than that of the casuist or the prophet.

Decisions and Virtues

Is Barth's moral theology too focused on the human agent's decisions to the neglect of her dispositions or virtues? We have seen that Barth shares with casuistical ethics an orientation to the particular situation of choice or decision as central to ethics. He thereby opposes a kind of abstraction he finds in forms of ethics that operate only at the level of general principles. We have also seen that

[133] CD II/2, 655/729 f.
[134] Barth, 'Political Decisions,' 158/13.

he avoids the opposite abstraction, in which the moment of choice or decision is considered independently of the continuous series of choices and decisions that form one's life. Ethical reflection involves 'the examination [*Prüfung*] of the choice now before us in its connection with past and future choices' and our present deeds are always accompanied by the examination (*Prüfung*) of the will of God with respect to prospective deeds.[135] We have seen that like the divine decision, and in correspondence to the latter, the human decision is part of a narrative history yet is not determined by that history. As the very structure as well as the content of Barth's doctrine of creation indicates, that narrative history consists of the self's interwoven relations to God, to other human beings, to itself, and to its temporal location.

The continuity of our decisions as just described is now widely recognized by Barth scholars.[136] However, this continuity is only a necessary condition for virtue to play a role in ethics; it is not sufficient. Does Barth actually assign virtue a positive role in the hearing of the command of God? The answer is that he does, but that this role is inadequate. We begin by recalling that the ethical activity par excellence, ethical reflection, is itself primarily an attitude or a disposition; it is a readiness to encounter the decision of God on one's own decision. Beyond this, Barth identifies certain virtues or dispositions as conditions of decisions made responsibly in the risk of obedience. These include intellectual virtues such as sobriety in weighing arguments and insight and perception in testing possibilities of action in relation to the will of God, as well as moral virtues such as courage and humility, and other states such as joy, assurance, and a good conscience in venturing a decision and proclaiming it to others.[137] Regrettably, Barth says very little about the intellectual virtues. (If he had said more about them we might have a clearer picture of what is involved in testing possibilities of action with respect to the will of God.) The moral virtues and related states or dispositions, on the other hand, appear frequently. For example, the command of God demands a combination of courage and humility of one who refuses military service;[138] their unwillingness to disregard their own lives (which would have required courage and resoluteness) indicates to Barth that those who plotted to assassinate Hitler did not receive, or perhaps did not hear, a command of God to do so;[139] and Barth

---

[135] CD II/2, 634/705 (revised), 639/710.

[136] Credit for this happy circumstance is due above all to William Werpehowski ('Command and History in the Ethics of Karl Barth') and Nigel Biggar (*The Hastening that Waits*, especially 127–45).

[137] These virtues are explicitly enumerated in 'Political Decisions,' 159–63/14–18. The intellectual virtues are seldom mentioned elsewhere, but in numerous places in his discussions of concrete moral issues, Barth explicitly mentions or alludes to these moral virtues.

[138] CD III/4, 467 f./535 f., 468 f./537.

[139] CD III/4, 449/513 f.

refers to the joy and good conscience required for anyone to venture a decision for suicide or abortion.[140]

The contexts in which these moral virtues and related states appear indicate that they have to do with the risk that is necessarily involved in human decisions. Courage is necessary to venture an understanding of a human action as the fulfillment of the divine will and to choose it and proclaim it to others as such. Humility is necessary in order to treat the decision made and proclaimed in this venture as only conditionally the command of God, and thus to remain open to correction from one's fellow hearers. By connecting joy with faith in the reconciling work of Christ, Barth appears to hold that one can venture such a decision, with the risk that one may be wrong, only if one is confident of God's forgiveness in Christ. But Barth almost always mentions joy in connection with having a good conscience and assurance in the face of a decision—and most often the decision is for an act on the boundary of a domain. In this context, however, joy is problematic and even dangerous. The boundary is already a danger zone; to venture there in joy and a good conscience seems reckless, an invitation to the worst kinds of evil. Is it not better—far less dangerous—to go there with an uneasy conscience and in regret, in fear and trembling? In one sense, to be sure, the recommendation of these dispositions is appropriate. For the question raised by the boundary case is not whether an extreme or paradoxical act can be unambiguously right (as opposed to being, say, the best of two or more acts all acknowledged to be evil, or an act that is good overall but has in it some residue of evil) but whether or not God has actually commanded such an act in this instance. If God has commanded it, it *is* unambiguously right—right by definition—and a good conscience is therefore appropriate. The only question, of course, is whether God has indeed commanded it. The recognition that one may be wrong in one's judgment about the latter entails the need for joyous assurance of God's forgiveness. However, joy and good conscience in combination seem to support or constitute a resoluteness which acknowledges but disregards the danger and uncertainty involved in a boundary case.[141] Unlike the courage that is complemented by humility, this resoluteness is not offset by any disposition that does justice to the danger involved. We may ask whether it is not therefore a perversion of courage—in Aristotle's terms, a deviation from the mean of courage in the direction of rashness. For all of the caution he counsels in leading up to the boundary case, Barth encourages a kind of moral recklessness once the decision has been made. We do well to warn against this recklessness.

---

[140] CD III/4, 410/468, 412/470, 423/482. How Barth thinks these conditions can be met in these cases is a question he does not answer.

[141] We shudder when we read the following, cited by Yoder: 'The more calmly we perceive and concede that we all alike stand under God's judgment in this war ... the more cold-bloodedly and energetically will it be waged, for then one ... will have a good conscience amidst this hard and horrible affair' (Barth, *Eine Schweizer Stimme*, 279, cited in Yoder, *Karl Barth and the Problem of War*, 61 n. 2).

The role Barth assigns these virtues is clearly limited. Apart from the intellectual virtues, about which Barth says so little, these virtues are not intrinsic to deliberation itself; that is, they do not, even in a provisional way respectful of the limits of ethical reflection, enable the deliberator to pick out the possible action that corresponds to the will of God. Moreover, these virtues, taken singly or as a whole, are not right-making features in the strict sense. In the strict sense, God's decision is both necessary and sufficient to make a human decision right or wrong. However, they are necessary though not sufficient conditions for human decisions to be undertaken responsibly (that is, in accountability to God and thus in a right relation to God's command even when they are mistaken); as such they constitute a kind of subjective or provisional obedience.

There is a more substantial role for virtue in Barth's ethics of the command of God. In the various domains, certain attitudes and dispositions are themselves constitutive of obedience to the command of God, at least at a general level. We have already noted, in the domain of life, the attitude of reverence for life and the affirmation of life and resolution to act in accordance with reverence for life. Most of Barth's instruction on the responsibilities of parents to their children specifies the general requirement of parents to represent the parenthood of God in certain attitudes and patterns of behavior towards their children.[142] Indeed, nearly the whole of Barth's description of the domains is occupied with articulating the criteria and standards that hold sway in each domain and the attitudes, dispositions, and patterns of behavior that embody these criteria and standards. This is true even of the domain of life which, because of the importance of the boundary case, requires more attention to the decision itself than do the other domains. Of course, by no means are these attitudes, dispositions, or patterns of behavior sufficient to determine the decision one risks in obedience to God. But just as any obedient decision always meets in some way the criteria or standards that hold sway in a domain, so any obedient decision expresses in some way the attitudes, dispositions, and patterns of behavior that are themselves required by these criteria or standards.

To bring these observations together in reverse order of their presentation, we may conclude that for Barth, certain virtues, dispositions, and attitudes are constitutive of obedience to the command of God at a general level and are specified in decisions at the level of actual or concrete obedience. Other intellectual and moral virtues are necessary for the inevitable risk involved in understanding and deciding to be incurred responsibly and thus obediently. Finally, the disposition of readiness to encounter God is necessary to fulfill the primary ethical requirement of accountability to God. To this extent Barth succeeds in showing how an ethic focused on human decision and its encounter with the divine decision can accommodate virtue. What is almost entirely missing,

---

[142] CD III/4, 276–85/311–20.

however, is an account of how we come to have these virtues and dispositions.[143] As we saw in the previous chapter, it is not that nothing happens in ourselves. Indeed, the task of special ethics is to describe how the sanctification of human beings accomplished by the Word of God comes to human beings; 'what it performs in [them] . . . what becomes of them in consequence.'[144] But Barth's special ethics is almost entirely about the actions, dispositions, and virtues the Word of God commands, not about how we may become people who perform those acts and cultivate those dispositions and virtues. And Barth has obvious reasons for avoiding such an account. His entire moral theology urges us to begin by turning our attention away from what happens in us to what happens in Christ and confronts us from outside ourselves. Still, we may wonder why the same Barth who was able to deny to casuistical ethics a role in the determination of the command of God while assigning to casuistry a role in the instruction that prepares one to hear that command could not also find a role for virtue acquisition in preparing one to hear the command of God. Without some practice of moral formation to accompany it, Barth's notion of ethical instruction can only appear as an intellectualist abstraction.

Presence and Absence

In Chapter 2, we asked whether Barth's ethics of the command of God reflects nostalgia for the pure presence of the command of God given to Adam. Nostalgia of this kind is deeply problematic for two reasons. First, like all nostalgia it harbors dangers of fanaticism bred by the sense of the loss of a primordial past and the lure of its recovery. Barth, of course, spent more than a decade of his life fighting this kind of fanaticism. Second, if the command of God is fully present to the hearer, then the meaning of Barth's entire ethics of the command of God will have been that God is the guarantor of the modern dream of total transparency of the right and the good to human knowing. Ironically, Barth will have reestablished the modern moral subject as judge of good and evil at precisely the point where he directed his sharpest challenge to this subject.

---

[143] Stanley Hauerwas charged that while Barth recognized that the sanctification of human beings by the Word of God imparts real direction to human lives, his concern to preclude the misunderstanding of this direction as a human possession makes it unclear how this direction becomes embodied in human agency. The result, Hauerwas says, is that Barth tends to treat the life of the Christian as a succession of atomistic acts (Hauerwas, *Character and the Christian Life*, 171 f.). Werpehowski and Biggar have successfully refuted the second part of the charge by showing how Barth does not and cannot assume any kind of atomism. However, neither Werpehowski nor Biggar refutes Hauerwas's first charge. In his attempt to do so, Biggar admittedly relies on what he thinks is implicit in Barth's account, and even with this move he does not satisfactorily answer Hauerwas's charge (Biggar, *The Hastening that Waits*, 142–5).

[144] CD III/4, 5/3.

We have seen that Barth denies that the specific command of God is accessible to human knowing. There is certainly no transparency here. However, the contrast between the ethics of the prophetic ethos and casuistical ethics is quite clearly a contrast between divine presence and absence. Barth associates the historical rise of casuistical ethics with a loss of confidence in the Holy Spirit and the prophetic voice, and with the consequent effort to determine what God commands by establishing legal codes.[145] These codes are marked by two features: their textuality (the legal code as *Gesetzetext*) and the generality of their laws (in contrast to the fully specified divine command). Both features associate casuistry with a loss of the divine presence in the Spirit and the prophetic voice, and this loss is implicated in the human appropriation of the command of God. Showing an acute instinct for the nature of textuality, Barth associates the legal code with the unending need for a supplement (*Zusätze*) to explain and extend the law. Under the regime of casuistical ethics the command of God turns out to be 'like every human law, concealed, wrapped in a cloud of further human laws...'[146] In its distance from the presence of God the legal code makes possible, indeed inevitable, human appropriation of the command of God by the endless substitution of new (human) laws. Moreover, the textuality of the legal code is closely connected with its generality, for it is precisely the generality of these laws that requires this chain of substitutions to interpret and apply them. By contrast, for Barth the command of God is already specific. Moreover, God is directly present in the specificity of the command, while the generality of the law abstracts from the divine presence.[147] And because God is properly acknowledged as lawgiver and judge only when God is present in the directness and specificity of the divine command, generality, too, makes human appropriation of the command of God both possible and inevitable.

Spirit or prophetic voice on the one hand and legal code on the other hand thus appear to fall under a binary opposition of divine presence and absence, and this opposition appears to be repeated in other oppositions: command vs. law; event vs. text; (prophetic) risk vs. (casuistical) method or technique. Together, these oppositions appear to undergird the central opposition between prophetic ethos and casuistical ethics. These oppositions are dubious for many reasons, one of which is their perpetuation of the now discredited dichotomies of prophecy vs. law and Spirit vs. law. This brings us to the question of anti-Judaism in Barth's thought. Recalling his description, noted above, of the Jew or the Pharisee, we can now see a broad identification of the Judaic with immanence, textuality, and generality, and thus with divine absence, in contrast to Barth's ethics of the command of God which involves transcendence, prophecy, and specificity, and thus divine presence. Of course, we saw that Barth ascribes the same features

---

[145] CD III/4, 7 f./6 f. See also CD II/2, 700/782.
[146] CD II/2, 700/782.
[147] CD II/2, 675 f./753 f.

indiscriminately to Catholic ethics since the second century and to much of Protestant ethics, and we remarked that he wrongly ascribes the feature of generality to Jewish ethics—another instance of misrepresenting Judaism for the sake of intra-Christian polemics.

We could respond to Barth by arguing that the rabbinic tradition denies the opposition between prophecy and textuality (understanding God to be present in both the direct revelation of the law at Sinai and in halakhic reasoning) and that according to the Christian tradition the Spirit may be present in casuistical hermeneutics. The binary opposition of Spirit/law or prophetic voice/legal code would then collapse, bringing down with it the binary opposition between the ethics of the prophetic ethos and casuistical ethics as an opposition between divine presence and absence. We could argue further that by placing presence and absence in a binary opposition and privileging the former, it is Barth who delivers the ethical over to the human subject, who thus stands secure in the divine presence despite lacking knowledge of good and evil in the strict sense. However, we will instead argue that the issue of divine presence and absence in the command of God as Barth describes it is more complex than these binary oppositions indicate. First, we will consider the relation of the ethical encounter to time. Next, we will examine the senses in which human beings know and do not know the command of God. Finally, we will explore Barth's treatment of the secrecy of God's decision.

While Barth speaks of an encounter of the human with the divine decision, that encounter is not characterized by any immediacy or transparency. The divine decision itself occurs in a complex relation to temporality in Barth's portrayal. It seems at once to precede and to follow our own decision: On the one hand, it is the prior decision made from eternity and in the midst of time and at every moment; on the other hand, it decides on our own decision, which must therefore be prior.[148] In what time, then, does the encounter occur? If encounter means transparency then it can occur only in the eschatological time of the final judgment. 'What we will and do is subject to this decision of God [that is, the decision that is made from eternity and repeated in Jesus Christ and again in each moment] and awaits the disclosure of it. . . . The judgment seat of Christ, before which we obviously do not stand here and now, has already been set up, and whether we have done, do or will do good or evil has already been decided from it.'[149] Human beings decide in a time between the primordial and always repeated decision and its eschatological disclosure, not in the full light of disclosure. The present encounter of our decision with the divine decision is therefore not a moment of transparency; rather, the divine decision is concealed in this encounter even as the specific directive of that decision is revealed to the one who asks sincerely in ethical reflection. And even that directive, as we have

---

[148] CD II/2, 632–6/702–7.
[149] CD II/2, 633/703 (revised).

seen, is not heard in its full clarity. God is absent precisely in the divine presence, or in Barth's terms, God is concealed precisely in God's revelation.

The non-presence of the divine decision implies a lack of knowledge of the specific command of God in the present. This brings us to the second point, namely the senses in which human beings do and do not know the command of God. Here, we expand on a theme we briefly reviewed in Chapter 2. The unbridgeable gap between our knowledge of the domains and the command of God itself has profound implications for our knowledge of the answer to the question of ethical reflection, 'What should we do?' 'If our action were to occur in the knowledge [*Wissen*] of that about which this question asks, our account-ability to God fulfilled in our action would mean our justification before God.' To ask the ethical question in the knowledge of its answer would be to identify ourselves with God who decides on and judges us in our actions. Morally, we would exist in likeness to God. 'Our decisions would run parallel to God's own decision and would be to that extent identical with it.' There would be no need, Barth points out, for ethical reflection, nor for the command of God as distinct from what we say to ourselves, nor even for Christ as mediator of the covenant. In fact, however, we do not exist in any such likeness to God. 'Our sanctification is God's work, not ours. Therefore the encounter, the confrontation of our exis-tence with the command of God is absolutely necessary. We must therefore inquire after the command of God, asking, What should we do? without already having the answer ready and without being able to supply it ourselves.'[150] As we have seen throughout this study, for Barth our goodness is in Jesus Christ; it comes to us from outside ourselves and is ours only by participation in Christ. The capacity to decide what corresponds at any point in our lives to the fulfillment of electing grace in Christ comes to us only in confrontation with the gracious God.

When we ask the ethical question in this way there is nevertheless a sense in which we do know the command of God. We know (*kennen*) it as something we must receive from God and not from ourselves, and we know our own decision as subordinated to God's decision.[151] When we seriously ask the ethical question 'we confess already that we know [*kennen*] the divine command, that it is present to us, that it has been disclosed to us, and therefore that the necessary ethical reflection which sets this question cannot be made in vain. . . . Not knowing [*wissend*] but asking what we ought to do, we confess that God knows about us [*um uns weiss*]. We subordinate ourselves to what he wills and orders, and our action is brought into line with his command.'[152] In other words, we do not know (*wissen*) the command of God as something over which we dispose with the power to decide and judge the rightness and goodness of actions and of

---

[150] CD II/2, 644 f./717 f. (revised).
[151] CD II/2, 652 f./727.
[152] CD II/2, 657/732 (revised). See also 648 f./722, 653/727.

ourselves in our actions. The knowledge we would have of the command of God—the light and clarity of *Wissen*—is rather the knowledge God has of us (*Gott um uns weiss*) in the divine decision and judgment on our conduct. Because God has this knowledge of us and our conduct that is denied to us, we must ask after the command of God. But in the very act of seriously asking after it we know (*kennen*) the command as something which we must receive from God and to which our decisions are subordinated.[153] Barth assures us that our asking is not in vain: that with our asking we receive the specific order (*Befehl*) of the command and our conduct is brought into alignment with the divine will. The key to Barth's position here is the shift it effects from the question of how we can know the command of God to the question of how we stand in relation to it. This brings us back to the meaning of the ethical question. For Barth, when we genuinely ask the question 'What should we do?' we show that we already know (*kennen*) the command of God even though we do not know (*wissen*) it. Genuinely to pose it before God is not simply to pose it rhetorically, as a question whose answer we already know or expect to be able to discover on our own, and genuinely to pose it is to pose it knowing that in it, we ourselves *are asked* concerning our obedience; to pose it in this way is already to respond properly to the command of God and is thus the first step of obedience.[154] This is why 'the crucial thing is that we ask seriously,'[155] and why Barth can say that '[i]nsofar as our action is determined and governed by this asking after [the command of God] it becomes obedient action.'[156] For this reason, we can exist in a right relation to the command of God even if we mistake its concrete directive.[157]

The gap between human knowledge and the command of God is bridged from the side of God, who gives the specific command (*Befehl*) as we ask. 'From God's side nothing is hidden at this point.'[158] Does it follow that having received (*empfangen*) what we asked for, namely this specific order, we now know (*wissen*) it? This brings us to the conscience (*Gewissen*), which Barth defines as 'the totality of our self-consciousness insofar as it can receive [*Empfänger*] and then proclaim the Word and therefore the command of God that is given to us, insofar as we . . . can become co-knowers [*Mit-Wisser*] (*suneidotes, conscientes*) with God. That Word and command that is given to us is as such the promise that we can become this.'[159] As the reference to the promise makes clear, this knowledge is

---

[153] The distinction we are drawing here between *kennen* and *wissen* should not be confused with the distinction between intuitive and discursive knowledge. Barth is not saying that we know the command of God perfectly well but cannot offer a chain of reasoning for it. Rather, the distinction for him is between knowledge of an object that is within our capacity to grasp whether intuitively or discursively, on the one hand, and knowledge of an object that is known only as it addresses us.

[154] CL, 32.

[155] CD II/2, 653/727 (revised).

[156] CD II/2, 645/718 (revised).

[157] CD III/4, 272/305, 273/306.

[158] CD II/2, 704/786.

[159] CD II/2, 667/744 (revised).

eschatological; Barth goes immediately on to say that conscience is not an anthropological but an eschatological concept. It follows that we do not possess this knowledge of the specific command of God this side of the eschaton.[160] The gap is bridged from God's side, but not from our side. From our side the command of God is obscure and its hearing is characterized by 'embarrassments and misunderstandings.'[161] Ethical reflection can and must proceed in the confidence that asking is not in vain, that God's specific command will be given. But this is not a confidence that the command will be heard clearly or rightly, either in deliberation and testing or in a retrospective judgment. The human decision involves an insurmountable risk.

The lack of knowledge of the divine command in the present brings us finally to the theme of the secrecy of the divine decision. For Barth, we test our prospective action knowing that God tests it, and us, in the divine decision on our action. Our action is the proof or authentication (*Bewährung*) of our status as covenant partners of God. But only God is capable of accomplishing this proof or authentication. Barth makes this point in terms of the scriptural notion of God as the one who tests and judges the heart, which is inaccessible to us. 'Absolutely and properly, only the divine judge is capable of this proving and testing of our works. He sees both our actions and also ourselves, the heart from which they proceed, *ta krypta tōn anthrōpōn* [the secret or hidden aspects of human beings] (Rom. 2: 5, 16).'[162] If we knew our conduct as right or wrong, good or evil, we would be able to pronounce the judgment of approval or disapproval on ourselves, to judge in God's place. But as we have seen, this is precisely the judgment we must receive from God and in the readiness for which we approach the divine decision. 'We cannot be approved [*Bewährte*] of ourselves and therefore we cannot claim ourselves to be such. Otherwise we exalt ourselves as judges of ourselves. . . .'[163] Our conduct as the proof of our status as God's covenant partners is therefore hidden from us; it is a divine secret. It belongs to the divine decision itself as the measure and criterion of our conduct. We and our actions stand under an examination whose result we do not know. It follows that we never have full knowledge of the goodness or rightness of our conduct, that is, we can never know in the strict sense the mutual relationship between the possibility we choose and the will of God. A 'relative manifestation' of the

---

[160] William Werpehowski, who along with Biggar did so much to draw attention to the continuity in Barth's ethics of the command of God, erred in concluding that while we cannot anticipate God's specific command before the fact we can understand, explain, and justify it after the fact by analogical correlations between our own action and God's action. Significantly, Werpehowski cites no texts of Barth that support this conclusion. See Werpehowski, 'Command and History in the Ethics of Karl Barth,' 310–12.

[161] CD III/4, 12/11; CD II/2, 709/792.

[162] CD II/2, 637/708.

[163] CD II/2, 637/708.

proof of our status is the most we are capable of.[164] Our lives are hidden with Christ in God.

All of this means that the testing of our conduct and of ourselves in our conduct takes place in ignorance of the divine decision. *Prüfung* takes place in the gap between our approval or disapproval in the secrecy of the divine decision on the one hand, and the proof we are required to furnish by our conduct on the other hand. The revelation of the ultimate decision of God on us in our conduct is eschatological; the present is the time of the secret. This secrecy itself has ethical implications. Barth offers the example of the Apostle Paul who, being in no position to supply the proof of his own approval before God, must submit to interrogation by the Corinthians.[165] The divine secrecy entails that everyone is subject to being held morally accountable by his or her neighbor—although, as Barth points out with reference to the apostle's reply to the Corinthians, the proper response to such interrogation by the neighbor involves reminding him or her that our moral approval is in Christ, whose own approval was manifest only to God. The divine secrecy—the hiddenness of our lives in Christ—is thus the ground of a moral solidarity in which the inability of anyone to guarantee his or her own moral approval is the occasion for mutual moral accountability. This condition of mutual accountability is the exact opposite of the condition (which, as we have seen, Barth identified as the primary manifestation of sin) in which each person presumes to judge herself and others.

To ask the ethical question in the trust that God reveals the divine decision even while concealing it is presumably what Barth means by the confidence in the guidance of the Holy Spirit which, for him, Christian ethics lost, and for which it tried to compensate by seeking to determine the order of the command through casuistical ethics. Without such confidence, the lack of knowledge of the divine decision becomes a problem for casuistry to solve. By contrast, ethical reflection asks without knowing, or rather it asks knowing that it cannot know of itself (which is precisely why it takes the form of prayer). Confidence in the guidance of the Spirit is not an expectation of full disclosure. It does not entail that human beings know through the Spirit rather than through casuistry what God decides —this would simply mean that Barth will have recovered through the divine a certainty he renounced as a human achievement—but rather that they need not institute their own casuistical ethics in order to be aligned with the will of God. In this confidence, Barth assures us, human beings can live morally without the capacity to ascertain the command of God for themselves.

From this perspective, the ethics of the prophetic ethos and casuistical ethics appear as two different ways of dealing with ethics after the fall, when the command of God is no longer directly present. With the loss of direct presence,

---

[164] CD II/2, 638/710.
[165] CD II/2, 637/708. The reference is to 2 Cor. 13: 3 f., which Barth understands in light of 2 Cor. 10: 18.

ethics can proceed in confidence that God is present in the prophetic voice or in the Holy Spirit, or it can engage in casuistical interpretation and application. Barth was surely wrong to conclude that the latter approach excludes the prophetic voice or the Holy Spirit; these two opposed forms of ethics may instead be two very different ways of understanding the divine presence after the fall. They are also two different strategies of preventing human appropriation of the command of God. Barth was wrong again to see in casuistic textuality as such the human appropriation of the command of God. For the endless substitution Barth rightly ascribes to casuistic ethics as a form of textuality can be invoked to ensure that the right and good are always beyond the reach of the appropriating subject. Once again, the ethics of the prophetic ethos and casuistical ethics can both be understood as alternatives to the modern effort to render the right and good transparent to the human subject. Moral theology has the legitimate task of deciding which of these is the proper postlapsarian ethic, but the charge that Barth's ethics of the command of God is an exercise in nostalgia for a lost immediacy is as rash as Barth's own charge that the alternative to his ethics inevitably banishes God from ethics and enthrones humankind.

5. CONCLUSION

The problem of ethics in its most concrete form arises at the point where human beings venture a judgment, choice, or decision, identifying a particular action or course of action as that which corresponds to the gracious action of God. On the one hand, there is no moral life in the absence of such a judgment, choice, or decision. On the other hand, how can human beings judge, choose, or decide without repeating the primordial and paradigmatic sin of asserting themselves as judges of good and evil, usurping a divine office that can only destroy them and their fellow human beings? This is the problem Barth seeks to resolve by describing ethics in its most concrete form as the practice of ethical reflection, which is the encounter of our decision, as fully informed as possible by ethical instruction rooted in the Word of God, with the decision of God. Barth shows how it is possible for special ethics to obtain knowledge of the command of God to some point of approximation to that command while also insisting on an unbridgeable gap between our knowledge and the command of God itself. He thereby (at least in principle) avoids the extremes of voluntarism and rationalism. Moreover, he preserves the notion of ethical inquiry and decision as a spiritual practice in which the ethical question 'What should we do?' is a question posed to God in prayer. Finally, in leaving the ultimate judgment on our decision, and thus on our entire life conduct, to God, Barth locates the proof of our election—the congruence of our active existence with our status under God's electing grace—not in our conduct but in the secrecy of the divine decision, which has already been made in Jesus Christ. Our lives are hidden with Christ in God.

Barth's special ethics, and indeed his ethics as a whole, are unintelligible apart from his conviction that human beings bring themselves and others to ruin when they act as judges of good and evil. Wanting to be the judge, '[man] and his whole world is in conflict with God. It is an unreconciled world, a suffering world, a world given up to destruction.'[166] Barth wrote these words in the early 1950s, during a period of frustration at a post-Christian world torn apart by two opposed moral and political visions each claiming to represent the cause of civilization against the other. Yet this moral polarization was hardly restricted to its geopolitical manifestation. 'The history of every man is, in fact, the history of their many and constantly arising and mutually contradictory and intersecting views. . . . The battle is between what is supposed to be good and what is supposed to be evil, but in this battle all parties—how could it be otherwise?—think that they are the friends of what is good and the enemies of what is evil.' In this situation 'the theory and practice of what we call tolerance seems to be the final refuge and one which we have to discover again and again.'[167] In this passage, Barth captures the moral and political character of the bourgeois era and its post-war afterlife, with its presumptions of moral certainty, its resulting conflicts between moral visions, and the principle of tolerance it proposes as a solution to the conflict. Barth decries the threat to human solidarity posed by moral certainty, yet he also knows that tolerance offers at most a semblance of solidarity. Solidarity, he is convinced, is possible only as we know ourselves to be placed under a command that is given to all of us yet is transparent to none of us, for the knowledge of which we must continuously ask God, and in our ultimate ignorance of which we must continuously reaffirm our accountability to one another.

[166] CD IV/1, 220/241 (revised).
[167] CD IV/1, 446 f./495 f.

Conclusion

From his 1916 lecture on 'The Righteousness of God' to his unfinished material on the ethics of reconciliation, Karl Barth pressed a consistent theme: It is God who accomplishes the good, and the task of moral theology is to attest in the language of ethics how human moral life and activity are constituted in and by that fact. Barth, of course, was acutely aware that the language of ethics was customarily employed in the service of other themes, and we have critically examined his strenuous effort to discipline that language in order to render it capable of attesting rather than betraying its proper theme. In his mature work that theme is expressed in an ontological and analogical form. God resolves on the good from eternity in the determination of humanity in Jesus Christ to commission and service as active witnesses of God's glory; fulfills it in time in the incarnation, life, death, resurrection, and ascension of Jesus Christ, who performs this commission and service in place of all of humanity; and summons, empowers, and directs human beings in every time to correspond to this fulfillment in their conduct. Ontologically, ethics is grounded in the eternal relationship of the Father and the Son and of all of humanity in the Son; in the incarnate Christ who is both the electing God and the elected human; and in the relationship of the humanity of other human beings to Christ's humanity. Analogically, the obedience of Jesus Christ is a reflection of the eternal obedience of the Son to the Father, and it is in turn reflected in the obedience of human beings to Jesus Christ, whose own obedience was exercised in place of these others.

This movement of the actualization of the good from eternity to the midst of time to every time reverses the direction of the pedagogical conception of ethics, according to which our capacities and desires are formed, with the assistance of grace, into a gradual approximation to the good that is their end. In accordance with his theology more generally, Barth breaks with all portrayals of the moral life as a journey from here to there; ethics can only be grounded in a journey God has already taken from there to here. This movement of the good from there to here would seem susceptible of conscription by a narrative of the secularization of ethics. Barth himself narrates it this way in his early account of the fate of the Reformed tradition, in which an ethic focused on the transcendence of God was transformed into an ethic of an immanent good, 'striding off from God into the world.' The paradigmatic narrative of this kind, of course, is that of Hegel, for whom the divine empties itself into history in the Christ event, its reality now constituted by immanent human action. What keeps Barth's ethics from these and other manifestations of the bourgeois ethos is not only his insistence that the movement of the good is from eternal election to creation, reconciliation, and redemption, and thus back to its origin in eternal life with God. It is also his insistence that the actualization of the good is accomplished by God's grace in Jesus Christ and not by our action. Our action is not implicated in an economy of grace but participates in the divine work of grace by corresponding to it and thereby exercising the commission and service to which grace itself summons human beings.

It follows from Barth's solution that human life in the world is meant to be a series of signs of grace, a lifelong song of praise glorifying God whose glorification consists in fulfillment of the divine will to be with and for human beings. Understood in this way, moral theology can focus earnest attention on life in the world without delivering ethics over to a purely this-worldly perspective. If Barth succeeds here, he resolves one of the most pressing problems of moral theology at least since the dawn of the modern era: How can ethics do justice to ordinary life without taking a naturalistic and ultimately a strictly humanistic form? How can moral theology direct its attention to the good as it is found in our lives in the world without ending up with a good that does not refer to anything beyond the horizon of natural human life and its capabilities? How can our ordinary lives— the protection of life and preservation of health; the nurturing of family bonds; the fulfillment of a vocation in the world; the sustaining of social, educational, and political institutions; the quest for human righteousness in the face of pervasive racial, economic, sexual, and legal injustice; and also, as the condition in which all the foregoing occur, our daily discipleship with its decisive break with the 'givens' that commend themselves to us as requisites of life in society— reflect what Christian faith proclaims as the ultimate meaning and purpose of our lives without either placing demands on our lives that exceed our human capacities and limitations, on the one hand, or simply attaching the name of grace to a form of life that is indistinguishable from one lived within a wholly secular or natural horizon, on the other hand? How can the turn to ordinary life resist the bourgeois ethos in which the world understands itself through itself, as the product of its own moral activity, as a counter-narrative to the narrative of grace?

Contemporary Catholic and Protestant moral theologians have struggled to meet this challenge of the ethics of ordinary life. Catholic moral theologians have increasingly qualified the sharp dichotomy they once maintained between a natural end having to do with ordinary life, for which natural human moral capacities are in principle adequate, and a supernatural salvific end that takes us beyond ordinary life and natural capability. In place of this dichotomy lies a tension reflected in many current debates. Do we find grace in ordinary life as lived in its fully natural horizon, so that the content of moral theology is natural morality while specifically Christian elements supply motivation or a context of meaning? Or are extraordinary acts of self-giving love and martyrdom interwoven into ordinary life itself, where natural morality, itself already open to the transcendent good found in Christ, supplies a set of conditions which already anticipate (and participate in) that higher end? A parallel tension exists in Protestant theological ethics between approaches that seek to identify the goods found in the various natural and social contexts in which human life is lived with theology articulating or symbolically expressing the ultimate ground or meaning of these goods, on the one hand, and approaches that focus on the language and practices of the church as the context in which goods are identified and pursued, on the other hand.

If Barth's moral theology deserves our attention today, it is at least in part because it seems to have overcome such tensions. For him, the life to which human beings are summoned by the sanctifying command is a genuinely human life, the life of those who always remain the creatures God created; and in this sense he stands with the first pole of the Catholic and Protestant tensions mentioned above. Yet for him, this life is meant to signify, in its characteristically human forms and activities, not what it is by virtue of its own capacities and achievements but what it is in and by God's grace, and in this sense he stands closer to the second pole, though with his characteristic emphasis on his conception of grace. Barth's position is best stated by way of a comparison with the *older* Thomistic conception, with its sharp distinction between the natural and the supernatural. That conception must carefully distinguish different levels of good and different ways in which grace is related to human characteristics and capacities. Barth's conception cuts through these distinctions by recognizing one good (the ultimate good, fellowship with God) which is entirely beyond our capacities but which has been actualized by God's grace in Jesus Christ and which, as such, is signified in our lives as they correspond to grace in all their humanness. Where the older Thomistic conception saw a supernatural good and the elevation of our nature beyond its natural capability, Barth sees an ultimate good that is accomplished in our place by grace alone. And where that conception saw a natural good with its own integrity, however provisional in relation to the supernatural good, Barth sees creaturely signs of the ultimate good—human nature in all its diverse aspects reflecting in its creaturely reality God's determination to bring God's human partner into communion with God. Human actions are thus fully human, yet they exist in both mimetic and testimonial relations to the ultimate good that has been accomplished by God in Jesus Christ. In all its finitude, in all its ordinariness, human life has the dignity of signifying grace, and it is in these signs of grace, most explicitly recognized in the life of the church but also found in the natural, social, and political dimensions of life, that human life bears witness to its purpose, which is the glorification of God in the world. Barth thus accounts for much of what is attractive in both of the newer Catholic models—human life is affirmed in its natural horizon yet that horizon points beyond itself to a reality that exceeds it—while avoiding the problems associated with them—most fundamentally, possible tendencies to either assimilate grace to nature or nature to grace.[1]

Another important implication of Barth's claim that God accomplishes the good in our place has to do with his relation to the Protestant Reformation tradition and the significance of that relation for ecumenical engagements in moral theology. To the extent that it followed Luther, the Protestant Reformation drew a sharp distinction between justification and sanctification. The contrasting terms in which the distinction was drawn in its strongest versions—righteousness was said to be in the one case 'alien' and in the other 'proper,' in the one case 'imputed' to us and in the other 'imparted,' in the one case an event and in the other a process—combined with the tendency to identify the first term in each pair as what is most paradigmatic of grace as grace, made it difficult to say how human moral action is related to divine grace. In the Lutheran tradition this could simply mean that the relation between divine grace and human moral action was left unclear (as with Luther), or it could mean that ethics was destined to be marginalized in a theology which focused so strongly on justifying grace. In the Reformed tradition, which was less vigorous in policing the distinction between justification and sanctification, this could simply involve ambiguity over the relation of divine and human action in sanctification (as with Calvin), or the Reformed emphasis on sanctification could eventually set in motion a process that would sever human moral action from divine grace altogether. It seems inevitable, given their fundamental convictions, that in the Reformation traditions inspired by Luther either grace would marginalize ethics or ethics would compromise grace.

Of course, the Lutheran and Reformed traditions are far more complex than this simple problematic suggests, but it is difficult to deny that the Protestant Reformation in its Lutheran and Reformed versions found it difficult to establish a stable relationship between divine grace and human moral action capable of providing a genuine alternative to the broadly Augustinian tradition that prevailed in Catholic theology with its understanding of justification and sanctification as two aspects of a single process. It is therefore unsurprising that one tendency among Protestant moral theologians today in their ecumenical engagements with Catholics is to emphasize their potential commonality with the Catholic tradition where sanctification is concerned, rescinding from or simply bracketing the strong claims about the sufficiency of divine grace entailed by classical Protestant understandings of justification. This approach risks resulting in a weak and somewhat hesitant version of the position the Catholic tradition embodies with much greater strength and confidence. It is here, however, that

---

[1] To put it somewhat crudely, the problem is how to resist tendencies to 'naturalize the supernatural' or to 'supernaturalize the natural.' See John Milbank, *Theology and Social Theory* (London: Blackwell, 1993), 206–55. The two tendencies are best thought of as ideal types; to attach them to proper names as Milbank does is a risky enterprise.

Barth's significance is apparent. While Barth maintains the distinction between justification and sanctification, he also transcends it in two key respects. First, insofar as for him Christ accomplishes both kinds of righteousness in our place, Barth ascribes both justification and sanctification to the kind of working of grace that is characteristic of justification in classical Protestant theology. Second, in both cases Christ also summons, empowers, and directs us to confirm this accomplishment in our own properly human action. Notwithstanding their important differences, then, justification and sanctification stand under the same Christological principle and exhibit the same general structure of divine and human action. It is therefore by upholding the most robust Protestant notion of the sufficiency of divine grace across the full range of dogmatic topics that Barth secures the stability of ethics in Protestant theology, and it is through this hyper-Protestant notion of grace, and not apart from it, that he is able to incorporate into his moral theology robust versions of the inseparability of justification and sanctification and of the cooperation of divine and human action that are worthy of comparison with their counterparts in the broadly Augustinian tradition of grace. Here, at last, is a viable alternative to the Augustinian tradition, one that is both truly distinct from the latter and capable of entering into a genuine and potentially fruitful conversation with it. If Protestantism has something of permanent importance to contribute to the universal church in the field of moral theology, it is more likely to be found in Barth's reformulation of the Reformation tradition represented by Luther and Calvin than in inferior versions of positions preserved and cultivated in the Catholic tradition.

Barth's insistence that we understand and live our moral lives as addressees of a command that has already been fulfilled by Jesus Christ in our place has several other significant implications which have been discussed at various points in this study and which therefore can be treated with brevity here. We have noted on more than one occasion the significance of Barth's conviction that we stand under the divine judgment of good and evil, a judgment in which we participate rationally and volitionally but which we ourselves do not make. As those who cannot presume to know good and evil but must prayerfully ask for God's judgment, prepare to hear it through others, and submit to the interrogation of others in our always provisional judgments, we are free for obedience to God and accountability to others and free from the presumptions of moral certainty and responsibility for the cause of the good that continue to threaten human lives and societies, even in an allegedly postmodern era.

The same accountability to the other acknowledged by those who know themselves to be the addressees of God's command is reflected in the readiness of moral theology to recognize moral truth wherever it is found and, more specifically, to receive instruction and correction from moral philosophy, even while denying the principled authority of these other discourses over moral theology, which is rather bound to the Word of God which speaks in all these places. To know oneself as the addressee of the command of God is to renounce identity with it, mastery over it, and exclusivity with respect to it. It is instead to recognize that the Word of God is always free to speak in places where it is not explicitly acknowledged and thus to always be prepared to hear the command of God in strange and unfamiliar voices. For Barth, there is no trade-off to be made between an ecclesial ethic and a so-called public ethic. The church must be faithful above all to its service of explicit witness to God's command. But this very service requires a willingness to hear this command wherever and through whomever it is spoken.

Finally, we have also discussed how the command that issues from Christ's fulfillment of the good in our place establishes us as moral subjects who are both genuinely bound to the good and genuinely free for it. The grace that interrupts our moral striving does not remove us from morality but places us in it on a firmer ground than we could ever discover or lay down for ourselves. Barth thus confronts us with a moral vision which opposes the bourgeois vision with its central conviction that the moral world in which we live is one of our own making. The latter vision will always be subject to a twofold pull on our humanity. In one direction, we will be tempted to exaggerate our moral knowledge and capability to meet the demands of the good. In the other direction, we will be tempted to scale back our understanding of the good, proportioning it to what we are capable of achieving by our own powers. To move in either direction, or in both at once, as is commonly done, is to violate our humanity.

If Barth's moral theology does commend itself to us on these grounds, how likely is it to exercise a significant influence on contemporary moral theology? On the one hand, Barth's moral theology enjoys much more attention today than it did during his own lifetime. The scholarship of recent years has established him as a moral theologian of the first rank of importance, securing for him a status in this aspect of his theology that has long been recognized in regard to the rest of it. It has also refuted many common misrepresentations: that the command of God as Barth articulates it is voluntaristic or occasionalistic and is heard by a solitary individual; that his emphasis on divine grace leaves no room for human action; that he collapses everything into Christology, rejects all extra-scriptural moral insight, and disrespects the integrity of created nature. If this study is successful, it will have reinforced some of these refutations and broken new ground on others.

On the other hand, however, the field of moral theology is probably less hospitable to Barth's approach to ethics today than it was during his lifetime. This situation is only partly due to the fact that certain flaws in Barth's moral theology identified in this study—lack of clarity over the precise role of reason in hearing the command of God, reticence regarding growth in the Christian life, the truncated role of virtue, and the tendency toward a rationalistic account of the activity of the Holy Spirit in the moral life that leaves little room for sacramental mystery—weigh more heavily on the scales today than they did during his lifetime. More significant, perhaps, is the resistance to any ethic in which the basic apparatus of command and obedience is central, a resistance that seems inevitable today even when this apparatus is deployed in as subtle and even subversive a way as Barth deploys it. Yet the most significant factor in the inhospitality of contemporary moral theology to Barth's ethics is surely our distance from the Reformation-era conception of grace that never ceases to determine the latter. While this conception was hardly popular in Barth's lifetime, it nevertheless held power to provoke and inspire which Barth was able to harness to great effect in his moral and political thought but which is largely spent today. And so, as with much of the Barth renaissance of the past two decades, work on his moral theology swims against the stream of the discipline as a whole. Barth, of course, would have expected nothing other.

For Barth, it is only when we let grace do what it is able to do (or has already done) that we are enabled to do what we, by the power and direction of the Holy Spirit, are able to do. The bourgeois era, with its ethic of responsibility, forgot that lesson, or never learned it in the first place. It proved that much more could be done for the good of humanity by ignoring that lesson than was done by nominally following it in previous eras. Yet it also unleashed forces and passions that diminished and even imperiled humanity, and continue to do so. Barth's articulation of the lesson belongs to the end of the bourgeois era. But while that era is technically over, much of its ethos is still with us, both within the church and without; and as long as that is the case, his moral theology will remain relevant however popular or unpopular it is. And if the lesson itself is true, then he has also contributed something of permanent significance to the universal church, however strange the voice in which he has spoken.

Bibliography

WORKS BY KARL BARTH

I. German Texts

'Der Christ in der Gesellschaft.' In *Das Wort Gottes und die Theologie*. Munich: Chr. Kaiser Verlag, 1925.

Die christliche Dogmatik im Entwurf, i: *Die Lehre vom Worte Gottes*. Edited by Gerhard Sauter. Zurich: Theologischer Verlag, 1982.

'Christliche Ethik.' In *Zwei Vorträge*, Theologische Existenz heute NS 3. Munich: Chr. Kaiser Verlag, 1946.

Das christliche Leben: Die kirchliche Dogmatik IV/4: Fragmente aus dem Nachlass, Vorlesungen. Zurich: Theologischer Verlag, 1976.

Ethik. Zurich: Theologischer Verlag, 1973.

'Die Gerechtigkeit Gottes.' In *Das Wort Gottes und die Theologie*. Munich: Chr. Kaiser Verlag, 1925.

'Das Halten der Gebote.' In *Vorträge und kleinere Arbeiten, 1925–1930*. Edited by Harmann Schmidt, 99–139. Zurich: Theologischer Verlag Zürich, 1994.

Die kirchliche Dogmatik. Zollikon-Zurich: Evangelischer Verlag, 1945–67.

'Politische Entscheidung in der Einheit des Glaubens.' *Theologische Existenz heute*. Munich: Christian Kaiser Verlag, 1952.

'Das Problem der Ethik in der Gegenwart.' In *Vorträge und kleinere Arbeiten 1922–1925*. Edited by Holger Finze. Zurich: Theologischer Verlag Zürich, 1990.

Die protestantische Theologie im 19. Jahrhundert: Ihre Vorgeschichte und ihre Geschichte. Zurich: Theologischer Verlag, 1952.

'Reformierte Lehre, ihr Wesen und ihre Aufgabe.' In *Vorträge und kleinere Arbeiten 1922–1925*. Edited by Holger Finze. Zurich: Theologischer Verlag Zürich, 1990.

Der Römerbrief. 1st edn. Zurich: Theologischer Verlag, 1985.

Der Römerbrief. 2nd edn. Zollikon-Zurich: Chr. Kaiser Verlag, 1926.

Die Theologie Zwinglis, 1922/1923. Edited by Matthias Freudenberg. Zurich: Theologischer Verlag, 2004.

Unterricht in der christlichen Religion, i: *Prolegomena*. Edited by Hannelotte Reifen. Zurich: Theologischer Verlag, 1990.

Unterricht in der christlichen Religion, iii: *Die Lehre von der Versöhnung/Die Lehre on der Erlösung*. Edited by Hinrich Stoevesandt. Zurich: Theologischer Verlag, 1990.

II. English Translations

'The Christian Community and the Civil Community.' In *Community, State, and Church: Three Essays with a new Introduction by David Haddorff*, 149–89. Eugene, Ore.: Wipf and Stock, 2004.

'Christian Ethics.' In *God Here and Now*. Translated by Paul M. van Buren. New York: Harper and Row, 1964.

The Christian Life: Church Dogmatics IV/4, Lecture Fragments. Grand Rapids, Mich.: Eerdmans, 1981.

'The Christian Proclamation Here and Now.' In *God Here and Now.* Translated by Paul M. van Buren. New York: Harper and Row, 1964.

'The Christian's Place in Society.' In *The Word of God and the Word of Man.* Translated by Douglas Horton. Gloucester, Mass.: Peter Smith, 1978.

Church Dogmatics. Edited by Geoffrey M. Bromiley and T. F. Torrance. Edinburgh: T. & T. Clark, 1969–80.

'The Doctrinal Task of the Reformed Churches.' In *The Word of God and the Word of Man.* Translated by Douglas Horton. Gloucester, Mass.: Peter Smith, 1978.

Ethics. Translated by Geoffrey W. Bromiley. New York: Seabury, 1981.

'Fate and Idea in Theology.' In *The Way of Theology in Karl Barth: Essays and Comments.* Edited by Martin Rumscheidt. New York: Pickwick Publications, 1986.

'The Gift of Freedom: Foundation of Evangelical Ethics.' In *The Humanity of God.* Translated by Thomas Wieser. Atlanta: John Knox Press, 1976.

'Gospel and Law.' In *Community, State, and Church: Three Essays with a New Introduction by David Haddorff,* 71–100. Eugene, Ore.: Wipf and Stock, 2004.

The Göttingen Dogmatics: Instruction in the Christian Religion. Vol. i. Translated by Geoffrey W. Bromiley. Grand Rapids, Mich.: Eerdmans, 1991.

The Holy Spirit and the Christian Life. Translated by R. Birch Hoyle. Louisville, Ky.: Westminster/John Knox Press, 1993.

'Humanism.' In *God Here and Now.* Translated by Paul M. van Buren. New York: Harper and Row, 1964.

'The Humanity of God.' In *The Humanity of God.* Translated by John Newton Thomas. Atlanta: John Knox Press, 1976.

'Philosophy and Theology.' In *The Way of Theology in Karl Barth: Essays and Comments.* Edited by Martin Rumscheidt. New York: Pickwick Publications, 1986.

'Political Decisions in the Unity of the Faith.' In Barth, *Against the Stream: Shorter Post-War Writings, 1946–52.* Edited by Ronald Gregor Smith. London: SCM Press, 1954.

'The Problem of Ethics Today.' In *The Word of God and the Word of Man.* Translated by Douglas Horton. Gloucester, Mass.: Peter Smith, 1978.

Protestant Theology in the Nineteenth Century: Its Background and History. Valley Forge, Pa.: Judson Press, 1973.

'The Righteousness of God.' In *The Word of God and the Word of Man.* Translated by Douglas Horton. Gloucester, Mass.: Peter Smith, 1978.

The Theology of John Calvin. Translated by Geoffrey W. Bromiley. Grand Rapids, Mich.: Eerdmans, 1995.

The Theology of the Reformed Confessions. Translated and edited by Darrell L. Guder and Judith J. Guder. Louisville, Ky.: Westminster/John Knox, 2002.

WORKS ABOUT KARL BARTH

Balthasar, Hans Urs von. *The Theology of Karl Barth.* Translated by Edward T. Oakes, SJ. San Francisco: Ignatius Press, 1992.

Beintker, Michael. 'Das Krisis-Motiv der Römerbriefphase als Vorstufe von Barths Zuordnung von Gesetz und Evangelium.' In *Theologie als Christologie: Zum Werk und Leben Karl Barths: Ein Symposium.* Edited by Heidelore Kökert and Wolf Krötke. Berlin: Evangelische Verlagsanstalt Berlin, 1988.

Biggar, Nigel. *The Hastening that Waits: Karl Barth's Ethics.* Oxford: Oxford University Press, 1993.

Busch, Eberhard. *The Great Passion: An Introduction to Karl Barth's Theology.* Translated by Geoffrey W. Bromiley. Edited and annotated by Darrell L. Guder and Judith J. Guder. Grand Rapids, Mich.: Eerdmans, 2004.

—— *Karl Barth: His Life from Letters and Autobiographical Texts.* Translated by John Bowden. Philadelphia: Fortress Press, 1976.

—— *Karl Barth and the Pietists: The Young Karl Barth's Critique of Pietism and its Response.* Translated by Daniel W. Bloesch. Downers Grove, Ill.: InterVarsity, 2004.

Clough, David. *Ethics in Crisis: Interpreting Barth's Ethics.* Aldershot: Ashgate, 2005.

Couenhaven, Jesse. 'Grace as Pardon and Power: Pictures of the Christian Life in Luther, Calvin, and Barth.' *Journal of Religious Ethics* 28 (2000): 63–88.

—— 'Law and Gospel, or the Law of the Gospel? Karl Barth's Political Theology Compared with Luther and Calvin.' *Journal of Religious Ethics* 30 (2002): 181–205.

Cullberg, John. *Das Problem der Ethik in der Dialektischen Theologie.* Uppsala: Appelbergs, 1938.

Gestrich, Christof. *Neuzeitliches Denken und die Spaltung der Dialektischen Theologie.* Tübingen: J. C. B. Mohr, 1977.

Hunsinger, George. 'A Tale of Two Simultaneities: Justification and Sanctification in Calvin and Barth.' In *Conversing with Barth.* Edited by John C. McDowell and Mike Higton. Aldershot: Ashgate, 2004.

—— *How to Read Karl Barth: The Shape of his Theology.* New York: Oxford University Press, 1991.

Joest, Wilfried. 'Karl Barth und das lutherische Verständnis von Gesetz und Evangelium.' *Kerygma und Dogma* 24 (1978): 86–103.

Johnson, William Stacy. *The Mystery of God: Karl Barth and the Postmodern Foundations of Theology.* Louisville, Ky.: Westminster John Knox Press, 1997.

Jüngel, Eberhard. 'Gospel and Law: The Relationship of Dogmatics to Ethics.' In *Karl Barth: A Theological Legacy.* Translated by Garrett E. Paul, 105–26. Philadelphia: Westminster, 1986.

—— 'Invocation of God as the Ethical Ground of Christian Action: Introductory Remarks on the Posthumous Fragments of Karl Barth's Ethics of the Doctrine of Reconciliation.' In Eberhard Jüngel, *Theological Essays.* Vol. i. Translated and with an introduction by J. B. Webster. Edinburgh: T. & T. Clark, 1989.

Klappert, Bertold. *Promissio und Bund: Gesetz und Evangelium bei Luther und Barth.* Göttingen: Vandenhoeck & Ruprecht, 1976.

Körtner, Ulrich H. J. 'Noch einmal: Evangelium und Gesetz: Zur Verhältnisbestimmung von Gesetz und Evangelium bei Karl Barth und Calvin.' *Theologische Zeitschrift* 49 (1993): 248–66.

Loverin, Matthew H. 'Obedient unto Death: The Person and Work of Jesus Christ in Karl Barth's Theological Ethics.' Unpublished doctoral dissertation, University of Notre Dame, 2009.

Lovin, Robin. *Christian Faith and Political Choices: The Social Ethics of Barth, Brunner, and Bonhoeffer.* Philadelphia: Fortress Press, 1984.

McCormack, Bruce L. *Karl Barth's Critically Realistic Dialectical Theology: Its Genesis and Development, 1909–1936.* Oxford: Oxford University Press, 1995.

Macken, John. *The Autonomy Theme in the Church Dogmatics: Karl Barth and his Critics.* Cambridge: Cambridge University Press, 1990.

Mangina, Joseph L. *Karl Barth and the Christian Life: The Practical Knowledge of God.* New York: Peter Lang, 2001.

Matheny, Paul. *Dogmatics and Ethics: The Theological Realism and Ethics of Karl Barth's 'Church Dogmatics.'* Frankfurt: Peter Lang, 1990.

Niebuhr, Reinhold. 'Barthianism and the Kingdom.' *The Christian Century* (July 15, 1931). Reprinted in Niebuhr, *Essays in Applied Christianity: The Church and the New World.* Edited by D. B. Robertson. New York: Meridian Books, 1959.

Nimmo, Paul. *Being in Action: The Theological Shape of Barth's Ethical Vision.* New York: T. & T. Clark, 2007.

Oyen, Hendrik van. 'Gibt es eine evangelische Ethik der Grenzfälle?' *Evangelische Ethik* 1 (1957): 2–17.

Rae, Simon. 'Gospel Law and Freedom in the Theological Ethics of Karl Barth.' *Scottish Journal of Theology* 25 (1972): 412–22.

Reckoning with Barth: Essays in Commemoration of the Centenary of Karl Barth's Birth. Edited by Nigel Biggar. London: Mowbray, 1988.

Rendtorff, Trutz. 'Der Ethische Sinn der Dogmatik.' In *Die Realisierung der Freiheit: Beiträge zur Kritik der Theologie Karl Barths.* Edited by Trutz Rendtorff, 119–34. Gütersloh: Gütersloher Verlaghaus Gerd Mohn, 1975.

Ruschke, Werner. *Entstehung und Ausführung der Diastasentheologie in Karl Barths zweitem Römerbrief.* Neukirchen Vluyn: Neukirchener Verlag, 1987.

Ward, Graham. 'Barth, Modernity, and Postmodernity.' In *The Cambridge Companion to Karl Barth.* Edited by John Webster, 274–95. New York: Cambridge University Press, 2000.

Webster, John. *Barth.* 2nd edn. London: Continuum, 2004.

—— 'Barth, Modernity, and Postmodernity.' In *Karl Barth: A Future for Postmodern Theology?* Edited by Geoff Thompson and Chrisitaan Mostert, 1–28. Hindmarsh: Australia Theological Forum, 2000.

—— *Barth's Earlier Theology: Four Studies.* New York: T. & T. Clark, 2005.

—— *Barth's Ethics of Reconciliation.* Cambridge: Cambridge University Press, 1995.

—— *Barth's Moral Theology: Human Action in Barth's Thought.* Grand Rapids, Mich.: Eerdmans, 1998.

—— 'The Christian in Revolt.' In *Reckoning with Barth: Essays in Commemoration of the Centenary of Karl Barth's Birth.* Edited by Nigel Biggar, 119–44. London: Mowbray, 1988.

Werpehowski, William. 'Command and History in the Ethics of Karl Barth.' *Journal of Religious Ethics* 9 (1981): 298–321.

—— 'Narrative and Ethics in Barth.' *Theology Today* 43 (1986): 334–53.

Willis, Robert E. *The Ethics of Karl Barth.* Leiden: E. J. Brill, 1971.

—— 'Some Difficulties in Barth's Development of Special Ethics.' *Religious Studies* 6 (1970): 152–5.

Yoder, John Howard. *Karl Barth and the Problem of War and Other Essays on Karl Barth.* Edited by Mark Thiessen Nation. Eugene, Ore.: Cascade/Wipf and Stock, 2003.

OTHER WORKS

Althaus, Paul. *The Divine Command.* Translated by Franklin Sherman. Philadelphia: Fortress Press, 1966.

Bonhoeffer, Dietrich. *Creation and Fall: A Theological Exposition of Genesis 1–3.* Dietrich Bonhoeffer's Works, Vol. iii. Edited by Martin Rüter and Ilse Tödt. English edition edited by John W. de Gruchy and translated by Douglas Stephen Bax. Minneapolis: Fortress Press, 1997.

Brunner, Emil. *The Divine Imperative: A Study in Christian Ethics.* Translated by Olive Wyon. Cambridge: Lutterworth Press, 2002.

Calvin, John. *Institutes of the Christian Religion.* Edited by John T. McNeill. Translated by Ford Lewis Battles. Philadelphia: Westminster Press, 1960.

Derrida, Jacques. *The Gift of Death.* 2nd edn. Translated by David Willis. Chicago: University of Chicago Press, 2008.

Ebeling, Gerhard. *Word and Faith.* Translated by James W. Leitch. Philadelphia: Fortress Press, 1963.

Foucault, Michel. *Ethics.* Edited by Paul Rabinow. New York: The New Press, 1992.

Gustafson, James. *Can Ethics Be Christian?* Chicago: University of Chicago Press, 1975.

—— *Ethics from a Theocentric Perspective.* Chicago: University of Chicago Press, 1981/84.

Hadot, Pierre. *Philosophy as a Way of Life: Spiritual Exercises from Socrates to Foucault.* Edited and with an introduction by Arnold I. Davidson. New York: Blackwell, 1995.

Hampshire, Stuart. 'Fallacies in Moral Philosophy.' *Mind* 58 (1949): 466–82. Reprinted in *Revisions: Changing Perspectives in Moral Philosophy.* Edited by Stanley Hauerwas and Alasdair MacIntyre, 51–67. Notre Dame, Ind.: University of Notre Dame Press, 1983.

—— *Innocence and Experience.* Cambridge, Mass.: Harvard University Press, 1989.

Hauerwas, Stanley. *Character and the Christian Life: A Study in Theological Ethics.* San Antonio, Tex.: Trinity University Press, 1975.

—— *The Peaceable Kingdom: A Primer in Christian Ethics.* Notre Dame, Ind.: University of Notre Dame Press, 1983.

Hegel, G. W. F. *Elements of the Philosophy of Right.* Edited by Alan W. Wood. Translated by H. B. Nisbet. Cambridge: Cambridge University Press, 1991.

Heidegger, Martin. 'Letter on "Humanism."' In *Pathmarks.* Edited by William McNeill, 239–76. Cambridge: Cambridge University Press, 1998.

Hütter, Reinhard. *Evangelische Ethik als kirchliches Zeugnis.* Neukirchen-Vluyn: Neukirchener Verlag, 1993.

Kant, Immanuel. *Die Religion innerhalb der Grenzen der blossen Vernunft. Kants Gesammelte Schriften,* vi. Berlin: Walter de Gruyter & Co., 1969. Translated and edited as *Religion within the Boundaries of Mere Reason* in *Religion and Rational Theology* by Allen W. Wood and George di Giovanni. Cambridge: Cambridge University Press, 1996.

—— *Der Streit der Facultäten. Kants Gesammelte Schriften,* vii. Berlin: Walter de Gruyter & Co., 1969. Translated and edited as *The Conflict of the Faculties* in *Religion and Rational Theology* by Allen W. Wood and George di Giovanni. Cambridge: Cambridge University Press, 1996.

Levinas, Emmanuel. *Totality and Infinity: An Essay on Exteriority.* Translated by Alphonso Lingis. Pittsburgh: Duquesne University Press, 1969.

Lindbeck, George. *The Nature of Doctrine: Religion and Theology in a Postliberal Age.* Philadelphia: Westminster Press, 1984.

McClendon, James Wm. *Ethics: Systematic Theology.* Vol. i. 2nd edn. Nashville: Abingdon, 2002.

Marion, Jean-Luc. 'The Original Otherness of the Ego: A Rereading of Descartes' *Meditatio* II.' In *The Ethical.* Edited by Edith Wyschogrod and Gerald P. McKenny, 33–53. New York: Blackwell, 2003.

Milbank, John. *Theology and Social Theory: Against Secular Reason.* London: Blackwell, 1993.

Murdoch, Iris. *The Sovereignty of Good.* London: Routledge and Kegan Paul, 1970.

Neibuhr, Reinhold. *The Nature and Destiny of Man.* Vol. i: *Human Nature.* New York: Scribner's, 1941.

—— 'We Are Men and Not God.' In *The Christian Century* (October 27, 1948). Reprinted in *Essays in Applied Christianity: The Church and the New World.* Edited by D. B. Robertson. New York: Meridian Books, 1959.

Nietzsche, Friedrich. *Beyond Good and Evil: Prelude to a Philosophy of the Future.* London: Penguin, 1990.

—— *On the Genealogy of Morality.* New York: Cambridge University Press, 1994.

O'Donovan, Oliver. *Resurrection and Moral Order.* 2nd edn. Grand Rapids, Mich.: Eerdmans, 1994.

Rendtorff, Trutz. *Ethics,* i: *Basic Elements and Methodology in an Ethical Theology.* Philadelphia: Fortress Press, 1986. Translation of *Ethik: Grundelemente, Methodologie und Konkretionen eine ethischen Theologie.* Vol. i. Stuttgart: W. Kohlhammer Verlag, 1980.

Schleiermacher, Friedrich. *Brief Outline for the Study of Theology.* Translated by Terrence N. Tice. Atlanta: John Knox Press, 1966.

—— *Introduction to Christian Ethics.* Translated by John C. Shelly. Nashville: Abingdon Press, 1989.

Schneewind, J. B. *The Invention of Autonomy: A History of Modern Moral Philosophy.* Cambridge: Cambridge University Press, 1998.

Schweiker, William. *Responsibility and Christian Ethics.* New York: Cambridge University Press, 1995.

Sockness, Brent. *Against False Apologetics: Wilhelm Herrmann and Ernst Troeltsch in Conflict.* Tübingen: J. C. B. Mohr, 1998.

Taylor, Charles. *A Secular Age.* Cambridge, Mass.: Harvard University Press, 2007.

Thielicke, Helmut. *Theological Ethics,* i: *Foundations.* Edited by William H. Lazareth. Philadelphia: Fortress Press, 1966.

Troeltsch, Ernst. 'The Social Philosophy of Christianity' and 'Stoic-Christian Natural Law and Modern Secular Natural Law.' In *Reason in History.* Translated by James Luther Adams and Walter F. Bense, 210–34, 321–42. Minneapolis: Fortress Press, 1991.

—— *The Social Teaching of the Christian Churches.* Vols. i and ii. Translated by Olive Wyon. Chicago: University of Chicago Press, 1931.

Weber, Max. *The Protestant Ethic and the Spirit of Capitalism.* Translated by Talcott Parsons. New York: Scribners, 1958.

Williams, Bernard. *Ethics and the Limits of Philosophy.* Cambridge, Mass.: Harvard University Press, 1985.

Index